PRIMATE ETHNOGRAPHIES

Edited by

Karen B. Strier

Boston   Columbus   Indianapolis   New York   San Francisco   Upper Saddle River
Amsterdam   Cape Town   Dubai   London   Madrid   Milan   Munich   Paris   Montréal   Toronto
Delhi   Mexico City   São Paulo   Sydney   Hong Kong   Seoul   Singapore   Taipei   Tokyo

Editor in Chief: Ashley Dodge
Publisher: Nancy Roberts
Editorial Assistant: Molly White
Development Editor: Ohlinger Publishing Services
Director of Marketing: Brandy Dawson
Executive Marketing Manager: Kelly May
Marketing Coordinator: Jessica Warren
Managing Editor: Denise Forlow
Program Manager: Mayda Bosco
Senior Operations Supervisor: Mary Fischer
Operations Specialist: Eileen Corallo
Art Director: Jayne Conte
Cover Designer: Suzanne Behnke
Cover image: Martha M. Robbins
Director of Digital Media: Brian Hyland
Digital Media Project Manager: Tina Gagliostro
Digital Media Editor: Learning Mate Solutions, Ltd.
Full-Service Project Management and Composition: Nitin Agarwal/Aptara®, Inc.
Printer/Binder: Courier Corp.
Cover Printer: Courier Corp.
Text Font: 10/12, Times LT Std

On the Cover: Silverback male mountain gorilla, Bwenge, and his son, feeding on the bark of planted eucalyptus trees outside Karisoke National Park, Uganda, in 2010. Photo credit: Martha M. Robbins

Credits and acknowledgments borrowed from other sources and reproduced, with permission, in this textbook appear on appropriate page within text.

Library of Congress Cataloging-in-Publication Data
Primate ethnographies / editor, Karen B. Strier.—1st ed.
   p. cm.
  Includes index.
  ISBN-13: 978-0-205-21466-2
  ISBN-10: 0-205-21466-5
  1. Primates—Fieldwork—Anecdotes. 2. Primates—Research—Anecdotes.
  I. Strier, Karen B.
  QL737.P9P672456 2013
  599.8072—dc23

              2013023258

10 9 8 7 6 5 4 3 2 1

ISBN-10: 0-205-21466-5
ISBN-13: 978-0-205-21466-2

CONTENTS

FOREWORD

The Value of Long-Term Research

Primatology is a maturing field with an incremental increase in primatologists and study sites. Primates are a diverse group found in almost all tropical regions with many variations in body size, social structure, and feeding habits. It is not easy to understand our close relatives. Primates, whether they be lemurs, monkeys, or apes, have long lifespans and following individuals from birth to death in the wild may take over 30 to 50 years of trekking in steep, mountainous forests, or parching deserts. Some field stations have hosted primate studies for decades, and the long-term research on distinguishable individuals has offered opportunities for understanding processes and behaviors otherwise impossible to comprehend. For the first time in a textbook, Karen Strier has collected a set of case histories of primate lives for you to enjoy. Whether you are a primatologist or just a primate fan, you are in for a treat.

One of the key behavioral factors, which is essential to understanding the flow of genes in a population, is dispersal. Theories of population genetics for predicting gene frequencies require precise knowledge of breeding structure, including dispersal distances and patterns. But dispersal of males and females from one group to another is difficult to track because of the vast expanses they travel and the unpredictable timing of group changes. Many primates don't breed until they are five to twelve years old. Knowing when an individual will leave the natal group and go to other groups to breed requires long-term following. In many long-term studies, such as Jane Goodall's chimpanzees, Karen Strier's muriquis, and my own studies with sifakas, we have data not only on the first generation of offspring, but the grandchildren. We see patterns of dispersal that we could never have dreamed possible when we first started our studies. And these patterns give us information necessary to understand population genetics, as well as intergenerational behaviors.

Primate dissertation research usually spans one or two years of following a few groups in the wild. These in-depth studies provide a slice of those primates' lives but just a short window into a lifetime. The behaviors seen could be idiosyncratic, or seasonal or transient. With long-term studies in the wild, patterns of behavior are repeated, and demographic trends become apparent, giving us insights into the evolutionary drivers of primate behavior.

Long-term studies also catch rare but important behaviors, such as "lethal aggression" (in humans called murder), or infanticide (infant killing by immigrant males), or long-term affiliations, coalitions, and friendships. Predation is a rare occurrence, but in a long-term study it is more probable that predation events will be observed. Interspecific competition for food among primates may be seen only at some times of year, or only every ten years in a drought situation. All of these rare events that impact so heavily on the evolution of a primate species are best documented in long-term studies.

Understanding variation in population densities is key to conservation of endangered primates. Documenting rainfall and temperature and the corresponding responses of key food items to environmental variation in a long-term study coupled with data on variation in primate reproduction, mortality, and demography offers understanding of population growth or reduction. In our long-term studies of eight species of diurnal lemurs, we have seen populations double or halve over 26 years. The food specialists—the golden bamboo lemur, the greater bamboo lemur (eating 95 percent bamboo), the black-and-white ruffed lemur (fruit specialist feeding on 90 to 95 percent fruit), and the aye-aye (bark larvae)—remain rare throughout the park and throughout the years. The congeners (red-bellied and red-fronted brown lemurs) seem to compete, with their population troughs and spires mirroring one another. Droughts and ENSO climate fluctuations affect the Milne Edward's sifakas' survival, but that of the bamboo lemurs not so much. Predation by the fossa has negatively affected populations, but we have seen these primate populations rebound within six to ten years. It takes concerted effort over years to understand these patterns, and it is important to the long-term conservation of these endangered species to understand the drivers of individual and group survival.

This is a changing world, and whether it be the changes caused by immediate anthropogenic change, such as selective logging, forest fragmentation or hunting, or from global climate change, we need the baseline data to understand the resulting changes in the primate's individual and population behavior, ecology, and demography. By following populations through time, we can document resilience or collapse, and by using long-term ecological and climate data, we can propose with some success cause and effect. Recognizing a "crisis" situation when a species may become extinct is possible only with a baseline for comparison.

In 1978, ecologist Donald Tinkle wrote that novel theory and continual testing of predictions are key to science. But theory tested with short-term data could lead to erroneous results. In the fields of population genetics, community ecology, life history theory, and sociobiology, good theory requires testing with long-term field studies. We need to test predictions from theory through an accumulation of quantitative data on individuals and population ecology over a time sufficient to measure variances in the relevant parameters. When we are talking about primates, the time sufficient might be decades.

This book gives an intense and revealing view of some of the long-term primate sites and what we have learned from them. These sites and these studies have made our understanding of primate behavior and evolution much richer, revealing new insights into primate diversity and the possible variation in our human ancestors. My hope is that funding agencies, which now award in one- or three-year cycles, will see the value of long-term studies and make room for funding long-term research.

Enjoy each chapter of this book as you travel throughout the tropical world and through time. Researchers who have studied long in wild places will share their lives and those of their subjects with you. You will join them in cherishing the richness of our Order and appreciating the diversity of our close relatives.

Patricia C. Wright
Centre ValBio, Madagascar
August 31, 2012

PREFACE

The idea for this book had been percolating for years. It came to mind with increasing regularity at professional meetings and in conversations with colleagues, as the different worlds I inhabit as a field primatologist and as an anthropologist began to converge. *Primate Ethnographies* is a collection of essays about the excitement of studying wild primates and the multifaceted challenges involved in conducting field research. Most similar accounts describing these aspects of field research in an accessible way are found in book-length monographs on particular species, and even some of the classic essays from popular magazines such as *Natural History* tend to focus on the primates, with little or no mention of the local human communities and the socio-political, economic, and ideological contexts in which the studies take place. The purpose of this volume is to provide readers with auto-ethnographic accounts by primatologists whose diverse experiences with primates, people, and institutions reveal the broader nature of the primatological field experience.

The essays are loosely organized into four sections with overlapping foci, instead of by the taxonomic or geographic affinities of the primates discussed. I did, however, use the goal of maintaining taxonomic diversity as a guide in my decision to classify an essay in one section instead of another. Thus, in *Starting Out*, the authors' reflections on their own lives are woven most explicitly into those on their research, whereas in *Social Complexities*, the authors describe in detail different aspects of primate social behavior and provide information about the methods they employed. The essays grouped in *Comparative Lenses* include explicit comparisons of the differences and similarities encountered in studies of different populations and species. These comparisons span contrasts between wild and captive populations, and between wild populations living under different ecological conditions as well as different species that occur sympatrically. The essays in *Changes with Time* describe the shifting perspectives that long-term studies on wild primates can provide, and the changing dynamics of place over time.

Although the partitioning of the essays into sections is intended to highlight particular parts of the narratives, most of the essays could easily have been grouped in alternative subsets. To help readers identify the many affinities among the chapters and alternative ways they could be sorted, I compiled an Appendix with cross-listings across regions described, species studied, and key themes and concepts that are common to the essays independent of their placement in this book.

The essays in this volume also illustrate the shared environments of primates and humans and the urgent and complex conservation issues that permeate contemporary primatology. Consequently, my net royalties from the sale of this edition will be donated to a special fund administered by Primate Conservation, Inc., a nonprofit organization established by Noel Rowe to support the study and conservation of primates and their habitats (www.primate.org). Pearson, the publisher of this book, has committed to contribute to this fund as well. The "Primate Ethnographies Fund" (PEF) will be dedicated to supporting primate field studies that contribute to conservation and to the local communities in which the studies take place. I am grateful to Noel Rowe for agreeing to help us administer this fund through Primate Conservation, Inc., and to Nancy Roberts, my editor, for negotiating Pearson's side of the arrangement.

I am indebted to Nancy Roberts for many other reasons, as well. Nancy's unfailing enthusiasm about this project transformed a rather vague idea into a unique and, I hope, useful volume for students and other interested readers to learn about the excitement of discovery and challenges of primate field research. Our shared vision is that *Primate Ethnographies* will serve as a textbook or companion reader for a wide variety of courses from primate behavior, ecology, and conservation, to cultural anthropology and biological anthropology; we also expect that the essays will be of interest to students of science studies, and of nature and science writing. Nancy's professional expertise and practical advice with this book, as well in her role as editor of my other Pearson textbook, *Primate Behavioral Ecology,* 4th edition, have been fundamental.

Nancy also deserves credit for reconnecting me with Jennifer Jacobson, the other person without whom this book would not have been completed. Jennifer had been my editor on the third edition of *Primate Behavioral Ecology,* when it was published by Allyn & Bacon where she previously worked. In her current position as an editor with Ohlinger Publishing Services, Jennifer has been my sounding board and a careful second reader on all of the essays in this volume. Jennifer's skills as an editor contributed to the consistency and flow of the diverse writing styles represented here. She has also played an essential role in cross-checking all of the details and standardizing format. Her energy for this project was sustaining.

In addition to Jennifer and Nancy, I am grateful to Michael Fischer and especially Jonathan Marks for feedback and ideas for this volume, and to Mary Pollock for stimulating me to think about my own field research story (or, as I learned from her, my narrative) through a more literary lens. My UW-Madison colleagues, in particular Anatoly Khazanov, Maria Lepowsky, Kirin Narayan, and Larry Nesper, were most helpful in answering what must have seemed like random questions that I asked them about ethnography and writing. My husband, Tom Martin, has been a great ally during this project.

And of course, I am indebted to all of the contributors, for accepting my invitation to participate in this project and for their generosity in making the time to think and write about their field research and experiences. It was a pleasure to work with colleagues and friends who provided such high-quality manuscripts and were so responsive and attentive to making revisions and meeting deadlines. It is an honor to share their stories here.

Karen B. Strier

Vilas Professor & Irven DeVore Professor
Department of Anthropology
University of Wisconsin-Madison
Madison, WI 53706
USA

LIST OF CONTRIBUTORS

Louise Barrett
Department of Psychology
University of Lethbridge

Jacinta C. Beehner
Departments of Anthropology
and Psychology
University of Michigan

Thore J. Bergman
Departments of Psychology and Ecology and
Evolutionary Biology
University of Michigan

Colin A. Chapman
Department of Anthropology and McGill
School of the Environment
McGill University

Marina Cords
Department of Ecology, Evolution and
Environmental Biology
Columbia University

Anthony Di Fiore
Department of Anthropology
University of Texas-Austin

Linda Marie Fedigan
Department of Anthropology
University of Calgary

Eduardo Fernandez-Duque
Department of Anthropology
University of Pennsylvania

Stephen F. Ferrari
Department of Ecology
Universidade Federal de Sergipe

Agustín Fuentes
Department of Anthropology
University of Notre Dame

Kenneth Glander
Department of Evolutionary Anthropology
Duke University

S. Peter Henzi
Department of Psychology
University of Lethbridge

Michael A. Huffman
Section of Social Systems Evolution
Primate Research Institute
Kyoto University

Peter M. Kappeler
German Primate Center and Department of
Sociobiology and Anthropology
University of Göttingen

James J. Moore
Department of Anthropology
University of California, San Diego

Leanne T. Nash
School of Human Evolution and Social Change
Arizona State University

Jill D. Pruetz
Department of Anthropology
Iowa State University

Ulrich H. Reichard
Department of Anthropology
Southern Illinois University

Martha M. Robbins
Department of Primatology
Max Plank Institute for Evolutionary
Anthropology

Charles T. Snowdon
Department of Psychology
University of Wisconsin-Madison

Craig Stanford
Anthropology and Biological Sciences
USC Jane Goodall Research Center
University of Southern California

Karen B. Strier
Department of Anthropology
University of Wisconsin-Madison

Robert W. Sussman
Department of Anthropology
Washington University

Patricia C. Wright (Foreword)
Department of Anthropology
University of Stony Brook

PART I

Introduction

Primate Ethnographies
The Biological and Cultural Dimensions of Field Primatology

By Karen B. Strier[1]

Like other researchers in the biological sciences, primatologists employ empirical methods to collect systematic data that permit quantitative analyses of behavioral, ecological, and evolutionary hypotheses. We are not ethnographers trained to study or write about human cultures. During the course of our primate field studies, however, we spend years, sometimes decades, living and working in close proximity to local people whose lives we also come to know. Perhaps this is why the ethnographer's challenges of conducting fieldwork far from home, often in a secondary language acquired solely for that purpose, resonate so closely with my own experiences in a small rural community in southeastern Brazil over the past 30 years.

Although my research has focused on the northern muriqui (one of the most critically endangered primates in the world) rather than on humans, it has not taken place in a cross-cultural vacuum. Indeed, even the most reclusive primate field researchers become embedded in the socio-political, economic, and ideological contexts of the local human communities within and around which their research takes place. These human dimensions of primate fieldwork can be as diverse and as tricky to navigate as the tropical habitats in which most primates live. They can also influence the directions that our studies ultimately take, and thus impact what we learn about the primates. Yet in the scientific literature on primates, the cultural contexts of the field research and the effects of these interacting dynamics on both the primates and the primatologists are stories that seldom get told.

Primate Ethnographies is intended to span this gap between the biological and the social science sides of primate field research. The essays in this volume are written by established

[1]About the author: Karen B. Strier has studied the behavioral ecology of the critically endangered northern muriqui in southeastern Brazil since 1982. Her main research interests are to understand how stochastic demographic fluctuations and individual life histories affect population persistence and behavior and to contribute to conservation efforts on behalf of muriquis and other endangered species. She is a Fellow of the American Association for the Advancement of Science and a member of the National Academy of Sciences and the American Academy of Arts and Sciences. She is the author of *Faces in the Forest: The Endangered Muriqui Monkeys of Brazil* and of *Primate Behavioral Ecology, 4th Edition.*

Contact information: Department of Anthropology, University of Wisconsin-Madison, 1180 Observatory Drive, Madison, WI 53706, USA, kbstrier@wisc.edu

Citation: Strier, K. B. 2014. "The Biological and Cultural Dimensions of Field Primatology." In Strier, K. B. (ed.), *Primate Ethnographies*. Upper Saddle River, NJ: Pearson Education, Inc. (pp. 2–10).

FIGURE 1.1 Northern muriqui females and their offspring at the RPPN Feliciano Miguel Abdala, in Caratinga, Minas Gerais, Brazil. **Photo credit:** Carla B. Possamai.

primatologists whose experiences, backgrounds, and motivating questions provide glimpses into the different pathways one can follow into the field of contemporary primatology. The contributors include biologists, psychologists, and physical anthropologists, whose interests range from the evolution of social behavior and communication, to feeding and community ecology, socio-ecology, and reproduction and life history theory. Their methodological approaches span the continuum from hands-off observational studies, to capture-and-release projects, to comparative investigations of captive and wild populations. The expertise of the contributors encompasses a broad taxonomic, geographic, and ecological diversity of primate species. Some of the contributors were among the first generation of primatologists to test explicit hypotheses about primate behavior in the field; some, like myself, have worked on the same populations of primates for decades. Still others have conducted comparative studies of different populations of a single species or of different species, requiring them to traverse continents, encountering new cultural conditions at each site.

I explicitly encouraged the contributors to weave into their essays key stories about the people who played pivotal roles in their particular studies, and this deliberate reflection on the human dimension provides one of the unifying themes in the volume. However, the choice of whether the contributors wrote about collaborators, field assistants, park guards, local farmers, students, government officials, hunters, or other memorable personalities was entirely up to them. For some of the contributors, this meant acknowledging people who had influenced their career decisions or who have participated in their research and whose appearance in the accompanying photos (all generously provided by the authors) is testimony to the importance of their

MAP 1.1

presence on the projects. For other contributors, the focus remained on the animals and how their behavior or circumstances have changed over time; nonetheless, when people do enter these stories, it is usually without names but with power or responsibility for imposing or communicating policies and official actions that impact the animals and the authors' scientific plans. This diversity of interpretations of the assignment is extremely informative, as it illustrates the different social and cultural dimensions in which primate field researchers work.

The dynamics of the cultural dimensions of primatological fieldwork differ not only by place, but also over time. For example, when I first visited the forest at Fazenda Montes Claros, a private coffee plantation and cattle ranch in the municipality of Caratinga, Minas Gerais in 1982, I was a 23-year-old graduate student exploring the possibilities of studying the behavioral ecology of the muriquis for my Ph.D. research. All of my interactions—whether with the owner of the forest and his family, or with the local people who lived and worked on the surrounding lands, or with the Brazilian university students (my peers), their professor (who became my first official Brazilian sponsor), or the ex-hunter who worked as his assistant—were constrained initially and most obviously by my rudimentary knowledge of Portuguese. Many of those early interactions were also undoubtedly shaped by a suite of conventions attached to someone of my foreign nationality, age, gender, and (single) marital status. I remained only vaguely aware of these conventions, even after I returned in 1983 for the 14-month field study that marked the onset of what was to become the ongoing, long-term research and conservation project that it is today.

Along with habituating one of the two muriqui groups that inhabited the forest and then documenting the feeding, ranging, and unusually peaceful social patterns of the 23 individuals in the group at the time, that first 14-month stretch of fieldwork also set the foundation for friendships and collaborations with Brazilian researchers and some of the local farming families that have persisted over the years. However, whereas the clues to deciphering the muriquis' unique egalitarian society and distinct way of life came from systematically observing their behavior while silently following them on their daily routines in the forest, my relationships with the people depended on my ability to communicate with them in Portuguese, on their patience with my frequent language lapses, and on our mutual efforts to find topics about which to relate.

Initially I sought refuge from awkward social interactions by spending as much time as I could in the forest. Those long working days at the outset were probably responsible for the rapidity with which the muriquis stopped fleeing and began tolerating my presence, and thus contributed to the advancement of my research goals. Although motivated at least as much by shyness as by dedication to the research, those long days in the forest also contributed to the reputation I soon acquired for working hard and for being *apaixonado,* (passionate) about the muriquis. The local people also worked long days, especially when there were crops (mainly coffee, beans, or sugar cane) to plant or to harvest, so this work ethic became something we had in common. We got to know each other in passing, especially early in the morning, along the dirt road that bisected the forest and that led me to my trails and the farmers to their fields.

My passion for the muriquis, by contrast, had a somewhat different effect than my long working days, for although it was a source of mild amusement, it also stimulated interest and curiosity about what could possibly be so special about the animals. The enigma was particularly puzzling to some of the kids, who were growing up in the countryside surrounding the forest but had no frame of reference with which to appreciate its importance as one of the last remaining sanctuaries for the muriqui and other endemic species of the Brazilian Atlantic forest ecosystem.

Today, this has mostly changed. By now, after three decades of research involving many dozens of Brazilian students and collaborators who have participated in the long-term monitoring of the 330-plus individuals in the entire population at this writing (now divided into four social groups), general knowledge about many facets of the muriquis' behavior and ecology and an appreciation for the forest that supports them has spread. In 2001, the owners of the forest transformed it into a permanently protected nature reserve. Although the Fazenda still exists, the forest is now known as the Reserva Particular do Patrimônio Natural (RPPN) Feliciano Miguel Abdala, in honor of the individual who defended the muriquis from hunters and preserved the forest long before laws to protect endangered species and their habitats had been passed. The research on the muriquis and the conservation of the forest have attracted international media attention and documentary filmmakers, as well as journalists familiar to everyone in the region because of their celebrity status on Brazilian television and in the Brazilian press. No one is surprised anymore by these activities or the attention that the muriquis generate.

Conversations early on with Russell Mittermeier (currently President of Conservation International) and two of the pioneers in Brazilian conservation and primatology, Dr. Adelmar Coimbra-Filho and Professor Célio Valle, encouraged me to consider the many ways in which maintaining a long-term research presence could contribute to conservation. For example, employment opportunities associated directly with the research and indirectly through the conservation NGOs (including the Brazilian NGO, *Preserve Muriqui,* established to administer the Reserve) have been essential to the research infrastructure. Although it is difficult to evaluate the full effects on the local economy, these activities have been going on for the past thirty years. This has been long enough for children of our long-term employees to become the first in their families to graduate from college. Some of those curious kids I first met in 1983 have cleared trails, collected temperature and rainfall data, or monitored the camera traps we now use in the research; they also have guided tourists and film crews that visit the Reserve and have worked in the NGO's nursery, where seeds of native tree species are collected and nurtured until the seedlings are ready to be sold for reforestation programs in the region. Many of those kids, now parents themselves, have invited me to their families' weddings, birthdays, and funerals. I have known the people in this community for more than half of my life.

The same can be said for some of the muriquis, which were present in my original study group at the outset and are still alive. These surviving muriquis were among the first individuals I could identify on the basis of their natural fur and facial markings. Based on what we now know about female age at first reproduction, some of those original adult females carrying infants in 1983 would have to be in their mid-to-late 30s by now; based on the long-term monitoring of their extended genealogies, we know that at least some of these females now have great-great-great-grandoffspring in the population.

Unlike male muriquis, which remain in their natal groups for life, most muriqui females leave their natal groups at about 6 years of age, before the onset of puberty. For years, my students and I confirmed that the emigrant females were associating with other muriquis from one of what had grown to two other groups, but then we lost contact with them when we resumed observations on members of the main study group. By the late 1990s, however, curiosity about these females' fates—and about the size and status of the rest of the primate population—led me and my long-time friend and collaborator, Sérgio Mendes (currently a professor at the Universidade Federal de Espirito Santo, or UFES), to organize a forest-wide census of the primate community with more than a dozen previous students who had worked on the project and were willing to donate a week of their time.

The census confirmed that there were as many muriquis living on the northern side of the forest as there were in our main study group in the south, and some of the females that had emigrated from the study group were still recognizable to the students who had spent years observing them. It was obvious that if we wanted to track individual females' life histories from birth through their entire reproductive lives, and to monitor the size, health, and long-term viability of the population, we would need to expand our research scope. This was accomplished, initially, through the collaboration of a post-doctoral fellow, Jean Philippe Boubli, and some of the students who had previously worked with the main study group, including Carla Possamai (who joined the project in 2001 and now holds a Ph.D. from UFES). Since 2003, the entire population of muriquis in the 957-hectare (or 2,365-acre) Reserve has been monitored.

The muriquis' endangered status has always played a role in my decisions about the kinds of questions to prioritize in the research and in my commitment to noninvasive research methods, which have included parasite, hormonal, and genetic studies based on analyses of the muriquis' dung that we could collect and preserve when it dropped to the forest floor. But it was not until I began thinking at the level of the entire population, instead of concentrating on my long-term study group, that I fully appreciated the importance of understanding the dynamics of the demography underlying the long-term persistence of the population. This shift in my priorities was stimulated, in part, by documented changes in the muriquis' behavior, which could most plausibly be attributed to the population's growth and shifts in the age structure and sex ratios of the groups. This has led us to pursue new investigations into the plasticity in their social and ecological adaptations, including the expansion of the muriquis' habitat use into an increasingly terrestrial niche.

With some 335 individuals (as of June 2013), our study population now represents more than one-third of all of the northern muriquis in the world. Its growth illustrates the promising potential of small populations to recover when they and their habitats are well protected. Our concerns now have shifted from the muriquis to include the constraints of the small size of the forest on further population growth. Now that the original forest fragment is protected for perpetuity, we

FIGURE 1.2A Some of the students and colleagues who participated in the first census of primates in 1999 at the RPPN Feliciano Miguel Abdala, in Caratinga, Minas Gerais, Brazil. The author (and the editor of this collection) is standing on the far left. Her collaborator, Sérgio Mendes, is standing in the middle row, sixth from the left (in a jacket). **Photo credit:** Courtesy of Karen B. Strier.

FIGURE 1.2B Commemoration of the twentieth year of the muriqui field study in 2002 at the RPPN Feliciano Miguel Abdala, in Caratinga, Minas Gerais, Brazil. The author (and the editor of this collection) is fifth from the left in the back row. Her collaborator, Sérgio Mendes, is standing in the back row, second from the left. Also mentioned in the text and visible are Jean Boubli (standing back row, far left) and Carla Possamai (far back row, second from the right). **Photo credit:** Courtesy of Karen B. Strier.

FIGURE 1.3   An aerial view of pasture outside the boundary of the Reserve. Efforts to establish corridors through these pastures, into other forest fragments, are underway to increase the habitat available to the muriquis. **Photo credit:** Carla B. Possamai.

need to find ways to increase its size. The most efficient way to do this is through the establishment of forest corridors, which the muriquis could use to move into other neighboring forest fragments.

Establishing these corridors is one of the primary initiatives being led by *Preserve Muriqui* and other conservation NGOs concerned with the northern muriqui. The corridor project has expanded the sphere of our interactions with people living beyond the Reserve and its owners' adjacent properties even further into the surrounding countryside. Just to the south of the Reserve, for example, are some other forest fragments, belonging to other farmers; protecting these forests and connecting them with the Reserve would increase the habitat available to the muriquis by almost 50 percent. A few years ago, Carla and another former muriqui student, Fernanda Tabacow, discovered that five females from our study population had dispersed into these fragments after leaving their natal groups. In April 2012, Fernanda confirmed that one of the females, who had returned to the Reserve for a brief visit early in 2010, was back in the neighboring fragment but this time carrying a young infant. These muriqui females have shown us where to focus our efforts for expanding their forest; the next step will be up to us.

Fernanda and Carla, like many of the dozens of other Brazilian students who have participated in the long-term field study, used some of the behavioral data they had collected for their master's dissertations, and they are still actively involved in conservation, in general, and with the muriquis, in particular. Along with other former students and ongoing collaborators, they have also contributed to the Brazilian National Action Plan for the Conservation of Muriquis. Some of the earlier cohorts of students who participated on the project are now university professors, with their own students and research projects; others are leaders in the conservation community. There is tremendous satisfaction when former students become respected colleagues; I attribute much of my current optimism about the future of the muriquis to them and other Brazilian colleagues, whose ongoing commitment and contributions to science and conservation are filling important niches in the field.

Conservation and concern for the future of wild primates is also a major theme that unites many of the other essays in this volume. I did not prompt the contributors to consider conservation in the way that I asked them to reflect on the human and cultural dimensions of their field experiences, yet the emergence of conservation in one form or another across many of the stories was neither unexpected nor unmerited. With half of the world's primate species now threatened with extinction as a result of anthropogenic activities, there is real cause for alarm—and for action.

The specific challenges to primates differ by species and by region, where traditional attitudes toward primates and their habitats are difficult to separate from the contemporary realities of global economic and political pressures. As conservation advocates, field primatologists can work at local, national, or international levels. This work generates many associations—it brings us into social, economic, and political contact with different spheres of society, depending on the scale of our activities and the accessibility of our targets. In Brazil, for example, there is a strong and vibrant conservation community, as well as an increasingly powerful scientific research tradition. There is also an increasingly informed and engaged public, whose interests in local issues of resource sustainability are forging new alliances with conservationists. I experienced one such initiative when, on the occasion of the thirtieth anniversary of my long-term muriqui project in June 2013, I became an Honorary Citizen of Caratinga, a growing community of about 90,000 inhabitants in whose jurisdiction my research is based. During a unique, multiday event, the Mayor's office and governing council launched *Caratinga +30, Agenda para o Futuro*, an ambitious plan aimed at stimulating various urban improvement programs including sustainable development projects over the next 30 years. Through the muriqui design that featured prominently on the poster and the vision of linking the city's plan for future sustainability with a 30-year research and conservation project, this community has provided proof of the potential for positive impact that primate field studies can have.

Because of its connection to anthropology, field primatology has been among the most introspective of the natural sciences. Critical analyses of these reflections and of the history of primate-human interactions have been conducted by other scholars, some of whose recent works are listed below. *Primate Ethnographies* is intended to be complementary to those. At the same time, I hope *Primate Ethnographies* will open up new avenues for reflection by scholars seeking to include the cultural contexts and the impact of these human dimensions on the field studies that advance our understanding of primates and ultimately inform us of our own place in nature.

Suggested Readings

Fuentes, A., and L. D. Wolfe, eds. 2002. *Primates Face to Face: The Conservation Implications of Human and Nonhuman Primate Interconnections*. New York: Cambridge University Press.

Kappeler, P. M., and D. Watts, eds. 2012. *Long-Term Field Studies of Primates*. New York: Springer.

Rees, A. 2007. "Reflections on the Field: Primatology, Popular Science, and Personhood." *Social Studies of Science* 37/6: 881–907.

Robbins, M. R., and C. Boesch, eds. 2011. *Among African Apes: Stories and Photos from the Field*. Berkeley: University of California Press.

Strier, K. B. 1999. *Faces in the Forest: The Endangered Muriqui Monkeys of Brazil*. Cambridge, MA: Harvard University Press.

Strum, S. C., and L. M. Fedigan, eds. 2000. *Primate Encounters: Models of Science, Gender, and Society*. Chicago: Chicago University Press.

Acknowledgments

My long-term fieldwork with muriquis began when my Ph.D. advisor, Irven DeVore, told me about them. Russ Mittermeier introduced me to them, and Célio Vallé encouraged me to study them. It has been possible to maintain the study thanks to: permission from the Brazilian Research Council, CNPq, and the Abdalla family; sponsorship at different times over the years from Célio Valle, César Ades, Gustavo Fonseca, and Sérgio L. Mendes, who continues to be an essential colleague, collaborator, and friend; and the support of many funding agencies including the National Science Foundation, National Geographic Society, Liz Claiborne and Art Ortenberg Foundation, Fulbright Foundation, Sigma Xi Grants-in-Aid, the Joseph Henry Fund of the NAS, World Wildlife Fund, L.S.B. Leakey Foundation, Chicago Zoological Society, Lincoln Park Zoo Neotropic Fund, Margot Marsh Biodiversity Foundation, Conservation International, the Graduate School of the University of Wisconsin-Madison, and a Hilldale Professorship and a Vilas Professorship from the University of Wisconsin-Madison. I also thank the Sociedade para a Preservação de Muriqui (Preserve Muriqui), Conservation International, and CI-Brasil for administrative support, and Pablo Fernicola, Sonia Souza, and the Microsoft Corporation Employee Matching Gifts Program, and other donors to the project. I thank the many dozens of students and colleagues who have contributed to the long-term demographic monitoring, behavioral research, and logistics in the field. I am especially grateful to Sérgio L. Mendes, Carla B. Possamai, Fernanda P. Tabacow, Marcello Nery, Fabiano de Melo, and Ramiro Abdalla Passos—and to all of the Muriqui Project's other "special" friends (Miriam Leitão, Sérgio Abranches, Cláudio Leitão, among others) for their encouragement and enthusiasm over the years past, and to come.

PART II

Starting Out

There and Back Again
A Primatologist's Tale

By Jim Moore[1]

I write this about 140 kilometers and 37 years from the hillside where, in retrospect, I think I became a primatologist because Delta screamed at me. She was an adolescent baboon in A Troop at Gombe National Park, Tanzania, and had no obvious reason for being upset with me. I had been taking notes on the females of A Troop for weeks, doing an undergraduate project on the acquisition of rank by females as part of my Human Biology major at Stanford. Delta was thoroughly used to my presence, and I wasn't even following her at the moment. Yet, she screamed. And it frightened me; not that *she* could do much harm, but the adult males were looking to see what the threat was, and with their 2–inch-long canine teeth they were decidedly another matter. And there was the injustice—I had done NOTHING to upset her! In the end, the males basically shrugged, she stopped, and I realized that I had seen her behave like this with older female baboons. The penny dropped: If I had been worried about how the males would react, maybe those females had worried too, and that worry had made them nervous enough to defer to Delta. Repeat that trick a few times, and maybe Delta could rise in rank. How doubly cool was that? She appeared to be using males as social tools, and she accepted me as an honorary baboon worthy of trying to dominate. I was hooked. I decided to apply to a graduate school where I could study adolescent female baboons from an evolutionary perspective. The only such program I knew of at the time was at Harvard, so I figured that when I was rejected I would go on, as planned, to study marine biology (intertidal invertebrates, to be precise). Baboons were a longshot diversion.

Three years later I was in grad school and ready to do a pilot study, but all the beds at my advisor's baboon study site were spoken for. Sarah Hrdy suggested I spend the summer in Mt. Abu, India, looking at male langurs. Her recent interpretation of infant-killing by langur males in terms of sexual selection theory had sparked a major controversy; to argue that evolution could

---

[1] About the author: Jim Moore has studied monkeys and apes in Tanzania, India, R.P. Congo, Mali, and Taiwan, and has had a wonderful time there and elsewhere. He now lives just outside Arcata, with redwoods and chickens in the yard. In his next life, he plans to study pygmy killer whales (*Feresa attenuata*).

Contact information: Department of Anthropology, University of California, San Diego, La Jolla, CA 92093, USA, jjmoore@ucsd.edu

Citation: Moore, J. 2014. "There and Back Again: A Primatologist's Tale." In Strier, K. B. (ed.), *Primate Ethnographies*. Upper Saddle River, NJ: Pearson Education, Inc. (pp. 12–24).

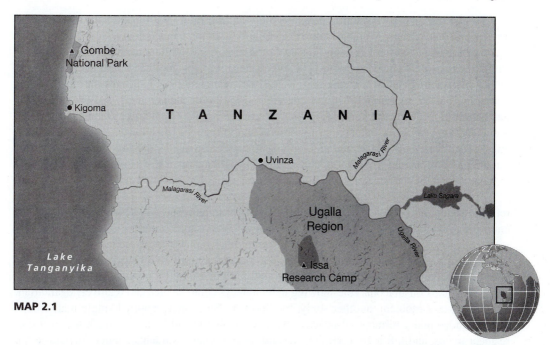

MAP 2.1

produce a behavior so complex (certain males under certain circumstances targeting infants within a narrow age range), counterintuitive (if evolution is about raising more offspring, what's with killing babies?), and just plain nasty (those babies are seriously cute) seemed outrageous to many. A better understanding of male langurs was needed, and I was available—reluctantly. I feared I would be diverted from studying female baboons, and that was just NOT okay.

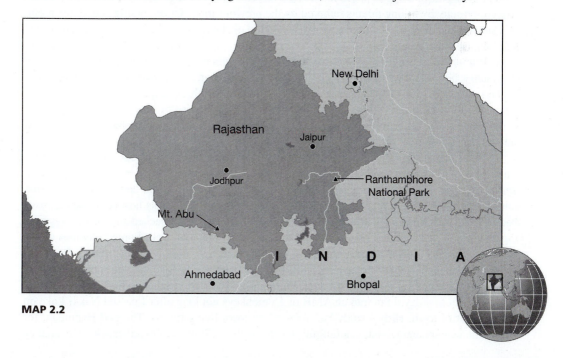

MAP 2.2

It's amazing what academic pressure plus funding (and lack of alternatives) can do. I arrived in Bombay (now Mumbai) knowing virtually nothing about India or langurs. My worst fears were realized as the late-night taxi from the airport passed hundreds of shrouded bodies along the roadside—obviously victims of some catastrophic plague that would likely claim me within days (subsequently realizing they were simply sleeping outside because of the heat was reassuring but brought home just how unprepared I was for the summer). Following Sarah's instructions, I made my way to Mt. Abu and rented a room at the Hotel Surya Darshan (about five rooms, no kitchen or hot water, and my introduction to the joys of bedbugs—many, many bedbugs). Thanks to a tasty but injudicious drink of crushed sugarcane during the day-and-a-half train ride, it was in a fevered, diarrheal daze that I bought a map of town and set out on the road to Sunset Point, on the edge of town, hoping to see langurs for the first time.

In 1977 I knew gray (or Hanuman) langurs, *Semnopithecus entellus*, as a bundle of theoretical puzzles. Two classic studies in different parts of India seemed to describe entirely different monkeys. Phyllis (Jay) Dolhinow found troops composed of multiple males and females, with low rates of aggression and mothers allowing other females to investigate and carry their infants even within hours of birth. They were a marked contrast to the aggressive and (apparently) male-dominated baboons described around the same time by my advisor Irven DeVore, and langurs took on an iconic role showing that monkeys could be nice and relatively egalitarian. But there was a problem; another study, by Yukimaru Sugiyama, reported single-male troops with excluded males forming all-male bands (AMBs) that would violently attack troops, expel resident males, and kill babies. (Huh?) Several of Dolhinow's students studied langurs in the Himalayas and found them multimale and noninfanticidal; when DeVore's student, Hrdy, reported infanticide at Mt. Abu, Dolhnow's group suggested that some sort of social pathology related to living in town might be responsible, with the implication that Hrdy's monkeys were not "normal." If true, that would obviously eliminate her proposed explanation: that males faced with the prospect of being deposed in a couple of years could enlarge their window of reproductive opportunity by killing infants fathered by the previous male. Once nursing ended, the mother's lactational amenorrhea would end and she would ovulate, giving the infanticidal male a head start on his own reproduction.

But why were single-male troops, AMBs, and infanticide seen only at some sites? And for that matter, how could a single male possibly keep an AMB of, say, a dozen males his size at bay in the first place? And if the AMB was really a "band of brothers" expelled from a troop, why were takeovers followed by fighting among the band and the rise of a new single troop male? Lots of questions, all bearing on one of the paradigmatic examples—or debacles—of the new field of sociobiology.

None of that captures the graceful beauty of the langurs themselves—silvery-white fur trimmed with black gloves and face, tails carried in a long, looping arc up and over their backs, wonderfully elegant as long as one ignores the gassy results of their fiber-rich diet. Langurs are colobines, a Family known as leaf-eating monkeys. Their specialized foreguts host cellulose-digesting bacteria, and by fermenting leaves in a microbial stew, cell walls are breached and the monkeys can digest not only the ruptured plant cells but the microbial fauna as well. Some colobines are so attuned to this leafy diet that sugary fruit will make them ill (by lowering the pH of their forestomachs), but Hanuman langurs are atypical and eat a lot of fruit. I have fond memories of snacking on *Carissa* and mango fruit alongside my subjects, while data collection halted for lunch.

On that first day, I ran into an AMB of 15 monkeys not long after I passed Nakki Lake on the way out of town. Hrdy's study had focused on town-living troops. The god Hanuman, for whom the langurs are named, is a faithful devotee of Lord Rama and together with his monkey

FIGURE 2.1 Urban langurs scrounge near a Mt. Abu shop, ignored by its customers.
Photo credit: Jim Moore/Anthro Photo.

and bear followers helped Rama rescue his wife Sita from the demon king of Sri Lanka; Hindus protect and sometimes feed the langurs in return. They get on fairly well alongside people, even in some cities (though sloth bears, capable of killing people yet not inclined to do so, don't seem to have earned the same welcome status).

The tolerance shown for langurs by the people of Mt. Abu was remarkable, especially in contrast to a similar situation one might encounter in the United States. In San Diego, ground squirrels and rabbits are periodically poisoned off when they become "problems," and swallow nests under balconies are destroyed to avoid the messiness of droppings. Now try to imagine a group of 25 large monkeys (adult males weigh up to about 18 kg) jumping on laundry lines, raiding gardens and market stalls, and defecating wherever they please. And yet the langurs were welcome.

I haven't been to India in almost thirty years. I hope that the commensal langurs of Mt. Abu town have remained even as the human population has more than tripled since the mid-1970s. But it is well known that as India has modernized, the balance between cultural/religious-based tolerance for monkeys and the very real nuisance they present has shifted. Some populations are still going strong, such as at Jodhpur where long-term research by S. M. Mohnot, Lal Singh Rajpurohit, and others has contributed to the langurs' preservation (Google "Jodhpur monkeys" for some YouTube videos of the monkeys). But overall, monkey numbers have fallen as traditional values change.

Those traditional values took some getting used to. I was initially hesitant to follow monkeys through people's courtyards, but when town kids started wandering into my hotel room to watch me work if I left the door open, I realized American privacy concepts didn't really hold. Even on the hillsides I was rarely alone for long; there were always woodcutters or kids tending their goats, and a hermit lived in a cave within my study group's range. His hair was matted and dirty, and he dressed in soiled, ragged robes. Imagine my surprise when I finally talked with him and learned that in addition to knowing the individual members of my focal group well, he'd been to South America and now sold drugs to some of the European and American seekers of enlightenment (or adventure, or escape) who wandered into Mt. Abu's ashrams. Never, never jump to conclusions based on appearances!

Still, I preferred the relative solitude of the hillsides outside of town, a Forest Reserve where leopard, bear, and sambhar deer still lived (and, at least once, a tiger visited for a while). This was a good thing, as I quickly learned that while langur troops were found all over town, AMBs were effectively excluded from the rich pickings of the bazaar. With lots of people-provided provisions, troop ranges could be small and the relatively close packing of troops meant that anytime an AMB ranged townward, they were immediately detected and seen off by a troop male. So how did troop males, acting individually, not only hold their troops but keep AMBs entirely out of town?

The first part of the answer follows from the asymmetry in payoffs. A troop male fights for his existing offspring and females; a challenger fights the troop male only for the chance to take on all his erstwhile AMB compatriots in the subsequent struggle to become the new troop male. Who wants to risk injury under such circumstances? And then there's the fact that troop males fight dirty. On several occasions I was with an AMB that was minding its own business, relaxing, resting, or feeding nowhere near a troop when a troop male burst in at speed, attacked a surprised male, and ran off whooping. Each time, there was blood. (In one case, the juvenile victim's abdominal wall was nearly ripped open; his survival was to me miraculous.)

For an AMB male, attacking a troop is dangerous and the payoff is uncertain; even being near a troop is risky. I believe what goes on is that an AMB monitors several troops (on average,

FIGURE 2.2 A coalition of two males harasses a male of another coalition, all within the same all-male band (AMB) at Ranthambhore, India. The nested interest levels (individual, coalition, and band) make for real social complexity; allies in today's interband fight or intraband coalition squabble are tomorrow's enemies when it comes to the final stages of a troop male replacement. **Photo credit:** Jim Moore/Anthro Photo.

about four to six), probing each one every week or so, challenging the troop male but then withdrawing, waiting for something to happen to him—illness, injury, predation—and only then moving in.

And this explains the absence of AMBs from the town of Mt. Abu. The people of the town often fed monkeys; there were crops to raid; leopards rarely entered past the outskirts. Mt. Abu town was a great place to be a langur, and the density of monkeys ($87/km^2$) was nearly three times greater than in the forest reserve immediately adjacent. Any AMB that moved into the center of town would have been buffeted by troop males continuously, so the "surplus" males held to the periphery, waiting, waiting. The local population density had predictable consequences for how male tactics would play out, resulting in a change in the relative distribution of troops and AMBs.

It's a nice story, and the theme of population density having predictable consequences for behavioral tactics is one to which I'll return, but it's pretty abstract. And aside from the sneak-attack phenomenon, most of it was at least guessed at before my arrival. As Sarah Hrdy had pointed out years earlier, what is really great about watching langurs is the ongoing soap opera as individuals (appear to) play high-stakes strategic games.

I had been following my first focal AMB for only a week or so when I arrived one morning to see two of them copulating. Yes, definitely intromission, but who was it? I compared my notes of facial scars, ear-nicks,and so on, and couldn't make the ID. The band was unsettled that morning—lots of running around—and to my surprise I saw another pair copulating. As I recall, it was several hours before it occurred to me that I should take another look at the rear ends of the individuals I'd seen mounted—sure enough, they were females (in my defense, this was all less than two weeks after my first glimpse of a langur!). It piqued my curiosity: What was going on?

The two females stayed with the band all day, sexually presenting repeatedly. The next day, a second AMB showed up, and the forest was chaotic as males fought each other over these promiscuous ladies. In one unforgettable episode, the two bands were fighting around a small clearing, while I perched atop a small cliff on the uphill side from which I could watch, comfortably sitting on a ledge. The males would surge back and forth, attacking and counterattacking (without the motivational asymmetry of troop male-AMB encounters, interband fights could be long and violent). Then, during a pause, one of the older males, breathing hard, came over and sat down within a foot of me and together we surveyed the battlefield. There is something profound about such moments of shared being: He and I both wanted to know what was happening, were both tired, and solved the problem identically. Then one of the females walked deliberately into the middle of the clearing and, without singling out anyone, began to crouch and shake her head rapidly in a sexual solicitation; males charged and the fight was back on. My memory is that my companion actually sighed and shrugged his shoulders as he stood to dive back into the fray, but perhaps that's projection.

The whole scene reminded me of elephant seals. Or rather, of a recent paper by Cathy Cox and Burney Le Boeuf on female incitation of male-male competition, stimulated by their observations of elephant seals at Año Nuevo in California. Females loudly vocalized whenever a male attempted to copulate; that would get the attention of any nearby male and, unless the copulating male was the undisputed dominant of the area, a fight would ensue. Cox and Le Boeuf realized that the effect of the female's vocalization was that only the most dominant male would ever complete a copulation with her—her cries provoked male-male competition and thus, were actually mechanisms of female choice.

Could this female langur be inciting competition "deliberately"? The result of presenting to about 15 males from two AMBs from the middle of a clearing certainly was male-male competition, not sex. But had she *intended* to provoke a fight? Or was she simply enslaved by raging hormones, sexually presenting whenever she saw a likely male, and this time it misfired? It is tough to be sure, but on other occasions I saw females slip away into the middle of dense, cactus-like *Euphorbia* bushes with preferred males to mate without the risks of being harassed. (It was always funny to watch as they tried to accommodate each other's motions without being poked by thorns.)

On the third day, the females returned to their original troop. The other AMB had gone its own way, while my AMB was close on the females' heels. To my surprise, no troop male waited; something must have happened to him, and the two females had in effect gone looking for a replacement, provoking competition between bands.

The result was a summer of high drama, as the two AMBs and several lone males battled to take over the females' troop. Within my focal group, Brand, the #4 male, began to target the higher-ranking males, and after Corwin left (for unknown reasons), he rapidly rose over Eric to become the dominant male of the group. Hrdy had speculated that a wise male ought to act subordinate prior to a takeover, in order to convince his friends/rivals that they were going to win (and so motivate them to do most of the fighting). Brand's behavior fit that pattern, but was it actually a strategy? With only a single such episode, it's impossible to tell.

The field season hooked me; having gone to grad school because I wanted to study adolescent female baboons in Kenya, I was now determined to work on male langurs in India and try to get large enough sample sizes to validate the intuitions I'd formed that first summer. I returned two years later, full of excitement. Things started well, with several months at Mt. Abu and then shifting to Ranthambhore Tiger Sanctuary (now a National Park, where "human disturbance" could be excluded as an influence on langur behavior). An assistant of Sarah Hrdy's was watching a large troop that ranged near the two AMBs I was studying; our hope was that we'd get to see a takeover from both sides. We almost did, but the morning that one of my AMBs invaded Sylvia's troop, we got word that the Government of India had suspended our research clearance pending investigation of the charge that we were working without proper permissions.

It was a circus for which I was unprepared. Prime Minister Indira Gandhi got involved; there was a decades-old grudge between senior Indian scientists; there was an unfaithful husband locked in a room with a bottle of whiskey and a shotgun; there was Indo-American tension over India's nuclear policy; there was a front-page article blaming us for the killing of a troop of langurs by villagers almost 200 kilometers away; and the list goes on. I spent six months in India waiting for the problem to be resolved and gave up only when I learned that our file had been sent to Group Captain Balakrishnan of the Aeronautics Division for his approval. I pictured him thinking, "Why has this come to me? It's totally unrelated to anything I do. There must be a catch. I've got to send it on to someone else and let them worry about it." I realized the situation was hopeless.

I came back to Harvard with a fraction of the data I'd been aiming for and a visceral reaction against working on what I did have. To this day, looking at my notebooks floods me with bitter memories. But, as the saying goes, when one door closes another opens.

During the six months spent waiting, I had traveled some and that included a visit to Rauf Ali, who was working on bonnet macaques in Tamil Nadu. Though I wasn't officially doing research, I was interested to see an adolescent female nilgiri langur in what otherwise looked like an AMB, and Rauf showed me a different young female in a troop of Hanuman langurs nearby. Over beers, we wondered what was going on and talked about writing a short note describing these observations. Some months after I got back to the United States, Rauf sent me a draft, and

I was struck by the second paragraph's brief statement to the effect that our report was interesting because female primates almost never left their troop of birth; in all but a handful of species, dispersal was done by males in order to avoid inbreeding.

I wanted to be sure these were accurate statements and started reading papers on emigration by females and explanations for dispersal in general. Several years and hundreds of pages later, my dissertation consisted of a chapter on langurs and several papers on primate dispersal; I had finessed my problems with the AMB data by doing mainly theoretical literature reviews. All well and good, and it got me a job at UC San Diego, but I wanted to do fieldwork and India was closed. What to do?

While I was writing up, I sat in on a course co-taught by Barbara Smuts (primate behaviorist), David Pilbeam (paleoanthropologist), and Glynn Isaac (paleoarchaeologist) in which the three looked at how we could integrate our understanding of modern primate behavioral ecology with evidence from fossils and artifacts to form testable theories about Plio-Pleistocene hominins. It was fascinating. And around the same time Bill McGrew and Caroline Tutin—friends and mentors from my first Gombe experience—together with their students were publishing papers describing savanna-dwelling chimpanzees in Senegal. They noted that such savanna populations live in habitats similar to those in which early hominins lived and that population densities were much lower than those of better-known forest populations. Aha! Population density! I had a plan.

But first I need to explain about population density as a variable that affects behavior. There is a tendency to assume that if population density explains variation in a phenomenon such as the occurrence of langur infanticide, it should do so linearly—none at low density, some at intermediate densities, and lots at high densities. That would fit with popular views of high population density leading to pathological behavior (drawing on the work of John Calhoun with captive rats and the "behavioral sink," as well as lurid news accounts of crime in big American cities). The problem was that langur infanticide showed no such linear correlation with density across sites, and so population density had been rejected as an explanatory variable.

The thing is, population density doesn't "do anything" itself; it sets the stage upon which behavioral tactics unfold. For langurs living at very low densities, the troops are so widely spaced that the AMB tactic of monitoring four to six troops on a regular basis doesn't work—the cost of searching for troops is too high, so subordinate males do better by shadowing a single troop (which in effect makes it multimale, with confused paternity and infanticide not favored). At very high population densities, encounters are frequent and "intruder pressure" is so high that no single male can monopolize a troop; multimale troops result, again without infanticide because infants might be sired by different males. Only at intermediate population densities does troop male aggression and AMB monitoring come into equilibrium, resulting in a high proportion of single-male troops and setting the stage for sexually selected infanticide. Thus, the key advance came from thinking about what population density does to individual behavioral options, not about density as an independent "force" acting on populations.

This was a transformative realization to me, because of what it might say about the putative inevitability of human violence. I grew up during the Cold War, and vividly recall one afternoon hearing civil defense sirens in San Francisco and seriously wondering if I would be vaporized within minutes. John Brunner's masterful novel *Stand on Zanzibar* made a powerful case for the human dystopia in store if Calhoun was correct about his rat model for human pathological behavior. But what if the general interpretation of Calhoun's work was wrong? Don't misunderstand me—I believe that high population density can create conditions that leave people with dismal options. But *options* are . . . optional, and we can work on finding better ones.

FIGURE 2.3   Dé, on the last day he was seen alive. While he had no major visible external wounds, he moved painfully and was emaciated; the ridges of his scapula and spine are clearly visible. His eyes had a haunted look that was painful to see. **Photo credit:** Jim Moore/Anthro Photo.

I'm not so naïve as to think better understanding the biological bases for human violence will save the world, but it is a debate with some real meaning. And low-density savanna chimpanzees may be a piece of the puzzle.

This is because, like humans, (forest) chimpanzees practice "lethal coalitionary raiding," in which males of a community will stalk, attack, and sometimes kill individuals (usually male) of neighboring communities. I saw the results of such attacks as an undergrad at Gombe, when I followed Kahama male Dé for a day, about three weeks after he was beaten by Kasakela males; it was the last time he was seen alive. Richard Wrangham and colleagues have suggested (I believe correctly) that this behavior stems from chimpanzees' unusual fission-fusion social system.

Because of it, there is always the potential for an intergroup encounter between a small group from one community and a large group from another; such imbalances of power allow virtually risk-free aggression. The degree to which observations of chimpanzees tell us anything about the "roots" of human violence is hotly debated and finely nuanced, so here I'll just assert that understanding chimpanzees is interesting in its own right, might be relevant to us, and so is a worthy goal until proven otherwise.

For male chimpanzees there can be a social cost to traveling alone; political rivals can form alliances in one's absence. So the fission-fusion system (and resulting potential for power imbalance) presumably depends in some way on the ability of individuals to separate for hours or days to feed but then come together relatively often for social reasons. This must be a function of territory size. (If everyone is crammed together in a small range, "fission" loses meaning because one's allies are likely to be within calling distance; in a vast range, how do

FIGURE 2.4   Alex Piel and Busoti Juma listening for chimpanzee calls overlooking the Ugalla Primate Project's main study valley at Issa, Ugalla. We arrived before sunrise and, hours later, hadn't heard anything. Some days are like that, but it sure beats office work! **Photo credit:** Jim Moore.

individuals find each other to form parties?) And since community sizes are relatively constant (usually 30–80 individuals), territory size is related to population density. As best as we can tell, some savanna chimpanzees live at population densities 30–50 times lower than those of forest chimpanzees—and that HAS to do something interesting to fission-fusion dynamics and, potentially, the expression of intercommunity violence.

So after graduate school I switched from langurs and went back to (near) where I started, to a site primatologists call "Ugalla"—a little more than 3,000 square kilometers of miombo savanna woodland in western Tanzania. The contrast with Mt. Abu couldn't be greater.

On my first visit, I hitchhiked down a dirt road for half a day and then, equipped with a hand-drawn sketchmap given to me by Toshisada Nishida, I set out to investigate the region. I found chimpanzee nests almost immediately and was thrilled to see a small herd of zebra not far from them. What I did not see, for about four days, was any other human or any flowing water. On the second day, I filled my canteen from a puddle in which I'm sure a hyena had wallowed— it was awful. (I treated it with plenty of iodine tablets.) The tsetse flies were merciless, their bites sometimes unnoticed and sometimes feeling like a red-hot needle. I came away vowing not to return, but I had been hooked.

Here were chimpanzees living in a relatively intact savanna ecosystem with iconic animals like elephant, lion, antelope, hippo, and buffalo, as well as at least seven other primate species, barely 500 kilometers from Olduvai Gorge. That was worth some discomfort.

When I started working there, the only electricity in Uvinza, the nearest town, was at the local salt factory. I pitched my tent near the house of a young minor official, Juma Mkondo, and

FIGURE 2.5 Visiting CARTA graduate students and Ugalla Primate Project field assistants take notes on some old chimpanzee nests in open woodland just above a patch of streamside evergreen forest; such forest makes up only about 2 percent of the habitat. **Photo credit:** Jim Moore.

while in Uvinza, I would play with his toddlers and watch chickens chase snakes in the dust. When electricity finally reached the main town, someone got a TV and VCR, set them on a table with a fence around it, and it was the town's first theatre. Today, the town headquarters of the Ugalla Primate Project (UPP) is on land owned by Juma. Juma's children are grown, and he is now a district agricultural officer based in Kigoma. There are two guesthouses in town (each with its own TV), and the market is bustling every day rather than just weekends. A madrasah 'Islamiyyah has opened, and the chanting of the children's lessons competes with radio hip hop.

Those are superficial changes. Also new since I started work at Ugalla are AIDS and conflicts in Rwanda, Burundi, and Congo that have flooded Tanzania with refugees. I visited one of the refugee camps in 2001 with a TV crew and felt powerless when confronted by a young man who very politely but firmly noted that the visit and resulting show would benefit our careers and asked what the Congolese in the camp would receive. I mumbled something about "increased awareness of your plight," which fooled nobody. I didn't tell him that I had earlier advised the United Nations High Commission on Refugees to site the camp there, on the north side of the Malagarasi River, knowing that as I did so to protect the wildlife to the south, I was probably condemning the last chimpanzee community known on the north bank. (As of this writing, the camp has finally been disbanded, but it isn't known if any chimpanzees remain of the Lilanshimba community.) Indeed, the combination of general economic development and refugee influx in western Tanzania has had an impact on all wildlife, becoming severe in the late 1990s. Zebra might still be present in Ugalla, but none have been sighted by project members for years; and while I don't miss the tsetse bites themselves, it is sobering to realize that fewer flies result from fewer animals.

FIGURE 2.6   Field assistant Busoti Juma collects fresh chimpanzee feces from a dry streambed in Ugalla, while Amani Kenge looks on. Such samples provide us with information about community size and association patterns (using DNA), diet (lots of washing and sieving), and health. Our collaborators have identified six protozoan and two nematode parasite species, and found a 30 percent prevalence of Simian Immunodeficiency Virus (SIV). **Photo credit:** Jim Moore.

India has been urban for as long as Europe, so wildlife there had reached an equilibrium of sorts long before I first visited; tolerated species are doing fine and others are restricted to reserves, with numbers small enough that conservation is relatively straightforward—a matter of trying to save what's left. In Tanzania, such an equilibrium is still in the future, with all the conservation potential and risk that entails. Ugalla is uniquely valuable as a scientific resource, but its value lies precisely in the low population densities that make it an apparently cost-ineffective location to save large numbers of animals. We don't know what the future will bring; meantime, our presence helps to prevent poaching, and the long-term data contribute to the value of saving this unique chimpanzee habitat.

Though I began this essay at Issa Camp, Ugalla, I complete it where I now do most of my work—Northern California, where my interest in chimpanzees has me balancing checkbooks for the UPP and advising students/collaborators via e-mail. We still don't know how low density affects community structure and intercommunity relationships, but the best available evidence suggests that the 70-plus individuals who use the area near camp have a community range of hundreds of square kilometers, larger than the ranges of all other non-savanna chimpanzee research communities combined. Thanks to a variety of indirect methods, including noninvasive DNA sampling (which I helped Phil Morin to pioneer some twenty years ago) and acoustic monitoring/tomography (using methods adapted by my student Alex Piel from marine bioacoustics), we've made notable discoveries and have hints of more to come. See http://ugallaprimateproject.com/ for more on our work.

What an amazing path Delta's screams pointed me toward.

Suggested Readings

Gagneux, P., J. Moore, and A. Varki. 2005. "The Ethics of Research on Great Apes." *Nature 437*: 27–29.

Hrdy, S. B. 1976. *Langurs of Abu*. Cambridge, MA: Harvard University Press.

Moore, J. 1984. "Female Transfer in Primates." *International Journal of Primatology 5*: 537–589.

Moore, J. 1996. "'Savanna' Chimpanzees, Referential Models and the Last Common Ancestor." In McGrew, W. C., L. Marchant, and T. Nishida (eds.), *Great Ape Societies*. Cambridge: Cambridge University Press (pp. 275–292).

Moore, J. 1999. "Population Density, Social Pathology, and Behavioral Ecology." *Primates. 40*: 5–26.

Ogawa, H., G. Idani, J. Moore, L. Pintea, and A. Hernandez-Aguilar. 2007. "Sleeping Parties and Nest Distribution of Chimpanzees in the Savanna Woodland, Ugalla, Tanzania." *International Journal of Primatology 28*: 1397–1412.

Acknowledgments

What a futile task, to attempt to thank everyone to whom I owe heartfelt thanks for a career that has spanned continents and decades (and then there's the funding agencies and institutions which have made it possible, and family and friends who accepted it). Without Don Kennedy, David Hamburg and Jane Goodall I'd never have started; Bill McGrew ensured (more than once) that I continued. Chuck Baxter, Richard Wrangham, Sarah Hrdy, Steve Gaulin, David Pilbeam, Barb Smuts, Alan Walker, Irven DeVore, Jack Bradbury . . . and so many others . . . shaped my thinking. Shirley Strum, Katerina Semendeferi, Margaret Schoeninger, and Pascal Gagneux made "work" at UCSD an oxymoron, and Ajit Varki spearheaded CARTA. Carole Sussman— I owe you. Thanks to Juma Mkondo, Adriana Hernandez-Aguilar, Moshi Rajabu, Alex Piel, Fiona Stewart, Busoti Juma and the rest of the Issa group for past, present and future at Ugalla. Thanks to Anton Collins for 40 years and counting of advice, and the rest of the watu wa Gombe; Jules. Karen, you're a star; Sue, Caite, Ben and Maeve, you're wonderful. Among those who have supported my work, special gratitude is due to the LSB Leakey Foundation, and also to UCSD's Center for Academic Research & Training in Anthropogeny (CARTA) for incredible intellectual stimulation as well as ongoing support for the work at Ugalla. I was a victim of a series of accidents, as are we all—I have been fortunate that most were lucky ones.

3

Moonlit Walks
A Serendipitous Journey from Baboons and Chimpanzees to Nocturnal Primates

By Leanne T. Nash[1]

Listening to a lashing thunderstorm hit the desert, I am transported from my office at Arizona State University (ASU) back in time and place to field sites in Africa and Madagascar as I recall other thunderstorms that evoked feelings of wonder, excitement, welcome relief from the heat, a bit of fear, and a sinking feeling in the pit of my stomach. I sit huddled in a poncho, high on a hill, watching the edge of the rain storm sweep across Lake Tanganyika, while near me sits a soaked baboon mother, infant on her chest, water dripping from her nose. My reveries fade into dusk at a forest growing on the ruins of an ancient walled town on the Kenyan coast on a night fortunately without a storm. Another mother, this time a tiny nocturnal galago (or bushbaby), emerges from a tree hole with her baby in her mouth, like a mother cat carries a kitten. For the very first evening since it was born just over a week ago, the mother is moving her infant from its birth nest. With that burden in her teeth, she takes a startlingly long leap and scampers away. "Parking" baby on a branch, she forages for a time nearby before returning to move and park it again, repeatedly, for a night of bouts of foraging "alone." Another vivid recollection: a bushbaby only a few feet away—I could almost touch it but don't—turns its back on my headlamp and clearly uses the light to scan for insect prey.

This mix of emotions that the storm brings comes from having often worked and lived where the rains come suddenly and violently. My intellect knows that rains are often sorely needed after a long and unpredictable dry period. Both people and the animals depend on the arrival of that rain. I tell newcomers to Arizona that the desert will be home when they stop to watch it rain. But that churning in my stomach comes from remembering what it was like trying

---

[1]About the author: Leanne T. Nash grew up in Sacramento, California, attended the University of California, Davis as an undergraduate psychology major (B.A. 1967), and did graduate work in biological anthropology at the University of California, Berkeley (Ph.D. 1973). She did fieldwork on primates in Tanzania, Kenya, Madagascar, South Africa, and briefly in China. Her husband, Michael P. Nash, aided by multiple cats and dogs, has been an important partner supporting her career, and her "offspring" are the 26 masters students and 9 doctoral students, all wonderful, whom she was privileged to supervise, as well as many other students she was able to mentor, across a 41-year career in anthropology at Arizona State University.

Contact information: School of Human Evolution & Social Change [SHESC], Arizona State University, Tempe, AZ 85287-2402, USA, leanne.nash@asu.edu

Citation: Nash, L. T. 2014. "Moonlit Walks: A Serendipitous Journey from Baboons and Chimpanzees to Nocturnal Primates." In Strier, K. B. (ed.), *Primate Ethnographies*. Upper Saddle River, NJ: Pearson Education, Inc. (pp. 25–33).

FIGURE 3.1 At Gedi (or Gede) Ruins National Monument, Kenya, a *Galagoides cocos* (formerly *Galagoides zanzibaricus*) female with her few-days-old infant in her mouth, carrying it away from her nest hole for the first time since the infant was born. **Photo credit** (and copyright): Leanne Nash.

to follow nonhuman primates in the rain, especially as most of my fieldwork was conducted at night. Work is less appealing in the rain and sometimes impossible: harder, messier, and possibly more dangerous. One slips and falls. Carrying a radio-tracking antenna around at night over your head in a lightning storm is not highly recommended. My students hear me chant that "the animal is never doing nothing . . . ," but in a hard rain, it seems like it.

Thinking about my changing perspectives on the rain makes me think about other changes of perspective I have gained throughout my career. In two words, my mantra has become "embrace serendipity." I have been lucky to have opportunities and also to be forced by circumstances to abandon career paths for different ones. Right now (in 2013), I am at retirement and over 45 years have passed since I discovered my fascination with the behavior of primates in my junior year as a psychology major at the University of California, Davis. As a sophomore, I took a "breadth requirement" from an inspiring teacher of "Introduction to Psychology," Gordon Bermant, who subsequently became my undergraduate mentor. Consequently, I switched my undergraduate major from medical technology to psychology (having simultaneously hit the third semester of chemistry like a brick wall). The next year, in his animal behavior class, I serendipitously did *not* get my first choice for a term paper topic (cetaceans) and instead got my second choice, apes. George Schaller and Jane Goodall were just beginning to publish their pioneering fieldwork on gorillas and chimpanzees. The next term, I took an anthropology class in primatology from Phyllis Jay Dolhinow. After that class, she encouraged me to switch to anthropology for graduate school and would become my Ph.D. mentor at UC Berkeley. At the time that I needed a Ph.D. field project, she also served on the Ph.D. committee of Tim Ransom, who initiated work on baboons at Gombe National Park, Tanzania. Serendipity: I wanted to go to Africa

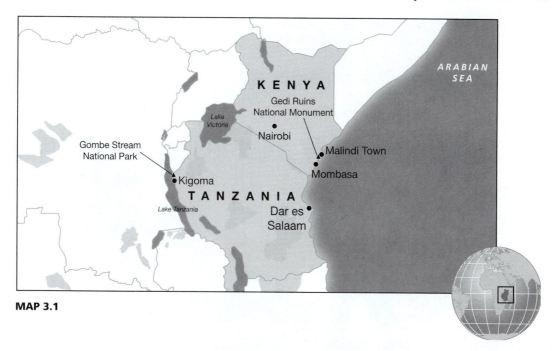

MAP 3.1

and study mother-infant behavior; he wanted someone to continue working on the baboons he had habituated.

After my dissertation work at Gombe in 1969–1970 on baboon mother-infant interactions, and a second field season in 1972 (with new husband in tow), my interests in long-term behavioral development, individual differences and temperament, and sex differences were solidified. I was thrilled when Jane Goodall suggested I continue long-term baboon work at Gombe. As a beginning assistant professor at ASU, I felt that I had a solid career plan established. That would change.

In 1975, rebels kidnapped four members of the research team at Gombe. Fortunately, eventually all were released, but it was a scary and worrisome time. Then Gombe was closed to most expatriate researchers for many years, and a door slammed on my fieldwork plans. As an untenured assistant professor, I was selfishly disappointed and unnerved. But other serendipitous events had come together at ASU: Anthropology had a newly renovated building with space for a possible "primate lab," and I had come to Arizona with a bushbaby that had been the pet of a former Peace Corp Volunteer. Bushbabies, also called galagos, are small, nocturnal, arboreal, and illusive strepsirrhine primates found in Africa. He had brought "Frodo" (named for its hairy toes) from Kenya and could not keep it. At the time, it was legal and fairly common for bushbabies to become pets in East Africa and they could be imported into the United States. However, an animal that marks its territory by wiping its urine on its feet, and has a really strong bite for its size, really is not an appropriate pet. This animal inspired me to develop a small colony of bushbabies in the available indoor space where the light-cycle was reversible. ASU maintained that colony for about 20 years. With the help of many students, we collected data on mother-infant interactions, sex differences in behavior, and behavioral development. The early stages of development of bushbabies are hard to see in the field due their nesting in tree holes and the "parking" behavior described earlier. Many students learned how to make careful, quantified observations

FIGURE 3.2   Two adult *Galago senegalensis* in the lab show interest in the food just eaten by a third. Note methods of identification of individuals: the fur clipping on the tail of one galago, a tag (a washer) on another animal's neck chain, and nothing on a third. **Photo credit** (and copyright): Leanne Nash.

of primate behavior by watching our bushbabies. Simultaneously, I began a long collaboration with the Primate Foundation of Arizona, which maintained a chimpanzee colony dedicated to the improvement of the well-being of captive chimpanzees. I, and my students, especially Sue Howell, assisted them in developing systems for data collection on longitudinal behavior development in chimpanzees born there and on the efficacy of behavioral enrichment options.

I had always wanted to combine the advantages of fieldwork and captive work, given that classic ethology and comparative psychology had shown that each were suitable for different sorts of causal questions about behavior. Due to the events at Gombe, I would change my field work career from baboons—large, diurnal, terrestrial, easily observed monkeys—to "none of the above." I sought to initiate fieldwork on the same species of bushbaby, *Galago senegalensis*, that we had at ASU. In pioneering fieldwork on nocturnal primates, what we thought at the time was that species had already been studied in South Africa by Simon Bearder and Gerry Doyle, and other bushbabies and pottos had been studied in West Africa by Pierre Charles-Dominique. In East Africa, where I had previously studied baboons, there was an "empty niche" for galago studies.

In the summer of 1976, after first consulting with Bearder in England, I surveyed for a field site in Kenya where I could, like Charles-Dominique, examine "my species" from the lab in sympatry (living in the same location with potential access to the same resources) with a close relative, a greater thick-tailed galago. Charles-Dominique had shown that sympatric nocturnal species would, as expected, have some differences in resource use, often related to the influence of body size on diet. Socioecological theory predicted that species' social behaviors should differ in ways related to contrasts between the distribution of different foods in time and space. At the time, few people thought that the nocturnal primates differed much in their social behavior. In fact they were considered "solitary" and were dismissed in most discussions of primate socio-ecology. Sometimes they still are.

Thus far in this essay, I have mostly avoided giving proper taxonomic names to the animals I have studied. The accepted scientific names for the animals I studied in the field have changed several times over the past 40 years. I've been dragged, kicking and screaming a bit, into issues of primate taxonomy. Mercifully, the animals I had in my lab have stayed *Galago senegalensis* (so far) but for many nocturnal primates there has been extensive taxonomic revision and species "splitting" due to changes in (1) the dominant philosophy of doing taxonomy and of defining a species (species concepts), (2) new discoveries about the animals as they were better studied in the wild, partly due to new genetic techniques (e.g., PCR, fecal DNA methods), (3) the incorporation of more genetic information into defining species and phylogenies, along with the more traditional morphological ("skins and skulls") data, and (4) the pressures on taxonomy imposed by how conservation laws and treaties are written. The latter tend to protect taxa, not habitats, so taxonomy must accurately reflect biodiversity.

Since the 1970s the number of species of nocturnal primates recognized has exploded as people discovered methods that made studying these challenging species more practical. The smaller bushbaby that I studied on the coast of Kenya has been called "*Galago senegalensis*," "*Galago zanzibaricus*," "*Galagoides zanzibaricus*," and is currently best referred to as *Galagoides cocos* (though there was a proposal at a conference in summer, 2013 by Judith Masters, Luca Pozzi, and colleagues that it belongs in a completely new genus as "*Paragalagoides cocos*"). The larger bushbaby has been known, and published on as, "*Galago crassicaudatus*," "*Galago garnettii*," and now *Otolemur garnettii*. Led by scholars like Simon Bearder, using the specific mate recognition species concept, attention has focused on the varying acoustic structure of loud "self-advertisement" calls of different populations of galagos. These calls, which communicate "mate recognition" criteria, are more distinctive and diverse than visible features that morphologists had previously used. After sorting populations by these call patterns, both genetics and subtle morphological distinctions (facial mask markings, relative ear size, palmer "fingerprints," and detailed penile anatomy) correlate with these vocal differences.

It turns out the ASU galagos were not the same species as those studied in South Africa after all. Working with Kaye Izard at the Duke Lemur Center, we found that we were studying very similar bushbabies from eastern Africa and from southern Africa, respectively, but that the two sets of animals had significant differences in body size, a propensity to have twins, and about a twenty-day difference in gestation length. Now, the galago we had at ASU is still recognized as a *Galago senegalensis,* separated from the Duke species, now called *Galago moholi*. All other nocturnal primate clades (lorises in Asia, pottos in Africa, nocturnal lemurs in Madagascar, tarsiers in Asia, and owl monkeys in South America) have all had similar taxonomic "splitting" for similar reasons. Thus, care must be taken when reading the older literature on these primates to "unscramble" the taxonomic history of the last few decades and understand which taxa are really discussed in each case.

What were those changes that made field studies of nocturnal primates easier to pursue? Some have been specific to working in the nocturnal environment, such as improved sources of light for the diurnal observer to see the animals and radio-tracking, which allows identifying and keeping track of individuals. The earliest observations of these animals' behavior were made with lights powered by heavy batteries, which required access to a source of electricity to recharge them and had to be carried. There was little or no way to identify individuals or follow such small, fast-moving animals at night. Making notes while following the galagos, either with paper and pencil or as recordings on a heavy and temperamental portable tape recorder, was very awkward. Early methods of radio-tracking involved transmitters and batteries that were often too large for the animal's size; they were also expensive, and often required the investigator to have the skill to assemble them in the field. When I began graduate work in primatology, I never imagined I would learn skills like soldering delicate wires to attach a battery to a tiny transmitter (about one-quarter of an inch square) or covering such an assembly with the same mix of materials used to make false fingernails! Body size limits transmitter weight, most of which is the battery, and battery size equals battery life. Transmitter failures were fairly common, not to mention the effort involved in capturing the animal to put the collar with transmitter on it. And even with radio-tracking, at night you can be right under the animal and not be able to see it at all or not for long. Also, hours would be spent transcribing and tallying up observations with, at best, a typewriter and an electric calculator. Today, batteries for lights, transmitters, and receivers are all smaller, lighter, and longer-lasting. LED technology has produced head lamps that use very limited amounts of battery power. Improved solar recharging technology has meant that work can be done in much more remote locations, far away from sources of electricity. Radio-tracking technology now includes capabilities like GPS, body temperature and heart rate monitors, and activity level and "death" sensors.

Other changes have made all fieldwork easier. Hand-held devices are used to record behavior and feed data directly into computers for analysis. Those computers may be an ocean away, connected by the Internet. For me, a key change is ease of quick global communication, including the ability to manage money from accounts around the world in remote locations. Until recently, an airmail letter from the United States to Africa could take a couple of months to get a response, even if the correspondent answered immediately. International telephone was difficult and very expensive—if the correspondent even had access to a telephone. Managing research funding could require carrying large amounts of cash and waiting for slow and fee-laden transfers. Today, even small towns have Internet cafés and automated teller machines. One "Skypes" to make research arrangements, and to stay in touch "back home," which is critical psychologically. Of course, technology has probably raised the bar for researchers' productivity expectations, an example of "be careful what you wish for."

Those two galago species I studied on the coast of Kenya did turn out to differ from each other in their social behavior and in the ecology of their main foods and of the forest canopy layers used. But neither was the species I had in the lab. Subsequent efforts to get back to fieldwork on that species opened another serendipitous window into the use of a rare food for most primates—plant gums (or "exudates"), a staple for *Galago senegalensis* and *G. moholi*. Because exudates pose digestive challenges similar to those of cell walls in leaves, we don't expect to see small bodied primates eating those foods. The oddity of this led me to study both exudate eating in the lab bushbabies and the diet and behavior of a small Malagasy folivorous lemur, *Lepilemur*. Both have to solve similar digestive challenges, given their main foods and their small size; exudate eating might have been an evolutionary route to folivory.

Improved feasibility of fieldwork on the nocturnal primates has revealed social diversity among these species that was, and still remains, often underappreciated. The four species I have worked most on all are more or less different in their sociality. Their active (nocturnal foraging) sociality is "dispersed" versus "gregarious"—mediated in space and time by scent marking and vocalizations, and they come together in regular sleeping groupings. Their varying social patterns have analogies to diurnal monkeys and apes living in "pairs," "multimale, multifemale groups," and "one-male groups." Perhaps someday we will have the detailed ecological and

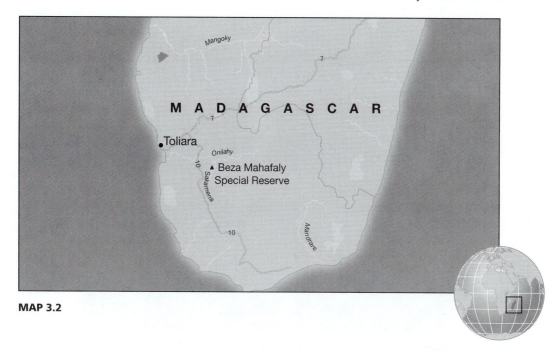

MAP 3.2

FIGURE 3.3 Leanne Nash and her Malagasy field assistant, Tana Bertrand, ready to go out for a night of observations of *Lepilemur*. Both must wear headlamps, which are powered by the solar panels in the background. Nash also carries a clipboard with notepad, radio-tracking receiver and antenna, binoculars, and a "fisherman's vest" filled with things needed in the field at night, including spare flashlight and batteries, spare bulbs for lights, compass, pens wrapped in reflective tape, and bottles for samples of feces as well as other "necessities" (e.g. hard candy). **Photo credit:** Mike Nash; **Photo copyright:** Leanne Nash.

FIGURE 3.4 *Lepilemur leucopus* (= *Lepilemur petteri*) at Beza Mahafaly Special Reserve in Madagascar sitting at the opening of its nest hole. **Photo credit** (and copyright): Leanne Nash.

behavioral information to test how well the "the socioecological model" for the evolution (i.e., "ultimate causes") of diurnal primate sociality will account for the social diversity in the nocturnal primates.

But why "be social" (gregarious) at all? Sharon Gursky's clever field experiments on tarsiers with models have suggested that predators may have driven the evolution of gregariousness among nocturnal primates. I did not realize that terrestrial puff adders might prey on agile galagos until a galago's alarm call drew my attention to such a snake at my feet. Later we found that some galagos spent a good deal of time on or near the ground foraging for insects. Comparative work on various mouse lemur species suggests that competition for tree holes to sleep in, as a place for behavioral thermoregulation, may lead some species, but not others, to cooperatively rear their young. Why the species differences?

When I first began studying primate social behavior, the evolutionary paradigm was so steeped in what was "good for the group" (group selection) that the scale of analysis was focused on gross species differences. Differences between individuals, or the sexes, were not of much interest. But from my dissertation on, I could not avoid focusing on individuals as "case histories." I have watched one baby galago in the lab scream when picked up, while another nestles in my hand. In the field, one galago is clever about stealing the bait in a trap without getting caught; another is repeatedly trapped and (anthropomorphically) just seems to enjoy the meal; and another won't go near a pile of fragrantly overripe bananas to enter the trap at all. And these individuals are consistent in these behavioral differences. Why? How do these differences influence their fitness? Recent work on the genetic differences of neurotransmitters has been correlated with such differences in temperament among monkeys. Rearing patterns differ in various mothers of the same species. So we also need to focus on these mechanisms, these "proximate" causes of behavior. These individual differences offer up opportunities for natural selection to shape differences among populations and species.

If my story seems all over the place, that is because it is: I've gone from baboons to galagos and chimpanzees, from mother-infant interactions and sex differences, to why eat plant gums. The connections emerge from what causes differences—differences between individuals, sexes, species, and how evolution or other factors contribute to causing differences in behavior. My route started out along a coherent plan, but serendipitous bumps, shoves, and doorways led me "all over the place."

Suggested Readings

Goodall, J. 1986. *The Chimpanzees of Gombe: Patterns of Behavior*. Cambridge, MA: Belknap Press of Harvard University Press.

Nash, L. T. 2004. "Kinship and Behavior among Nongregarious Nocturnal Prosimians: What Do We Really Know?" In Chapais, B., and C. M. Berman (eds.), *Kinship and Behavior in Primates*. Oxford: Oxford University Press.

Nash, L. T. 2007. "Moonlight and Behavior in Nocturnal and Cathemeral Primates, Especially *Lepilemur leucopus*: Illuminating Possible Anti-predator Efforts." In Gursky, S., and K. A. I. Nekaris (eds.), *Primate Anti-Predator Strategies*. New York: Springer.

Nash, L. T., and A. M. Burrows. 2010. "Introduction: Advances and Remaining Sticky Issues in the Understanding of Exudativory in Primates." In Burrows, A. M, and L. T. Nash. (eds.), *The Evolution of Exudativory in Primates*. New York: Springer.

Nekaris, K. A. I., and S. K. Bearder. 2011. "The Lorisiform Primates of Asia and Mainland Africa: Diversity Shrouded in Darkness." In Campbell, C. J., A. Fuentes., K. C. MacKinnon, S. K. Bearder, and R. M. Stumpf (eds.), *Primates in Perspective,* 2nd ed. Oxford: Oxford University Press.

Acknowledgments

This paper is dedicated to Gordon Bermant and Phyllis Dolhinow, who shaped my career opportunities, and to the memory of Jo Fritz, co-founder of the Primate Foundation of Arizona, an amazing lady who helped chimpanzees, me, and many, many students. I also extend great thanks to all the other people, especially Mike, and to the animals, without whom I would not have had this career. Jessica Harding gave most helpful comments on the manuscript. Thanks to Karen Strier for strong editing and lots of patience.

4

The Lure of Lemurs to an Anthropologist

By Robert W. Sussman[1]

I first arrived in Madagascar in August 1969 to study the behavior and ecology of ringtailed and brown lemurs from an anthropological perspective. I was a Ph.D. student at Duke University at the time. After two closely related species of early hominin (*Australopithecus spp.*) had been found living contemporaneously, the question had arisen as to whether two related species of primates could coexist and, if so, how. So, I was to study two closely related species of lemur, the ringtailed lemur (*Lemur catta*) and the brown lemur (*Eulemur fulvus*), in southwestern Madagascar. These two species were similar in size and skeletal morphology. If you had only the bones of the two species, you would not be able to tell them apart unless you knew exactly what to look for.

The questions for my dissertation were pretty straightforward: "In what type of forests were these species found living together, and when together, did they coexist peacefully, or were they in competition?" I first had to determine a good method to collect quantitative data on the animals, and once in Madagascar, I had to find suitable research sites. I say sites because it was necessary to compare the behavior of each species when living together and alone to see if the interaction between the two species had any effects. I had never done field work before and, in fact, had never been outside the United States, except to visit Mexico by car with high school pals, a fairly common jaunt for teenagers from Los Angeles. It was going to be a true adventure and I was quite excited.

Madagascar was (and is) one of the most exotic places in the world, both in its culture and in the amazing plants and animals found nowhere else on earth. When flying into Madagascar, one lands in the capital, Antananarivo (or Tana), a truly beautiful city built on a series of hills

[1]About the author: Robert W. Sussman is a professor of anthropology at Washington University. He is past editor of *American Anthropologist* and *Yearbook of Physical Anthropology,* and is Secretary of Section H (Anthropology) of the American Association for the Advancement of Science. He has written many articles and authored and edited many books in primatology and anthropology, among the most recent being *Man the Hunted* (co-authored with Donna Hart) and *Origins of Altruism and Cooperation* (co-edited with C. R. Cloninger).

Contact information: Department of Anthropology, Washington University, St. Louis, MO 63130, USA, rwsussma@artsci.wustl.edu

Citation: Sussman, R. W. 2014. "The Lure of Lemurs to an Anthropologist." In Strier, K. B. (ed.), *Primate Ethnographies*. Upper Saddle River, NJ: Pearson Education, Inc. (pp. 34–45).

FIGURE 4.1   The author with habituated ringtailed lemurs (*Lemur catta*) at his field site. **Photo credit:** R. W. Sussman.

with winding roads and lovely architecture in the Central Plateau of the Island. Madagascar is the fourth largest island on earth, about 1,000 miles long and 300 miles wide. Little forest remains on the central plateau, and most of the remaining endemic forest (unique to Madagascar) is found in the lowlands on the perimeter of the island, along the coasts.

Before beginning my actual field work, I spent some time in Tana to gather supplies and get various permits to do my research—a common necessity for field workers, which often takes longer than one anticipates. I also had to wait for my Ph.D. advisor, John Buettner-Janusch, to

FIGURE 4.2   A brown lemur (*Lemur fulvus*). **Photo credit:** R. W. Sussman.

finish the human genetics work he was doing on the island so that I could inherit his Land Rover. I required a vehicle for my work, both to find adequate sites in remote areas and, once they were found, to be able to get into and out of them. During this preparation time, my then fiancé (now my wife), Linda, was to join me.

When I first arrived in Madagascar, the human population was around 6 million people. It has now more than tripled, with approximately 22 million in 2011, 85 percent of whom live on less than two dollars per day. This is quite noticeable in Antananarivo, the most densely populated area on the island. In 1969, Madagascar was a cosmopolitan, bustling city with excellent shops, hotels, and restaurants—some of them reflecting five-star ratings in French Michelin Guides. A wonderful open market covered a good portion of the city, with vendors under massive umbrellas selling an enormous assortment of goods. The market had an Indonesian flavor to it with the people of the Central Plateau of Madagascar mainly of Indonesian origin. Although Madagascar had gained its colonial independence from France ten years earlier, the city was still very much under French influence. It was a wealthy city with many foreign visitors: businessmen, government officials, and tourists. The pedestrian and automobile traffic reminded me of New York City. There was some poverty, but it was not pervasive, and although there were some beggars in the streets, these were few and each of them seemed to have some handicap and to be known to the people of the city and treated well.

The conditions in the city have changed dramatically over the years. After major financial perturbations, related to the global financial crisis beginning in the 1970s, the country has undergone a major economic downturn. Now, there is massive poverty. Antananarivo, though still a charming city, is now very poor, with massive overcrowding, and a large number of homeless people, many of whom are children. As with many "developing" countries, the global financial situation has essentially ceased any major new development and begun to slow or reverse any development that may have begun in the past. Rapid population increase, of course, has exacerbated the problem.

In 1969, Linda and I enjoyed Tana immensely, but we became very anxious to begin our adventure into the mysterious lowland forests of the southwest. Finally, after several weeks and with the Land Rover packed to the hilt, we were able to head south to begin our research adventure. "We" included Linda and me, and our Malagasy assistant, Folo Emmanuel. Folo had worked with a number of English-speaking biologists and was to be our research assistant, guide, translator, interpreter, and go-between. He spoke Malagasy, French, and English eloquently and, as we soon found out, was also a great story teller with a great sense of humor and a charming personality. He stayed with us for the first several months and was indispensible, especially in our surveys of the region, in finding exceptional sites for my thesis research, and in helping us establish a good relationship with the local people. Folo was one of many of the Malagasy, both in a professional capacity and otherwise, with whom we have worked in Madagascar and with whom we still maintain professional ties and personal friendships.

Our first destination was to the forests west of the large southwestern port town of Tulear (now called Toliara). Madagascar has some of the worst roads on earth. On the Central Plateau they are paved, but the pavement was not always in good repair, with holes in some places as large as elephants, or one might say elephant birds (the largest bird that ever existed—10 feet tall, with 20-plus-pound eggs—was endemic to Madagascar, but alas is now extinct). On top of this, they were very narrow, sometimes with hardly enough space for two small cars but often filled with large trucks. Also, the Central Plateau is basically mountainous, so the roads are very windy; we never knew what type of vehicle was around the next corner, a massive truck; a bush taxi (taxi brouse) overloaded with passengers, unwieldy packages, chickens, and other random

FIGURE 4.3 A large funeral procession on the narrow road south of Antananarivo.
Photo credit: R. W. Sussman.

items; a bicycle or motorcycle; a herd of zebu (African humpbacked cattle, *omby* in Malagasy); an *omby* cart; or a large funeral procession.

It also often rains on the Central Plateau—sometimes very, very hard. Thus, after a treacherous two-day ride, one reaches the turning point (a town called Ihosy), where after a night's "sleep" one heads towards Toliara. I put quotations around sleep because this town was notorious for its feral dogs, which howled through the night. The road west was flat, but it was a dirt road graded like a corrugated tin roof, and one needed to keep a certain speed—a fairly good clip—or you felt that your teeth would fall out. Intermixed with fairly nice graded road, depending on the last rain or the last large truck, tremendous pot holes or washed out spots littered the way, and you could be in for a big surprise, like unexpectedly falling into a great largely invisible hole, or a broken axle.

So on the third day of travel, we reached Toliara, a charming, relatively large port town, with some nice beaches. At that time, like Antananarivo, this was quite a rich town with many foreign residents and a tourist center. It also still had many French businesses and residents, remnants of Madagascar's colonial past. Like Antananarivo, it has changed a great deal over the last 40 years.

After a couple of days in Toliara getting final supplies, we started the final portion of our journey, now heading north to the administrative town of Manja and then from there south again to the Mangoky River. It is along the banks of this river that the brown and ringtailed lemurs were known to co-exist. We faced more corrugated and dirt roads, even worse than those we had just driven. I had never been an "off-road" enthusiast (this wasn't a popular sport at the time), but I was getting to be an expert at it by necessity. At one point we had to cross a long stretch of pure beach sand—I was very worried that we would get stuck, but the Land Rover was up to the task.

At the end of the sand stretch was a motorized bac (a flat primitive wooden raft) on which a few vehicles would mount in order to cross the wide Mangoky River. To board the bac, I needed to drive onto two planks, each of which was only as wide as each tire! I wanted to close my eyes, but of course, that would have been disastrous. The pilot of the bac guided me aboard, and I am sure that Linda and Folo *did* close their eyes.

It was a long, hot day's journey with mosquitoes as large as small birds and big, fat "horse" flies—or to be more precise, "zebu" flies. During this trip, Linda and I got our first indication of Folo's sense of humor. These big flies bit, and the bites hurt. Once one of them got into the Land Rover and gave Folo a good bite. Using his quick, primate hand–eye coordination, Folo grabbed the fly and, looking into its compound fly eyes, he pulled off its head, exclaiming, "You bother me, I bother you!"

In Manja we gathered our final supplies and made some very important acquaintances, some of which would last a lifetime. For example, there was one small colonial-like hotel with pumped water and generated electricity—in fact, all electricity was powered by individual generators—where we established a sort of base to which we could return in the future when we needed to resupply. Manja would be the last place we could get items like batteries, fresh food, and canned goods. The town had the ambiance of the U.S. old west, often with cattle being herded through the streets. The hotel was run by three generations of a Greek family, the Varellas family, including the grandmother (the grandfather had died), mother and father, and three sons, completely integrated into Malagasy society. Two of the sons were slightly older than Linda and me, and the third son was younger, in his late teens. The family was extremely helpful to us and became life-long friends. The sons are now all married to Malagasy women and still assist us whenever we return to that region of Madagascar.

Finally we headed more than 50 kilometers south to the Mangoky River. We set up tents on the banks of the river, just south of the village of Vondrove. We learned that both of my study species, along with the beautiful white sifaka, *Propithecus verreauxi,* were in the forests bordering the south side of the river, and we began to study them there. However, it was not an ideal spot. It was a narrow strip of forest, the banks were fairly steep in some places, and there weren't many lemur groups. I also had to learn to pole an outrigger canoe across the river. With the strong current, it was necessary to head way up the river to about halfway across in order to end up where I needed to be on the other side.

We also did some surveying up the river and although we found lemurs, the area was remote and difficult to access. Once, while surveying up the river, we heard a loud splash. The local people told us that there were no crocodiles on this part of the river, but Folo had grown up in a village in the east of Madagascar where crocodiles were quite common and frequently attacked and killed humans. Thus, after we had heard the splash, Folo would never again swim in the river. When Linda and I swam, he would sit on the river bank, shake his head, and mutter, "Crocs! Man with the beard, die soon sure."

Although I collected some data on the lemurs on the banks of the Mangoky, we kept searching for better research sites. A local man, Bernard Tsiefatao, spoke French—one of the few people in the village who did. Linda and I spoke French but very elementary Malagasy at that time. Bernard was very knowledgeable about the local forests, and he soon became our main local assistant. Soon after we got settled in Vondrove, Folo returned to Tana.

Bernard informed us of two forests that sounded perfect for my research plans. Tongobato was a small forest just 2 kilometers north of Vondrove. It was an ideal gallery forest with a number of groups of brown lemurs but no ringtailed lemurs. The second forest, Antserananomby, was a lemur paradise. It was only 15 kilometers from Vondrove, but because of the road, or lack thereof, it took at least an hour to get to it. However, this forest contained all of the lemurs endemic to the region, as well as all of the other mammals and birds of the area. There were at least three groups of ringtails, with one centered in the forest, plus twelve groups of brown lemurs, and many groups of sifakas. The forest also contained at least five species of nocturnal lemur: at least one species of mouse lemur, Coquerel's giant mouse lemur, the fat-tailed dwarf lemur, the sportive lemur, and the fork-marked lemur—all with very healthy populations. The forest was truly remarkable. I have never found another in western Madagascar so densely popu-lated with lemurs, both in numbers of individuals or of species. I soon learned, however, that I could not find a forest with the ringtailed lemur alone within the area. Thus, my third study for-est, Berenty, was in southern Madagascar where the ranges of the ringtailed and brown lemurs did not overlap.

Within a few weeks of arriving at the Mangoky, we were invited to live in the wonderful, small village of Vondrove, populated by around forty families. There was one small shop where we could get a few canned goods (sardines, powdered milk, spam), some small tools, fabric, candles, matches, and other items. One home opened every few months as a wine bar, when the proprietor felt like taking his *omby* cart to Manja to purchase a couple of 20-gallon bottles of red wine. We had the only motorized vehicle and all other transportation was by *omby* cart or by foot. Of course, there was no running water or electricity. None of the children had ever seen a *vazaha* (white person). The village was idyllic, and we were welcomed as family. When we were working at Tongobato, we stayed in a small, cozy, and very nice one-room mud house provided to us by the village. At Antserananomby, we lived in a tent in the forest. Although we were in the most remote place we had ever been (or would ever be), it was the ideal spot to do my thesis

FIGURE 4.4   Linda and Folo in front of our house in Vondrove being observed by curious village children who had never seen a *vazaha* (white person). **Photo credit:** R. W. Sussman.

research and a truly remarkable, amazing, and most wondrous place to live, both with the local people and within the fairytale-like forest.

Linda and I were able to settle into the village, and living in Vondrove was extremely calm and pleasant. The village was picturesque and the people were kind, accepting, and made us feel like we belonged, like family. In many ways, it was like going back 10,000 years, living in a self-sufficient agricultural/herding community. Over the year and a half, we learned a great deal about the people, including the local practice of divination, traditional games, and Malagasy cuisine and rituals. We learned that people from very different cultures are indeed very different while being much the same. For example, the language, of course, was different, as was the way the people recognized kin. At certain periods, the dead were dug up and reburied, and the Malagasy stories of creation differed from ours. However, we shared emotions and could laugh and cry together about certain events. We could always communicate about certain wants and needs, and we could understand and share the pleasures of friendship.

In living, and feeling at home, in this small village I realized that, even though my main work was in primatology, I was primarily an anthropologist. You might ask, how and why does one become an anthropologist in the first place, and why would an anthropologist study lemurs? Of all the subjects and professions that one pursues in college, this is not a particularly likely choice. Few high schools even offer anthropology courses, and few high school students have heard of the subject. Why somebody interested in anthropology would be studying lemurs might seem equally odd. Anthropology, after all, is the study of humans, and although lemurs are primates, they are only distant relatives. Nonetheless, I believe that being an anthropologist is extremely important to the work that I do, and that *why* one becomes an anthropologist (rather than a biologist, for example) usually governs how one does his or her work, the questions one asks, and the methods one uses to answer those questions.

A major aspect of doing anthropology is the ability to stand outside your own culture and to have an open mind about different cultures. Being somewhat alienated from your own culture allows you to see it and others with an open mind. Growing up, I always felt a little like I was on the outside looking in. My father and mother were both Jewish immigrants who came to the United States from Russia as children. My father was nineteen years old when the Great Depression began in 1929 and, although he was extremely interested in higher education, he could not afford to attend college. After a short stint in the Merchant Marines at the end of World War II, he became a blue-collar laborer, first building ships and then aircraft. Our family was quite poor. The first winter holiday season that I remember was when my mother, sister, and I were living in government housing in Seattle (when my father was at sea). We received presents from the local fire department.

When I began school, my father wanted to make sure that we lived in one of the better school districts, and this influenced where we lived when we moved to Los Angeles when I was in the fifth grade. I was always among the poorest kids in my class and among my friends, and one of the only Jewish students in my classes. In fact, there were only two other Jewish students in my high school, and when one of my classmates learned this, he exclaimed, "You can't be Jewish, you're not black!" At that moment, I developed a natural interest in how little most people understood about human variation and what led to racial prejudice.

Needless to say, being Jewish and being quite poor in a relatively affluent, mainly Christian school, I was a bit of an outsider. This sense of being different was reinforced by growing up with a father who was a relatively low-paid blue-collar laborer (often working two jobs), but who had also always been a scholar. Our house was full of books, and my father took many correspondence courses, earning certificates from them, and he read passionately in areas like mathematics, history, philosophy, and the classics. When I asked him questions about my school work, he often answered with more detail and greater nuance than my teachers. I grew up knowing that teachers and authority figures might not always be the best or only sources of knowledge and could often be wrong.

Although at the time I did not know anything about anthropology, my personal background had a great deal to do with my later choice to pursue anthropology, and my often skeptical view of "accepted theory" or what might be called "conventional wisdom." At UCLA, I took my first sociology class and became interested in the study of race and race prejudice, but it wasn't until my junior year that I decided to become an anthropologist. My first course in physical anthropology was taught by Jack Prost, an amazing professor who focused not only on the subject but also on the history of anthropology, the philosophy behind it, the methods used in pursuing anthropological questions, the importance of knowing scientific methodology, and the history of science, in general. I was hooked. The whole field of anthropology, both sociocultural and biological, fascinated me and was directly relevant to my interests, which had shifted from the study of race *per se* (at least for the time) and more towards the study of human behavior and the evolution and nature of human nature.

I decided to major in anthropology with a focus on physical anthropology. However, Prost studied primate locomotion. So this is where I started my professional training. Wanting to continue to work with Prost, I planned to remain at UCLA for graduate school. However, the next year, Prost took a position at Duke University, so the following year, I followed him there. I began working on primate locomotion and on lemurs, as Duke University had a primate facility that specialized in these Malagasy primates. It was a wonderful facility filled with these beautiful animals. My research interests soon became broader. I was interested in human adaptations and human nature, and in the evolution of human behavior. I guess you could say I was interested in why we do what we do.

For the most part, primatologists within anthropology differ in their perspective and approach, and also often in the questions they ask. I have always considered myself an anthropologist first, with a subdisciplinary focus on primatology. This is because I had become interested in anthropology and in primate behavior ultimately to answer questions about human evolution and the evolution of human behavior.

Prost had been a Ph.D. student of Sherwood Washburn. Washburn (1911–2000) was the prime mover in incorporating field primatology into anthropology. Many papers by him and his students, which stressed the need for primate field research, appeared in the 1960s. As he wrote on the inside cover of his edited volume *The Social Life of Early Man* (Aldine, Chicago) in 1961:

> The social relationships that characterize man cannot have appeared for the first time in the modern human species . . . Since Man is a primate who developed from among the Old World simian stock, his social behavior must also have evolved from that of this mammalian group. Thus the investigation of man's behavior is dependent upon what we know of the behavior of monkeys and apes.

Following his paradigm, my research focused on a question being debated in the early human evolution literature at that time. Hence, the discovery of two species of australopithecines living in proximity led to the question of whether two closely related species of humans or primates could co-exist in the same area; my research on whether and how ringtailed and brown lemurs might co-exist was an obvious extension of this.

Thus, I had become an anthropologist somewhat by accident and somewhat by a conglomeration of chance events, particular interests, and particularly influential people including my father and my first anthropology professor. Being somewhat alienated from my own culture, I gravitated towards anthropology; my interest in studying racial prejudice got me interested in physical anthropology; the complexity of race and racism made me interested in the evolution of human nature and human behavior; Prost's influence kindled an interest in how the study of primates could help us understand the evolution of human behavior and human nature, and in scientific methodology and history; and doing my Ph.D. at Duke—the only primate center focused on Malagasy primates in the United States—led me to study the lemurs in Madagascar. While I was in the field, Prost moved to University of Illinois, Chicago, and his colleague John Buettner-Janusch became my Ph.D. advisor.

As a Ph.D. student, one of my major concerns about conducting my field research was how I could quantitatively compare the behavior of two different species living in the same and different forests. There were many studies of primates in the field by that time but the information was mainly descriptive. How could one tell if animals were doing things similarly or differently in any significant way without some quantitative method? I needed to have statistical comparisons; I was very concerned with measuring accurately. I scrounged the literature and finally discovered one paper, published in 1968, in which the time that animals spent in various activities, on what substrates, and in eating various items was actually measured. Crook and Aldrich-Blake, two British psychologists who had studied bird behavior and ecology, had introduced a method of scan sampling—sampling the number of individuals doing a particular activity at a particular time (say every five or ten minutes), much like an instantaneous photograph—that enabled them to quantify and compare three sympatric ground-dwelling primate species in Ethiopia. I decided to use this method. Their paper was the first in which this method had been used on primates, though now it is one of the major methods used in collecting data on primate behavior in the field.

When one first goes into the forest to study primates like the two lemurs I was to study, the animals are very nervous; how nervous depends upon their past experiences with people. They need to get used to the primatologist's presence. If they have been hunted, this might take a long time. Fortunately, the forest of Antserananomby was protected by the local people and habituating the animals was an easy and quick process. Within a few weeks, I was essentially accepted into the groups. I realized this one day when I was observing a group of around 18 ringtailed lemurs as they were calmly feeding in the dry river bed. I was sitting among them on the bank at a curve in the river. Suddenly, a flock of guinea hens came strolling around the corner and, when they noticed me, they panicked, loudly squawking their predator calls, and wildly flying off in fright. The lemurs thought there was a predator in their midst and immediately scattered and disappeared into the forest. About fifteen minutes later, using their cat-like meows as a regrouping call, they came back together, and I again found myself at the center of the group. When accepted like this by a group of primates, it is hard to explain but one really feels privileged, like you are one with nature, part of an ancient and connected universe.

The two species that I was studying were very different from each other. I began with the brown lemurs because they were the easiest. They would awake very early in the morning and begin to eat high up in the trees, sometimes when it was still quite cool. Then by as early as 9:30 or 10:00 a.m. they would begin to rest in clumps. The groups were small, around 7–10 animals. They would not venture far and would eat what was available in a small area, mainly the leaves of the most common tree species in the forest. I was surprised to observe that they would essentially snooze away the whole day, only rising again towards dusk, and even into the night, to feed in the same trees. I would mainly sit under a tree in the shade and watch them sleep most of the day. This could become monotonous. I was anxious to see what the ringtailed lemurs were doing as I saw their relatively large groups, of around 18 to 20 animals, intermittently wandering through the forest while I sat under my tree.

So, I was very curious, after a few weeks, to follow the ringtailed lemurs, which couldn't have been more different. They would wake up about the same time as the brown lemurs, but then they would sit, either high in the forest or in a clearing on the ground, and sun themselves—virtually spreading their arms and legs out while sitting and facing the sun. The temperatures at night could drop to below 12 degrees Celsius, so they were using behavioral thermoregulation to adjust their temperature. To me it seemed much like having a morning coffee or two to raise your metabolism. And I soon found out why. After sunning, the animals would head out of the forest on the ground and then spend most of the morning searching for fruit and herbs in the open areas surrounding the canopy forest. Although I had been able to sit in the shade and keep cool while observing the brown lemurs, it could get extremely warm outside of the canopy cover, and I found myself very hot and sweating while trying to keep up with the ringtails. It was a real relief when they took their short, 1- to 2-hour break in the hottest portion of the day. Then, between 2:00 and 3:00 p.m., they woke up again and traveled and fed until dusk.

Thus, the two lemur species stayed mainly in different parts of the forest, had different activity cycles, ate different things, and had very different daily and long-term (home) ranges. They also had very different types of social groups and social organization. Even the lemurs seemed to recognize their differences, as they rarely got in each other's way. Rather than compete, the two species had evolved completely different lifestyles, using different parts and different resources while living side by side in the same forest, often feeding or passing each other in the same trees. Each species' behavior was essentially the same whether living together or alone; they had little or no effect on one another, revealing that early human ancestors also may have lived side by side without conflict.

Nearly ten years later, I did a long-term study of long-tailed macaques in Mauritius and found them to have an entirely different personality or "gestalt" from either the brown or ringtailed lemurs. The macaques were much more intelligent and manipulative of their environment. They lived in much larger groups of more than 65 individuals; they had much more complex social interactions; and they manipulated the environment in more complex ways, searching under rocks in the rivers for snails and other critters, and opening hard nuts by banging them against tree trunks. The macaques had been hunted for years and although we did succeed in habituating them to some extent, they were never as trusting of us as were the lemurs.

Approximately twenty-five years after my thesis research, two of my colleagues, Guy Ramanansoa of the University of Antananarivo and Alison Richard of Yale University, and I established a forest reserve in southwestern Madagascar—the Beza Mahafaly Special Government Reserve. The reserve was created to promote research, conservation, education, and development in the region. Beza Mahafaly was several hundred miles south of Vondrove and outside of the geographic range of the brown lemur. The amazing forest of Antserananomby was just too remote to set up an accessible reserve. I also believed that the human population in the region of Vondrove was so small and the forest so isolated that there would be time later to create a reserve at Antserananomby. But I was wrong. Although the forest still existed in satellite images taken in 2000, when a Malagasy colleague, Joelisoa Ratsirarson, and I actually surveyed the area in 2005, we found that Antserananomby had been cut down to grow corn for cattle feed. Thus, assuming that this forest was safe for the immediate future instead of working to establish it as a reserve turned out to be one of my biggest mistakes and greatest regrets. It is amazing that a forest that existed for hundreds of thousands of years, one of the most remarkable forests on earth, could disappear in essentially a moment of time. Thus, I plan to go back and survey this region to see if any other forests like Antserananomby remain.

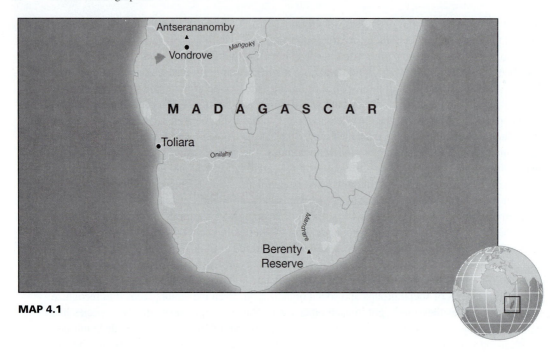

MAP 4.1

Besides the lemurs and macaques, over the years I have now studied a number of neotropical monkey species and have found each to have its own gestalt. I also have found that in each country I have worked (Madagascar, Mauritius, Panama, Costa Rica, and Guyana) the people and their cultures differ in many ways. However, at another level, as was discovered by anthropologists in the early 1900s, the ways humans think and feel emotionally are much the same throughout the world. While each species of primate that I have studied has a different "nature" from every other species, humans all share the same human nature, and different cultures enable humans to present vastly different variations on this basic human theme. And, after all of these years, I am still interested in discovering more about the evolution and nature of human behavior; why we do the things we do.

Suggested Readings

Jolly, A., R. W. Sussman, N. Koyama, and H. Rasamimanana. 2006. *Ringtailed Lemur Biology: Lemur catta in Madagascar*. New York: Springer.

Sussman, R. W. 1999. *The Biological Basis of Human Behavior: A Critical Review*. Upper Saddle River, NJ: Prentice Hall.

Sussman, R. W. 2003. *Primate Ecology and Social Structure, Volume 1: Lorises, Lemurs and Tarsiers*. Boston: Pearson.

Sussman, R. W. 2010. "Human Nature." *American Anthropologist 112*: 514–515.

Sussman, R. W. 2011. "A Brief History of Primate Field Studies: Revised." In C. J. Campbell, A. Fuentes, K. C. Mackinnon, S. K. Bearder, and R. S. M. Stumpf (eds.), *Primates in Perspective,* 2nd ed. Oxford University Press: New York (pp. 6–11).

Acknowledgments

I would like to thank Karen Strier for inviting me to contribute to this volume and for her comments on the paper. I also thank all the people in Madagascar who have assisted me, Linda, and my students in our work in Madagascar over the years. Washington University has supported me and provided assistance in my research endeavors, as have many government and nongovernment agencies, and without this support this research would not have been possible. Finally, I acknowledge the support and love of my daughters, Katya and Diana, my favorite and most successful accomplishments.

5

On the Ground Looking Up

By Kenneth Glander[1]

The Wisconsin dairy farm where I grew up was far away on that July day in 1970 when I stepped off a bus at Hacienda La Pacifica, in Guanacaste Province of Costa Rica. Along with 23 fellow students in the Organization for Tropical Studies (OTS) course, I had just traveled four hours from the capital city of San Jose. As my feet hit the ground, I was startled when the resident howling monkey male began howling in a cacophony of sound. Though I did not know it at the time, I had embarked on a life's journey that since has taken me to many parts of the world including Belize, Brazil, Colombia, Ecuador, Honduras, Mexico, Madagascar, Panama, Peru, Puerto Rico, Trinidad, Uganda, Venezuela, Vietnam, and Zanzibar but has always brought me back to Hacienda La Pacifica, a research oasis that I discovered on that fateful day more than 43 years ago.

The male who had so vigorously reacted to my presence as I stepped off the bus would play a significant role in my career. I documented his life until he died from natural causes five years later at the age of 19. I also came to know the life histories of many of his 230 cohorts who live in the forests of La Pacifica. They and many of their kin have dropped feces on me, urinated on me, and appeared to aim dead branches at me. As a scientist I know that these actions were not intentional, but as a victim of those materials I am convinced that I was a carefully selected target paying the price for being in their life space. Such are the hazards of being on the ground looking up.

Objects falling from the trees and hitting me are still part of my career that began when I decided in the fall of 1965 to go back to night school. At the time I was in the United States Air Force stationed at Brooks Air Force Base (now known as Brooks City-Base) in San Antonio, Texas.

[1]About the author: Born on June 14, 1940, Kenneth Glander grew up on a dairy farm in Wisconsin as the oldest of five brothers and two sisters. He joined the U.S. Air Force in 1962 and spent four years as, first, an animal handler and then a manager of monkeys used to test the safety of human space flight. This experience precipitated a desire to conduct research that would benefit nonhuman primates and led directly to his attending night school while still in the Air Force, completing undergraduate and graduate school, and then carrying out basic research on lemurs and monkeys in Madagascar, Costa Rica, and nonhuman primate habitats around the world.

Contact information: Department of Evolutionary Anthropology, Duke University, Durham, NC 27708, USA, glander@duke.edu

Citation: Glander, K. 2014. "On the Ground Looking Up." In Strier, K. B. (ed.), *Primate Ethnographies*. Upper Saddle River, NJ: Pearson Education, Inc. (pp. 46–56).

FIGURE 5.1   Adult male mantled howler monkey, howling. **Photo credit:** Ken Glander.

Monkeys were a part of my life in the Air Force. Brooks AFB was the NASA training base (no longer active) for our Mercury 7 astronauts. I worked in the veterinary section with the rhesus monkeys that were used as test subjects for radiation and acceleration studies. One of the monkeys assigned to me was SAM (an acronym for School of Aerospace Medicine—a part of Brooks AFB that still exists today as part of Brooks City-Base and is known as the United States Air Force School of Aerospace Medicine). SAM was the first primate in space, not HAM the chimpanzee as is so often reported. SAM was a VIP who was visited by members of Congress and the Senate. NASA initiated these visits, which usually occurred just before the House and Senate voted on whether NASA would get any future funding.

My four years working with monkeys in the Air Force triggered a fascination with nonhuman primates that has continued unabated. I also felt an obligation to do something to benefit nonhuman primates to compensate for contributing to the deaths of many monkeys as research subjects. This commitment motivated me to take night classes while still in the Air Force and then to enroll at the University of Texas at Austin in January 1967 after being honorably discharged the month before.

One of my early dreams was to complete a graduate degree and maybe even earn a Ph.D. Some might say that this dream was nothing but a flight of fancy because at the time I was facing three more years of military obligation and had previously achieved a 1.2 grade point average out of 4.0 during one and a half semesters at the University of Wisconsin at Oshkosh (the dean "suggested" that I withdraw).

Night school and Rudyard Kipling helped bring my grade point average up to 2.6 (I did quite well in my English literature night classes and discovered Kipling's "Jungle Book" and his poem "If"). Living in Texas for four years while in the service got me into UT at the low state resident fee. I completed an undergraduate degree in anthropology and made a trip to Mexico

FIGURE 5.2   The author (Ken Glander) looking up at howlers during his dissertation research. **Photo credit:** Ken Glander.

City to talk to Dr. Russell Tuttle, a professor in the University of Chicago's Anthropology Department whose research blended functional morphology and naturalistic behavior. (My undergraduate training in anthropology convinced me that I needed a mentor with this emphasis.) He agreed to accept me as his graduate student. I was 29 years old.

When I came to Chicago in 1970, my research interests were diet and African monkeys. My goal was to study the diet of black and white colobus monkeys on the slopes of Mount Kilimanjaro. Folivorous primates were believed to have unlimited food (leaves) in those days, but my readings about plant defensive strategies introduced me to research on the diets of insects and how that diet impacts their population size. These studies demonstrated that plants have the ability to reduce insect health and reproduction by investing their leaves with toxins. If insects were being limited in their food choices by the tree's strategies, I believed that leaf-eating primates also would be impacted.

I had discussed my interests and reservations about the unlimited food hypothesis with Dr. Tuttle in Mexico City and again when I arrived in Chicago. During the middle of my first semester he mentioned the OTS course and suggested I consider studying howling monkeys in Latin America. His rationale was that they had similar diets to colobus monkeys, and Latin America was a lot closer and cheaper to visit. He indicated that the OTS course might prove useful for a budding primatologist and encouraged me to apply for their summer program in Costa Rica.

I was accepted in April of 1970. (THANK YOU, RUSS!) On July 1, 1970 I arrived in San Jose, Costa Rica to begin working toward what were to be significant milestones in my life. I met Dr. Norman Scott, the teacher of the summer OTS course. Norm taught me much of what I know about tropical biology, helped my dissertation research by finding a safe method of capture for

MAP 5.1

arboreal monkeys, and became a true friend and colleague. And, on July 8, 1970 I met Scar, the male howler who welcomed me to Hacienda La Pacifica with his booming roar as I stepped off the OTS bus for my first visit and led me to consider La Pacifica as a future study site.

Neither I nor Dr. Tuttle knew about La Pacifica or its unique approach of environmentally friendly ranching prior to my arrival. La Pacifica just happened to be the first of seven OTS field sites visited by the two-month summer course of which I was a member. My goals in taking this course were to learn about tropical ecology and to find a field site where I could study the diet of wild leaf-eating primates. The male howler's welcoming roar was a promising start to my search for a research site and it foreshadowed my return. After 11 days at La Pacifica, the course left for similar length visits to the other six sites. I evaluated each of them as a future dissertation site, but none of them had the appeal of La Pacifica.

The primary goal of my dissertation study was to understand the relationship between the howlers and the trees that presumably provided their food. I did not anticipate the role that my research results would play in the conservation biology of howlers nor that the ranch owner would use what I discovered about the howler's diet to increase his beef production and to begin conserving the forests.

At the end of the two-month OTS Tropical Ecology course I went back to La Pacifica to do a three-week preliminary study before returning to Chicago. I spent the next two years completing course requirements and planning for a return to Costa Rica and the howlers of La Pacifica. That June day in 1972, when my wife Molly and I boarded a plane at O'Hare Airport and flew off to Costa Rica, we were completely unaware of what was ahead of us. We had no keys on our key rings and our life savings was $4,000. When we returned to Chicago 14 months later, we still had no keys on our key rings and no money in the bank.

When we arrived in Costa Rica in June 1972, it had been only two years since my earlier visit during the OTS course, but Costa Rica had changed a lot. The upscale hotel in San Jose

FIGURE 5.3   A Guanacaste tree left standing in one of the La Pacifica pastures (left) and an older Guanacaste tree on the edge of the forest (right). **Photo credit:** Ken Glander.

where I had stayed in 1970 was now a brothel, and instead of colorful streets there was a postal strike and Molly and I were sprayed with mace while shopping for field supplies. After spending the first two nights in San Jose, we were glad to head out to the relative quiet of Hacienda La Pacifica, where we only had to dodge falling feces, urine, and branches. We fell asleep to the pleasant sound of howling monkeys greeting the sunset with their calls and were calmed during the night by a symphony of tree frogs and owls. The next day Molly and I began collecting the data that led to my dissertation.

Hacienda La Pacifica is located in Guanacaste Province in northwestern Costa Rica. This area is called the Texas of Costa Rica because of all the cattle ranches. La Pacifica was at that time a cattle ranch that was also a tourist center and research station. In 1972 it consisted of 1,300 hectares (3,120 acres) with approximately 600 hectares (1,440 acres) of forest remaining in windbreak strips, on hilltops, and along all rivers. In 1996 an additional 680 hectares (1,632 acres) were added. The Province of Guanacaste is named for a distinctive umbrella-shaped tree (*Enterolobium cyclocarpum*) that is common on La Pacifica. The Guanacaste tree is also known as the monkey-ear tree because of the shape of its seedpods.

La Pacifica was established in 1955 when Ciba-Geigy (a Swiss drug company) bought 1,300 hectares in Guanacaste in order to grow pharmaceuticals (i.e., cultures of medicinal plants), among them *Dioscorea* or wild yam. In 1951 Carl Djerassi, a chemist in Mexico City, had developed an orally active contraceptive by synthesizing hormones from Mexican yams. He and his colleagues shared their creation with other laboratories and Ciba-Geigy believed that they could grow yams in Costa Rica, but their attempt failed. This left the drug company with what was nonproductive land, and in 1959 they hired Werner Hagnauer of Switzerland to evaluate the situation and develop a business plan for the property. There were a few large Pochote (*Bombacopsis quinata*) trees left from the original primary forest and under Mr. Hagnauer's supervision these became the seed stock for many of the present Pochote trees both on La Pacifica and elsewhere in Costa Rica. ICE (Instituto Costarrecense de Electridad) representatives collected cuttings from the La Pacifica Pochote trees in the early 1960s to plant at ICE sites around Costa Rica. These Pochote seedlings served as central points for regenerating the forest on La Pacifica and elsewhere because they provided refuge for birds and other animals, which distributed the seeds of other trees and plants necessary for regrowth of the forest. These regenerated forests became the home for the howling monkeys that I (with Molly's assistance) had come so far to study.

Money from a large corporation (Ciba-Geigy) that led to cutting down forest ultimately was directly responsible for the forest regeneration under the careful guidance of Werner Hagnauer's plan to make La Pacifica a viable eco-friendly business long before it was politically correct. In 1960 Mr. Hagnauer planted cotton but stopped in 1968 because the cost of spraying to control insects became too expensive. After 1968 the focus shifted to the production of beef. At that time about 800 hectares (1,920 acres) of pasture were developed. Natural flowing canals designed by Mr. Hagnauer irrigated the pastureland. These pastures were able to sustain 1,100–1,300 head of beef cattle, the maximum number of cattle that could be economically and environmentally carried on the land and far more than the neighboring ranches that did not irrigate.

In 1971 Mr. and Mrs. Werner Hagnauer bought La Pacifica from Ciba-Geigy. They continued to run it as a cattle ranch. In 1972, they added tourism to the ranch business. A restaurant, motel, and swimming pool were opened in December of 1972. Also, several houses with cooking facilities were built to accommodate the many researchers who visited and worked on La Pacifica, including Molly and me. These researchers studied a wide variety of flora and fauna ranging from grasses to trees, bees to birds, monkeys to lizards, and cows to bats. One of the first studies of vampire bats was done at the same time that we were observing the monkeys.

In 1975, Mr. Hagnauer developed a dual-purpose system that resulted in the production of Grade-A milk and beef from the same herd. In this system the calves were separated from their mothers in the early evening and spent the night apart. The next morning the cows were milked and then put out to pasture with their calves. The calves would nourish themselves during the day until just before dark when they would be separated from their mothers again to allow accumulation of milk for the following morning's milking. This unique approach was economically and ecologically sound because, without negatively impacting the environment, it yielded milk and beef from the same cattle herd that had previously produced only meat.

In December 1985 Stephan Schmidheiny purchased La Pacifica. The new owner continued to operate La Pacifica as a beef cattle operation with the previously described milk production, tourist trade, and research facilities until 1999 when the cattle were sold and tilapia farming was started. La Pacifica again changed hands in 2008 and beef cattle were brought back and the tilapia farming increased. Forests had been cut to accommodate the tilapia tanks, but other areas were allowed to regenerate.

From its beginning in 1955 to today, La Pacifica has undergone considerable change both in ownership and business plan, but the one constant has been the maintenance of approximately 600 hectares of forest. It is this forest that has allowed the continued existence of the monkeys and other wildlife and provided me with my first contact with wild monkeys. Surveys conducted by one of my long-term collaborators, Dr. Margaret Clarke, have shown that the howler population has been fairly stable at 230 individuals since the start of my dissertation research in 1972.

Collecting the data for my dissertation meant often getting up at 3:30 a.m. because the monkeys would begin moving and feeding before dawn, particularly in the hot, dry season from December to April. Molly and I would spend all day or until 6:00 p.m. with our study group, recording everything they did. In 14 months we averaged 12 hours/day of observation for 172 days, numbered 1,699 trees (every tree in the study group's 10-hectare [24-acre] home range to determine what total resources were available to the monkeys), and immersed ourselves in the local community of human and nonhuman primates. I never could have collected so much data without Molly's full-time voluntary assistance.

FIGURE 5.4 Lacey, an adult female howler with her 4-month-old infant in a Guanacaste tree at La Pacifica. **Photo credit:** Christopher Vinyard (author's collaborator).

My research questions focused on individual feeding and behavior strategies and could only be answered with unequivocal individual identification (e.g., individual strategies that require consideration of complete life histories of known individuals). Some of the monkeys had unusual physical features, but these could not always be seen; thus, the only way to unquestionably identify them was to capture and uniquely mark them with visible collars and brightly colored tags. These provided unambiguous identification but required capture and recapture to replace lost or damaged collars and tags. It was important to ensure that precise, secure, and permanent identification of research individuals was maintained even if they lost their collar/tag before the next recapture. In 1998 we began using the same type of implantable RFID (Radio Frequency Identification) microchips for my howlers that are used in the United States for domestic pets like cats and dogs.

Capture of wild animals for any reason can lead to injury or death and must be undertaken with care and consideration for the health and safety of the captured individuals. Both the initial capture and subsequent recapture require scientifically based justification. The behavior and physiology of free-ranging primates results from the interaction of numerous factors that cannot be adequately replicated in the laboratory. These factors include food supply, food quality, predation, social interactions, and three-dimensional variation in forest weather conditions. Thus, existing data from lab studies may not provide an ecologically, and therefore evolutionarily, relevant explanation of most primate behavior or physiology in response to environmental variation.

Capture allows standard measurements and samples to be collected and the application of such formerly lab-based technologies as the collection of blood glucose levels, core and subcutaneous body temperatures, heart rate, activity levels, and the actual three-dimensional distance traveled. All of these can be continuously recorded and monitored (i.e., in real time) over 24-hour periods. Collectively, these environmental and physiological data can then be analyzed

FIGURE 5.5   Two student field assistants holding a net that is used to catch monkeys falling from the trees after being darted. They are darted because my research questions require positive identification; thus, I needed a safe way to capture monkeys that live in trees, do not enter traps, and seldom come to the ground. In 1971 Norm Scott discovered a darting system manufactured by Pneu-Dart, Inc. that was used by city pounds to dart stray dogs. He contacted Robert Waldiesen of Pneu-Dart., Inc., who was interested in a possible new application of his system. Norm acquired the necessary equipment and together we learned to use it on monkeys living in the trees of La Pacifica during June and July of 1972. The initial system has been modified over the years as I strive for maximum safety for the primates. During the past 40 years I have used this system to safely dart 2,869 primates. My overall mortality rate is 1.6 percent and I continually strive to achieve zero deaths. **Photo credit:** Ken Glander.

to better understand how behavior is related to variable weather conditions, available energy, and food choices, thus, relating environmental variation to behavioral and physiological data from wild primates.

I still remember the first howler that I darted. His name was Number 1. His group was No. 1. This group disbanded eight years later and a group that I later called Group 2 now occupies Group 1's former home range and is one of my four main study groups.

Each individual is named when it is first captured. The names for the original 12 animals of my 1972–1973 study group (Group 7) were based on the unique color of their identifying collars and tags, for example, Green, Red, Blue, and so on. Some were named for a distinguishing physical or behavioral category, such as, for example, Scar for a large scar on his upper lip, which he received in a fight that I witnessed on my second day as a beginning primatologist. There was Houdini, named for his ability to escape our attempts to observe him, and Bandit from the movie "Smoky and the Bandit." Then there were Able, Baker, and Charlie. These names were a carryover from my stint in the U.S. Air Force.

Scar, Baker, and Bandit have a special place in my life, as their soap opera lives became as familiar to me as my own. In addition to being the first wild howler that welcomed me to La Pacifica when I stepped out of the OTS bus in 1970, Scar was the resident and only male of Group 7 when I began my preliminary study two months later. On my second day following Group 7, I witnessed a short violent fight between a new male I later called Baker and the resident Scar, who before this fight was unmarked. The fight lasted 89 seconds and was silent. Scar ended the fight by running away from Baker. He had a severely lacerated lower lip and a small slash on the inside of his upper left arm. Baker was uninjured and announced his victory with a loud grunt followed by a short howl as he assumed the alpha male role in Group 7. After three weeks of recovery, Scar rejoined Group 7 but as subordinate to Baker. Scar and Baker were still present in similar roles when I returned for my dissertation study in June 1972, but by then, the group had increased from 13 to 22 individuals.

Bandit was presumed to be Baker's son based on Baker's mating behavior with Bandit's mother. On May 18, 1978, when he was just 8 months old, Bandit was attacked by Macho, a male who had just taken over Group 7 after winning a fight with Baker, just like Baker had done in 1970. Such attacks against infants less than 12 months old by the newly dominant male are now known to be a common pattern in howling monkeys. Bandit was fortunate in that he was able to escape from Macho's grasp with only a three-inch gash on his tail.

Macho continued his harassment until December 1978, when Bandit at 15 months old finally left Group 7 and became a solitary individual. He took up residence on the opposite side of the river from his natal group in an area unoccupied by other howlers primarily because it included the motel and restaurant built by La Pacifica's owner to take advantage of the many local and foreign tourists who stopped for refreshment as they drove the Pan American Highway. We met many of these tourists and answered their questions about why we were sitting in chairs taking notes while staring up at the trees at a monkey with a distinctive kink in his otherwise fully healed tail. Bandit soon became one of the primary tourist attractions as he ran across the restaurant's roof, peered over the roof's edge as the tourists ate breakfast, and taunted the resident dogs by hanging by his tail in branches just out of their reach.

The fact that Bandit survived Macho's initial attack and subsequent harassment, and the isolation of being alone at an extremely young age is extraordinary. Indeed, none of the other 138 individuals whose departures from their natal groups have been documented left before they were 24 to 30 months old.

Bandit's presumed son Roo and then his grandson José succeeded him as the alpha males in Group 19, the group that Bandit and a young female named Ruby started in 1980, with the restaurant at the center of their home range. When they established the group, Bandit was only 37 months old while Ruby was an older female of 40 months. Group 19, another of my four primary study groups, has ranged in size from these two founders to 17 individuals over the years. This is within the range of sizes of the 32 howling monkey groups, which average 13 individuals, at La Pacifica. Unfortunately, Bandit died from natural causes in December of 1994 at the age of 17, much younger than the normal life span of 30 years for these monkeys. Group 19, however, still occupies the same home range around the restaurant.

Bandit and I developed a love-hate association worthy of any highly rewarding relationship. Our most intimate and challenging interactions occurred every six months when I attempted to capture him for his bi-yearly exam and measurement. My original dissertation research required only one capture of each study animal, but following its completion, I wanted to broaden the scope of the study and focus on morphological and physiological changes from birth to death. This requires obtaining infants during the first year of their life for weighing, measuring, and marking and then recapturing them every six months for similar data collection. No individual of less than one year old is darted, but clinging infants become part of the database when their mothers are darted and fall into our catching net. My database currently contains body weights, measurements, and biological samples from 78 female and 92 male infants who were less than 12 months old. Fully three-quarters of them were one month or less with many being one or two days old at the time of first sampling. Such detailed morphological and physiological data on the same wild individual throughout their life spans are rarely available, and these data from the La Pacifica howling monkeys are providing unique, longitudinal insights into their life history stages.

I know many of the present-day La Pacifica howlers on a personal basis, but none of them have touched me like Bandit and his father Baker. They were special individuals and I miss them both. Bandit lives on in my dreams and will probably always be a part of my life. Plus he and his fellow howlers played an unexpected role in the economy of La Pacifica.

The results of my dissertation research on the monkey's diets had a direct impact on the cattle business of La Pacifica because Mr. Hagnauer incorporated my findings on plant secondary compounds into his feeding program for his beef cattle. My research showed that the monkeys were obtaining all of their food from only 331 of 1699 trees available in their 10-hectares home range. In fact, they got 79% of their food from only 88 trees. They were selecting leaves that contained higher amounts of protein and lower amounts of plant toxins than those leaves not selected.

One of their most important food trees was a legume known locally as Madera Negro. My chemical analysis revealed that the leaves of individual Madera Negro trees with yellow cambium did not contain toxic compounds, but the leaves of individual Madera Negro trees with black cambium did contain significant amounts of toxins, while both contained about 20 percent protein. Based on these results, Mr. Hagnauer instructed his farmhands to begin harvesting branches only from the nonpoisonous Madera Negro trees, grind the leaves, and mix them 50/50 with ground sugar cane to feed his young stock. This inclusion of a diet with higher protein resulted in his beef cattle achieving market weight one month quicker than when he was using only the high-carbohydrate but low-protein sugar cane diet. A side benefit of this procedure was that he and his workers no longer cut down what they had believed to be "weed" trees, thus, maintaining and actually increasing a valuable food tree for the howlers and cattle living on the ranch.

Even prior to my research, Mr. Hagnauer was committed to preserving windbreak strips of forest and larger patches of forest occupying nontillable land because their presence protected the soil from the strong winds that blow during the five-month dry season. The wind barrier yielded reduced desiccation and made economic sense. These strips and patches of forest not only protect the soil but also serve as safe havens for many animals and plants. The subsequent owners have maintained this practice, thereby making the 1,980-hectare La Pacifica a refuge for local wildlife, particularly howlers, while still allowing it to be a productive farm operation that actually benefits economically by maintaining 500 to 600 hectares of forests. Surrounding ranches are clear-cut and their crops and cattle have difficulty surviving the five-month dry season. La Pacifica is proof that good business practices can also benefit the environment.

Many of the ranch-hands working on La Pacifica became interested in my research. Before my study, the monkeys were just a relatively uninteresting part of the landscape and ignored or hunted. During my dissertation study and the subsequent years, the humans became much more aware of the nonhuman primates and now serve as my "eyes" on the ranch when I am not there. They tell me of events that happen between my visits. The lead cowboy was instrumental in helping me track seven howlers that were translocated into the La Pacifica population in 1991 (six rescued from a dam site and one albino rescued from another ranch). The Costa Rican Electric Company (ICE) initiated the dam rescue by asking if I would safely remove the howlers from the soon-to-be flooded forest behind the dam, another example of a large company doing something that benefited conservation because of our research presence.

Local people know me as the "crazy gringo" who studies monkeys. Some of them cannot comprehend why someone would spend 10–12 hours a day, occasionally in a driving rainstorm, watching the monkeys that they take for granted. They came to appreciate my persistence and the fact that I am committed to studying these monkeys. In this way I believe that my continuing research and presence on the ranch has benefited the howlers of La Pacifica and possibly other monkeys in the nearby forests.

Suggested Readings

Glander, K. E. 1994. "Nonhuman Primate Self-Medication with Wild Plant Foods." In N. L. Etkin (ed.), *Eating On The Wild Side: The Pharmacologic, Ecologic, and Social Implications of Using Noncultigens*. University of Arizona Press: Tucson & London (pp. 227–239).

Glander, K. E. 1992. "Dispersal Patterns in Costa Rican Mantled Howling Monkeys." *International Journal of Primatology 13*: 415–436.

Glander, K. E. 1977. "Poison in a Monkey's Garden of Eden." *Natural History 86*: 34–41.

Glander, K. E., L. M. Fedigan, L. Fedigan, and C. Chapman. 1991. "Capture Techniques and Measurements of Three Monkey Species in Costa Rica." *Folia Primatologia 57*: 70–82.

Glander, K. E., and R. A. Nisbett. 1996. "Community Structure and Species Density in Tropical Forest Associations in Guanacaste Province, Costa Rica." *Brenesia 45–46*: 113–142.

Acknowledgments

The success of the La Pacifica Howler Project is due to the contributions of many individuals too numerous to mention individually, but my gratitude goes to each one with special thanks to Professor Russell Tuttle, Lily and Werner Hagnauer, Verena and Anthony Leigh, Jorge and Lydia Hagnauer, Stephan Schmidheiny, Fernando Estrada, Francisco Campos, and The Organization for Tropical Studies. Many collaborators have had a significant impact on this project with special recognition to Professors Margaret Clarke, Timothy Keith-Lukas, Paul Opler, Norman Scott, Mark Teaford, Susan Williams, and Christopher Vinyard.

6

Learning to Become a Monkey

By Michael A. Huffman[1]

"Coo! Cooi! Cuii!" As I climb up the steep winding trail, I hear the familiar high pitched chorus of contact calls coming from the 236-member-strong Arashiyama B troop of Japanese macaques. It is a balmy autumn day in the first week of October 1983 in western Japan, and the sweet, fresh scent of the clusters of tiny orange Osmanthus blossoms fills the air. Above I can also hear Nobuo Asaba, the Iwatayama Monkey Park's director, calling out to the monkeys with a hearty "Hoooi! Hoooi!" This ritual exchange is performed to encourage the monkeys to leave the forest and come out to the provisioning site. It is 12:00 p.m., the second of three daily provisioning times when sweet potatoes or wheat and fresh vegetables and fruits are spread out over the feeding grounds. This has been the practice here since 1955, when provisioning of the resident macaques—the only nonhuman primates native to Japan—was first started at several sites by scientists and local entrepreneurs.

Perched high up on the mountain, carved out of the steep slopes of Mt. Iwatayama, the Arashiyama study site lies on the western edge of Kyoto City. By the time I reach the station, the food is already half gone. Excited to be here again after three long years, I call out, "Ohisashi-buri!" (it's been a long time), as I run across the feeding ground to greet Asaba san, who in addition to serving as park director since 1976, is the man who has become like a second father to me, providing every kind of support in my study of the Japanese monkeys. We move inside the station building to talk and greet the other staff. I catch up on what the monkeys have been doing in my absence, how everyone's families are doing, and explain my future research plans.

Suddenly, like the pelting of hail on the roof, comes a loud din of noise. Because it's sunny, I am puzzled by the commotion from above and rush outside to see what is going on. Unexpectedly, I find a gathering of about 15 juvenile monkeys up on the metal roof with stones

[1]About the author: Michael Huffman was born in Denver, Colorado in 1958, and first came to Japan in 1978. Moving there permanently in 1983, he received an MSc (1985) and DSc (1989) in Zoology from Kyoto University. He has conducted long-term field research in Japan, Tanzania, Uganda, and more recently in Sri Lanka and Vietnam.

Contact information: Section of Social Systems Evolution, Primate Research Institute, Kyoto University, 41-2 Kanrin, Inuyama, Aichi 484 JAPAN, Huffman@pri.kyoto-u.ac.jp

Citation: Huffman, M. A. 2014. "Learning to Become a Monkey." In Strier, K. B. (ed.), *Primate Ethnographies*. Upper Saddle River, NJ: Pearson Education, Inc. (pp. 57–68).

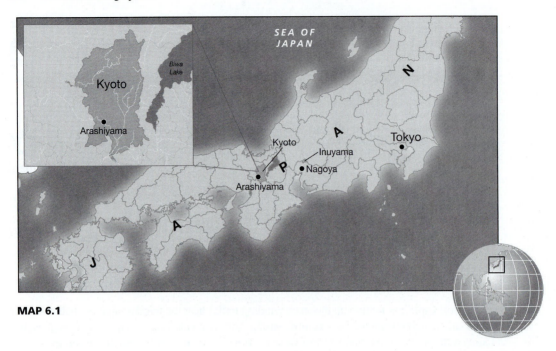

MAP 6.1

of various sizes—rubbing them across the metal surface, gathering them together, and scattering them about again.

During the 12 months that I first studied this troop between 1979 and 1980 as an undergraduate, I had never seen or heard anything like it. I asked Asaba san when all this started, and he replied that it became noticeable about two years earlier, shortly after I left the mountain in August of 1980. It was his impression that the handling of stones had become increasingly more frequent, especially after he dumped a large pile of stones that had been left over from some trail repairs on the side of the provisioning grounds.

For more than 30 years now, Japan has been my permanent home base, and for nearly as long (since 1979), I have been affiliated with Kyoto University. I have spent most of my career to date investigating the behavior and ecology of Japanese macaques and chimpanzees. In 1989 I completed my master's and doctorate in zoology. In 2001, after a series of postdocs, lecturing jobs, and fieldwork in Tanzania (1985–2005), Uganda, and Guinea on chimpanzees, I became the first tenured North American faculty member in the university's Graduate School of Science. I work in the Department of Ecology and Social Behavior at the university's Primate Research Institute (PRI).

Typically, students are encouraged to change universities several times in their careers to broaden their experience, but for a young primatologist in Japan, like myself, there was no better institution to be affiliated with than Kyoto University. This is where primatology in Japan began and today continues to be one of the longest, most productive focal points of primatological activity in the world.

In 1948 a small group of young undergraduate students (Junichiro Itani, Masao Kawai, and Shunzo Kawamura) in the Laboratory of Ecology began their observations of monkeys under the guidance and inspiration of Professor Kinji Imanishi. The group was officially christened the "Primate Research Group" in 1951 and published many early findings from nationwide surveys

FIGURE 6.1 Japanese macaques at the Iwatayama feeding station (Arashiymama). The alpha male at the time, Deko 64, is eating grain on the tree stump, surrounded by females and their offspring.
Photo credit: Michael A. Huffman.

as reports under this name on mimeographed copies for distribution among colleagues. Imanishi is considered the founder of primatology in Japan, and these three young protégés became the pioneers of primatological fieldwork and the academic fathers of perhaps one of the most diverse lineages of primatologists in the world.

Primatology at Kyoto University then and now remains focused at the Laboratory of Human Evolution Studies (established in 1962 as the Laboratory of Physical Anthropology) in Kyoto City and the university's Primate Research Institute (PRI, founded in 1967) located in the small town of Inuyama, north of the large port city of Nagoya in central Japan. The Japan Monkey Center, located next door to PRI, houses the editorial office of *PRIMATES*, the world's first international journal dedicated entirely to the study of primates (founded in 1957). Articles from this journal over the years offer a good sense of the development of primatology.

My fascination with primates and my quest to enter the "monkey business" began even before I can remember, sometime around 1960 at the age of three. My mother succumbed to my incessant pleading every night before bed to be read one of the many adventures of Curious George (by Margret and H. A. Ray). Many years later, with several trips to Africa already under my belt, my mother told me that as a child I had asserted, "Someday I will travel to Africa and live with chimpanzees." Among my earliest memories of chimpanzees is a life-sized, furry, stuffed toy version, whose big, floppy ears I can still remember chewing on. I met my first live chimpanzee, a young male named Dooby, in high school while volunteering in the veterinary department of the Denver Zoo, where I helped to care for injured animals in the collection and quarantined new arrivals. Dooby was donated to the zoo by a family who could no longer manage him. He and the male zoo keepers had a distrust of each other, but somehow the two of us got

FIGURE 6.2   The author (Michael A. Huffman) in 1980 at the Iwatayama feeding station (Arashiymama), enticing a juvenile to come closer so that its facial features could be studied better. **Photo credit:** Photo taken by Michio Nagarmune. Photo owned by Michael A. Huffman. Used with permission.

along well. Perhaps it was the hair beginning to sprout on my chin, which made him think we were somehow related! I must admit, though, he managed to get retribution for his "kin" by chewing on my ankles and hands more than once!

Curiously, around the same time I was learning about the adventures of George, I also had my first exposure to Japanese culture. My closest friends in elementary school were two Japanese-American brothers. We called each other's parents "Mom" and "Dad," and during weekends and summers I practically lived at their home, frequently eating "Mom's" Japanese meals. In all my worldly sophistication, I knew Tokyo was where Godzilla and King Kong "duked it out," but it never crossed my mind that the realization of my earliest dreams of chimpanzees in Africa and my life's work in primatology were to begin in Japan. My fascination for nature and science was kindled when my second grade teacher, Ms. Sloan, showed our class under the microscope the community of micro-organisms living in the pond water of my local swimming hole. In high school I subscribed to Scientific American and Science News. I filled spiral notebooks with notes from the wildlife programs on TV. I was the guy with the ponytail and a pocket protector, who spent weekends technical rock climbing or skiing in the Colorado Rockies when I wasn't working at the zoo, but everybody knew me as "Monkey Mike"!

Still yearning for Africa, I had written to several organizations including the National Geographic Society about opportunities to participate in a field research project overseas. Finally I was accepted by a program called International Expedition Training Institute. I dropped that bombshell on my unsuspecting parents one day after I came home from my job mopping floors at my old elementary school. I had enough money to cover the trip from my savings. My family and teachers were very supportive, though initially quite surprised by my persistence at overcoming obstacles and finding a way to make my dreams come true. I spent a few weeks after high school graduation, in the summer of 1977, on the British West Indies island of St. Kitts watching vervet monkeys.

In May near the end of my senior year, I received the long-awaited letter of acceptance into the undergraduate program in biology at Fort Lewis College (FLC) in Durango, Colorado. I had spent three weeks the previous summer on campus participating in a split course on the cultural anthropology and ecology of the Southwest, a summer program organized by the science and social studies faculty of my high school. The location of the campus at the foot of the San Juan Mountains and the thought of being able to observe nesting bald eagles along the river from the parking lot of K-Mart at the edge of town and following signs of coyote up on the mesa behind campus sold me on the idea of going there for undergraduate studies.

As fate would have it, in the same envelope as my admissions package, there was an invitation to join a group of six other students from FLC to go to Japan for a six-month study program at Kansai University of Foreign Language Studies (Kansai Gaidai) in Osaka. A catalogue of world-wide study abroad programs also had arrived that same day. The feeling came over me almost instantly that something was waiting for me in Japan, and I had to go at all costs. This time, the biggest hurdle was convincing my father that it really wasn't going to cost him that much! My savings were not enough to cover this adventure.

In February 1978, after a semester of preparatory classes at FLC, I traveled to Osaka. I quickly took to life in Japan, spending the first six months with a host family commuting an hour by train each way every day to school. A fateful chain of events and the supportive friendship of a few sensei at Kansai Gaidai paved the way to my eventually settling down in Japan. The term "sensei" is an important word in Japanese that means teacher, or in more general terms, is used as an honorific term for one's elder colleagues or mentors in all aspects of life.

In addition to my required studies at the international students' complex, I decided to see if I could audit some biology classes on the main campus to improve my Japanese and learn more about science in Japan. I was befriended by the Dean of Student Affairs on the main campus, Shimizu sensei, when I approached him for permission to audit classes there. He had a passion for nature, and as I found out later, some good friends at Kyoto University. One evening at his home, Shimizu sensei gave me three books in Japanese, two about the pioneering research on the ecology and social behavior of Japanese macaques, written by Kawai, Kawamura, and Itani. From that day on, I set out to improve my Japanese reading and writing skills with Kawai sensei's book, *The Ecology of the Japanese Macaque* (1963). Sometimes I would stay up all night, translating the book sentence by sentence. My enthusiasm sometimes cost me by making me late for morning classes and not do well on surprise language quizzes. (Unfortunately for me, there were no questions about consort behavior, seasonality of diets, or the matrilineal social structure of Japanese macaques!) Although the structured language course was very important, the most meaningful lessons in both language and cultural skills came from my daily interactions outside the classroom talking with people and corresponding with them in Japanese. I gave my first guest seminar on the ecology of the Japanese monkey, in Japanese, to a class of anthropology students on the main campus of Kansai Gaidai around the sixth month of my stay in Japan.

Trading my ponytail and pocket protector for geta (traditional wooden clogs) and a cloth bicycle saddle bag normally used for carrying large bottles of sake for home delivery as my book bag, I moved out on my own. I had managed to obtain a teaching scholarship to cover my tuition and a few lucrative English conversation jobs from my senior classmates returning to their home countries. Not able to afford my own apartment yet, I was staying in a one-room flat with one of my classmates from the main campus when there was a "vacancy" on the floor (i.e., when his girlfriend wasn't staying over!). As a result, I lived a rather nomadic life but was always well fed and taken care of by the many generous friends that I had made.

One night over dinner with Shimizu sensei and his family, I mentioned how interesting Kawai sensei's book was. Without my knowing, he wrote a letter of introduction for me, and two weeks later Shimizu sensei told me that if I could go to Inuyama, I could meet with Professor Kawai at the PRI. I was both thrilled and a bit intimidated at the thought. On July 20, accompanied by one of my Japanese classmates whose family lived not far from Inuyama, I met Kawai sensei at his office in the Section of Life-History Studies (now the Department of Ecology and Social Behavior). We chatted about his book and the work he was doing in Ethiopia on gelada baboons. He signed my copy of his book and offered the all-important formal introduction for me to his old friend and colleague in Kyoto, Junichiro Itani! Kyoto was closer to where I now lived, and a week or so later I went alone by train and bus to his office in the Laboratory of Physical Anthropology (currently the Laboratory of Human Evolution Studies), on the main campus in northeastern Kyoto. My appointment was for 30 minutes, but we must have talked for more than 3 hours.

He was an incredibly gracious host, considering the scruffy young visitor who showed up at his office. I was mesmerized by Itani sensei's stories about research on Japanese macaques and his pioneering travels across central and East Africa in the late 1950s in search of places to study gorillas—and chimpanzees! In 1960 while looking for a field site in Tanzania, against the advice of Louis Leakey, he visited Gombe Stream, not knowing that he was the first visitor Jane Goodall and her mother had received. They began a friendship that lasted Itani's lifetime. I told Itani sensei of my dreams of Africa and to study chimpanzees. He gave me the last copy he had of one of his many books in Japanese, *In the Forest of Gorillas and Pygmies* (1961), now a classic in modern Japanese literature. This meant more sleepless nights up reading. Then and there I was convinced that my road to Africa passed through Japan, and that this was the sensei from whom I would learn about being a primatologist and a mentor.

Before leaving his office, Itani sensei invited me to attend the laboratory's weekly seminars and suggested that Arashiyama would be a good place to observe Japanese monkeys. He introduced me to his student, Yukio Takahata, who was then just finishing his master's research on the reproductive biology and socio-sexual behavior of the Japanese macaques at Arashiyama. A few days later, I arrived at Arashiyama Station, an hour and a half by bicycle, bus, and train from the Kansai Gaidai campus. It was 8:30 p.m. and already dark when I arrived. I had to give an English lesson that evening, so I left directly after work with a large backpack filled with my sleeping bag, an umbrella, a little food, and the 8 millimeter movie camera that I had used on St. Kitts. After the many long mountain climbing trips in Colorado, I had no qualms about sleeping up on the mountain, but I naively thought that once there I would bivouac and go looking for the monkeys in the morning.

I found my way to the park entrance, a quiet isolated spot just above the river behind a Shinto shrine. A short steel gate at the beginning of the narrow trail led up a steep, dark, densely forested path. The gate was locked and a sign hung on it warning against entering after hours due to dangerous feral dogs and wild boar! A bit unsure of it all, I ended up sleeping by the river near Arashiyama station in my sleeping bag on a stone bench with the umbrella over my head. Here, I was in the company of a drunken businessman who had missed the last train home. I was pestered by mosquitoes and light rain all night but was excited about hiking up the mountain the next morning for my first encounter with the Japanese macaques of Arashiyama.

I arrived as the park was opening around 8:30 a.m., Itani sensei's business card in hand with a meticulously written introduction in small writing on the back. That was the key to my start, and I was warmly welcomed by Asaba san when I gave it to him at the feeding station.

FIGURE 6.3 The Iwatayama feeding station (Arashiyama) in the winter, with snow-covered Mt. Atago (1,000 meters above sea level) in the background. **Photo credit:** Michael A. Huffman.

My first year with the Arashiyama B troop began on August 2, 1979. Itani sensei's first advice to me was "To learn about monkeys, you have to become one first. Experiencing their lives to know them is more important in the beginning than any textbook."

As a young undergraduate living in a foreign land with monkeys in my backyard, I had the luxury to do just that. I had finished my studies at Kansai Gaidai. My new routine was to teach a few English classes at the beginning of the week and then go to Arashiyama after my last lesson on Wednesday. I would climb down the mountain on Friday after a few hours of observations in the morning, attend Friday seminars, and return to Arashiyama in the evening after dark. For the next 12 months, I slept up on the mountain 3–4 days a week in the small building that Asaba san had constructed as an office and meeting place for the Arashiyama Natural History Society. As there was no shower, during the summer and early fall I would wash up out in the open on the grassy slope behind the feeding station grounds. The spigot, sticking out of a concrete slab tee-tering on the edge of the clearing, was the last remnant of a building long torn down. It was supplied with cold water diverted from a stream to the feeding ground. At dusk, solitary male macaques, small groups of wild boar, and an occasional deer would pass by for water too. The view from the "watering hole" was a spectacular one of Kyoto in the sunset, not enjoyed by any-one else in the entire city. I would cook my rice in the hut along with a stir-fry of whatever was available from the monkey's provisions in the station kitchen—usually onions, carrots, cabbage, and potatoes. Every few weeks Asaba san would say I was looking a bit thin, and he needed to get me something good to eat! This always meant going to one of several of the local restaurants owned by his school day buddies, and after it closed we took them along with us to the next place, usually a bar, until it closed! Unlike the partying businessmen who missed their trains and had to sleep in the park by the river, after our nights out I had a snug bed to return to on the mountain with the monkeys. I felt guilty later on to learn that Asaba san would take the earnings of the day from tourist admissions and spend it on provisioning a primatologist!

Typically, at the end of the day after transferring my field notes into spreadsheets and adding highlights of the day into my diary, I would go back up into the forest with a head lamp, walking thirty minutes or so along game trails to locate where the monkeys were sleeping for the night. There are vipers in the forest, so I was advised to bring a walking stick at night to tap on the trail as I moved. This also doubled as a "rear break" when sliding down the steep slopes in the daytime following behind the monkeys. In the winter, things got interesting with 1–2 feet of snow, but that also made finding and following the monkeys easier, that is, until they decided to go straight down a steep mountainside!

I focused on two projects during this initial year: the cataloguing of the troop's natural plant food diet, and the effect of female mate choice on the social grouping of adult males and females during the nonmating season. I was interested in the work that Takahata had completed on the formation of nonsexual partnerships, what he termed "PPR" (peculiar proximate relationships) between adult males and females from the following year on after consort relations. After my year of observations, it seemed to me that females played a key role in the maintenance of the nonsexual status of these relationships as part of their mate choice strategy.

My language abilities had improved to the stage that I no longer used English in my daily life, writing my field notes in a combination of Japanese and shorthand symbols. I had also begun dreaming and talking to myself in Japanese by the end. I reluctantly left Japan in August of 1980 but promised myself that I would return and test these ideas for my graduate studies. Back in the United States and totally reverse culture shocked, I spent the next two and a half years at FLC finishing up my undergraduate degree. My studies were challenging and enjoyable, but I could think of nothing but returning as quickly as possible to resume my research at Arashiyama and to establish my career as a primatologist in Japan. I graduated with a Bachelor's of Science, earning a specialty degree in the natural sciences with a secondary emphasis on anthropology. I supported my way through college with loans and part-time jobs on campus, one of which was teaching Japanese to American students preparing to spend a semester abroad in Japan. I received the long awaited news in the summer of 1983 that I was granted a Japanese government scholarship for graduate studies at Kyoto University in the laboratory of Itani sensei! The day I got the news, I quit a part-time job at a Japanese restaurant in Durango and began preparations to return once again to Japan in October, this time for what I assumed was going to be for a very, very long time.

After my first day back up on the mountain in October of 1983, on the train ride back to Kyoto, I began to think about those young monkeys playing with stones on the roof. I suddenly remembered seeing a young female playing with stones at the feeding site one day in December of 1979. The proverbial light bulb above my head went on, and I became excited about the prospects of having possibly witnessed the start of a new cultural behavior for Japanese macaques. I returned to the lab that afternoon and told Itani sensei what I had seen at Arashiyama. He was very interested and encouraged me to look into it in more detail. A few days later, after I had unpacked all my books and records from Arashiyama, I went through my photo and slide files and found the picture I was looking for—the young female playing with stones! Using the date imprinted on the slide, I went to my notes and found the entry:

> "December 7 1979, A few minutes after the 12:00 feeding time, a young female is out in the center of the feeding site, a few minutes after the group is provisioned with wheat and soy beans. The 3-year-old female, Glance 6476, is stacking and rearranging blocks of stones."

FIGURE 6.4 Three-year-old Glance 6476 handling stones in the feeding grounds of the Iwatayama Monkey Park (Arashiyama) on December 7, 1979. This is the first observed and photographed episode of stone handling at the site. **Photo credit:** Michael A. Huffman.

I remember being struck by how human-like the behavior seemed. Up until I left in August of 1980 I never saw this behavior again. But by 1985, after a proper census could be made, I found that this behavior had spread to 60 percent (142/236) of the troop: all born before 1984, but none earlier than 1978. With long-term study, this was indeed shown to be a new case of cultural transmission in primates, the first of a play behavior having no immediate adaptive value to those who acquire it. Nonetheless, this tradition has continued to persist, being transmitted to all infants in the group within the first six months of life, every year for the last 30 years.

Over this time, with the collaboration of students and postdocs, we have found that the behavior has grown in complexity, with an increase in the number of behavioral innovations from the original five types recognized in 1980 to 35 in 2008. Not only did the number of behaviors increase, but their complexity and variation also increased. Perhaps most surprising of our findings from Arashiyama, a result of long-term research based on individual recognition, is that unlike typical play behaviors that cease to be exhibited by individuals as they reach adulthood (5 years), stone play behavior continues to be practiced by the oldest females in the group who acquired it when they were young. This led us to propose that beyond a functional explanation for play in young (i.e., development of motor-neural and perceptual skills through synaptic development), in adult and aging individuals, the continued practice of handling stones may provide important neurophysiological benefits by stimulating new neural growth (synaptic development) around damaged or deteriorating parts of the brain, as shown for elderly humans.

Stone handling was a secondary topic to my primary research at Arashiyama on female mate choice and partner preference in the Japanese macaques. I continued with this topic as the focus of my master's and doctorate research building on the observations that I had started in

FIGURE 6.5 A young adult female holding onto an arm full of stones, appearing to be in total bliss. **Photo credit:** Michael A. Huffman.

1979 because it allowed me to follow the development of mating relations between specific pairs over the short and long term. It was important to take this approach, as there was little information about the role of female choice and its impact on primate mating systems. To that point, the emphasis in studies on baboons and macaques was traditionally placed on male dominance as the determinant of reproductive success. Interestingly, work from Arashiyama in the 1960s by Gordon Stephenson proposed that the maintenance of a preferential mating system was controlled by male dominance. But it was the long-term efforts of Takahata and me that showed in the end that females really do have a strong influence on reproductive success and the maintenance of the Arashiyama macaque mating system.

From the onset, primatologists in Japan strongly emphasized the role of social relationships and their influence on group social structure, concepts that only took hold in the west much later on. While most primatologists world-wide are familiar with the role of matrilineal dominance in troop fission, male transfer, and incest avoidance, few may be aware that these concepts were first described and documented in detail at Arashiyama. Indeed, research at Arashiyama can be seen as a microcosm of primatology in Japan. Observations on the monkeys began in 1948 with the first detailed report of encounters with the troop by a local elementary school biology teacher. From 1951, Japanese researchers from Kyoto University and Osaka City University, joined periodically from 1969 by a number of international scientists, have systematically investigated this troop. Because of this collaborative effort, Arashiyama is one of the longest continuously studied populations of free-ranging primates in the world, with a complete genealogy for the entire period! This was possible only through

FIGURE 6.6   Arashiyama B troop's matriarch, 30-year old Mino, with a nursing offspring. **Photo credit:** Michael A. Huffman.

individual identification, collaboratively managed, long-term studies, three hallmarks of Japanese primatology.

I first came to this country with the goal of learning about the culture of Japan as a participant observer on the terms of her people, learning the language and accepting what I saw for what it was, rather than comparing it to the culture I was brought up in. This philosophy has served me well in the many countries and cultures that primatology has taken me to over the years. While learning to become a monkey, I was also learning to be a Japanese primatologist.

Suggested Readings

Asquith, P. 2000. "Negotiating Science: Internationalization and Japanese Primatology." In Strum, S. C., and L. M. Fedigan (eds.), *Primate Encounters*. Chicago: Chicago University Press (pp. 165–183).

Fedigan, L. M., and P. Asquith, eds. 1991. *The Monkeys of Arashiyama: Thirty-Five Years of Research in Japan and the West*. Albany, NY: State University of New York Press.

Leca, J.-B., M. A. Huffman, and P. L. Vasey, eds. 2012. *The Monkeys of Stormy Mountain: 60 Years of Primatological Research on the Japanese Macaques of Arashiyama*. Cambridge: Cambridge University Press.

Nakagawa, F., M. Nakamichi, and H. Sugiura, eds. 2011. *The Japanese Macaques*. Tokyo: Springer.

Takasaki, H. 2000. "Traditions of the Kyoto School of Field Primatology." In Strum, S. C., and L. M. Fedigan (eds.), *Primate Encounters*. Chicago: Chicago University Press (pp. 151–164).

Acknowledgments

It goes without saying that had it not been for the hard work and dedication of the pioneers of primatology in Japan, many of whom are mentioned in this essay, my own research would have taken a quite different direction. For their friendship, generosity, and unfailing support over the years I am forever grateful. I also give my heartfelt appreciation to Karen Strier, a good friend and supportive colleague, for the opportunity to write this essay. It was a wonderful opportunity to think back and reflect on the years spent here in Japan, how it all began and where it has taken me. I dedicate this essay to the memory of two dear friends and very special people, Junichiro Itani and Nobuo Asaba.

PART III

Social Complexities

7

The Accidental Primatologist
My Encounters with Pygmy Marmosets and Cotton-Top Tamarins

By Charles T. Snowdon[1]

The day began as the worst birthday of my life. For the last four days we had been chugging upstream from Iquitos, Peru on tributaries of the Amazon. Our boat was old and listed about 30 degrees to port. The only seats were benches on either side of the diesel engine, and at night, no matter how we strung our mosquito netting, we could not avoid being bit countless times. The water level was low and we frequently ran aground on sand bars. What was I doing here? I despaired of ever getting to see any monkeys, let alone do the research I had hoped to do. Toward the end of this hot, humid day we reached landfall at the camp and I met my research guide, Pekka Soini. Within a few minutes of landing, he took us into the forest and I saw wild monkeys for the first time in my life. A group of pygmy marmosets foraged around the edges of a small clearing made by a fallen tree, some eating exudates, the sap, and other excretions emerging from holes they had gouged in trees, and others catching insects. In less than an hour the animals began to call to one another, and they traveled single file to their night nest. My birthday turned out to be wonderful after all.

I was excited to finally see the pygmy marmosets and looked forward to staying for a long time, but Pekka had other ideas. We would leave the next morning to find another site further upstream. I had heard lots about Pekka from others who had worked in the Amazon. A native of Finland, Pekka had moved to the Peruvian Amazon for its much warmer climate. His first love was herpetology, and he had written a guidebook to the snakes and turtles of the Peruvian Amazon. But now he was working for the Pan American Health Organization (PAHO) to capture saddle-back and mustached tamarins for researchers in the United States. He had developed a method to attract monkeys to traps by walking along with a captive monkey that would call frequently and attract the local monkeys who were interested in the stranger. The monkeys were

[1] About the author: Charles Snowdon has studied tamarins and marmosets for more than 30 years both in captivity and the field. He has served as editor of *Animal Behaviour* and the *Journal of Comparative Psychology* and associate editor of *Behaviour, the International Journal of Primatology* and *Advances in the Study of Behavior* and has edited several books. He enjoys working with bright undergraduates and has published papers with more than 35 undergraduate co-authors.

Contact information: Department of Psychology, University of Wisconsin, 1202 West Johnson Street, Madison, WI 53706, USA, snowdon@wisc.edu

Citation: Snowdon, C. T. 2014. "The Accidental Primatologist: My Encounters with Pygmy Marmosets and Cotton-top Tamarins." In Strier, K. B. (ed.), *Primate Ethnographies*. Upper Saddle River, NJ: Pearson Education, Inc. (pp. 70–80).

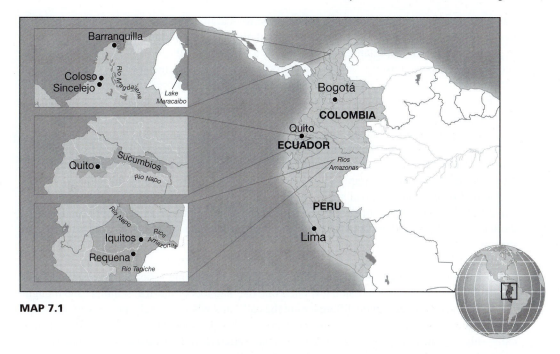

MAP 7.1

trapped and held in small wire cages, and the boat we had taken was supposed to return every two weeks to bring fresh supplies and to take the monkeys back to Iquitos. It mattered little that no one had successfully bred mustached tamarins in captivity. U.S. researchers wanted these small primates for research, and PAHO was willing to oblige.

The next morning we moved upstream, and with the help of local workers we modified a small shack for ourselves. Pekka and his Argentinean girlfriend, Maria, built a new house, roofing it with palm thatch that he carried with him from one place to another. Every day my then wife, Alexandra Hodun, and I went out to look for pygmy marmosets with little success. There was much logging in the area, and we would see several floats of logs pass down the river daily. The local population had burned much of the river edge forest for planting crops. As a result there was little suitable habitat for pygmy marmosets and those monkeys we did see were more shy around humans than the ones we had seen on the first day. Nonetheless, we made the most of our time and completed two studies, one on subspecies differences in the calls of saddleback tamarins that had been caught for PAHO and the other on individual recognition of group members by mustached tamarins. We found that if we simply moved an individual monkey to the opposite side of the clearing, it would begin to produce long calls. We observed the responses of other monkeys and found that only animals from the same group as the calling animal responded with answering, long call vocalizations.

In the evenings we each made our own meals but gathered for coffee later. Pekka carried a battery-operated turntable everywhere, and each night we would listen to a different Sibelius symphony. Pekka was making Maria read books by Kafka so she would have a better understanding of European culture, and it was a surreal experience to sit in the middle of the Amazonian rainforest listening to Sibelius and discussing Kafka in Spanish.

But our main purpose for coming to the Amazon was to study vocal communication in pygmy marmosets and this was not going to happen if we stayed with Pekka. As soon as the boat returned, we hitched a ride back to the place where we had first seen marmosets and we spent the next 7 weeks on our own. What was I as a psychologist doing in the Amazon and why were pygmy marmosets so important? I was trained as a behavioral neuroscientist, and all of my dissertation work as well as my work in my early years as a faculty member involved the neural controls of food intake in rats. However, I became increasingly bored with this work, and one day an undergraduate student told me of some monkeys in a back room at the Wisconsin National Primate Center on campus. I was intrigued and discovered that they were pygmy marmosets that had been purchased because they were the size of rats, and a researcher had hoped to make direct comparisons between monkeys and rodents using the same apparatus. However, he quickly found that while the marmosets seemed to understand the tasks rapidly and solve them quickly, they were easily bored and simply sat in the middle of the mazes for an entire session. When I had started in my position, I had hoped to study birds as well as rodents and had asked the University of Wisconsin Psychology Department to build some indoor aviaries for me. The bird work never really took flight, and so when I discovered that pygmy marmosets were arboreal and that my aviaries might be suitable structures, I negotiated with the Primate Center to transfer the monkeys to my lab.

I quickly discovered that pygmy marmosets have a fascinating variety of vocalizations, and my first undergraduate collaborator, Yvonne Pola, had had lots of musical training. She thought that she could hear many subtle differences in the calls, and when we analyzed the acoustic spectrum of the calls, we found her intuitions were correct. We observed a complex of trill-like calls—high-pitched, frequency modulated calls that varied in duration, bandwidth, loudness, and in whether the call was continuous or had a series of interrupted notes. Most of the calls appeared to be used interchangeably in captivity even though they differed greatly in structure. Two calls, the Open Mouth Trill and Closed Mouth Trill, had similar acoustic structure except that the Open Mouth Trills were always longer. We observed that the Open Mouth Trills were produced more often when animals were aggressive and Closed Mouth Trills were more often associated with affiliation, such as when the animals called before joining each other. We were able to synthesize these calls electronically and through a playback study, we showed that the marmosets responded differently to these two call types.

But that left us with three other trill variants that appeared to be used in similar contexts. The Quiet Trill is given at low amplitude and has a very narrow bandwidth. The Closed Mouth Trill has a larger bandwidth and is produced with greater amplitude. The J-call has the same frequency modulation as the Closed Mouth Trill but is a series of interrupted notes with only the ascending part of the trill appearing in spectrograms, looking very much like the letter "J," hence the name. The differences between these calls got me thinking about the acoustics of sound localization. We and other animals can localize sound easily based on timing cues that arise from several repeated notes and also from the frequency range of a call. (A pure tone is harder to localize than a noise burst or a tone that sweeps through a wide range of frequencies.)

What does this mean for pygmy marmosets? In the field, vocal communication is a trade-off between interacting with others of one's species and allowing possible predators to eavesdrop. The three calls differed in how readily they could be localized in the wild, with the Quiet Trill being the most cryptic and the J-call being the easiest to detect. When marmosets are close to each other, they can localize each other easily, and so they should use the Quiet Trill. When they are separated further from other group members, they should use the Closed Mouth Trill, and when they are farthest apart, they should use the J-call. This was the hypothesis we wanted to test in the field.

Two weeks later we left Pekka, and Maria and returned to the pygmy marmosets we had seen on my birthday. We quickly set about gathering data. Each morning we carried our recording equipment to the clearing and attempted to record Quiet Trills, Closed Mouth Trills, and J-calls from the marmosets. When we recorded a monkey's calls, we quickly looked around to find the next nearest monkey and noted where it was. Using tape measures we could measure the linear distance on the forest floor between the callers and the nearest listener, and using a ranging scope we could estimate the hypotenuse from us to the monkey and then use trigonometric equations I had not used since high school to solve for the actual distance between the two monkeys.

Over the next several weeks we were able to record several hundred calls and were able to measure the distance from the caller to the nearest neighbor. Each night we reviewed our tapes and were distressed that we could barely detect the calls that were so salient to our ears during the day. It was not until we were home and could use a sound spectrum analyzer to visualize the calls that we felt a sense of relief that we would have some data to analyze. The data supported our hypothesis that pygmy marmosets used calls according to properties of sound localization, giving more cryptic calls when close together and saving more detectable forms of calls for when they were separated. We also found that there was lots of ambient noise—from birds, frogs, and insects—and that was why we could barely hear the calls in our tent each night, but from the spectrum analyzer we saw that the pygmy marmoset calls virtually floated above the ambient noise, making the calls distinct. Not only did the marmosets adapt their call structure to how close or far they were from their neighbors, but they also used a frequency range for vocalizations that was above the ambient noise level (and above the prime hearing range of many birds that prey upon monkeys as well).

I have to admit I was not terribly excited about going to the Amazon the first time. I was in my late thirties and enjoyed the comforts of home and lab. And after the boat dropped us off at the site, it would be another seven weeks before a boat returned, and when it did, we were down to our last three days of food (rice and beans), and I had lost at least 30 pounds. We had expected the boat to resupply us every two weeks. We learned that the first boat had mechanical difficulties with replacement parts unavailable in the Amazon, and it took an unexpectedly long time to find another boat to fetch us. Needless to say, we were delighted to return to Iquitos. Before our trip I had completed a sabbatical with the noted primatologist, Thelma Rowell (now Professor Emerita at the University of California, Berkeley). She kept insisting that results from captivity could never be as valid as results from the wild, and in order for my conclusions to be valid, I must do field work. When we spoke with her later about our ordeal of being on our own with no supplies for seven weeks, she admitted that she never spent more than two weeks at a time in the field and always returned to a city for a hot shower and a good meal of meat and potatoes.

Instead of finding that my captive work had been useless, I learned that my captive monkeys and the wild monkeys showed the same behavior and had similar vocalizations, with the major value of the field being that I had a much greater appreciation of the context in which the behavior occurred and I had the satisfaction of knowing that my theoretical ideas actually made sense in the wild.

More than twenty years passed before I observed wild pygmy marmosets again. In the interim my students and I had completed several studies on call perception and classification. The next trip was to the Ecuadorian Amazon where my then student, Stella de la Torre, now Dean of Biology at the Universidad San Francisco de Quito, was doing her dissertation work on pygmy marmosets. We traveled in the dry season, and after a flight to the city of Coca, we traveled in the back of a pickup truck along newly built roads lined with oil pipelines, eventually reaching a stream that would be our entrance to Isla La Hormigo (the Island of Ants). The water level was too low for a boat, so we slept on a concrete slab and, fortunately, it rained during the night, providing just enough water to float the motorized dug-out canoe. At several places the stream was blocked by fallen trees, but the boat operator simply gunned the engine to raise the front of the boat, and as we slid over the trees, he pulled up the motor and we slid back into the stream. La Hormigo Island had two tourist camps and Stella had been studying three groups of pygmy marmosets. She was apologetic because when she had last visited she had failed to find the marmosets and now here I was to check up on her work!

The first morning out we heard the unmistakable babbling sounds of infant marmosets and we quickly ran to discover one of the groups Stella had been studying. Why should young marmosets make themselves so audible? In our captive studies I had found that the more a young marmoset "babbled," the more quickly it developed adult vocal structures, suggesting that vocal practice is important. We also found that babbling leads to rapid social responses from adults. A subsequent study on human infants found that greater maternal responsiveness to infant babbling promoted more rapid development of speech. Thus, the babbling of marmosets subsequently served as model for a study on how mothers' responses to infant babbling speeds human language development. In addition, a babbling marmoset may also be showing off its vigor to its parents and thus promoting greater parental care.

We eventually encountered the other two groups during the week but they were shy and quickly fled from us. Stella later learned that between her prior visit and when we arrived, someone had captured a young monkey from each of the groups to sell as pets. Stella regained some trust from the remaining animals and went on to compare these groups with those living in a pristine environment and found reduced vocalizations and reduced reproductive success in those groups living close to tourist camps and where the animals had been captured.

In subsequent work Stella replicated the study we did in the Peruvian Amazon, and she also showed that calls degrade in the natural habitat at different rates so that the close-distance

FIGURE 7.1   Pygmy marmoset eating exudates in Ecuador.
Photo credit: Pablo Yépez.

calls are more rapidly distorted by the habitat than the longer-distance calls. She has also found evidence of dialects, with each of five different populations having distinctly different forms of trills and J-calls. We had shown in captivity that when animals from two different groups are paired they adjust their individual calls structure to create a common pair version of a call. Thus marmosets learn to adjust their calls to their neighbors and mates, and we suspect that some type of vocal learning may underlie the formation of dialects in wild marmosets. Stella and her partner, Pablo Yépez, also found population-specific preferences for the species of trees from which marmosets collect exudates, and these preferences are not related to the abundance of each tree species. With vocal dialects that can be learned and population preferences for certain tree exudates, do we have a basis for culture in pygmy marmosets?

In contrast to the accidental discovery that led to my research with pygmy marmosets, it was a divorce settlement that gave me my first colony of cotton-top tamarins. During my sabbatical with Thelma Rowell, I was studying cotton-top tamarins. One of Thelma's graduate students had been married to another professor, and the student asked her ex-husband and Thelma to write a grant proposal to support her to study the hormonal basis of paternal care. The grant was funded and tamarins were imported from Colombia shortly before they were declared an endangered species. After six years, the student had dropped out, the grant had ended, and Thelma was stuck with a colony of endangered monkeys. I was fascinated by the wide range of vocal signals they used, and so when Thelma offered to give me the tamarin colony, I quickly accepted.

I moved the eleven tamarins from Berkeley to Madison and immediately faced a dilemma. Many tamarins had been imported for biomedical research in the 1950s and 1960s (an estimated 20,000–30,000 tamarins), and yet captive breeding success was poor, with only wild caught animals regularly rearing infants successfully. Captive born animals had poor reproductive success. If I was to do meaningful research of any kind, I would have to develop methods for sustained captive breeding.

An analysis of breeding success in a related tamarin species offered some clues. Tamarin parents who did not have experience caring for another's infants as they grew up proved to be

FIGURE 7.2   Group of cotton-top tamarins. **Photo credit:** Carla Boe.

terrible taking care of their own infants. Unlike many other primate species and our views about our own species, there appeared to be no innate "parenting instinct" in tamarins. They needed to learn to be parents by helping others do infant care. Tamarins and marmosets are known to be cooperative breeders, meaning that two parents are not enough to rear infants successfully. Non-reproductive helpers are critical. We were able to show later, both in the field and in captivity, that tamarins did not reach 100 percent infant survival until they had families of two parents and at least three helpers.

When we started we did not know this, but we did know that young animals needed to grow up in environments where they could stay long enough to learn parenting skills. To accommodate larger groups of tamarins, we built large cages. Family cages had 450 cubic feet, and the floor space was equivalent to a human home of 5,800 square feet based on size differences between them and us. Tamarins have claws rather than nails, and to mimic their natural arboreal environment, we placed lots of tree branches, ropes, and other climbing structures. Most of these were placed high in the cage so that the monkeys could be above human observers. Every two to three months we removed all structures and replaced them with a new configuration. This helped provide for sanitation and also provided a changing environment so that tamarins could be stimulated by new sensory and motor patterns. These changes proved highly successful, and we bred multiple generations in captivity. (It takes about three years for tamarins to reach sexual maturity and learn good parenting skills.) Over the course of 30 years we maintained a population of 75 animals and have donated nearly 300 tamarins to zoos, sanctuaries, and other research institutions.

We also realized the value of noninvasive methods to maintain healthy, reproductively successful animals and found ways to move a scale into the cage to weigh animals without capture, to use air conditioning ducts to move animals from one cage to another, to build apparatuses that we could move to test animals in their home cages, and to provide medications by placing them in preferred food. Many of our animals spent their entire lives without ever being handled by a human.

One of our most successful noninvasive methods was the collection of urine for hormonal assays. The idea was first suggested by Jeffrey French, now Professor of Psychology and Biology at the University of Nebraska, Omaha, and extended by my long-time colleague, Toni Ziegler at the Wisconsin National Primate Center. We quickly found that another advantage of our large cages was that we could enter the cage and follow an animal with a bucket until it urinated. We quickly learned that these monkeys, much like humans, urinate when they first wake up in the morning, so if we enter the cage as the monkeys are just waking up, we can collect a urine sample that represents the last 12 hours of hormonal activity. We recruited eager undergraduates to show up early each morning to collect samples for us. Initially, we ran into objections from other scientists who did not accept urinary measures. We had to demonstrate with each new assay that we were measuring something valid. Over the years the use of urine and feces has become much more acceptable, and Toni Ziegler has collaborated with many other researchers to develop and validate assays for more than thirty different species of primates, and urinary assays are now readily accepted as noninvasive measures in human research.

Our first hormonal question was why helpers were not trying to breed on their own. We sampled tamarin daughters living at home with their mothers and found that not a single one (of more than thirty sampled) ever ovulated when living with her mother. Yet when we removed a daughter to pair with a new male, ovulation (and often conception) occurred rapidly. (Eight days was our record.) However, if we transferred the scent marks of the mother to a daughter's cage,

FIGURE 7.3   Cotton-top tamarin male carrying an infant.
Photo credit: Carla Boe.

the daughter would not ovulate, and if we removed daughters from their mothers but housed them with their fathers or brothers, they would not ovulate. This suggests that a female has to be away from cues from her mother but also needs to be stimulated by a novel male in order to ovulate. Interestingly, measures of the stress hormone, cortisol, showed very low levels in suppressed daughters, so the lack of ovulation was not due to stress. Sons showed no evidence of any hormonal suppression and in fact are sexually active with all group members of both sexes in the home cage.

We were also interested in the mechanisms of paternal care. Nursing mothers naturally produce high levels of the hormones prolactin (involved in milk production and maternal care) and oxytocin (involved in uterine contractions at birth and in the milk let-down reflex in nursing). We and others found to our surprise that fathers carrying infants had prolactin levels as high as nursing mothers, and we found elevated prolactin levels in males before the birth of infants. We then moved backwards through pregnancy, measuring hormone levels, and found that fathers began increasing several hormones around mid-pregnancy of their mate, and experienced fathers showed hormonal changes earlier than first-time fathers. Humans talk with their partners about pregnancy, but how does a male tamarin "know" that his mate is pregnant? We found that halfway through pregnancy mothers begin to secrete high levels of glucocorticoids in their urine and that within a week after this began, experienced fathers began to show a variety of hormonal changes in testosterone, estrogens and prolactin. Could they be sensing cues from the mother's urine? The likely cause of the mid-pregnancy increase in glucocorticoids is the maturation of the adrenal gland of the fetus and the mother's body clearing out the excessive hormones. Could the fetus be using its mother to communicate to the father to start preparing for paternal care?

Tamarins in captivity appear to form lasting pair bonds, and this raises the issue of what behavioral and hormonal mechanisms are involved in pair bonding. We know from studies of monogamous rodents that oxytocin plays an important role in females developing bonds with their mates. We collected urine samples and behavioral measures from several pairs of tamarins and found a close correlation between males and females within a pair in oxytocin levels. There was great variability in oxytocin measures, and the variability was correlated with sexual and affiliative behavior. In males, variation in oxytocin was best explained by how often they had sex, and in females, variation was best explained by how much cuddling and grooming they received—not much different from humans! In the pairs with the highest oxytocin levels, females solicited sex more often, and males initiated cuddling more often as if each knew what was best for their partner. We also found that challenges to the relationship, such as brief separations and odors from novel ovulating females, also increased sexual and affiliative behavior. All of these results suggest that sex and cuddling are important behavioral mechanisms for forming and maintaining pair bonds.

Although the work with mating, parenting, and hormonal controls is fascinating, we studied many other topics as well. Because cotton-top tamarins are an endangered species, we have felt compelled to learn as much about them as possible. Once they become extinct, we can never learn anything more. If we can show that they are interesting animals, we might motivate others to care about tamarins and, thus, to help conserve them. We studied vocal communication and found that cotton-tops have a large vocal repertoire with subtle variants used in very specific contexts as well as a rudimentary grammar. We have found that young tamarins must learn communication skills. We studied social learning and cooperation and found that tamarins learn from others much more readily than chimpanzees do, and they regularly engage in teaching their young, something rarely seen in great apes. They readily cooperate to solve tasks that require two animals working together and continue to work together even if only one animal receives a reward. These cooperative breeders are truly cooperative.

Relatively early in my research with tamarins, I encountered a remarkable undergraduate. Anne Savage, now Conservation Director, Disney's Animals, Science, and Environment, at Disney's parks and resorts, published her first paper based on work she started as a freshman, and her senior thesis won a best student paper award in competition with Ph.D. students. After working in my lab for a few years, Anne decided to become a graduate student with the goal of doing a field study of tamarins in Colombia. Only one prior field study had been done on tamarins in Colombia, and it left many questions unanswered.

In 1985 we were invited by Colombian officials to make a preliminary visit and arrived in Barranquilla early one January. We went to a government field station near the small village of Coloso, where there were several cages housing groups of animals that had been confiscated from the pet trade adjacent to a forest with several wild groups of tamarins. The forest was quite different from the Amazon. There is a distinct rainy and dry season in Colombia, and the forest consisted of remnant patches along a stream bed that was used by local farmers to water their cattle and for their families. It was far too noisy to record vocalizations, but over several years Anne made many important observations.

There were many similarities between what my colleagues and I saw in captivity and what Anne Savage and her colleagues in the field observed. Pairs in the field stayed together on the same territory over many years, breaking up only after a drought that left no surviving infants. Both parents as well as helpers looked after infants, and first-time mothers were less successful than experienced mothers in carrying infants and sharing them with others. There was clear time-sharing of infant carrying, with animals trading roles of carrying, feeding, and being vigilant throughout the day. For most of the time only one female in a family group was pregnant. The only exceptions that occurred were when a new male had migrated into a group before conception, just as predicted from our captive research.

There were also important differences and new discoveries. In captivity (both in our lab and in the captive groups in Colombia) females could give birth at any time in the year, but wild tamarins bred seasonally, with births occurring only at the start of the rainy season when presumably more food is available. We studied natural dispersal and ranging in the field and found that both sexes dispersed equally and that tamarins ranged close to the stream in the dry season but had much broader home ranges in the rainy season when fruit was dispersed widely.

For both pygmy marmosets and cotton-top tamarins, conservation has a high priority. Stella de la Torre and Pablo Yépez have developed educational programs in the languages of the native tribes of the Amazon and have worked to develop an ethnobotanical reserve for the Secoya people to preserve traditional uses of plants in medicine, house construction, and hammock making while incidentally preserving the wildlife. Despite these efforts, habitat destruction to build villages and clear land for subsistence farming continues, and many of the groups of pygmy marmosets that Stella studied a decade ago no longer exist.

In Colombia the situation is even worse. Anne Savage developed educational programs for schools and involved local communities in finding new ways to cook without cutting wood in the forest, and she has developed sustainable markets for local women to sell bags and purses that they weave from discarded plastic bags. Yet paramilitary and drug trafficking activities remain and have spread to several areas, disrupting families and villages and creating difficult environments for conservation education. A 2010 survey found a significant reduction in suitable tamarin habitat since 2000 and estimated that only about 7,000 cotton-top tamarins remain in the wild. On the hopeful side, Anne has worked with Disney's Animal Kingdom and the Nature Conservancy to create a new reserve for cotton-top tamarins.

Tragically, it may become increasingly rare for others to share my excitement and joy of seeing pygmy marmosets and cotton-top tamarins in the wild. Even doing captive research on these species is becoming increasingly difficult with budget cuts for scientific research and an increased focus on studies that have an immediate benefit to humans. It has been a great gift for my students and me to glimpse the lives of these amazing monkeys and to learn some of their secrets of survival.

Suggested Readings

De la Torre, S., and C. T. Snowdon. 2009. "Dialects in Pygmy Marmosets? Population Variation in Call Structure." *American Journal of Primatology*, 71, 333–342.

Savage, A., C. T. Snowdon, H. Giraldo, and H. Soto. 1996. "Parental Care Patterns and Vigilance in Wild Cotton-Top Tamarins (*Saguinus oedipus*)." In Norconk, M., A. Rosenberger, and P. A. Garber (eds.) *Adaptive Radiations of Neotropical Primates*. New York: Plenum (pp. 187–199).

Savage, A., L. Thomas, K. A. Leighty, L. H. Soto, and F. S. Medina. 2010. "Novel Survey Method Finds Dramatic Decline of Wild Cotton-Top Tamarin Population." *Nature Communications* DOI: 10.1038/ncomms1030.

Snowdon, C. T., and S. de la Torre. 2002. "Multiple Environmental Contexts and Communication in Pygmy Marmosets." *Journal of Comparative Psychology,* 116: 182–188.

Snowdon, C. T., and T. E. Ziegler. 2007. "Growing up Cooperatively: Family Processes and Infant Development in Marmosets and Tamarins." *Journal of Developmental Processes* 2, 40–66.

Acknowledgments

I thank my field collaborators, the late Alexandra Hodun and the late Pekka Soini in Peru, Anne Savage in Colombia, and Stella de la Torre and Pablo Yépez in Ecuador. I have also had many creative and wonderful collaborators in my captive work, with special mention going to Jeffrey French, Toni Ziegler, Anne Savage, and Jayne Cleveland in the early days of establishing the captive colonies. Many undergraduates contributed creative ideas and participated in the humane care of the animals. Supported by National Institute of Health Grants MH029775 and MH035215.

8

Of Monkeys, Moonlight, and Monogamy in the Argentinean Chaco

By Eduardo Fernandez-Duque[1]

I had been considering whether I needed to capture owl monkeys ever since I finished my first field season in June 1996. I had confirmed that it is not possible to distinguish male and female owl monkeys reliably based on morphological sex differences while they are running through the canopy. I struggled with my own impatience and with everyone's insistence to move ahead. I did not want to rush a decision; I could not take the risk of hurting or even worse, killing, one of my monkeys during the capture process, even though I had carefully consulted with veterinarians and colleagues about how to capture these small (1 kg) monkeys using a blowpipe and anesthetic darts. It took me three years to gain proper veterinary training and to secure all necessary local, national, and international permits.

On August 2, 1999, I finally felt ready. I woke up before dawn and after some toast and mate (pronounced like "mah-teh"), a typical Argentinean tea-like drink, I checked the equipment for the hundredth time and went off to the forest with my assistant, Marcelo Rotundo, who is now my close friend. We readily found a group of owl monkeys moving in the canopy, but as soon as dawn broke (and following a full-moon night with lots of activity) they promptly settled down to sleep, high in the canopy and huddled in an immobile clump, until 4 p.m. that afternoon! We went back to camp because we did not want to dart them at dusk when visibility is poor. The next several days were equally unsuccessful. Sometimes the monkey was close, but twigs and leaves interfered, and I could not get a clear shot. Sometimes the monkey was on an open branch but higher than 6–7 meters, where my accuracy with the blowpipe was not reliable.

We decided to switch tactics. On August 24, we went out early in the morning to look for groups unaccustomed to our presence. When contacting nonhabituated groups, one individual

[1]About the author: Eduardo Fernandez-Duque is a biological anthropologist interested in understanding the evolution and maintenance of social and mating systems. His research focuses on the mechanisms that maintain social monogamy and on male-female relationships, pair bonding, and paternal care in humans and nonhuman primates.

Contact information: Department of Anthropology, University of Pennsylvania, 431 University Museum, 3260 South Street, Philadelphia, PA 19104, USA, eduardof@sas.upenn.edu

Citation: Fernandez-Duque, E. 2014. "Of Monkeys, Moonlight, and Monogamy in the Argentinean Chaco." In Strier, K. B. (ed.), *Primate Ethnographies*. Upper Saddle River, NJ: Pearson Education, Inc. (pp. 81–91).

usually approaches us while giving alarm calls; we were hoping that a daring individual would give us a chance for our first capture. Sure enough, soon after finding a group, one monkey came low while vocalizing. I took a deep breath, blew, and immediately saw a yellow flash that suggested to me that I had hit my target. "Damn, you hit a twig again," cursed Marcelo. Twig or monkey? I wanted to remain calm because the animals did not show any indication that they were frightened or scared by our presence, but my legs were shaking and I was trembling; I was definitely more nervous and scared than the monkey. After a few minutes, when I saw what seemed to be a motionless monkey on a branch, Marcelo climbed an adjacent tree to have a better look. "Yes, completely asleep, will try to get it," but the monkey was about 4 meters away from Marcelo's reach. "Bring the poles!" yelled Marcelo in reference to the telescopic poles we had prepared for a situation like this, and that we had left about 1.5 kilometers away. We had only a few minutes before the monkey would start rousing from the anesthesia and move away. Despite the knee-high rubber boots on my feet, I went for what I felt was the run of my life, while Marcelo stayed on top of the tree with the blowpipe and a few darts in case the monkey started to wake up while I was gone. I got the poles, a holding cage, yelled for the help of two assistants who were somewhere else in the forest, and finally rejoined Marcelo. The monkey was still completely asleep, hanging only from its toes. Marcelo kept trying to reach the monkey with the basket at the end of one of the poles as the assistants and I held a net underneath. "Got it, got it" shouted Marcelo after a few trials. With the monkey in the basket, both came safely down from the tree.

I remember feeling in complete control of the situation. I had planned every detail of what to do in nine long pages of written instructions; we had discussed every step again and again; I had rehearsed the procedures with captive owl monkeys on my own in the United States and then practiced them with Marcelo and the others using stuffed animals in the field. Anything that could be contaminated by our handling of the monkey was done first: We pulled hair samples for

FIGURE 8.1 Physical exam of an anesthetized owl monkey of the Gran Chaco, Argentina. The author (Eduardo Fernandez-Duque) is shown on the left.
Photo credit: Courtesy of E. Fernandez-Duque/Owl Monkey Project, Argentina.

genetic analyses, and we rubbed Q-tips on the pectoral and perianal glands for analysis of olfactory communication. Next, we took two small skin biopsies from the inner thighs for establishing live cell lines. A complete physical exam, which included taking body measurements, getting its weight, and checking its fur for the presence of ectoparasites followed. The male—by now we knew after examining its genitalia—urinated quite a bit while asleep, so we collected two samples for hormonal analyses. We fitted the radio collar, and forty-five minutes after Marcelo brought him down, we were done. We placed him in the holding cage, and kept it at some distance visually isolated from us. After two hours, once we confirmed that he had regained consciousness and locomotion, we opened the cage. He climbed into a little tree and rested there while we watched. We had successfully captured, radio-collared, sampled, and released "Carrito"—a 1.2-kilogram male owl monkey, member of study group F1200.

The live skin cells we had collected needed to arrive at the San Diego Zoo in California, within 48 to 72 hours, to avoid contamination by growing fungus or microbes. We had to deliver a properly packaged and labeled shipment to the local courier in Formosa City by 11:30hs, so that it would go by air to Buenos Aires at 17:00hs, then connect to the United States in the evening. "We are good," we thought: It was only 09:00hs, and the city was only a half-hour drive away. Then we hit a snag. Our field site is located in a private ranch with an entrance gate, which I had always found unlocked. Every single day, for three years, when I drove in and out, the gate had been unlocked. Not once was it locked, not until this day. We were trapped inside the ranch, with live monkey cells in our hands and no time to waste! Ignoring common courtesy that would have required us to ask our host to let us out of his property, we cut the chain on the gate and took off. There would be time later for apologies and explanations.

At 11:25hs we walked into the courier store; just five minutes later, we would have missed the courier. With the samples out of our hands, we drove back to the forest and tracked down Carrito's radio-collar signal to see how he was doing. Happily, he was resting with his group, so at 16:00hs, I headed back to the city, went home, and took a wonderful shower and napped. Back at home, I kept thinking of all the implications of what we had just accomplished. So many times, sitting by the fire in camp, drinking "mate," we had imagined it: "Once we mark them, we will be able to study sex differences in parental care . . . we will be able to learn if the males really are the biological fathers." The next few months, as we captured a few more individuals, our confidence grew. We were about to seriously plan the first ever field study of identified and sexed owl monkeys. Little did I know that the peculiar owl monkey biology soon would be a source of a most embarrassing event.

Some months later, following another shipment of samples, I received an e-mail message asking me to confirm the sex of some material labeled as having come from an individual named Elina. Our sexing of Elina as a female did not match Dr. Oliver Ryder's genetic tests at the San Diego Zoo. A similar mismatch occurred on a second occasion, but only much later could I explain what had most likely happened those times. Both times we had misclassified the individual's sex; first someone wrote "male" on the check sheet, only to later cross it out and write "female." It is likely that as the anesthesia caused a drop in body temperature, the relatively small testes of the monkey retracted into the body cavity. Taking into account a small penis that sometimes isn't much bigger than a female's clitoris and the mistake of not checking for a vagina opening, it appeared that a tired field worker had made a mistake—human error as they call it. "Can you check their sex again?" my zoo colleague inquired. "Check again?" I screamed to myself. I explained that the captured individual was now running happily in the canopy of the gallery forests of Formosa, Argentina, and that we could not tell its sex from watching it. "We will not be able to tell if it is a female until it nurses . . . . if it ever does, and if we can then observe it in the poor light conditions when we normally watch these little creatures. That is why we are capturing and marking the monkeys!" read my message to the zoo's geneticist.

Welcome to the world of studying small-sized, arboreal, cathemeral (active during both night and day), sexually monomorphic, monogamous owl monkeys. Owl monkeys, like titi monkeys, gibbons, marmosets, tamarins, and many lemurs, show few obvious sex differences, and this lack of sexual dimorphism has long been thought to be related to other important aspects of primate behavioral biology. But, there are only a few primate taxa in which sexual monomorphism is also associated with the tendency to live in socially monogamous groups, share parental duties, and occupy relatively exclusive territories. I had already studied one of these taxa for my doctoral dissertation at UC Davis, the titi monkeys (*Callicebus cupreus*) of South America.

After finishing my Ph.D., I was interested in continuing my research on monogamy and pair bonds, but I also wanted to return to my country, Argentina. One of the four primate species found in Argentina was the monogamous owl monkey—this was the lucky part. Owl monkeys are arboreal, relatively small (3 lbs, 1.2 kg), spend a good proportion of time being active during the night, and males and females look much alike—this was the not-so-lucky part. With a $4,000 grant from the L. S. B. Leakey Foundation as my only available funds, two sons (ages 5 months and 3 years), a wife and colleague, and lots of dreams, I went home to start the Proyecto Mirikiná (as people call owl monkeys in Argentina).

In Argentina, owl monkeys are only found in the eastern portion of the Provinces of Formosa and Chaco. The geographic region is part of the South American Gran Chaco, a vast expanse of land that includes forests growing along rivers (gallery forests), savannahs, and patches of forests immersed in those savannahs. Most of the land is privately owned, and the main activity is raising cattle that graze in the open savannahs. There is little interest or activity occurring in the gallery forests where the owl monkeys live. After renting a small house in the

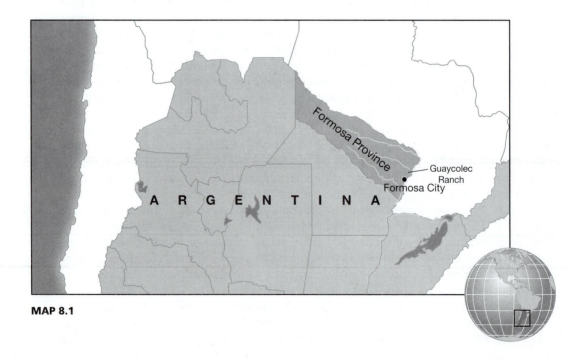

MAP 8.1

city of Formosa, I drove to the Guaycolec Ranch, a 25,000-hectare cattle ranch 25 kilometers away that had been owned by the same company based in Buenos Aires for 75 years. The manager, Don Gerardo Berger, gave me some directions, offered all of his support, and then left me to my own devices. The ranch functioned as a little village. The gauchos (somewhat similar to the "cowboys" of the United States) lived on the ranch; good times centered on the school: a national celebration, a birthday party, a wedding. Sad times took them to the cemetery, only a few hundred meters away from the school. My family and I slowly became part of their community, a "fútbol" game on Sundays followed by a shared "asado" (Argentinean barbecue) and lots of *mate* bringing us all together. We spent family weekends in the forest, with my sons' friends visiting the project's camp in the forest and the monkeys. During those first few years the forest became our own huge backyard.

It was also a crazy time, with a pace of life and research that I would not encourage my students to adopt. My wife, Claudia Valeggia, a biological anthropologist as well, was also beginning her field research on indigenous Toba communities of Argentina. We had to juggle our two projects with two kids attending school in the city and a large number of volunteers and assistants who needed my emotional and logistical support in the field. Some days I would start at 4 or 5 o'clock in the morning, with a 40-minute drive to camp, work in the forest until noon, return to town to pick up the kids from school, have lunch at home with the family, followed by a "must-have" Formosan nap, then drop the kids at school for their afternoon period, and race back to the forest for the late afternoon bout of activity of the monkeys. Other times, it was more efficient for me to stay in the forest for several days at a time, then take a day off to be with my family and relieve my wife of parental duties.

The first couple of years my goal was to quantify the extent of diurnal activity in the owl monkeys of the Argentinean Gran Chaco. I needed to know if they had enough diurnal activity to make studies of social behavior possible. From Panama in the north to Bolivia in the south, owl monkeys are strictly nocturnal animals, coming out of their sleeping holes in tree cavities late at dusk and returning to them at dawn. There had been some brief studies suggesting that in Argentina and Paraguay, the owl monkeys were also somewhat diurnal.

The evolution of nocturnality in primates has been for a long time a subject of interest to evolutionary biologists, primatologists, and anthropologists because it is still a matter of controversy whether ancestral primates were nocturnal, diurnal, or cathemeral. Although nocturnality is common among strepsirhines, owl monkeys and tarsiers are the only nocturnal haplorhines. But if one owl monkey species exhibited a pattern of activity that includes both diurnal and nocturnal behavior, then what were the key behavioral and physiological adaptations involved? Was this unusual temporal pattern of activity determined by available moonlight or by ambient temperature? I hoped that our research would provide some answers.

With the help of lots of students, we followed five groups of owl monkeys all day long or all night long and sometimes both day and night over the course of a year. For the first few months we stayed with the monkeys for 12–14 hours straight, until we realized we were burning out. So we organized ourselves into three teams doing 4- or 8-hour shifts. When we were doing a 24-hour *follow*, the first team would find the group at dawn and follow it until early afternoon; the second team would stay until 22:00hs; and then the brave "owl" team would watch them during the rest of the night. After 1,500 hours of following groups day and night, we confirmed that owl monkeys in the Chaco are, indeed, cathemeral, as opposed to strictly nocturnal like other owl monkey species elsewhere in the Americas. Cathemeral owl monkeys, which can be active anytime during a 24-hour cycle, still have two main peaks of activity—one at dusk and another one at dawn. It also became clear that light and temperature are the primary determinants of their

FIGURE 8.2   An owl monkey social group.
Photo credit: M. Corley/Owl Monkey Project, Argentina.

activity patterns. At full moon, they are active throughout the night and show reduced activity during the day. With a new moon, activity decreases during the dark portion of the night, peaks during dawn and dusk, and extends over the bright morning hours. During the cold winter months, the monkeys display twice as much activity throughout the warmer bright part of the day than during the other months.

These were novel and exciting results about behavior, but it was not until many years later that we could investigate the underlying mechanisms regulating these activity shifts. Thanks to new technologies involving automatic and continuous recordings of activity obtained with collars that include a motion sensor, which we were able to put on the monkeys, we discovered the complete shutdown of nocturnal activity during full moon eclipses. That was as close as you could get in the wild to running an experiment evaluating the effects of light on activity. Those years we learned quite a bit about the owl monkeys' activity patterns. Little progress was made on understanding their social behavior, however, because this required the identification of individuals, their age, or their sex. We simply could not recognize individuals: there were no visible natural marks, and we could seldom reliably distinguish their testes or protruding nipples. Occasionally, a few animals looked distinctive to us. For example, in 1998 we found an individual who had a tail significantly shorter (26 cm) than the typical 35–40 centimeters, and Cola Corta ("short tail" in Spanish) became one of our friends; he lived at least 14 years and sired five infants. Or, there were "Long and Skinny" with a long and skinny tail, and "Chopped" with the end of its tail severed. On several occasions we watched Long and Skinny mounting Chopped, and several months later, when an infant was born, it was "Chopped" that nursed the infant.

Thus, we classified Chopped as a female and Long and Skinny as a male in our field notes, but we still had to capture the animals, examine their genitalia, take measurements, and obtain genetic samples to be 100 percent sure. It was clear that collecting these data on other monkeys and fitting them with radio collars so that we could follow them through life was going to be a full-fledged project involving local students and communities and the local, national, and international support needed for capturing wild primates.

The new millennium brought me a "Millenium Postdoctoral Fellowship" from the Zoological Society of San Diego. Dr. Alan Dixson, an owl monkey expert and at the time Director of the Center for Reproduction of Endangered Species, offered me a five-year postdoctoral fellowship to concentrate on field research. Those years of field support were the final push the project needed to expand into one that combined basic primate research with applied conservation and education. The Owl Monkey Project would never be the same after those five uninterrupted years of field work.

We wanted to capture, mark, and sample an adequate number of individuals in an adequate number of groups to identify and sex individuals. As all biologists and primatologists know, there is variation in how each individual behaves over time, how individuals differ from one another, and how populations may vary from place to place. Variation is at the core of evolutionary biology theory and research. That is what we teach, and that is what we find in the field, but too frequently, time and resources limit our ability to sample variation. I was determined to develop a system that would be recognized for adequate sample sizes, but what is an "adequate" number? At a meeting with Dr. Dixson and Dr. Ryder during one of my brief visits to San Diego, we agreed that I needed to sample at least 35–40 animals in 6–8 groups. "Adequate" had been defined; I had something I could work on.

We made great progress in capturing and marking individuals. Owl monkeys were getting names, and the soap opera of their lives began to unfold. We had known for a while that there were fights among them, and many times we had the impression that the fights were between members of a group and a solitary animal. Esperanza, mother of Ernestina and Elegida, was one day expelled from the group following some dramatic fights with a strange solitary female that extended over two days. The fights left Elegida with severe wounds, which eventually led to her death. Ernestina disappeared from the area, and Esperanza ranged alone for a few months until she, too, died.

Our science changed dramatically once we were able to recognize individuals. We could finally address the questions about monogamy that had taken me to Formosa in the first place. One of our most significant findings was that the socially monogamous groups of owl monkeys are not always "families" of biological parents and offspring, but instead regularly include step-parents. Following radio-collared individuals as they left their natal groups, we learned that as they look for reproductive opportunities, both males and female show significant intra-sexual aggression that can sometimes result in deaths. This was an unexpected finding because it illustrated that despite remarkably little morphological and behavioral dimorphism, there can still be intense and frequent competition between individuals of the same sex.

We also gathered valuable information on the relationship between pair bonding, monogamy, parental care, and life history traits. Owl monkeys have a remarkably slow life-history trajectory for such a small organism: Infants are very dependent until six months of age, and following weaning, both males and females continue to grow until at least four years of age, at which time they tend to disperse from their natal groups. Reproducing for the first time when they are at least six years old, individuals may produce four to six offspring during their lives.

Although our study has not lasted long enough to establish conclusively the duration of their lifespan, we can safely estimate that some individuals have lived at least 14–15 years.

The new millennium also brought Fundación ECO of Formosa. As an Argentinean working in my own country, I wanted to integrate myself in the community while also contributing to conservation and educational activities. One evening at home I wrote a letter to my Argentinean close friends, with tears in my eyes, telling them about two mothers giving birth in the same hospital bed, kids going to sleep on an empty stomach, and teenagers having hardly any reason to dream about the future. My wife and I had grown up in Buenos Aires, as protected kids raised in middle-class families, and we could not believe these things were happening in our country. I needed to get active in trying to change things and I invited my friends to join us. For every problem we considered, for every potential solution we imagined, we kept going back to the need for more and better education.

We made a decision: We would establish Fundación ECO with the mission to "support and encourage academic and non-academic education in the region" (http://fundacioneco.wordpress.com/). Given the nature of my research, I have naturally found myself immersed in projects related to conservation, education, and the protection of habitats, flora, and fauna. The charismatic owl monkeys were an invaluable flag species, and having radio-collared individuals opened up a whole range of opportunities to organize educational activities with schools, local communities, and ranch owners. Being an elusive, small, and quite nocturnal primate, most locals have never seen it. Even though we tend to think that the local people know their forest well, the truth is that most of them have never ventured into the forest, much less at night! We could now reliably find and show owl monkeys to people. Owl monkeys became known to many people in Formosa—they were in the newspapers and TV. Japanese television and the BBC made the local news when they arrived in Formosa to film our project. Groups of ten-year-old students went to the forest at dawn to see owl monkeys for the first time. Adults signed up for one-day workshops. We offered field courses on primate conservation that trained 70 students from 10 different Latin American countries.

Slowly and steadily, Fundación ECO continues moving forward. Over the years, we have organized educational activities to promote the conservation of the fauna and flora of the Gran Chaco using owl monkeys as a flag species. We have participated in local science fairs, provided teachers with logistical support to incorporate material on local biology into their curriculum, and invited Formosa elementary school children to participate in field biology on the ranch. A successful scholarship program supports low-income students with the costs of postsecondary education. Fundación ECO remains a small, 100 percent volunteer-run organization but one that we hope is making a small difference in contributing to the education of the local communities in the Province of Formosa.

Our long-term commitment to the research project and to the local communities, and the significant economic activities that our work generated did not go unnoticed. Our relationships with the ranch owners and local and national authorities evolved in the sense that evolution works—without a purpose, without a linear progress towards a "better" relationship; relationships just changed over time, sometimes bringing us satisfaction, sometimes frustration. One of the most satisfying experiences occurred in June 2006, when the ranch owners hosted a one-day celebration to mark the tenth anniversary of the project that was attended by the National Director of Wildlife, the Formosa Minister of Production, and representatives of the National Parks Administration. They all visited the forest, had wonderful views of the monkeys, and a great lunch, all in the context of laying out concrete plans and commitments for the establishment of the "Mirikiná Reserve." Today the reserve is a reality: a 2,000-hectare area of gallery forests that

FIGURE 8.3   Dixie, a two-year-old juvenile being released with a radio collar. **Photo credit:** M. Corley/Owl Monkey Project, Argentina.

encompass our camp, our study area, and a long stretch of forest up and downstream from where we work. In December 2011, the Formosa provincial congress passed a law declaring the owl monkeys "Monumento Natural Provincial," a legal designation that gives owl monkeys and their habitat special protection. It is also very satisfying to realize that close to 300 students, assistants, and volunteers have had the wonderful experience of discovering the cultural and biological diversity of the Argentinean Gran Chaco thanks to our project.

But there were hard times as well. In April 2003, I was summoned to the ranch office by Mr. John Adams, the manager of the ranch at that time. Without any previous notice he told me that the ranch had changed owners and the new manager wanted to meet with me. "Eduardo, I need to ask that you and your team members leave the ranch before dusk today," said the new manager Ing. Cimino in an emotionless firm business tone. While sharing a drink, he explained that Bellamar Estancias, the new owners of the ranch, needed a formal agreement for our activities and that he could not allow us to stay in the ranch until those agreements had been signed. He promised it would take only a month or two at most to get all of the proper documentation signed. The meeting took place a few days after we had finished fitting six owl monkeys with the motion sensor collars that my German colleague, Dr. Hans Erkert, had provided for a study of activity patterns. Each of the collars was worth $1,100, and we had planned to monitor the animals day and night. Now, instead, I had to spend the next two long months getting this new documentation ready. When the agreements were signed, we went back to the forest; much to our despair, we found that three of the monkeys we had fitted with collars had been replaced in their groups by other adults. We learned the hard way that April–May, the time when we had fitted the motion collars to the animals, is a time of the year when there is a lot of competition among adults, and therefore not the best time to capture and release monkeys. Quite frequently, young solitary individuals challenge resident adults and succeed in replacing them as resident adults in the group. We never found the missing collars, but our studies in the ranch have continued uninterrupted since then and with a stability and support from the ranch that we could not have without a formal agreement.

An even more stressful event soon brought to light the crucial importance of having proper documentation with the private sector, as well as provincial and national authorities. Around that time, there was a second event that made me think of quitting. "¿Quien mata a los mirikinás?" (Who is killing the owl monkeys?), read the hand-written painted sign on the side of the highway in front of the entrance to the Guaycolec Wildlife Reserve, a small 200-hectare provincial facility adjacent to the ranch. The central page of the main local newspaper showed a picture of the sign. The Fundación ECO's office was being called by radio stations, and television crews were knocking on its doors. The Formosa Ecological Police requested my presence at the police station. For a few weeks, I feared everything would fall apart. But fortunately, the ill-founded accusations that our project was responsible for the death of numerous owl monkeys were rapidly dismissed by those (i.e., governor, minister, secretary, council of veterinary doctors) who had a full understanding of the project and who had signed all necessary provincial and national permits.

Despite the challenges and the demands of the project, the value of our mission and the importance of our findings have kept us motivated. The study of monogamy, pair bonding, and alloparental care is of special interest to anthropologists because it has been suggested that pair bonding could be a fundamental adaptation of early hominins. In societies everywhere, a man and a woman develop a relationship between them that is qualitatively different from the relationship that they have with other opposite-sex adults. Psychologists, historians, poets, anthropologists, behavioral ecologists, and economists all have testified to this ubiquitous phenomenon: a pair bond, attachment or love that develops between a man and a woman together with a commitment to share space, time, resources, offspring, and labor. Owl monkeys offer a simpler nonhuman primate model with a remarkably slow life history (like humans) where we can examine the biological bases of pair bonding free from the cultural variability associated with studies of marriage among humans. As the Owl Monkey Project of Argentina continues with studies on the third generation of identified, sexed, and aged owl monkeys, it offers one of the few primate models in which we can explore the interactions between behavior, ecology, demography, and genetics, as well as the possible role of historical events and infrequent climatic phenomena in shaping primate behavior and life history.

Suggested Readings

Fernandez-Duque, E. 2011. "Rensch's Rule, Bergman's Effect and Adult Sexual Dimorphism in Wild Monogamous Owl Monkeys (*Aotus azarai*) of Argentina." *American Journal of Physical Anthropology* 146: 38–48.

Fernandez-Duque, E. 2011. "The Aotinae: Social Monogamy in the Only Nocturnal Anthropoid." In Campbell, C. J., A. Fuentes, K. C. MacKinnon, S. K. Bearder, and R. M. Stumpf (eds.), *Primates in Perspective,* 2nd ed. Oxford: Oxford University Press (pp. 140–154).

Fernandez-Duque, E. 2012. "Owl Monkeys *Aotus spp* in the Wild and in Captivity." *International Zoo Yearbook* 46: 80–94.

Fernandez-Duque, E., H. de la Iglesia, and H. G. Erkert. 2010. "Moonstruck Primates: Owl Monkeys (*Aotus*) Need Moonlight for Nocturnal Activity in Their Natural Environment." *PLoS ONE* 5:e12572.

Huck, M. G., and E. Fernandez-Duque. 2012. "Children of Divorce: Effects of Adult Replacements on Previous Offspring in Argentinean Owl Monkeys." *Behavioral Ecology and Sociobiology* 66: 505–517.

Acknowledgments

Thanks to all the students, volunteers, assistants, and colleagues who made the research possible, to the owners and administrators who allowed us to work in Estancia Guaycolec, and to Ministerio de la Producción, Subsecretaría de Ecología and Recursos Naturales and Dirección de Fauna from Formosa Province who authorized the research. EFD acknowledges the financial support during all these years from the Wenner-Gren Foundation, the Leakey Foundation, the National Geographic Society, the National Science Foundation (BCS- 0621020), the University of Pennsylvania, the Zoological Society of San Diego, and Argentinean National Council of Research (Conicet).

9

Stress in the Wilds

By Jacinta C. Beehner[1]
and Thore J. Bergman[2]

It's about 5:30 in the morning. I'm crouched in a steel cage, smack in the middle of the African savanna. I squint into the waning darkness of the early African morning and try (in vain) to identify movement from the nearby bushes. The only sound I hear is my heart pounding. My morning began as every other morning had for the past seven months—rising before dawn, choking down some tea and bread before driving out to a nearby escarpment to find a group of baboons that I'd been dutifully collecting behavioral data on for my Ph.D. thesis. But, this morning my routine was interrupted by a primal fear that has surely shaped human survival for millions of years—*the urge to flee.* Remarkably, I have an option available to none of our hominid ancestors—a steel cage only 10 meters away. I immediately scramble into the cage where I now sit, wishing that my heartbeat wasn't so loud. I try to reassure myself, "This works with sharks, right?" Then, I hear it again—the low, rhythmic roars of a lion (or, more likely, a lioness) only a stone's throw away from me.

In behavioral fieldwork, the number-one rule is to maintain objectivity. Don't get too close or emotional with the subjects we study. Don't anthropomorphize. Maintain an appropriate scientific distance. Strictly speaking, I try to adhere to this policy. However, by necessity, fieldwork also causes our lives to become inextricably intertwined with our subjects in ways that we cannot avoid. We follow them up and down steep canyons; we wander with them across the plateau under a scorching sun; we rest with them in the sparse shade of acacia trees; we climb trees to

[1]About the author: Jacinta C. Beehner is an associate professor of Anthropology and Psychology at the University of Michigan. She is the co-director of the University of Michigan Gelada Research Project, which was established in Ethiopia over seven years ago. She continues to study behavioral stress and reproductive physiology in geladas.

Contact information: Departments of Psychology and Anthropology, University of Michigan, Ann Arbor, MI 48109–1107, USA, jbeehner@umich.edu

[2]About the author: Thore J. Bergman is an assistant professor of Psychology and Ecology and Evolutionary Biology at the University of Michigan. He co-directs the University of Michigan Gelada Research Project with Jacinta, focusing on gelada social behavior, cognition, and communication.

Contact information: Departments of Psychology and Ecology and Evolution, University of Michigan, Ann Arbor, MI 48109-1043, USA, thore@umich.edu

Citation: Beehner, J. C., and Bergman, T. J. 2014. "Stress in the Wilds." In Strier, K. B. (ed.), *Primate Ethnographies.* Upper Saddle River, NJ: Pearson Education, Inc. (pp. 92–106).

FIGURE 9.1   Thore Bergman baiting cages with corn in anticipation for trapping baboons. One baited cage, in the distance, already contains three Anubis baboons at the Awash National Park. **Photo credit:** Jacinta Beehner.

escape lions. Their stressful environment is simultaneously *our* stressful environment. Their predators are *our* predators.

This brings me back to why I am sitting here in this cage. After hearing the first set of roars, my mind scans the familiar landscape for a tree to climb. (Somewhere in my brain I do know that lions can climb trees, but brainpower has an inverse U-shaped relationship with stress, and I was certainly at the dysfunctional end.) Then, in the dim light of dawn, I catch a reflection from metal and am quickly reminded of the cages nearby. We (that is, me and Thore Bergman, my fellow graduate student) had set up six cages in anticipation of another "trapping season." About every other year the Awash National Park Baboon Research Project (led by Drs. Clifford Jolly and Jane Phillips-Conroy) would round up a group of eager American graduate students for a three-month trip to Ethiopia to trap baboons to collect morphological, genetic, and physiological data. These trips are festive and fun for the students, and even the baboons appear to appreciate these "seasons," with many of the males (particularly those trapped in previous years) voluntarily sitting in the open cages, presumably waiting for the corn bait to appear. But, this morning all the cages are empty—that is, all of them except the one I am crouched in.

It suddenly occurs to me that the baboons must not be on the cliffs below or they would be going bananas right now. During the night, the baboons' primary means of protection is to sleep on steep, rocky cliffs where predators (that is, lions, leopards, and spotted hyenas) can't get to them. But during the day, they protect themselves by mobbing predators with loud alarm calls and threats—in short, they create such a commotion as to discourage any and all predators (who mostly hunt by stealth). Even when the baboons are (enviably!) on the safety of the cliffs, this mob mentality affects their demeanor, and the mere sight or sound of lions sends them into a frenzy of alarm calls. All my fear is immediately replaced by irritation. The day could be entirely wasted if I don't find the baboons before they disembark from their sleeping cliffs. Despite the chaos generally surrounding a group of 103 baboons, they can be surprisingly difficult to locate on an open savanna. I wonder to myself whether Thore is having more luck finding baboons at the other sleeping cliffs. I could radio him, but although *theoretically* I'm safe in the cage, the thought of making a single noise is terrifying. I opt to just sit and wait.

Twelve years later, I can perfectly recall myself sitting in the cage. Little did I know that the next decade would bring many more close encounters with predators, but this one (being my first) is forever seared on my brain. I don't just remember what happened, I remember how it all felt—how difficult it was to see, how loud my heart was pounding, even how the cage smelled. I teach my undergraduates about these vivid, emotional memories in my Hormones and Behavior class at the University of Michigan. It's called "flashbulb memory" and it's not unusual for memories of stressful moments to be particularly salient. For example, most people can tell you in an instant where they were when they first heard about the terrorist attacks on September 11, 2001. The adaptive idea is that the hormones (known as glucocorticoids or "stress hormones") secreted as a result of just one experience immediately notify the brain as to the importance of the event, and presumably keep us (and other animals) from making the same mistake twice (in my case, romping around on the African savanna before the sun is up). These hormones are just one way that the body gets through a stressful situation and comes out alive in the end.

Perhaps as a result of many of our own experiences (such as sitting, petrified, in that cage for more than two hours that early morning), stress in wild primates is a major focus of Thore's and my research. From our Ph.D. work on baboons in the Awash National Park of Ethiopia, to our postdoctoral work on baboons in the Okavango Delta of Botswana, to our current project on geladas (a close cousin of baboons) that live only in the highest mountains of Ethiopia, we keep trying to figure out what is stressful for these animals as they navigate their environmental and social landscape. It's actually not that hard to figure out because we too must "live" with the monkeys to observe their natural behavior; we too subject ourselves to many of the same stressors that affect their physiology and behavior. Thus, we gain (all too) intimate knowledge of severe environmental conditions, life-threatening predators, and the psychological stress of living in a large social group.

Despite the vivid memory of myself in a cage that early African morning, predators were actually the least of our worries in the Awash National Park of Ethiopia. Across Thore's and my (combined) four and a half years of Ph.D. field research, we rarely encountered predators as we traipsed across the savanna. There just weren't (and still aren't) many of them left. Alas, the more salient "evil" dominating our days in Awash was the relentless and unforgiving sun.

The Awash National Park is situated right at the juncture where the Rift Valley opens up to the Danakil Triangle. Dust and sand rise up in funnel-shaped twisters that spin across the desert briefly and then collapse. It's dry, dry, dry here—and did I say *hot*? Very few crops are grown here, and most of the land is used by the nomadic pastoralists to graze their goats, cattle, and camels on the sparse vegetation. According to Wikipedia, the hottest place on earth is Dallol, Ethiopia with a recorded annual mean temperature of 93.9°F. *That's nothing,* I think. The temperature gauge outside our window regularly reads 97.0°F, *and that's in the shade.* (Temperatures during the rainy season probably lower the annual mean temperature enough that the Awash National Park escapes mention on the "Extremes on Earth" Wikipedia page.)

Today, as Thore and I lie under the kitchen table waiting for the cool cement floor to suck some of the heat out of us, I think about the possibility of a drought. The rains should have come more than a month ago, but we have yet to see a cloud in the sky. The oryx and kudu are starting to show their ribs, and the campsite baboons have taken up an almost permanent residence in the nearby staff village to raid the garbage pits. Everything around us is sore and cracked and in dire need of rain. Here in the Ethiopian lowlands it's pretty dry all year long, but in all the years that I've been traveling back and forth, I've never seen it so dry and barren. I wonder to myself

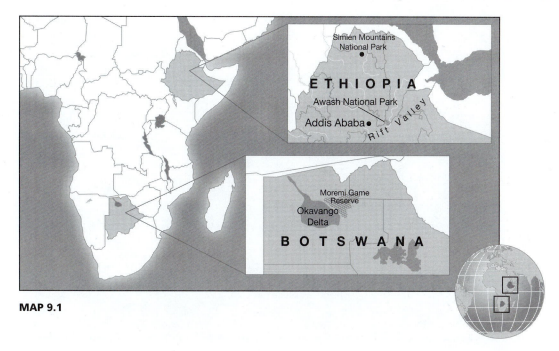

MAP 9.1

whether this drought will rival that of 1984—a drought and subsequent famine of epic propor-tions with 1 million deaths and millions more made destitute that came to define Ethiopia (in the mind of Westerners) as a country of starving children.

Ethiopia has long since recovered from the 1984 famine, but because the economy of Ethiopia is based almost entirely on agriculture (almost half of their gross domestic product, 60 percent of exports and 80 percent of total employment), droughts can have severe consequences. Survival here is still dependent on the annual rains, and they have yet to come.

Such extreme conditions also make life difficult for the baboons, a species that typically is found in more fertile habitats than this. Baboons, like humans, are "weed" species. In other words, they are able to inhabit and exploit most habitats that other, "nonweed" species cannot. Humans are found in every corner of the planet. Baboons, compared to most other nonhuman primates, are nearly as adaptable, found all throughout sub-Saharan Africa, and even in parts of the Middle East. Part of what makes them so versatile is that they can adjust their diet and rang-ing patterns with the local conditions. I'm continually amazed that, while we have to pack sev-eral high-energy bars and a large lunch to facilitate our daily journey with the baboons (sometimes up to 15 km), the baboons manage to survive on the scraps of leaves, insects, and seeds that they find along the way. Perhaps more amazing is that they are able to get a whole day's worth of water in one trip to the river. They take a long drink, sit for about 20 minutes, and then take another long drink. We regularly carry 5 liters of water (each), yet by early afternoon we have to go home because we've run out of water. (We've found that filling our stomachs with one extra liter of water before we set out in the morning helps.) But, even though baboons can survive in extreme environments, I wouldn't exactly say they thrive in it.

As any sensible animal would, the baboons avoid the sun as much as possible. Unfortu-nately, obtaining enough calories for the day usually depends on a long trek across the African savanna with the sun beating down on their backs. However, when the sun is at its hottest, they

FIGURE 9.2 A group of baboons resting on the edge of a cliff in the desertlike conditions of the Awash National Park. **Photo credit:** Jacinta Beehner.

typically nap in the sparse shade of an *Acacia* or *Grewia* bush. Unfortunately, a knee-high bush is adequate shade for a baboon, but it does very little for me and Thore, who must stand nearby baking in the sun. Much to our relief, during the most extreme times of the year, like right now, the baboons actually move around less when food is most scarce. It is as though the baboons have done the math and figured out that the energy expenditure out on the savanna is just not worth the scraps of food they might get. Better to just rest up in the shade of the cliffs. And, what shade it is! There are caves in the sides of the cliffs—providing enough shade for all of us. On these wondrous occasions, we eagerly scramble over the canyon edge and gingerly climb down to rest with the baboons in the caves. The relief is immediate. Surely, these caves are the coolest place in the entire Rift Valley. But, today was not one of the wonderful cave days. Today was one of the many days of walking at least a dozen kilometers in the blazing sun. The only reason we were able to keep up with the group was thanks to one of our adult females, Cecelia.

In the past two months, Cecelia has fallen ill. Her fur is missing on parts of her body and her ribs are showing. We don't exactly know what is wrong with her, but we do know two things. First, she hasn't shown signs of fertility in more than two months, and second, due to her lagging behind the rest of the group, she has made it much easier for us to continue following (and finding) our group. Although we are benefiting from Cecelia's plight, it is sad to think about her (likely) death and whether it will be an isolated event or the first of a series caused by the drought.

We worked in the Awash from 1997–2001, and then shifted study sites to the Okavango Delta of Botswana for our postdoctoral research from 2001–2005. By sharp contrast to the Awash, the Okavango Delta was a breadbasket of resources throughout the year. But, of course, an abundance of resources brings with it not just fat, well-fed baboons but animals that want to *eat* fat, well-fed baboons—that is, lots and lots of large predators. Predation is the biggest source of mortality for baboons living in the delta. And, as we went everywhere the baboons went, we were exposed not only to baboon predators (lions, leopards, and hyenas) but also to lots of other large animals that pose dangers to humans walking around on foot (hippos, elephants, and buffalo). We quickly learned that we had to think like prey, to avoid ending up as prey.

Baboon Camp (so called to distinguish it from other tourist and research camps in the delta—Crocodile Camp, Wild Dog Camp, Elephant Camp) is essentially an island for most of the year. A few months after the rains arrive in southern Africa, the rivers fill up in Angola and the overflow slowly creeps its way to Botswana. Ironically, the floodwaters don't reach Botswana until the rain has long since ceased across the continent. Therefore, during the "wet season" (when it rains nearly every day) the delta is actually empty, but during the "dry season" (when it never rains) the entire delta is full of floodwater, and Baboon Camp is nothing more than about a square kilometer of land in the middle of a swampy sea. The swamp waters never get very deep, and we can usually wade, waist-deep, from island to island to find our troop of baboons. The baboons actually swim from island to island in search of their next feast on figs or mangosteen fruits (an orange-colored, grape-sized fruit that the baboons just love). Although these water crossings are a necessary part of daily life during the flood season, they are nonetheless fraught with angst for both baboons and researchers. The water is frigid because during the flood season

FIGURE 9.3 Our research assistant, Mokupi, watching the chacma baboons as they muster up the courage to make another water crossing. We always let the baboons go first. Who knows what lurks at the other end of the crossing? **Photo credit:** Dorothy Cheney.

nighttime temperatures can drop to freezing. But, the most unpleasant thing about these crossings is what might be waiting for us on the other side.

One of the most unusual things about the Okavango Delta is that the 11 cubic kilometers of annual floodwaters never actually make it to the ocean. Most of this water is consumed through transpiration by plants while the rest evaporates. This constant inflow (with no outflow) means that the delta has a massive accumulation of minerals ("salts"). These salts cling primarily to the roots of plants and build up over time, eventually forming islands, which at the center are too salty to support plant life aside from the occasional salt-resistant palm tree, while the less salty, sandy soils at the edges are covered with dense tangles of trees, bushes, and grasses. The end result is often an island with a ring of forest growth surrounding a barren spot in the middle. This means that the forest abuts the water and must be immediately penetrated upon extracting ourselves out of the swamp. It is known (by both baboons and researchers) as a dangerous transition, and on more than one occasion has ended badly for the first baboon to venture ahead. (*We* certainly don't go first.)

Needless to say, after only one month at Baboon Camp, dormant instincts we didn't even know we had were awakened as we quickly learned to pay attention to our surroundings. Which way is the wind blowing? (We want to be downwind from elephants.) Was that an oxpecker? (Oxpeckers are good indicators that buffalo are nearby.) In rare moments, we lull ourselves into a feeling of safety while walking with the baboons. With 90-plus sets of eyes looking out for predators, we can be certain that we won't run into a lion or a leopard without warning. However, as Thore discovered during this first month, this safety disappears the moment a predator actually arrives on the scene.

Thore and Mokupi (our field assistant, who had been working for Baboon Camp for the past 10 years) were walking in the middle of the baboon troop through one of the more forested areas of a large island. It was one of those typical days when baboons surround you, and you have to be careful where you step, lest you trip over a small juvenile that is not paying attention. Thore was in the middle of recording a grooming interaction between an adult female and her daughter, when suddenly he was interrupted by the sharp staccato sound of a baboon's alarm bark. Thore looked up, and (much to his horror) he saw three lions running towards him and the baboons. Within a fraction of a second, all the baboons were up trees. He likens the scene to one of a dog running through a park littered with squirrels—chasing one up a tree and then looking for another (easier) target. Only the week before, Mokupi had given us a very academic rundown of what our appropriate response should be for each of the dangerous animals in the delta. So, in theory, Thore knew that, for lions, he should just stand his ground and stare back. *Never, never run from a lion*, he remembered from Mokupi's lesson. The lions around here typically don't see many humans. So, when they *do* see us, they really don't know what to do. But, as soon as we turn around and run, *they know exactly what to do*. If you act like prey, they will do what they do best—hunt. If you don't act like prey and meet their gaze, you represent somewhat of a loose cannon. They are confused (and, dare I say, maybe even a bit scared?) and make the conservative choice to move away. There are plenty of impala and kudu around.

Well, this theory seemed quite sensible while having an evening chat around the campfire, but with three hulking lions coming at him full speed, Thore will attest to the near impossibility of standing one's ground. As Thore instinctually turned to run, Mokupi put his hand firmly on Thore's arm and, without turning his head from the oncoming lions, said, "Do not move." The firmness of his hand and voice were enough. Thore froze. When the lions saw the two humans, they literally stopped in their tracks. After about two minutes (which seemed like a lifetime to Thore), the lions made an about face and walked away.

The most remarkable part about this entire incident was its effect on Mokupi. For him, it was back to life-as-usual about a minute later; he started recording the incident as part of our field notes. Thore had to sit down and recover for nearly 20 minutes before his heart was no longer in danger of bursting out of his chest. It then occurred to Thore that this *was* part of Mokupi's life-as-usual. He'd been staring down lions probably since he was a kid. He *knew* there wasn't any danger, as long as he responded appropriately. I suppose it's like traffic on a busy street. It could kill you if you jump into it, but if you know to look both ways before crossing, you needn't worry. For Mokupi, dealing with lions is nothing more than crossing a busy street. Thore came away from this incident with a sense of power over the world around him. A clear case of brains beating brawn (well, that is, Mokupi's brain).

A much greater threat to our safety while out with the baboons was the animals the baboons *don't* warn us about, such as hippos, elephants, and buffalo. We're told that hippos kill more people than any other animal in Africa. They are extremely aggressive and territorial (and not all that bright) and will attack anything that ventures into their path, whether on land or in the water. It's hard to know whether this is why they are so dangerous or whether it's their aggressive behavior *combined* with many tourists' misconception that hippos should be smiling and wearing pink tutus (as in the classic Disney animation, *Fantasia*). All I know for sure, is that the only animal-related human death in the Okavanga Delta over the four years that Thore and I worked there was caused by a hippo that attacked and killed a tourist who was out on an evening boat ride.

Even Mokupi is a little bit afraid when we have to deal with hippos or elephants. I suppose there's just an inherent danger to having a really big and unpredictable animal around you. Even trained circus elephants can kill a person quite easily; they turn their head unexpectedly to one side and inadvertently impale a trainer with their tusk. It's like the risk of encountering drunk drivers on the road: It doesn't matter how much you follow the rules, you still could get hit. And, in the Okavango Delta, *there's a lot of them* (hippos and elephants, that is).

Walking around in a place where elephants can sneak up on you, it is useful to know when you're in danger and when you're not. One of the first days we were out with the baboons, Mokupi gave us this lesson: Once an elephant smells you, he has three choices: (1) He can turn around and run away; (2) he can trample you; or, (3) (the most likely of the three) he will deliver a mock charge. This mock charge seems just like the real thing, until he gets as close as he wants (which is usually much closer than *you* want), and then he will suddenly stop, back up slightly, and go about his business. Mokupi told us that unlike buffalo (who *never* bluff; when buffalo charge, they mean to kill), elephants "give you three chances." Trying to get specifics, I asked Mokupi if this meant that *each* elephant gives you three chances, or if elephants as a group give you three chances (like points accumulated on your driver's license). And, does this mean that *I*, individually, have three chances, or does each elephant end his mock charges on the third human he sees regardless of whether he has seen her before? And, do three chances mean that the third charge is mock and the fourth charge is real, or the third charge is real? Mokupi, who thought his explanation was quite sufficient, had already moved off down the path. I had to be satisfied with Thore's succinct explanation: *Elephants bluff more times than not.*

Thore and I have actually completed an elephant trifecta: We've been charged by an elephant in the car, in the motorboat, and on foot. The boat and foot charges were (thankfully) both bluffs. The car charge was hard to tell, because we didn't wait around to see if it was a bluff. So, we still don't have enough data to adequately test Mokupi's theory. Nonetheless, Thore and I are now operating on the assumption that we've used up our allocation of mock charges. Female elephants are a bit more predictable. They travel in very large cow/calf herds of 20–100 animals (usually their mother, aunts, sisters, and all offspring). The matriarch of the group will make the decision to do one of two things: She will signal a retreat or she will signal a charge—and if they charge, you can be certain that it is *not* a bluff.

We don't have to be bigger than the animals; we just have to be smarter than them. This has worked for Mokupi for 30-plus years now (and hundreds of other guides in Botswana who make their livelihoods walking, boating, and driving around the delta in search of dangerously large game animals to impress their tourists). Certainly Mokupi's lessons to us have helped to mitigate the stress of living among so many dangerous animals. And, fortunately, none of us has been seriously injured by any of these animals. I only wish I could say the same for the baboons.

Predation is, without a doubt, the biggest source of mortality for these baboons. By day, the lions grab them, and by night, the leopards do. We don't generally witness the actual predation events themselves, but the telltale signs are difficult to miss. During the day, because we are usually with the baboons, predation events go something like this: (1) baboon alarm barks at the front of the group (this always makes me wonder—*who* in their right mind would ever want to travel at the front of the troop?); (2) complete chaos as baboons respond, running up trees and more alarm barking; (3) bewildered researchers trying to figure out what is going on; (4) an hour passing as baboons return to normal behavior (and researchers' heart rates return to normal). At this point, we do a quick census to see if anyone is missing, and often someone is. In these cases, if we haven't seen the predator, Mokupi can piece together a pretty accurate account of what happened with his expert tracking skills. (He can tell the species of predator, the size of the baboon, and exactly where the predator grabbed the baboon, all from a few fresh marks in the sand.)

Even nighttime predation is hard to miss. Nearly every one of the baboons' sleeping sites (that is, groves of trees that leopards have difficulty climbing, such as palms and knob-thorn acacias) is within earshot of our tent. So, I can say with some certainty that it's impossible to sleep through a baboon predation event at night. The cacophony of screams and alarm barks can pull even the soundest of sleepers (i.e., me) immediately out of a deep sleep. I can almost visualize each event. A leopard targets the straggler baboons that didn't get a prime sleeping spot on one of the palms or knob-thorn acacia trees (some sleeping spots are much better than others). The moment the leopard is spotted, the baboons begin alarm calling. But, as he climbs closer to a tree-bound baboon, the alarm calls begin to sound more like screams. As the leopard swipes at the baboon, the screaming swells to a deafening frenzy. Then it eases up as the leopard waits for his next swipe. It goes on like this until he catches his victim. And, he nearly always gets a victim. Although leopards are afraid of a troop of baboons during the daytime, it is difficult for a single baboon to defend against a leopard at night. (Other baboons will alarm call, but they never volunteer to defend the victim.) Once, a leopard with a keen taste for baboons picked off one baboon each night for a week. Those must be terrifying nights for the troop.

One year later, we discovered that, indeed, those *were* terrifying nights for the baboons. As with the Awash baboons, we collected weekly fecal hormone samples from all of our animals across the entire study. After analyzing samples in the laboratory, we weren't surprised to find that the baboons' stress hormones skyrocketed during times when predation was high. During these stretches, they were probably frightened for their lives each time the sun went down, and I'm sure they got little to no sleep.

We also discovered something even more interesting about the baboons' stress profiles. Although *everyone's* stress hormones tended to rise during these periods of high predation, one group of baboons seemed to have particularly high levels—the close friends and family of the

FIGURE 9.4 A rare moment of relaxation with the baboons. With baboons nearby, we know that we will always be forewarned if predators approach. **Photo credit:** Thore Bergman.

victims. The survivors, who had to continue on without their mother, or their daughter, or their close friend, not only exhibited the highest levels of stress hormones, but they also changed their behavior following the death of their companion. They increased their grooming network during the months immediately afterwards—as if searching to replace their loss. We don't like to assign human emotions to our animal subjects, but this was as close to "bereavement" that we had ever seen in our animals.

From our days in the Rift Valley to our treks through the Okavango Delta, we faced the stress of extreme heat and large scary animals side by side with the baboons that we followed around. But, neither of these experiences prepared us for our next assignment—the geladas (*Theropithecus gelada*), a close relative of baboons—who face neither source of stress. Geladas live in the highest mountains of Ethiopia in the Simien Mountains National Park. Because the park is so high in altitude, the temperature never gets too hot; and because so many people live within the park's boundaries, the predators have been nearly wiped out. But, that does not mean the geladas are worry free. We suspect yet another selective force might be at work here.

One of the most enchanting things about the geladas living in the Ethiopian highlands is their sheer numbers. To look out on a field *full* of over a thousand grazing monkeys is a sight that not many people get to see. It seems like an idea a child came up with: just replace cows with monkeys, and *presto!*—geladas. But, this field of fur actually presents some obvious problems. Mainly, how do geladas recognize (and deal with) so many neighbors? Or, do they?

By the time Thore and I started our own project on wild geladas in the highlands of Ethiopia in 2005, we had studied more than 250 individual baboons. Our ability to recognize and recall a baboon's name even from a quick glance at a baboon butt was, by this time, exceptional. So, after an entire month spent with our new population of geladas, you can imagine our dismay when the only individuals we could recognize were *Gimach,* a male with only half a tail (whose Amharic name means "half"), and *Tripod,* a female missing her front arm. Other than these two animals, it was still just a field of furry bodies. How would we ever begin to collect behavioral

FIGURE 9.5 Jacinta Beehner, trying to identify individuals among a field of furry bodies. Individual geladas are more difficult to distinguish than other primates the authors have studied. **Photo credit:** Thore Bergman.

data on known individuals with so many geladas that all look exactly alike? Although we thought the problem reflected our failure as researchers, we soon learned that the geladas, themselves, face a similar problem.

We were surprised to discover that, unlike most other primates, geladas actually do *not* recognize the other animals around them. With the exception of the animals in their own family, geladas (like humans living in the suburbs) showed no signs of recognizing their immediate neighbors—even animals that they spent more than half their time with. This is exceptionally rare for a primate. Most primates live in relatively small, cohesive groups that include only well-known animals (often close kin), where the mere sight of an unknown conspecific(s) is enough to trigger a call-to-arms: heightened vigilance, alarm calls, herding females and infants away from the intruder(s), and ultimately (if the intruder doesn't retreat) an all-out battle. Based on this xenophobic response, it's not surprising that encountering unknown conspecifics represents an extremely stressful situation for most primates. But, not for geladas. In fact, geladas seem to have the exact opposite response to unknown individuals; rather than finding such individuals threatening, they actually find them *attractive*. With visibility in the mountains exceeding several kilometers, we often can predict exactly where our geladas will move next, as it is usually towards another group of geladas in the distance. Even with binoculars, I'm unable to recognize who these distant animals are. I suspect the geladas don't either (nor do they care)—they just want to forage in the largest group possible.

Perhaps this tendency reflects a time when geladas had many more predators than they do now (larger groups means more eyes for spotting predators out on the exposed grassy hillsides). Or, perhaps reproductive males ("harem"-holding males) want to guard their females against the threat of "bachelor" males, and a dilution effect is one effective way to do this. Regardless of the selective force responsible, geladas are often found congregating in herds of up to 1,200 individuals—many of them complete strangers.

Although being surrounded by strangers is not stressful for geladas, it does pose some problems—specifically, how do you make decisions about animals you know nothing about? If you want to pick a fight with someone, how do you know who is weaker (or stronger) than you are? You can't rely on having seen them fight before, or their dominance rank, or anything else that requires remembering previous interactions. Instead, you have to make decisions based on what you can discern about the animal at the time you interact with them. In other words, you have to rely on "proxies" for physical condition. While this may sound quite complicated, it's actually one of the primary ways that nonprimate animals make decisions about each other. Such species have evolved a myriad of external signals such as morphological features that reflect high testosterone (a hormone responsible for male secondary sexual characteristics) and acoustic/visual displays that demonstrate an animal is in prime condition. Assuming these signals are honest indicators of fighting ability, they allow males to make decisions about who to fight and who to leave alone. Think of these signals as a karate belt. By glancing at the color of someone's belt, you can gain a pretty good idea about the fighting ability of the bearer. (A yellow belt, for example, would never challenge a black belt.) Since in karate (as in nature) fighting is costly for both the loser and the winner, assessing rivals before entering into a match you can't win is always a good policy.

So, how do geladas assess other geladas out there in the furry crowd? Gelada males have two potential signals that could allow strangers to assess their fighting ability. One is a visual

FIGURE 9.6   An adult male gelada flaunting his brilliant chest patch right next to our color chart. The color chart provides a standard for measuring chest color across different light conditions.
Photo credit: Jacinta Beehner.

signal—a red patch of skin on their chest that has given them the name "bleeding-heart baboon." We have discovered that the redness of the chest indicates something about the status of the male, with males in the best condition having the reddest chest patches. Thus, with only a quick glance at a rival's chest, a bachelor male can quickly gain information about the fighting ability of the harem-holding male nearby. Second, gelada males produce loud vocalizations during ritualized chases between potential rival males. These "display calls" are, in terms of energy, costly to make, and we suspect that only males in prime condition are able to give the best calls. We are currently investigating whether it's the calls themselves or the frequency of the calls that indicates something about male condition. Thus, gelada males may be able to detect weakness in a rival by just looking at him (if he's close by) or listening to him (if he's far away). So, rather than getting to know every gelada around them, advertising their "quality" appears to be a good solution for dealing with crowding among geladas.

The Simien Mountains National Park is crowded not just with geladas but also with people and their livestock (a problem paralleled across the country). Ethiopia (a country about the size of Texas) has a population of over 80 million people, and much of this population base is not located in the capital city (as in many overpopulated countries), but throughout the countryside. The Simien Mountains National Park, at some of the highest altitudes in all of Africa, illustrates a perfect example of this population explosion. Not long ago, the barren fields above the treeline were considered inhospitable for farming, but now overcrowding in the lowlands has pushed people into the highlands. Farmers are now trying to eke out an almost vertical existence on the sides of mountains. Thus, despite being both a National Park and a World Heritage Site, the Simien Mountains have been pushed to the limit by human population pressure.

The presence of so many people in the park certainly has taken a toll. There is severe erosion in the farmed areas. There is intense competition for the native grasses, which often are grazed down to the dirt by hungry livestock. People regularly harvest the native heather trees for firewood. Wild animals are occasionally poached for food, and leopards and hyenas are chased away or killed. These problems have landed the park on the list of *World Heritage Sites in Danger* and threaten the potential of the park to attract tourists and generate revenue for Ethiopia. The real tragedy is that all of this degradation doesn't really help anyone—the people struggling to survive in the inhospitable environment are among the poorest people on the planet. Surely the stunning scenery and unique flora and fauna of the Simien Mountains generate more money from tourists than from farming and grazing? The first problem is how to get this revenue from tourism to directly benefit the local people. The second problem is how to bring the local people together to work towards the common interest of preserving the park.

We know firsthand that the second goal is entirely possible. In 2007, one year into our gelada study, the entire park was threatened by a severe bush fire. I can honestly say that this was the only time that I felt grateful for the hundreds and hundreds of families that live in the park.

We were awakened one night by a knock on our door. It was two of the park rangers, Misgano and Ayzano, asking whether we could help fight a bush fire nearby. Thore and I had been plagued by bushfires while we were in Botswana and knew the damage they could bring. We quickly followed them outside to the top of a ridge where everyone was gathered. As we were walking, Misgano fired his gun into the air. Thore and I jumped at the gunfire. Then, two more scouts fired their guns into the air. I could not figure out how gunfire could possibly help the situation except to instill panic in everyone around. What we failed to realize at the time, was that the gunshots were essentially a "call to arms." At the moment the gunshots went off, in villages all throughout the area, every man in every household set out on foot (with no flashlights and many of them barefoot) into the thick of the night to come help.

In the meantime, Thore and six park rangers drove off into the darkness to check out the severity of the fire. The road wound away from the fire for a while, and then they came around a corner to see an entire hillside ablaze. Everyone let out a gasp at the sight. Thore knew that their twelve hands were not enough to slow the fire, much less put it out. Nevertheless, all the rangers jumped into action—breaking large, leafy branches off bushes to beat down the flames. Thore quickly decided to drive back to find more help (at the very least, to get me and to recommend that the villagers prepare to evacuate).

To his utter surprise, when he arrived back at the village the first huge crowd of breathless men had just shown up and piled into the back of our pickup truck. I jumped into the truck along with the hordes of men, and we all headed to the fire. I dumped that truckload of people (and Thore as well) at the fire. Then I turned the truck around to head back for more people. I made this same trip about four or five times. However, each crowd of men was running at top speed (as they had had been from their villages several kilometers away), and I was only driving them the last kilometer or so to the fire. My trips kept getting shorter and shorter. By the fifth trip, the men were so close, it took me longer to turn the truck around on the narrow dirt road than it would have taken the men to just finish the trip on foot. Still, everyone likes a commotion, and to arrive at a fire on the back of a pickup truck really seemed to psyche them up for the fight. Some people, I noticed, never actually got out of the truck, but were enjoying just riding back and forth shouting to everyone along the road, "The British are coming! They're on their way!", or something to that effect.

In Botswana, when we fought bush fires, the chaos came from the fire itself. In Ethiopia, the chaos came not from the fire, but from the masses of people, shouting and running, and overwhelming the fire with their sheer numbers. With so many people and relatively little fire, the fire never stood a chance. It was out before I finished my fifth trip back. I never even got to see battle—a testament to the strength of so many people working together that night. If a similar level of teamwork can be brought to bear on the long-term preservation of the park, I truly believe that even seemingly insurmountable obstacles can be overcome.

When I reflect back on my time in the field, I'm most often brought back to that memory of myself as a naive graduate student sitting in a baboon cage one early Ethiopian morning. In laboratories across the world, it's the animal subjects that sit in the cages. Yet, there I was, out on the African savannah—the researcher—sitting in the cage. One of the first people to study wild apes, an American zoologist named Richard Garner, went to West Africa in the 1890s and observed wild chimpanzees from a cage he built. Later, Jane Goodall put her son, "Grub," in a cage to protect him from the chimpanzees she studied. It's rather ironic that a cage provides the safety for us when we are in natural primate habitats. In many ways, perhaps our Western lives resemble those of captive animals more than wild ones. We have our survival needs provided for, but at the cost of living in sometimes overcrowded and perhaps unnatural environments. I am reminded of Desmond Morris's *The Human Zoo* where he compares the human inhabitants of a city to animals living in a zoo. Our sources of stress are no longer the elements—extreme temperatures, predators, or even living among strangers. No, our primary sources of stress are psycho-social and thus not true threats to our survival. I'll never forget the feeling I had when (two long hours after the last lion roar) I crawled out of the cage and squinted into the morning sun. I felt exposed and vulnerable out there in the wilderness. But, from an animal's perspective, I was free.

Suggested Readings

Beehner, J. C., and C. McCann. 2008. "Seasonal and Altitudinal Effects on Glucocorticoid Metabolites in a Wild Primate (*Theropithecus gelada*)." *Physiology & Behavior* 95 (3): 508–514.

Bergman, T. J. 2010. "Experimental Evidence for Limited Vocal Recognition in a Wild Primate: Implications for the Social Complexity Hypothesis." *Proceedings of the Royal Society B Biological Sciences* 277 (1696): 3045–3053.

Bergman, T. J., and J. C. Beehner. 2008. "A Simple Method for Measuring Colour in Wild Animals: Validation and Use on Chest Patch Colour in Geladas (*Theropithecus gelada*)." *Biological Journal of the Linnean Society* 94 (2): 231–240.

Bergman, T. J., L. Ho, and J. C. Beehner. 2009. "Chest Color and Social Status in Male Geladas (*Theropithecus gelada*)." *International Journal of Primatology* 30 (6): 791–806.

Cheney, D. L., and R. M. Seyfarth. 2007. *Baboon Metaphysics.* Chicago: University of Chicago Press.

Dunbar, R. I. M. 1984. *Reproductive Decisions.* Princeton: Princeton University Press.

Sapolsky, R. M. 2004. *Why Zebras Don't Get Ulcers.* New York: Henry Holt and Company, LLC.

Acknowledgments

We would like to offer our heartfelt thanks to each of our supervisors that we have had the privilege to learn from, including Drs. Jane Phillips-Conroy and Clifford Jolly, Dorothy Cheney and Robert Seyfarth, and Jeanne Altmann and Susan Alberts. Additionally, we would like to thank each country that helped facilitate our work: The Ethiopian Wildlife Conservation Authority, the Office of the President of the Republic of Botswana, and the Botswana Department of Wildlife and National Parks. None of these adventures would have been possible without our generous sources of funding, including the National Science Foundation, the Wenner-Gren Foundation, the Leakey Foundation, the National Geographic Society, Sigma Xi, Washington University in St. Louis, the University of Pennsylvania, and the University of Michigan.

10

Baboon Mechanics

By S. Peter Henzi[1]
and Louise Barrett[2]

Here, at Africa's southern tip, a cold front has moved in from the Antarctic. It announces its arrival with gale-force winds and walls of rain that you see long before they hit you and about which you can do very little. The baboons pay the rain and the wind almost no heed other than to turn their backs, hunching over while they forage. Their human observers, on the other hand, are frozen over water-proofed data loggers, undecided whether to brave it out or to call it quits and head home to stand in front of a heater. It's odd that this should be the first memory that pops up after all this time because, between fronts, the southern Cape is beautiful in July; it's a winter-rainfall region and the greenery and carpets of flowers make one forget the hot, dry, sere days of the summer to come. Nevertheless, the cold and the rain remind us of our reasons for being here.

"Here" is the De Hoop Nature Reserve in the Western Cape province of South Africa, some 70 kilometers south of Swellendam, the country's third-oldest town. Together with the missile test site that abuts it, it stretches for some 80 kilometers along the coast and extends about 10 kilometers inland. It was promulgated to protect both the local *fynbos* (endemic shrubland vegetation) and the offshore marine life. Ecologically, it is an island that is surrounded on the

[1]About the author: Peter Henzi received his PhD on vervet monkeys from the University of Natal in 1982. After a brief period researching herring gulls, he spent the next 25 years working on baboons at three sites in South Africa. He is now at the University of Lethbridge in Canada and runs a vervet monkey research program with Dr. Barrett.

Contact information: Department of Psychology, 4401 University Drive University of Lethbridge, Alberta, T1K 3M4, CANADA, peter.henzi@uleth.ca

[2]About the author: Louise Barrett worked on group dynamics in Ugandan grey-cheeked mangabeys for her PhD, which was awarded by University College, London in 1995. She took two years off from her teaching at the University of Liverpool to take up a prestigious post-doctoral fellowship in South Africa, working on biological market phenomena and infant development in chacma baboons at De Hoop. She now holds a Canada Research Chair in Cognition, Evolution and Behaviour at the University of Lethbridge.

Contact information: Department of Psychology, University of Lethbridge, 4401 University Drive, Lethbridge, Alberta, T1K 3M4, CANADA, louise.barrett@uleth.ca

Citation: Henzi, S. P., and Barrett, L. 2014. "Baboon Mechanics." In Strier, K. B. (ed.), *Primate Ethnographies*. Upper Saddle River, NJ: Pearson Education, Inc. (pp. 107–117).

FIGURE 10.1 Not all primates are tropical. Researchers Tanya Dhillon, Parry Clarke, Jo Halliday, and Louise Barrett make it only too clear that the southern Cape winters in South Africa impose thermal demands on human observers that the baboons seem to shrug off. **Photo credit:** © S. P. Henzi.

landward side by prosperous wheat farms and exists only because crops do not grow well on the alkaline soils of this limestone-dominated landscape. De Hoop ("Hope") derives its name from a farmstead dating back to the eighteenth century, and the reserve now incorporates a set of farms that, by the 1960s, were unable to provide a sustainable income for their Afrikaner owners. In earlier times, before the arrival of Europeans, it had been the haunt of Khoi pastoralists, whose features are still strongly evident in the local, mixed race communities—themselves now culturally Afrikaner—that make up the majority of the region's population. Long before them, even, it may well have been the wellspring of modern humans: Blombos cave, famous in archeological circles, is also on the reserve, yielding up more and more evidence of the emergence of behavioral modernity in our own lineage.

We, however, have come down here to find out how the baboons and their environment interact. A long-standing project in primatology has been directed at understanding social organization in relation to ecology. Here, the central questions relate, on the one hand, to past selection for attributes that underpin species or population-level modes of coexistence and, on the other, the extent of behavioral flexibility in the face of current variation in environmental conditions. Baboons have been a keystone species in this endeavor, partly because they are relatively easy to habituate, but mostly because they are very widely distributed throughout sub-Saharan Africa and show remarkable habitat tolerance. South Africa, in this regard, offers baboons an unusually wide variety of environmental conditions and habitat types, from hot, wet tropical woodland and hot, dry semi-desert, to cold, wet subalpine grassland. At the same time, the country has a well-developed conservation infrastructure that traditionally has been very

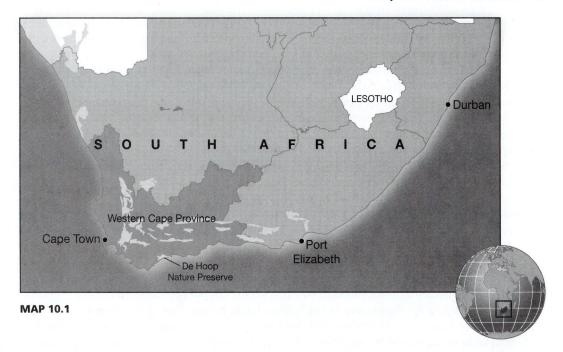

MAP 10.1

research-oriented and is logistically very easy to navigate. Small wonder, then, that one of us (SPH), as a South African, had opted for relatively short baboon projects in different localities, trading life historical depth for ecological breadth. Just prior to De Hoop, this effort had been directed at the baboon population of the Drakensberg Mountains of KwaZulu-Natal, in an ongoing attempt to understand how individual action and population processes feed into each other. The earlier period of research, undertaken with Dick Byrne and Andy Whiten of the University of St Andrews in the early 1980s, had provided the basic behavioral and ecological background and had suggested that social structure and dynamics were responses to specific features in the environment. After five years in the 1990s addressing these issues in more detail with PhD students John Lycett, from the University of Natal, and Tony Weingrill, from Hans Kummer's group in Zürich, there was a need to decide whether to settle in for the long term or to move on to something else—boredom, if nothing else, being the motivator. A chance encounter with a scientist from the provincial conservation authorities raised the prospect of a move south.

As the other of us (LB) clearly also needed some excitement after what a baboon researcher could only describe as the tedium of forest monkeys, we visited De Hoop in mid-1996 and liked what we saw. And what we saw was that the region looked and felt very little like "Africa," not only climatically but also floristically. Fynbos, while beautiful and botanically intriguing, doesn't really pander to the need for mammals to make a living. Together with the seasonal reversals (dry, hot, food-poor summers and cold, wet, food-abundant winters) we felt that the ecological variables had been shaken up enough to offer at least the prospect of seeing something new, if, in fact, baboon behavior was that environmentally labile. And so, after what passed for a formal negotiation with the regional conservator ("Well, would you like to work here?" "Yes, we would." "OK, then."), that was that. Together with Russell Hill as a PhD student from Robin Dunbar's lab in Liverpool and Tony Weingrill as a newly-minted

Swiss postdoc, we set up shop in December 1996 and maintained a continuous presence there until December 2007, when an incident, both unanticipated and unpleasant, led us to bring the project to an end.

It has to be acknowledged that our primary reason for choosing the new study site at De Hoop was no more than a broad belief, verging on blithe faith, that change would be good and that the animals themselves would inevitably reveal something interesting about themselves. Nevertheless, we did carry with us some intriguing theoretical possibilities that tied into our general interest in behavioral flexibility and for which we needed a new population of baboons if we were to develop them any further. In comparison to populations elsewhere, the unusual thing about females in mountain baboon troops is that they only very rarely contest resources; so rarely, in fact, that we were never able to allocate dominance ranks to our subjects. The reason for this apparently peaceful coexistence is that the subalpine grasslands simply do not provide food that is worth fighting over. The baboons rely heavily on the underground storage organs of various plants, and these are so small and widely dispersed, and so quickly swallowed, that they cannot repay the energetic expenditure needed to get across quickly enough to extort them from the finder. Despite this, these females continue to groom one another at rates comparable to those of female baboons in other, more conventional habitats, and our interest in explaining why this might be so offered us a more focused way into the lives of our new subjects.

The reason for the piquing of our interest lay in the fact that, at the time, the prevailing account of nonhuman primate sociality held that grooming served as "social glue," bonding females in anticipation of the need for support during the inevitable fights over scarce resources. In the absence of any aggression, therefore, why would mountain baboon females bother to groom one another to the extent that they did? It was pondering this question, put to us one night in a St. Andrews pub, that drew us back to Robert Seyfarth's earlier theoretical work on the functional significance of grooming. At the heart of Seyfarth's model lay the argument that grooming, by virtue of its hygienic function, was a service that females could provide in return for other services. While the general expectation was that the grooming allocated to other, particular females served to increase the probability of their providing coalitionary support, it struck us that the logic applied equally to the reciprocation of grooming. Rob Barton, now at Durham University in England, had shown that if a female was unable to groom all parts of herself with equal facility, then grooming was a service that another female could provide and was, by the same token, a service that one required of others. Mountain baboon females, it seems, persist in providing grooming simply because they themselves need to be groomed.

This small insight—that grooming was a service or commodity that could be traded for itself—drew us directly towards another body of theory that would guide our initial data collection at De Hoop. A year or two earlier, Ronald Noë and Peter Hammerstein had made the case that, where organisms are interdependent, the metaphor of a marketplace was likely to be a more productive framework in which to consider the evolution and maintenance of cooperation than was the currently dominant "Prisoner's Dilemma" approach, which emphasized the high likelihood of cheating instead of mutually beneficial exchanges. In the Biological Markets model, as the latter has come to be known, the distorting effects of cheating on cooperation are assumed to be circumscribed by the availability of alternative partners who offer better value. More importantly, for our purposes, by construing animals as traders seeking fair exchange, this model predicted that the value of a commodity, such as grooming, would be set by local supply and demand and so could fluctuate across space and over time. Instead of a notional or fixed value to grooming, then, we might expect it to be matched to the current value of the commodity for which it was being traded.

And so we had our first prediction: In the mountains, where grooming could realistically be traded only for itself, the amount of grooming given should match the amount received. There were, however, two problems with testing this. The first concerned the question of the time period over which to compare the investment in grooming between any two females, which is compounded by the fact that we knew of no cognitive capacity in baboons that would allow them to remember what they had done to whom and when. Indeed, Robert Hampton has shown experimentally that monkeys lack such episodic memory. Fortunately, the baboons themselves provided the answer. In the mountains, we had found that once a group had more than six or seven females, they no longer all groomed one another and that, even as groups grew larger still, the average size of a female grooming clique remained constant at six. This capping of numbers had the effect of reversing the decline in the length of grooming bouts seen as cohort size rose beyond six and, most impressive to us, this reversal occurred precisely when the duration of the grooming bout was the shortest it could be and yet still allowed grooming to be reciprocated immediately. From a baboon's perspective, this capping of clique size made immediate reciprocation possible. It was a very elegant solution to the problem of ensuring time matching, and our subsequent analyses simply compared grooming times within these reciprocated bouts.

The second problem was that there is an inherent unpredictability in the duration of grooming. How similar did times need to be to be considered a close match? In our view, the only way

FIGURE 10.2 One of the early projects at De Hoop focused on the idea that grooming was a commodity that could be exchanged for other commodities. Here we see a female grooming a mother before handling her infant. Mothers are reluctant to lose contact with young infants and our data indicated that the amount of grooming given is determined by the number of young infants in the group: When more infants are present, less grooming is necessary to get the mother to cooperate. Although these results were explained within the functional framework provided by biological markets theory, the proximate explanation for the relationship is likely to be that, in the absence of other young infants, a mother is the focus of a good deal of unwelcome attention and it takes more grooming to get her to relax sufficiently. **Photo credit:** © S. P. Henzi.

to address this was comparatively—work with a second population where grooming need not only be exchanged for itself and, therefore, might vary with other factors. The prediction was then that grooming times would be more closely correlated in the mountain baboons than they would be in this other population. We hoped De Hoop would be such a population (it was), and it turned out to be one where, even more fortunately, we were able to habituate two troops, one large and one small, whose female cohort sizes matched those of two of our mountain troops, making direct comparisons possible.

Life at De Hoop was always very comfortable. The logistic complexity of all fieldwork turns, in essence, on the ease with which three interrelated needs can be met. Of these, the first is food. Like armies, field projects march on their stomachs. It's noteworthy how much conversation effort is given over to dinner menus and how much attention is paid to the regimented rollout of the day's packed snacks. During the long days of summer, especially, the passage of time is marked, and the doldrums kept in check, by the apportioning of food: a biscuit at ten o'clock, perhaps, and then half of one's sandwiches at twelve, the other half at one—not a minute earlier and certainly not a minute later. The awful dead time between 2 p.m. and 4 p.m., particularly, is made tolerable only by the promise of an apple later on, while the last few hours of the day are given over to the contemplation of supper.

Now the truth is that just about anything is edible, if not always delicious, after a 14-hour day. But whereas our weekly diet in the Drakensberg was decided by what could be carried 8 kilometers up a mountain on our backs, De Hoop was sufficiently close to two towns—each with the large supermarkets without which no South African can make do—to allow for frequent expeditions to stock up on supplies. Just as pertinent, perhaps, is the fact that the southern Cape hinterland is given over to the production of wine and, with it, the inevitable restaurants, so that a short excursion sufficed to replenish the project cellar and assuage the rigors of the field. It's easy to mock being concerned with luxury, and it's certainly a very different African experience to the one related by the self-styled "Old Africa Hands," but the truth is that time saved on subsistence is time that can be put into fieldwork.

This was equally true of accommodation. Housing, often a problem in national parks and a source of considerable friction, was plentiful at De Hoop. With the rising wages that followed the election of South Africa's first fully democratic government in 1995, a number of reserve staff chose to purchase property in the nearby towns and commute to work, leaving houses available for occupation on site. With electricity, water, and plumbing, they matched the bourgeois comfort of the food and made it possible, at least in principle, to concentrate on the baboons.

If only the same could be said for our transportation, all would have been logistically idyllic. While getting to and from the baboons, at least for the first few years, could be managed on foot, movement off the reserve, in the absence of any form of public transport, required a project vehicle, and a project vehicle required funding, which was always in short supply. It's an oddity of life that, whereas funding agencies generally are happy to pay for large pieces of laboratory equipment, they tend to regard field vehicles as an expensive luxury, despite the fact that these are no less essential to the research and lose their value no more rapidly. The Natural Environment Research Council of the United Kingdom, for example, whose mission is to increase our understanding of the natural world, expressly refuses to fund the purchase of vehicles for use in the field. The upshot, at least for us, was a series of decrepit second-hand cars, each with several thousand kilometers on the clock at the time of acquisition, and a rapid insight into Marx's theory of capital, insofar as it applies to vehicle ownership. Each of the cars cost so much to keep on the road that it was never possible to accrue the capital needed to buy a sensible replacement. The inevitable demise of each merely ushered in an even less reliable successor. Memorably, our last project car was a large, gold Mercedes Benz sedan, bought from a farmer who had benefited in the distant past from farming subsidies paid in pursuit of the rural vote and who sold it to us with exquisite timing—its exhaust pipe fell off on the way back from town after the deal had been concluded. By the same token, not all of the blame could be laid at the door of the cars; they were, after all, being driven by students. The Mercedes lost its emblematic star badge in the first week when its driver failed to negotiate a bend in the road and rammed it into a tree. A similar failure to turn a corner found an earlier car marooned in a ploughed field after gouging its way through a barbed wire fence. One hapless driver contrived to smash a car into the post of a gate wide enough to accommodate two vehicles simultaneously, while another somehow managed to hit a porcupine at high speed, with terrible consequences for both porcupine and car. Most intriguingly, one student, apparently having hit a bump, failed to notice for some days that the upper mounting of the suspension had sheared so that, as he drove, the Macpherson strut hammered an increasingly conspicuous bulge into the hood. His only comment, when this was pointed out to him, was that that the car had started to sound a little noisier than usual. And so it went. The Mercedes gasped its last breath one gray day, an ill-starred omen of the project's own demise a few weeks later.

Regardless of vehicular travails, work could always continue because the baboons generally were within walking distance of the house. Once the two study troops were good to go, we began the collection of detailed grooming data and were ready to compare the patterns with those that we had found in the mountains by late 1997. The extent to which the initial results conformed to prediction surprised even us, supporting the contention that grooming was a commodity that could be exchanged for itself or for other commodities, and that its value fluctuated in response to local market structure. Mountain baboons, being able only to exchange grooming for grooming, maintained a tighter fit between the amounts given and received, than did the De Hoop females, while the latter's grooming, which we had hypothesized could be exchanged for access to resources, showed the predicted shifts in the relative allocation of grooming in response to the extent to which resources could be contested.

Perhaps the neatest demonstration of the markets metaphor as an explanatory device, however, came from what Ronald Noë called the "Baby Market." Baboon females are inordinately attracted to young infants, while baboon mothers are loath to let their infants out of their grip; not surprisingly, given the predilection for infanticide by immigrant males in this taxon. The females solve this dilemma by approaching and grooming mothers and then, at some point, stopping to reach out and purloin the infant for a few minutes' contact. We found that this point was determined by the relative availability of infants. The fewer the infants in the troop at the time, the longer females had to groom before mothers gave in to their blandishments. Female groomers behave "as if" they are aware of the current value of grooming, but in reality, they simply continue grooming until the mother is sufficiently relaxed. The fewer the number of available infants, the more harassed the mother and the longer it takes for grooming to work its magic.

At the time, this depiction of grooming as something to be bartered for immediate gain generated some interest. While others began to interrogate and build on these findings, however, we found ourselves drawn back to the comparative questions about the relationship between baboons and their local environments that had led us to De Hoop in the first place. Broadly speaking, socioecology has regarded the species to be the locus of gene recombination, with the consequence that observed differences in behavior among different animal taxa are assumed either to indicate that the taxa concerned are different species, where the differences are therefore "hard-wired," or to reflect the influence of differing local conditions on the same species. As Robin Dunbar expressed it, and as his elegant comparative time budget analyses of baboons and other primates have worked to demonstrate, a species will have a single "deep structure" whose specific expression in a particular troop or population reflects local ecological demands. Surprisingly, however, the longer that we spent at De Hoop, the more we were struck, not by the differences, but by the similarities in behavior with the chacma baboons we had worked on earlier, under widely differing local conditions.

Three things, in particular, caught our attention. First, we noticed that male chacma baboons had marked infanticidal tendencies, which they indulged at the time of their immigration into a new group. Then, we could find no evidence that males ever formed coalitions with other males. Finally, females frequently emigrated from their natal groups together with a single male and a variable number of other, unrelated females. These are noteworthy details, not only because they appear robust in the face of local environmental challenge but also because they are not features that are shared by yellow and olive baboons in East Africa. In these other, more tropical, taxa, infanticide is either very rare or absent, males form coalitions, and females leave their natal troops in the company of close female relatives on those infrequent occasions when large troops undergo fission. As it was equally evident that olive, yellow, and chacma baboons interbreed where their ranges overlap, it wasn't possible for us to play the different-species card in attempting to explain our observations. Baboons, it seemed, were all the same and yet all different.

Fortunately, Cliff Jolly, a paleoanthropologist from New York University, had long been attempting to uncover what he correctly discerned to be the species' complex biogeography, without ignoring the obvious morphological differences among the different baboon taxa (yellow baboons are, after all, "yellow" and olive baboons are "olive"). In his account, different populations, isolated in different habitats at different times and for differing durations, had come under selection in relation to particular local conditions without having speciated, in the sense that biologists used the term to mean "not capable of interbreeding." At the last count, the consensus, from the New York lab, is that what were once regarded as four superficially different baboon taxa, together with the hamadryas baboon, whose unusual social organization made its classification as a "standard" baboon somewhat problematic, are best seen as eleven or more allotaxa, or types of baboon. That is, while they are all baboons, each has characteristics that distinguish them from the others. Not only did our belated discovery of his work change our own approach to the problem, his lab's—and, more recently, Dietmar Zinner's—use of the newest genetic techniques meant that the evolutionary origins of modern baboons could be placed on a much firmer footing. This proved key for us. In essence, the data indicated that modern baboons began life about 2 million years ago in southern Africa at a time when conditions were, if anything, more arid than they are now. We wondered whether, perhaps, it isn't current ecological conditions that set the patterns that we see, but rather the conditions encountered by baboon populations during the periods when gene flow had been restricted by their isolation from other populations.

Our own comparative data on modern baboons showed that chacma baboons, living as they do in the relatively arid south, have much smaller average group sizes and more female-biased sex ratios than do baboons in more tropical locales. If anything, then, groups would have been smaller and sex ratios more pronounced at the time of their divergence from the ancestral stock. Here, then, are the conditions that explain the patterns that bind different chacma populations: Young males encountering small groups of females can best pursue their reproductive interests through infanticide because the absence of many other possible fathers renders infant defense less effective. One response to this by mothers is to emigrate with the likely father, either temporarily or permanently, in the wake of male immigration. Finally, we speculated that troops in the original chacma populations simply contained too few males for coalitionary behavior to emerge and be fixed by selection.

With the establishment of this comparative analytical framework and with the arrival of Parry Clarke from England, first as doctoral student and then as a postdoc, we turned our attention to the consequences of infanticide for the dynamics of association among males and females. Seen from a female's perspective, infanticide is clearly a disaster, as it is for fathers with vulnerable infants. The obvious solution—that mothers and fathers cooperate in the defense of infants—is hampered by the absence of the male reproductive coalitions seen in East African baboons. Alpha males in chacma troops have unimpeded access to reproductive females. Barring coincidental ovulatory synchrony among females, therefore, subordinate males can have little expectation of fathering offspring, which, in turn, means that they cannot be expected to carry the risks associated with defending infants that are not theirs. Not surprisingly, we found good evidence for the evolutionary battle of the sexes predicted by sexual conflict theory. De Hoop females are fully sexually swollen for longer than their East African counterparts, thereby reducing further the correlation between ovulation probability and swelling size, and they work very hard to get males to mate with them in the period before ovulation. Chacma males, in response, have become more resistant to such feminine wiles and are actually quite conservative, at least in restricting the timing of their matings to the most likely times for conception.

This conservatism drew our attention to the more interesting dilemma that infanticide generates for the alpha male. Whereas infanticide, by reducing the time taken for a mother with a young infant to return to sexual receptivity, is a great way for a male to maximize his reproductive opportunities during an alpha tenure of unpredictable length, it carries the implication that once an alpha male is bested by a challenger, the tables will be well and truly turned on him, a possibility that is exacerbated by the relatively high likelihood that he will actually be absent for a substantial fraction of the time that his own offspring are vulnerable to infanticidal attack.

We reasoned that the best option for alpha males might be to concede some conception opportunities to other males, thereby making it more likely that they would intervene during an attack directed at infants. To test this prediction, we were at last able to use the long-term data

FIGURE 10.3 Infanticide is common in chacma baboons. Here, the immigrant male on the right has attacked a mother who rushes to the side of the infant's father, who has arrived to defend his own reproductive investment. The infant itself is clinging on for dear life. **Photo credit:** © S. P. Henzi.

that had accrued to their full advantage, with pleasantly gratifying results. We found that fully one-third of all offspring had subordinate males as fathers, apparently because alpha males simply did not pursue every opportunity to monopolize receptive females. Interestingly, alpha males were most *laissez faire* when there were few other males about, suggesting that the proximate mechanism may turn on the extent to which alpha males feel pressured: the more males in the troop, the more stressed the alpha male and the likelier, therefore, that he takes up consortships.

Functionally, of course, conceding conceptions when there are few other males increases the likelihood that these males, being fathers, will stay. This reduces the possibility that, purely by chance, there will be no males available to defend infants. And the need for additional fathers is clear: Almost all of the deaths that were due to infanticide occurred in the absence of either real or surrogate fathers. Most unexpectedly, we were also able to show that alpha males were more likely to lose the battle against immigrant males if they were the only fathers in the troop. We surmised that this is because they are compromised by the need to protect their infants. Paradoxically, then, reproductive concession not only improved the survival of his current progeny but also, by extending an alpha male's tenure, allowed him to father more.

All of the data that went into these and other analyses were collected by a series of participants from various locations in Europe and South Africa, who, during their stay became members of a larger social community that helped shape and define their experiences. This community extended all the way from conservation staff, to local farmers, to shopkeepers in the region's towns. The "Baboon Mechanics," as we became known, were aided and abetted over the years, partly because people, of all hues, in the southern Cape are—at least to an Afrikaner from further north—incredibly friendly and hospitable. Arguably, the reason for this stretches all the way back to the eighteenth century, when the Afrikaner community in the Cape Colony divided on the question of British sovereignty with those who, in essence, didn't like being told what to do, departing for the deep interior where they were beyond command and where, in turn, they could impose their will on others, with ramifications that resonate still. Be this as it may, one thing that all South Africans share is a persistent reverence for education, an attitude from which we, as researchers, also undoubtedly benefitted, both in the community generally and, more particularly on the nature reserve, where research of whatever kind was considered legitimate, if not necessarily always valued.

Although we were its beneficiaries, this tolerance for research never translated into any actual interest in what we were up to. In fact, in 30 person-years of primate research in a number of different parks, no game ranger or warden ever made any effort to come out and spend time with the animals themselves, despite our repeated invitations. This hasn't, however, stopped them telling us what they thought we ought to know about our subjects. The country's other shared conviction, derived perhaps from its recent rural roots and echoed in any number of folk tales, is the considered view that baboons are hell's own minions—or, at least, if not satanic, then certainly morally recalcitrant. This anthropomorphic projection constantly reared its head, sometimes amusingly, and sometimes not so, as when reserve staff, having cheerfully suffered depredations on their gardens by antelope, would complain loudly that "our" baboons had had the cheek to trespass on their property.

The notion that one can transfer an urban lifestyle to the wild—and that the animals one is there to safeguard will appreciate and respect this disconnect—is, perhaps, peculiar to a developed country, where these distinctions are more easily blurred. In the last phase of our stay, De Hoop welcomed a new warden who brought with him to his new post two large dogs. While these were ostensibly meant to be confined, they were, in truth, free to roam the reserve. Apart from any other damage they might have done, one day they chased down an infant in a study troop only to run, as you might expect and hope, right into a protective male who chased one dog off and ripped the other to pieces. Nothing was said but, a few days later, the warden stepped out and shot, in cold blood, a male baboon—not even, as it happens, the one that had killed his dog—in order to "teach them a lesson."

With this act of violence, our stay at De Hoop came to an abrupt end. While we might have persevered—the warden was dismissed shortly afterwards for other, even more heinous manifestations of his personality—we felt that the relationship between ourselves, the place, and the animals had, in some fundamental sense, been dislocated. Put simply, the fun was over. More scientifically, we had stayed at De Hoop longer than initially intended in order to better appreciate population processes at the temperate margins of a tropical species' distribution. This presupposed the absence of human interference, something we could no longer take for granted. As it happens, our fears were well-founded: The need to generate money from tourism resulted in the decision to rebrand De Hoop as a tourist hotspot, run by private contractors. There is a restaurant there now, among other things—right in the center of the troop's home range—and there has been increasing conflict between the baboons, who see human garbage as rich pickings, and humans, who still think that baboons need to mind their own business.

And so we packed our bags and headed for the hinterland. On our long drives down to De Hoop from the city of Durban, we had always been intrigued by the apparent abundance of vervet monkeys in the inhospitable karoo—the dry, hot semi-desert that makes up much of the country's interior. We had made casual enquiries about possible study sites each time we passed through the region and were eventually presented with an offer that we couldn't refuse. At the time of writing, we've been at our new site for five years, working on an equally interesting species, but this is another story altogether.

Suggested Readings

Barrett, L., S. P. Henzi, A. Weingrill, J. E. Lycett, and R. Hill. 1999. "Market Forces Predict Grooming Reciprocity in Female Baboons." *Proceedings of the Royal Society London. Series B* 266: 665–670.

Henzi, S. P., and Barrett, L. 2003. "Evolutionary Ecology, Sexual Conflict and Behavioral Differentiation among Baboon Populations." *Evolutionary Anthropology* 12: 217–230.

Henzi, S. P., P. Clarke, C. van Schaik, G. Pradhan, and L. Barrett. 2010. "Infanticide and Reproductive Restraint in a Polygynous Social Mammal." *Proceedings of the National Academy of Sciences, USA* 107: 2130–2135.

Jolly, C. J. 2001. "A Proper Study for Mankind: Analogies from the Papionin Monkeys and Their Implications for Human Evolution." *Yearbook of Physical Anthropology* 44: 177–204.

Noë, R., and P. Hammerstein. 1995. "Biological Markets." *Trends in Ecology and Evolution* 10: 336–339.

Acknowledgments

We would like to thank Cape Conservation for permission to work at De Hoop and Werner Fourie, Rory Allardyce, and Ben Swanepoel for administrative and logistic assistance over the first few years. Among others, Drs. Russell Hill, Tony Weingrill, Mina Echeverria-Lozano, Dave Gaynor, Paul Dixon, and, especially, Parry Clarke contributed data to the long-term project. Our research was funded by NRF (South Africa) and Leakey Foundation awards.

11

The Graceful Asian Ape

By Ulrich H. Reichard[1]

It was pitch dark outside on a cold, cloudy January morning in 1993 when I left the research house to spend another day with the most graceful of the apes, the white-handed gibbons of Khao Yai National Park in Thailand. I had no idea then that I would soon be witnessing events I had only heard or read about in books on birds and a few mammals and had not imagined would unfold right in front of my own eyes. I entered the forest at the "village," a point where I regularly crossed over from my human world into the world of the rain forest and its creatures, a world I had all my life wanted to see. I had named this spot, which was nothing more than two small rows of old longhouses on stilts where a few rangers and their families lived, to create a reference point where I, being a proper scientist, would always note the exact time of "entering" and "leaving" the forest. Doing so gave me a precise measure of how many hours and minutes I had spent in there. My wristwatch read 05:56. I scribbled the time down in my tiny notebook—quickly so as not to lose precious "forest-time"—by the dim beam of my small hand-held torch, stuck under my left armpit for that purpose because I have never liked the much more popular head-lamps.

The village was one of four entry points into the forest. It was the one I most frequently used back then because it was closest to where I stayed and where the gibbon groups I visited nearly daily could be found. The stroll past the longhouses culminated in having to balance across some thin, always slippery planks put down by some men to cross a narrow section between the high Lam Takhong River Bank and the last longhouse. On bad days I imagined that they had installed it deliberately to see me or one of my research crew members slip, slide, or fall

[1]About the author: Ulrich Reichard is a biological anthropologist and behavioral ecologist whose research program focuses on the behavior and evolution of primates. His empirical work concentrates on a large community of white-handed gibbons at the Khao Yai National Park, Thailand, where he investigates topics such as female reproductive strategies, the threats of predation to gibbons and pig-tailed macaques, development and individuality of gibbon songs, and spatial intelligence with his students and colleagues. He is particularly interested in the evolution of primate mating systems and is a co-editor of the book *Monogamy Mating Strategies and Partnerships in Birds, Humans, and Other Mammals*.

Contact information: Department of Anthropology, Southern Illinois University, Carbondale, IL 62901-4502, USA, ureich@siu.edu

Citation: Reichard, U. H. 2014. "The Graceful Asian Ape." In Strier, K. B. (ed.), *Primate Ethnographies*. Upper Saddle River, NJ: Pearson Education, Inc. (pp. 118–130).

MAP 11.1

into the river while they giggled behind a glassless longhouse window; on good days I thought it was an act of friendliness to help me get into the forest. The truth was probably that the little wooden bridge had nothing to do with me at all but was installed by the villagers, for the villagers on their own way into the forest to collect forest products.

Past the plank, the trail was muddy. I was soon surrounded by 30-meter-tall trees, moisture evaporating from leaves heated up by the rising sun, and smells of foreign aromas. Beautiful forest sounds would slowly replace human voices, children babbling, and the rattling of motorbikes carrying still-tired rangers to work. The beginning of male gibbon solo songs would soon turn into a counter-calling chorus, the bowing of hundreds of cicadas, an awakening Asian fairy bluebird pair chit-chattering in a fig tree, and the spectacular back-and-forth screech-roar call of a pair of majestic Great Hornbills. Their song would soon be followed by a powerful departure from their nearby, hidden nesting hole in the crack of a large tropical tree with its unique, deep "wuff-wuff-wuff" sound as their wings pounded the fresh morning air.

My pace was fast and I sweated as I hurried along the trail, always worried about being too late for the gibbons, which might already have left their night-sleeping trees and then would be so much harder to find. I could walk fast because I knew the forest well even in darkness. The rough bark of erect trees along the trail and thin shadows of fallen trunks in faint moonlight had become familiar landmarks pointing to the trail's turns. I had begun my research in the Khao Yai National Park in 1989, and over the past four years I had come to recognize the sounds and smells of the forest life. I felt united with the seemingly endless shapes and life-forms that natural selection has created over millennia in this biodiversity hotspot, and I felt euphoric and privileged to be part of this, like I still do now—23 years later—when I'm in this forest alone with myself, when I see a new dawn through the canopy, when my senses are switched on high alert, and I am ready to absorb through eyes and fingertips whatever surprises the day is about to bring. Then, as now, I experience a tension in my body that I imagine must

FIGURE 11.1   Research trail in the forest at the Khao Yai National Park, Thailand.
Photo credit: Ulrich Reichard.

be similar to an arrow's feeling of tension seconds before its release from the bow by an archer, ready to fly. I knew that soon I would reach "my" gibbons and would follow them through the high canopy with my eyes pressed against the heavy, precious, beloved Leica 10x42 binoculars, to witness and document their daily life.

I went up and down a few more hills until I reached the night-sleeping area of group C. But before I got there I had to suddenly pause, at 7:28 a.m., breathing heavily and listening to the low, deep growls of a tiger at about 75° N and 500–600 meters from my current position. There was no time to ponder the tiger's intentions as I resumed my trot to find the gibbons. Back in 1993, signs of tigers such as fresh scent marks, large footprints, and occasional growls were still relatively frequently found or heard once every two weeks. In 1990 my first student, Jill Ebert, was lucky enough to see a tiger poke its head out into one of our trails while she was quietly watching gibbons in the late afternoon who had already settled into their night trees. Sadly, we've had no direct evidence of the presence of tigers in the study site for the past decade.

Heavily sweating, I reached the area of last night's sleeping tree of group C, close to the zone overlapping with the home range of group A and where a gentle slope along R-trail leads towards a small creek. Group C slept just across the creek, but over the past days they had had several encounters with group A on this side in an area sprinkled with large ficus trees in full fruit. My first sighting on this day was of *Cassandra*, a dark adult female, at 08:41 a.m. As she began to travel, I quickly identified the other five group members: buff adult male *Cassius II*, the group's second dark adult male *Claude*, buff young adult male *Chet*, his dark adolescent male

FIGURE 11.2 Adult male, Claude, feeding on figs.
Photo credit: Ulrich Reichard.

brother *Christopher,* and their much smaller, buff juvenile sister *Caleb*. It seemed like a regular morning until 11:17 a.m., when soft gibbon hoots were heard in the distance. Tension rose, and group C began traveling quickly and quietly towards where the hoots had come from. Soon members of group A and group C were together but on opposite ends of a tree crown feasting on ripe fig fruits, giving me an opportunity to quickly identify the buff adult female of group A, *Andromeda*, her dark adult male partner *Fearless*, the dark subadult male *Amadeus,* and the buff juvenile male *Aran.*

Such co-feeding in the same tree crown is infrequent and occurs in only about 35 percent of intergroup encounters at Khao Yai. Shortly after noon most members of group C had retreated from the fruiting tree, when Claude, who had not been feeding until now, tried to enter the fruiting tree but was blocked by *Fearless* who, demonstrating his dominance, sat with legs spread on the lead branch that gave access to the tree's crown. *Claude* seemed nervous but determined to feed, and began emitting soft, typical male encounter vocalizations. *Andromeda* approached *Fearless,* perhaps as a "back-up" or to encourage him in the revitalized encounter, and soon *Cassius II* was also near. When *Claude* retreated deeper into the crown of a neighboring tree, *Fearless* followed. This allowed *Cassius II*, who had been climbing up in the tree to nearly the same height as *Fearless*, to approach *Andromeda*. *Andromeda* retreated slowly, almost reluctantly, and while *Fearless* followed *Claude* in the opposite direction, *Cassius II* surprisingly continued pursuing *Andromeda* instead of chasing after *Fearless*, which would have been his typical response. Because of the unusual dynamics with *Cassius II* being close to *Andromeda,* and *Fearless* leaving in the opposite direction, I decided to switch from observing group C to group A so that I could follow *Andromeda* for a while. The canopy was dense where *Andromeda* had just disappeared, and I soon lost sight of her. When I next spotted her through my binoculars, she was arm-swinging in typical gibbon locomotor fashion towards the creek.

I anticipated her route, and I knew I had to rush to the creek's crossing to catch up with the gibbons along the slope on the other side. I followed the curving, narrow trail downwards with a clear idea of where I would find *Andromeda* again. Indeed, when I stopped to look up minutes later, she was only about 15 meters from me, quietly sitting with legs up against her belly, close to the trunk of a small tree and monitoring her surroundings. My vantage point was slightly higher than where she was sitting, and I had a clear view of her and *Cassius II*, who to my surprise was within only 6 meters of her. I could not see any other gibbons but continued to hear male encounter vocalizations about 30–50 meters away from the area we had just left. I sensed a tension between *Andromeda* and *Cassius II* that was different from the usual intergroup encounter atmosphere, and contrary to the many other times I have seen adults of two social groups, because *Andromeda* seemed unconcerned by *Cassius's* proximity. I knew that she could and would retreat deeper into her home range if she was uncomfortable or disinterested as she had done many times before. But today she remained as if expecting or anticipating something to happen.

When *Cassius II* approached, she crouched and suddenly emitted a sharp, short call, which was unfamiliar to me, but she stayed put until *Cassius II* was within arm's reach and only then did she let herself slide half a meter down the trunk. She looked up at *Cassius II*, who glared back at her, hooting softly. He approached again, this time circling around and below her, and then briefly paused to smell her genitalia. She remained still. Unexpectedly, juvenile *Aran* emerged from an adjacent tree, coming nearly into body contact with *Andromeda* and watching her and *Cassius II* closely. To my surprise, subadult *Amadeus* also came into view in a nearby tree. Within a minute after *Cassius II* had inspected *Andromeda's* genitalia, he lifted himself up while *Andromeda* slightly crouched. Then the pair copulated for 17 seconds with about 20 thrusts while *Amadeus* approached closer and *Aran* sat in front of *Andromeda*, intently watching the copulating pair.

Towards the end of the copulation I heard a series of short, strange, and unfamiliar vocalizations. I had never heard "copulation calls" before and couldn't determine whether they came from the female perhaps while the male ejaculated or the male called while ejaculating, or both, or neither, and it was one of the immatures. The immatures showed no signs of fear of *Cassius II*, who now hung slightly above *Andromeda* for only a few seconds after their intimate encounter ended and he retreated about 1.5 meters. As *Andromeda* sat upright, *Aran* clung to her, and *Amadeus* eventually sat beside them on a neighboring branch. For a minute no movement was seen and no sound heard, but when *Cassius II* approached again, the three A individuals slid lower down in the tree. Then soft vocalizations announced *Fearless's* return, upon which *Cassius II* quickly retreated. The two males passed each other as *Fearless* arrived from the creek low in the canopy while *Cassius II* high above swung away fast. I followed *Cassius II* with my binoculars and saw him crossing the creek and climbing up an emergent tree on the other side only seconds later. The encounter was over, and I remained with group A. The four of them sat close to each other for a little while before *Andromeda* invited *Fearless* to groom her. Although her initial grooming invitation was unsuccessful, it did not take long before the pair groomed one another as if nothing significant had just happened.

I, however, could barely contain my excitement while I quickly scribbled pages full of detailed notes in my tiny fieldbook. I had just witnessed an extra-pair copulation (EPC) episode in white-handed gibbons, something that was not supposed to happen and had never before been recorded in this species. But, had I possibly jumbled individuals? No, impossible! In addition to clear facial identification of *Andromeda* and *Cassius II*, who had been only roughly 10 meters away from me, *Andromeda's* long-term mate *Fearless* was of dark pelage color, and the male who has just copulated with *Andromeda* was as buff as she was. I couldn't contain the big smile that was slowly taking possession of me. It was one of those slow, happy smiles you can feel coming from inside and flowing through your body like a wave before hitting your lips. When I was finally done with my notes, the gibbons had left the area. The encounter had ended at 12:15 p.m., the midday heat tempered all forest animals' activities, and everything seemed to have gone back to its normal state. But my excitement stayed, and from that day on "normal" gibbon behavior had changed its meaning for me and nothing was the same anymore.

When I set out to study white-handed gibbons at Thailand's Khao Yai National Park in 1989, the script was clear: Gibbons are exquisitely elegant apes who gracefully sing and swing around the treetops of southeast Asia's rain forests. But the research on gibbons, so the story was told, was all about monogamy and stable, perhaps lifelong pair bonds. The gibbon nuclear family ideal probably originated a century ago when a desire existed to find animal examples for how humans ought to live. Animals' "natural behavior" was used to define humans' "natural behavior." In the case of the gibbons, the prescribed role they had been given was one of "animal care and love": two adults who partner in a sincere and faithful bond to raise their offspring until one of them dies. Until recently this model had been applied to gibbons based on suggestive, but incomplete observations and a lack of in-depth knowledge. The gibbons I studied, however, turned out to behave differently, and I discovered much social and mating flexibility beneath a shallow surface of pair living.

The gibbons' geographic range extends from northeastern India and southern China down to the southern hemisphere of the Indonesian island of Java. When I saw gibbons in Thailand, the general descriptions of gibbons proved correct. The gibbon world was magical and fundamentally different from my grounded existence on the tropical forest floor. Compared to the gibbons' fast and elegant ricochetal brachiation through the top canopy, my human bipedality, often heralded as an advanced mode of locomotion, immediately seemed clumsy. Their movements seemed capable of defeating gravity in an effortless way, holding the key to understanding why there is no reason for them to descend to the ground, not even to drink, as they quench their thirst from morning dew on large leaves of emergent trees and vines or from their daily portion of fleshy fruit, which for Khao Yai gibbons makes up more than 60% of the diet.

Khao Yai National Park was established in 1962, and in 2005 it became part of Thailand's large (6,199 km^2) Dong Phayayen – Khao Yai Forest Complex (DPKY), a UNESCO World Heritage site based on its high biodiversity. The forest complex is a conglomerate of five geographically close but distinct protected areas of which Khao Yai is the largest (2,168 km^2). The terrain is rugged, with elevations ranging from 200 to 1,351 meters above sea level. The climate is seasonally wet, averaging nearly 2,500 millimeters of annual rainfall following the Asian southwest monsoon cycle with a wet season from March–October and dry months from November–February. The dominant vegetation is classified as tropical seasonal forest or moist evergreen forest, and it supports the longest studied populations of gibbons in the world. In addition to white-handed gibbons, Khao Yai National Park is also home to a second gibbon species, the pileated gibbon (*Hylobates pileatus*). The two species are closely related, and a small zone of natural hybridization exists only 30 kilometers from the study area.

When I first arrived in the Park, in October 1989, research on white-handed gibbons had been ongoing for about a decade. The information I received was that Dr. Sompoad Srikosamatara, then a young man without the "Dr." title, was the first person to explore Khao Yai as a gibbon research site. Srikosamatara did not end up studying white-handed gibbons, but went to nearby Khao Soi Dao Wildlife Sanctuary, where he studied pileated gibbons. His fine master's thesis in 1980, together with an important book chapter on pileated gibbon ecology in 1984 and, a surprising publication about gibbon polygyny in 1987, were important contributions.

At Khao Yai, however, it was Dr. Warren Y. Brockelman and master's student Uthai Treesucon of Mahidol University who began studying white-handed gibbons. They were joined by a British couple, Patricia and Jeremy Raemaekers, for two years. Jeremy Raemaekers had studied white-handed gibbons and Siamang (*Symphalangus syndactylus*) for his dissertation research at Kuala Lompat on the eastern edge of the Krau Game Reserve in Pahang State, Malaysia, and both Raemaekers were instrumental in setting up the Khao Yai field site. The trails and trail tags they left proved invaluable to me in 1989, preventing me from getting lost all the time and guiding me out of the tangles of streams, gullies, and ravines back to the researcher house. I often thought of the Raemaekers while trotting along the elephant paths they had turned into a measured trail grid. The Raemaekers also began naming individual gibbons. However, despite my best efforts to use the names they had assigned to the same individuals, oral history failed a little. From the beginning, their research included group A, and I was told they had named the adult female *Andromeda*. It was only much later, and too late to change it back, that I found out that the female I was calling *Andromeda* had previously been named *Andromache* and had been carrying an infant known to my predecessors as *Actionbaby*.

It is this time-depth of decades that makes research on Khao Yai white-handed gibbons and other long-term mammal studies exceptional, fascinating, and scientifically outstandingly rewarding. When I began my study, only members of study group A were tolerant of human observers, but within a decade, thanks to the hard work of many students, volunteers, and myself, we managed to habituate another eight groups in addition to monitoring three other groups that had formed from dispersed habituated offspring of adults in our original study groups. Systematic social history records now date back to the beginning of the 1990s for a core of 14 study groups, whose ranges we have mapped. I still vividly remember the sweat and hours

FIGURE 11.3   Left to right: Kazunari Matsudaira, University of Tokyo, Japan; Rob Stroh, Southern Illinois University Carbondale, U.S.A.; Kristina Vintzens, German Primate Center, Germany; Tanja Wolf, German Primate Center, Germany and Ulrich Reichard, Southern Illinois University Carbondale, U.S.A., watching gibbons at the Khao Yai National Park, Thailand, 2009.
Photo credit: Norberto Asensio.

spent cutting new trails or looking for old tree tags to reopen the Raemaekers' trails, measuring out distances with a 50-meter measure tape, taking a compass bearing, and in the evening spending hours to convert the geographic field notes representing a three-dimensional space into a two-dimensional map! It was not an easy undertaking, and we were always aware that our map was only a relative approximation of what the real forest, ridges, and creeks in the gibbons' home ranges looked like.

What have we learned through the years? Compared to long-term studies of baboons and primates living in larger groups and having faster reproductive rates, our sample sizes are still small. Even after having studied gibbons for more than twenty years, our understanding still seems in its infancy. Is this perhaps the reason why most gibbon field researchers have switched to other models after a few years of studying wild gibbons? Insights into gibbons' life ways come slowly, yet funding agencies and universities are looking primarily for people with fast accumulating publication records and databases, and CVs sparkling with a string of publications like trophies.

Despite the challenges of studying a primate with a slow life history living in small groups, our understanding of the Khao Yai white-handed gibbons is much greater today than it was only a decade ago. *Andromeda* was probably the first individually recognized animal because of her distinct morphology of an unusually large, almost square-like upper torso compared to other females and even males; her golden-buff pelage; hardly visible eyebrows; and a white hair line around her mouth and chin that looked like a thin beard. She and her family illustrate both how much we have learned and how much more there is to discover, including such basic questions as how long wild white-handed gibbons can live. For example, we know from our long-term demographic records that white-handed gibbon females at Khao Yai do not give birth before the age of 10 years. Therefore, if the infant that *Andromeda* was carrying in early 1981 was her first, which seems likely given her lifespan, then she must have been born in 1970 or earlier. That would make her at least 42 years old as of 2012, the oldest known individual in our study population.

FIGURE 11.4   *Andromeda* with infant *Akira*, 1994.
Photo credit: Ulrich Reichard.

Significant changes in *Andromeda's* family were recorded as far back as 1984, foreshadowing what we know now about group composition changes. Contrary to the idea that gibbon pairs stay together as family units until an adult in the group dies, changes in *Andromeda's* group (group A) created a "patchwork family" unknown until then, when the group's adult male, *Achilles*, was replaced by the neighboring young adult male *Fearless* and subsequently *Fearless's* two younger brothers, *Felix* and *Frodo*, likewise immigrated into group A. For years, the unrelated juveniles, *Actionbaby* (*Andromeda's* infant) and *Frodo*, grew up together with their respective step-parents and "brother-uncle" *Felix*. The group was indistinguishable from other gibbon groups with the exception that the two juveniles were obviously much closer in age than related gibbon offspring usually are. For many years we believed that male and female dispersal patterns differed, because we were able to follow the natal dispersal of several males but lost track of most females who reached maturity. During the past decade, however, we were lucky to also record a few cases of female natal dispersal. These females also settled on neighbors' home ranges and quickly replaced the resident females just like dispersing males. The significance of these observations remained unclear until a recent genetic study further confirmed similar female dispersal cases onto neighboring home ranges. We now believe that adult replacement on a neighboring home range is the common pathway to find a first partner not only for males but also for females. Secondary dispersal may follow thereafter.

We have not only witnessed the creation of new family units, but also the formation of multimale groups when a male immigrant, instead of ousting a former resident, accepted the resident male's continued presence as the female's secondary partner. Our observations have confirmed that secondary males are able to maintain an intimate relationship with the female that includes grooming and occasionally copulating with each other, and they are active participants during intergroup encounters. Despite such insights, the ultimate reasons why some groups transition into multimale stages, particularly from a primary male's point of view, and others don't are yet unknown. Perhaps kin relationships play an important role in transfer decisions, as was seen early on in group A. Based on knowledge of individuals with well documented dispersal histories, we have documented multiple cases where a replaced older male joined a presumed kin, sometimes a presumed son and at other times a presumed brother. In group A, for example, years after *Fearless* replaced his predecessor, *Achilles*, he was replaced himself by the young adult male *Christopher* from group C. In early 2004, *Christopher's* presumed father in group C, *Cassius II*, was challenged by an unknown immigrant male, *Chana*. *Cassius II* lost the battle and subsequently joined group A, where he became a secondary male to *Andromeda* and resided on the home range with his assumed son *Christopher*, *Andromeda's* primary male partner. Soon after, the two males were also joined by *Christopher's* young siblings, the adolescent and juvenile males, *Chikyu* and *Chuu*, who likewise left group C. Similarly, *Fearless* settled in the home range of his assumed son *Amadeus* after *Christopher* had replaced him in group A.

The gibbons' social dynamics are mirrored in their sexual relationships, with *Andromeda* once again being the first female to exhibit what we now know to be much more flexible mating relationships than gibbons were previously thought to have. In her lifetime so far, *Andromeda* has had five long-term social partners with each of whom she has shared the same home range for many years. For some time, she lived with two and even three adult male partners and maintained intense successive and simultaneous sexual relationships with all of them. Additionally, she also copulated on occasion with at least seven of her eight adult male neighbors. A rough estimate of her sexual activity indicated that about one in ten observed copulations was with a neighboring male. As described above, extra-pair copulations happen fast. A neighboring male and a cycling female would not hesitate to copulate upon meeting in an overlapping zone between their home ranges and out of sight of the female's primary partner. If a primary male became aware of an extra-pair copulation, he would immediately break it up and vigorously chase the neighboring male away, but most of the extra-pair copulations we have witnessed have gone unnoticed by the primary males. Female cooperation during these sexual encounters is unquestionable, but what advantages females gain from engaging in extra-pair copulations and mating with multiple males is yet unclear. Females may even play a more active role in soliciting copulations from multiple males than we currently envision, because our hormone study of female ovarian functioning, which we have been monitoring by measuring sex hormone concentrations from feces, found that changes in sex hormone concentrations correspond with cyclical changes in the coloration and turgidity of female's anogenital region. A detailed study of Khao Yai white-handed gibbon females' sexual swellings found that females stimulated male sexual activity and that mostly primary, but occasionally also secondary and extra-pair males copulated with a female during her most likely period of conception. Female sexual swellings become maximal in size around ovulation, but the temporal overlap between swelling size and corresponding ovulation probability is not exact. This slight mismatch allows females to manipulate male mating activity, because males can only approximate the day of ovulation, which makes close male mate-guarding less effective in white-handed gibbons compared to other primates and allows females to choose different mating partners during the short window of conception. However, female mate choice in a primarily pair-living species like the white-handed gibbon has not been seriously tackled yet. Not surprisingly, a recent genetic study confirmed what the presence of sexual swellings and extra-pair copulations already suggested: Although the majority of infants in the Khao Yai population were fathered by females' stable social partners, approximately one in every five infants was sired by a neighboring male.

I still fly to Thailand to visit the Khao Yai white-handed gibbons and have maintained research on this population over the past two decades. After all of these years, I still feel the same inexplicable, deep satisfaction when I walk home to the research house in the afternoon, when the light coming through the forest canopy is soft, on the same winding trail I have walked hundreds of times after a full night-tree to night-tree observation day with the gibbons. A barking deer, a small ungulate, has become so accustomed to our presence that she simply freezes, so close to the trail that I could almost touch her if I wanted to when I pass by in my steady gibbon-researcher pace downhill towards the village. Slightly less pleasant forest inhabitants for us have likewise become so comfortable with our presence that they hardly run away—we also often encounter a particular Asian black bear and a Malayan sun bear along our trails. Another hour or two of sunlight usually remains when I leave the forest, because gibbons settle early in their night trees. The slippery bridge has been repaired and shifted slightly a few times, but otherwise it is still the same challenging gateway or obstacle, and when I cross back into the noisy human world my thoughts are largely also still the same as twenty years ago. What an amazing place and what a privilege it is to be able to work here! Once, white-handed gibbons, like all gibbon species, were only thought of as the gentle and faithful apes that live in small, exclusive family groups. Their lives seemed simple and were characterized by harmonic within-family relationships and somewhat reflective of a human family ideal. The picture has changed dramatically, and it is my hope that the research we conduct will continue to contribute to a refined, more realistic picture of the gibbons' reproductive strategies. We now know that white-handed gibbons take new partners at times and that they may simultaneously have multiple sexual partners, some of which sire infants, resulting in half siblings or unrelated offspring being reared together. We have also learned that most individuals upon reaching maturity disperse only one or two home ranges away from their natal home range. Because they tend to stay close to home, these migration

FIGURE 11.5 Subadult female *Rak*, 2009. **Photo credit:** Ulrich Reichard.

dynamics result in related individuals often residing in groups next to one other. Thus, the next logical step we need to take in our research is to develop a community model of gibbon society that closely integrates intra-group relationships with inter-group relationships. We have made the first steps towards a more accurate understanding of white-handed gibbons' flexible social and sexual life, but we also have decades of research ahead of us to ultimately answer the pressing question of what underlies the gibbons' dynamic behaviors, which will eventually be another piece in the puzzle of the evolution of the social behavior of animals.

Just as the gibbon families have changed over time, so have the Thai families living in the longhouses I pass on my way to the gibbons. After twenty years, children who once chased large, pretty butterflies in the afternoon sun when I walked out of the forest—looking at me with disbelief as I passed, dressed in heavy army clothes, sweating and dirty with binoculars dangling from my neck and a pen tied to a string so as to not lose this precious observation instrument—are now adults who always have a smile for me on their lips. They work as rangers as their fathers have, in the Khao Yai National Park office, or clean houses and guide tourists to see and experience the treasures of wildlife found in the Park.

Unfortunately, the threats to the gibbons and their forest have persisted over the years. Poaching continues to be a problem, but an equally great threat to the wildlife of Khao Yai continues to come from the perfume industry. Like many Asian forests, Khao Yai National Park is home to a tree family known locally as *Mai hom* (*Aquilaria crassna*). When this tree is injured, it produces a dark brown, aromatic resin to protect the wound against bacteria and fungus. Areas of the tree that contain the resin are chiseled off by poachers, who bag large quantities of the woodchips—also known as agarwood, aloewood, or eaglewood—and haul them out of the forest. Several small factories around Khao Yai National Park extract the valuable resin and sell the raw product to Japan, China, and the Middle East, where it is used as an ingredient of soap and, more importantly, incense sticks. We have helped Khao Yai rangers confiscate large bags of poached *Mai hom*, and once my student chased a poacher who was active in the home range of study group C for nearly an hour, despite the considerable risk given that most poachers these days are heavily armed. Despite numerous arrests every year, poaching has not decreased much because the jurisdiction of Khao Yai police ends at the park border, and convicted poachers are bailed out at local police stations by their criminal bosses.

The negative impact to the forest from this nontimber extraction is enormous. Specific trees are cut down, which damages the forest structure and reduces its biodiversity. Gibbons feed on the tiny sprout of the developing seed when *Mai hom* trees come into fruit, and when the trees are cut, they lose a source of food. Sometimes heavy machinery is brought in to carry away large *Mai hom* stems or woodchips, and once a poacher's provisions are depleted, he will live off what he can hunt in the forest. Gibbons are not a preferred target, but deer, wild boar, and pheasants are hunted frequently by *Mai hom* poachers. Tigers also have disappeared from the park, probably hunted for their value in the traditional Asian medicine market. Thus, even well protected areas such as Khao Yai National Park are not as safe as they should be.

I have learned the Thai language well enough to be able to communicate with the Thai field assistants who have worked for the Gibbon project over the years. Some families have grown close to me, particularly during the years when I could take my family with me to Khao Yai. When my then blond sons were 2 years and 6 months respectively, it was a common occurrence for Thai people to ask if they could touch or squeeze their skin, for they claimed they had rarely seen such a "white" baby. Certainly having young children with me in the field helped with winning the trust and cooperation of the Khao Yai people. By contrast, it has remained a struggle to establish solid, enduring working relationships with the park officials, in large part because the superintendent of the park changes every two or three years in an effort to minimize chances for bribery and kin favoritism. This has meant that I need to re-establish and explain my project at regular intervals. Most park superintendents are not scientists but administrators with backgrounds in forestry or wildlife management, and they have great expectations of what a scientific project can contribute to their National Park, including expecting the project to provide financial support in the form of donations and project personnel to lead tourist groups and give public seminars. In 2010 we organized a new gibbon exhibit for the Khao Yai Visitor Center with the help of Professor Suchinda Malaivijitnond and Chulalongkorn University, Bangkok. However, one thing I have learned is that whatever we do, it never seems to be enough and I am always surprised by what the next superintendent will ask us to do.

I am not sure if the people living and working in Khao Yai National Park understand our research and scientific aims and why I keep coming back year after year, but I do get a strong sense that they acknowledge my dedication to the graceful apes of Asia, and some of them seem to quietly share my strong love and passion for the gibbons and their tropical rain forest.

Suggested Readings

Barelli, C., M. Heistermann, C. Boesch, and U. H. Reichard. 2007. "Sexual Swellings in Wild White-Handed Gibbon Females (*Hylobates lar*) Indicate the Probability of Ovulation." *Hormones and Behavior* 51: 221–230.

Barelli, C., M. Heistermann, C. Boesch, and U. H. Reichard. 2008. "Mating Patterns and Sexual Swellings in Pair-Living and Multimale Groups of Wild White-Handed Gibbons, *Hylobates lar*." *Animal Behaviour* 75: 991–1001.

Reichard, U. 1995. "Extra-Pair Copulations in a Monogamous Gibbon (*Hylobates lar*)." *Ethology* 100: 99–112.

Reichard, U. H., and C. Barelli. 2008. "Life History and Reproductive Strategies of Khao Yai *Hylobates lar*: Implications for Social Evolution in Apes." *International Journal of Primatology* 29: 823–844.

Reichard, U. H., M. Ganpanakngan, and C. Barelli. 2012. "White-Handed Gibbons of Khao Yai: Social Flexibility, Reproductive Strategies, and a Slow Life History." In Kappeler, P. M., and D. Watts (eds.), *Long-Term Field Studies of Primates*. Springer, Berlin (pp. 237–258).

Acknowledgments

I am grateful to Warren Brockelman and Ramesh Boonratana for introducing me to the Khao Yai National Park and its gibbons. Christian Vogel and Volker Sommer have been an inspiration throughout my academic career. I thank Suchinda Malaivijitnond for her unfailing support and generosity to collaborate with me on gibbon research in Thailand. The Max Planck Institute for Evolutionary Anthropology, Leipzig, and the Director of the Department of Primatology, Christophe Boesch, have provided much financial, logistic, and intellectual support during critical years, for which I am thankful. I thank Southern Illinois University Carbondale and the L.S.B. Leakey Foundation for current and past support of my research.

PART IV

Comparative Lenses

12

Studying Lemurs
on Three Continents

By Peter M. Kappeler[1]

FIRST CONTACT

I was getting desperate. It was August 1984 and my year abroad at Duke University's Zoology Department had only started two weeks earlier. I had signed up for an animal behavior course—and I desperately needed a topic for my first independent project by the end of the next day. I had arrived at Duke as an exchange student from Tübingen University in Germany with a rather unfocused interest in organismal biology—and in mammals. During my orientation week, I had visited the Duke University Primate Center (DUPC, now Duke Lemur Center), where I first encountered these cat-sized grunting primates called lemurs that bore little resemblance to what I had gotten to know as primates from zoos and television. As I struggled to come up with a project idea, I remembered my visit to the DUPC and decided to do my project on lemurs, even though I did not know anything about them, and they came in all sizes and colors. Not knowing where to begin, I sat down in frustration in front of some outdoor enclosures. Before too long, I noticed a small, cute lemur climbing up the fence in front of me, reaching out with its arm towards me (visitors were allowed to feed them raisins in those days). The small plastic tag attached to the fence revealed that this curious beast was a juvenile female crowned lemur—then called *Lemur coronatus*. After interacting with her for a little while, my heart had melted, and my project was clear.

Consultation of the Biological Abstracts at the DUPC library revealed that, apart from the species description, there existed only one publication on crowned lemurs which described their karyotype, or number of chromosomes. So, here was a species of primate, in captivity no less, and it was virtually unknown to science! I quickly found out that the DUPC housed several more

[1] About the author: Peter Kappeler studied biology at the University of Tübingen (Germany) and Duke University, where he obtained a PhD in zoology in 1992. He has headed the Department of Sociobiology and Anthropology at the University of Göttingen and the BES Unit at the DPZ since 2003. Most of his publications have focused on the lemurs of Kirindy, where he established a field site with Jörg Ganzhorn in 1993.

Contact information: Department of Sociobiology/Anthropology, University of Göttingen, Kellnerweg 6, D-37077 Göttingen, GERMANY, pkappel@gwdg.de

Citation: Kappeler, P. M. 2014. "Studying Lemurs on Three Continents." In Strier, K. B. (ed.), *Primate Ethnographies*. Upper Saddle River, NJ: Pearson Education, Inc. (pp. 132–138).

family groups of crowned lemurs, and I began to design a study of their social, reproductive, and scent marking behavior during the upcoming breeding season. By the end of my year abroad, what had been my class project for the fall semester had extended into an independent study during the spring, and it ultimately formed the basis for my MSc thesis submitted at Tübingen in 1987, as well as my first three publications. Almost thirty years later, I am still studying lemurs. I am also beginning to get desperate again . . . but more on that later.

BACK IN THE USA

Three years later, I was back at Duke as a graduate student. I wanted to learn more about this radiation of primates that remained poorly known compared to other primates – despite the heroic efforts of pioneering scientists such as Jean-Jacque Petter, Alison Jolly, Bob Sussman, Ian Tattersall, Alison Richard, and Peter Klopfer and his students who put lemurs on the primatological map before 1980. In the 1980s, you could read virtually everything that had ever been published on the behavior of almost any lemur species in a day or two. On the one hand, this fact defined an exciting frontier. On the other hand, it was difficult to identify an appropriate species for any theory-driven project because so little was known about any of them, especially from the wild. I settled on the topic of female dominance for my PhD project. Field studies by Alison Jolly and Alison Richard on ringtailed lemurs and sifakas, respectively, had identified the phenomenon, in which females are able to elicit submissive behavior from all adult males. Later studies attributed this social pattern to all or most lemurs. I was hoping to learn something about social evolution and sexual selection by focusing on an apparent example of sex-role reversal in an entire adaptive radiation of primates that were relatively close kin of baboons, gorillas, and the like. The topic also offered several opportunities for different conceptual and methodological approaches, including the fundamental decision between studying lemurs in the wild or in captivity.

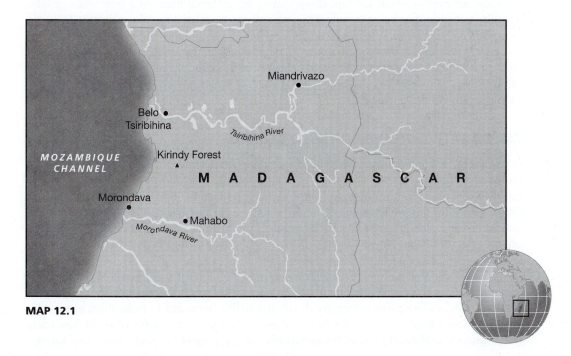

MAP 12.1

In 1988, I spent my first summer as a graduate student volunteering in two projects in Madagascar. My first mission took me to Jörg Ganzhorn's field site in the dry deciduous forests of western Madagascar known as Kirindy forest. There, I spent several weeks cutting and surveying transects for diurnal and nocturnal lemurs in habitats with different logging history. Little did I know then that this forest was going to become my second home for much of my entire professional career. With essentially no research infrastructure to fall back on, I had to master most difficulties of field work, ranging from giardia (intestinal distress from amoeba) to my first encounter with a fosa (the largest extant carnivore predator on Madagascar) with only a mosquito net as protection. Six weeks later, I exchanged the Malagasy forester camp for Ranomafana's rain forest, where Pat Wright had set up her research camp a year earlier. She provided me with an opportunity to habituate several groups of the then just recently discovered golden bamboo lemurs, and I learned a lot about some still unstudied lemurs from a cheerful bunch of other Duke students and knowledgeable local field assistants. I also picked up a lot of insights about successfully organizing and running a field site that would become handy later on because Pat had plenty of field experience from her previous studies of night monkeys and tarsiers.

Hundreds of leech bites later, I was back at Duke and had to make a decision. My impressions from the field were overwhelming, but they also clearly indicated that a detailed study of a subtle aspect of social behavior, such as male-female agonistic interactions, could better be done in captivity where observation conditions were more reliable. The DUPC offered uniquely suitable opportunities in the form of large natural habitat enclosures, where multiple groups of several lemur species roamed freely. It also took me only five minutes, instead of five hours, to locate a study group, and all the animals were habituated and individually marked whereas such working conditions were just being established at Ranomafana. Moreover, the DUPC colony provided the opportunity for comparative studies, even though the respective species were not sympatric in the wild. Furthermore, I had access to the histories of all groups and individuals, including information about kinship, at least along the maternal lines. At a time when genetic paternity tests were just being invented, this was clearly an asset. The colony records also provided data on body weights, which could be used for my specific interest in sexual dimorphism and growth. With these thoughts in mind, I opted to work at the DUPC, and by 1992, when I finished my PhD, I knew a lot more about lemur social behavior, sexual dimorphism and maternal investment. However, even after another 25 years of research, we still don't know why most female lemurs dominate males.

COMPARATIVE STUDIES OF WILD LEMURS

In retrospect, luck and chance seem to be just as important determinants of a scientific career as resolve and enthusiasm. I was very lucky in that completion of my doctorate coincided with the establishment of a new research group at the German Primate Center (DPZ) in Göttingen. Jörg Ganzhorn headed this group and kindly took me on as a postdoc. We decided to establish a permanent research station in Kirindy Forest, where Jörg continued to study community ecology and the effects of habitat fragmentation, and I turned to a new frontier: the social organization and mating systems of nocturnal lemurs.

Bob Martin and the members of Jean-Jacque Petter's team had pioneered the study of nocturnal lemurs years before, but their studies were short-term or mainly descriptive. Because the dry deciduous forests are extremely dense, it was first necessary to make them accessible, especially for working at night. We therefore established regular systems of small foot trails whose intersections could be used for systematic live trapping of the small, nocturnal lemurs.

FIGURE 12.1 After being captured in a life trap, a nocturnal Coquerel's dwarf lemur (*Mirza coquereli*) is individually marked with a subdermal chip, has its body proportions measured, and has a small tissue sample for subsequent DNA extraction removed before being released at its capture site at dusk. One of our field assistants (Bruno Tsiverimana, left) is demonstrating these methods to a Malagasy student under the supervision of Rodin Rasoloarison (right). **Photo credit:** Peter Kappeler.

Capturing individuals not only allowed us to measure and mark individuals, to furnish them with radio-collars, and to obtain small tissue samples for genetic analyses, but it also allowed us to discover that this forest actually harbored a second species of mouse lemurs. The newly discovered species, *Microcebus berthae*, weighs just 30 grams, making it the world's smallest extant primate. It is also one of the most endangered ones because of its tiny distributional range, which includes only Kirindy and a few adjacent forests.

I became interested in the population structure of nocturnal lemurs and began employing what have become much more readily available genetical tools to determine their kin structure and mating systems. Initially, I wanted to compare the closely related Coquerel's dwarf lemurs (*Mirza coquereli)* and fork-marked lemurs (*Phaner pallescens*) because previous work had indicated that they were solitary and pair-living, respectively. I never managed to capture a single *Phaner*, however; a nice demonstration of the fact that it is easy to design a beautiful study at your desk, but that some unknown constraints can easily ruin it. Years later, my PhD student, Oliver Schülke, had enough stamina to capture *Phaner* successfully, and he joined other students of mine who conducted the first systematic studies of the social systems of other sympatric nocturnal lemurs (Manfred Eberle: *Microcebus murinus*; Melanie Dammhahn: *M. berthae*; Roland Hilgartner: *Lepilemur ruficaudatus*). These lemurs continue to be stimulating subjects for comparative study because most of them belong to the same taxonomic family and sit in the same trees; yet, they exhibit very different social organizations and adaptations to deal with the pronounced seasonality of this forest. For example, only the mouse lemurs use torpor to sit out part of the cool dry season, and *Lepilemur* and *Phaner* are pair-living, whereas the mouse lemurs and *Mirza* live solitary lives in home ranges that overlap with those of many other conspecifics.

In 1995, I also established an individually-marked population of sifakas (*Propithecus verreauxi*), followed by the redfronted lemurs (*Eulemur rufifrons*) inhabiting the same study area a year later. I found these two species interesting because they represent two primate lineages (Indriidae and Lemuridae) that have evolved group-living independently and could therefore offer insights into various questions including the problem of female dominance, which remained unresolved. I hoped to learn something about it by focusing on the male side of the coin; in particular the mechanisms with which males compete with each other. Paternities are the evolutionarily relevant outcomes of male-male competition, but it took more than ten years before we

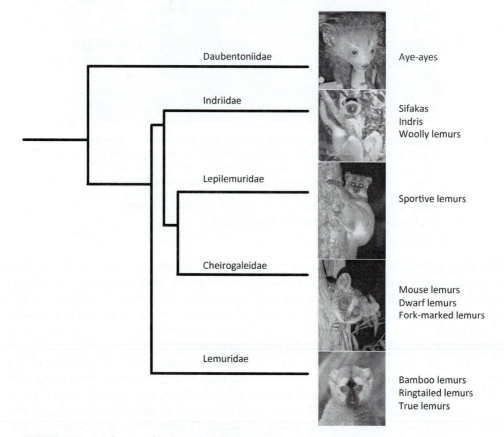

FIGURE 12.2   A schematic family tree of the lemurs of Madagascar. The more than 100 currently recognized species are divided into five families, of which one representative is depicted. Common names indicate the common names of most genera making up each family. The independent evolutionary origin of the Lemuridae and Indriidae was inferred from a phylogenetic reconstruction, using this tree and the available data on the social organization of extant species. **Photo credits** (from top to bottom): Peter Kappeler, Claudia Fichtel, Claudia Fichtel, Elise Huchard, and Claudia Fichtel.

had enough surviving infants for a meaningful analysis of the patterns and predictors of paternity. Even though we studied ten and more groups simultaneously, with primates such as mouse lemurs that reproduce at the end of their first year of life and whose average life span is only two to three years, it can take decades to understand their population dynamics. Over the years, these studies gradually developed into an unplanned long-term study of demography and life history, which revealed, among other things, that paternity in lemur groups is strongly biased in favor of one male; however, without the expected consequences of male-male competition for sexual dimorphism and male dominance.

LEMUR COGNITION: BACK IN CAPTIVITY

The continuous support of the DPZ has also afforded us the opportunity to begin studying lemurs at our home institution in 2010. This captive colony of three species provides us with opportunities to address questions that are difficult to study in the field. Long considered to be equipped with under-sized brains compared to other primates, systematic studies of lemurs' cognitive abilities have lagged behind. Together with Claudia Fichtel and her students, we have therefore established an agenda for comparative studies of physical and social cognition that may eventually provide yet another angle on lemur sociality. For example, we are interested in their numerical abilities and their propensities to engage in prosocial behavior—both questions that are currently being studied experimentally. In addition, this colony has also enabled us to intensify the transfer of methods between the field and the lab. In addition to non-invasive analyses of various physiological health indicators, we developed an apparatus that permits us to evaluate how lemurs respond to an experimental choice task in which they learn to access a food reward using one of two different methods; this is now being used by Anna Schnöll to investigate social learning in two wild lemur species.

FIGURE 12.3 Wild redfronted lemurs (*Eulemur rufifrons*) are being presented with a small food reward in a box that can be opened in two ways (push or pull). One individual in a group is being trained with one of these methods, and subsequent trials are conducted to determine whether naive group members learn this method socially (i.e., by observing others). **Photo credit:** Marie Theres Dittmann.

INTERIM RESUMEE

Studying lemurs for 25 years in different settings has generated a range of experiences and mixed emotions. Scientifically, it has been a rewarding endeavor because we have been able to learn a great deal about lemur behavior and ecology. Ironically, today's beginning graduate students are faced with an even larger number of completely unstudied lemur species than I was 25 years ago because the number of newly discovered lemur species has more than tripled in the meantime. It appears that most of them have very small ranges, so that there is a real risk that some will go extinct before we know more about them than their body size and the sequences of a few of their mitochondrial genes.

Organizing and managing a field site in a tropical country has proven to be a continuing challenge that also generated both desperation and optimism. As many other primate origin countries, Madagascar has suffered from several periods of political instability, whose ramifications can be experienced firsthand at Kirindy as well. The forest still has no legal protection, despite its recognized biological importance as one of the largest remaining tracts of deciduous forest with a number of locally endemic vertebrates. Analyses of a series of satellite images have confirmed our first hand impressions that illegal deforestation activities have peaked during periods of political instability. So, while it has been a pleasure to see how our local field assistants have become dedicated naturalists and conservationists, without political support and essential resources, their commitment may not be enough. I had to learn the hard way that the possibilities of a research institution such as the DPZ to make tangible contributions to conservation are limited. With the perspective of nearly twenty-five years of experience, I came to realize that time is one of the most precious commodities in this context; and mine is beginning to run out. About fifteen years ago, my then three-year-old daughter asked me, "Daddy, will you protect the lemurs until I am old enough to do it myself?" I hope that we have enough time and forest left for her to get a chance. I am counting on her and, importantly, on all twenty-seven children of our eight field assistants.

Suggested Readings

Fichtel, C., and Kappeler, P. M. 2010. "Human Universals and Primate Symplesiomorphies: Establishing the Lemur Baseline." In Kappeler, P. M., and J. B. Silk (eds.), *Mind the Gap: Tracing the Origins of Human Universals.* Springer, Heidelberg (pp. 395–426).

Kappeler, P. M. 1993. "Variation in Social Structure: The Effects of Sex and Kinship on Social Interactions in Three Lemur Species." *Ethology* 93: 125–145.

Kappeler, P. M. 1997. "Intrasexual Selection in *Mirza coquereli*: Evidence for Scramble Competition Polygyny in a Solitary Primate." *Behavioral Ecology and Sociobiology* 41: 115–127.

Kappeler, P. M., and C. Fichtel. 2012. "A 15-year Perspective on the Social Organization and Life History of Sifaka in Kirindy Forest." In Kappeler, P., and D. Watts (eds.), *Long-Term Field Studies of Primates.* Springer Berlin, Heidelberg (pp. 101–121).

Kappeler, P. M., and L. Schäffler. 2009. "The Lemur Syndrome Unresolved: Extreme Male Reproductive Skew in Sifakas (*Propithecus verreauxi*), a Sexually Monomorphic Primate with Female Dominance." *Behavioral Ecology and Sociobiology* 62: 1007–1015.

Acknowledgments

Thanks to all Malagasy cooperation partners for supporting our research activities at Kirindy over so many years, to all our local staff for making Kirindy what it is today, to Peter Klopfer, Jörg Ganzhorn, Eduard Linsenmair and the late Klaus Schmidt-Koenig for their supporting influence on my life history, and to Karen Strier for the invitation to contribute to this volume.

13

A Tale of Two Monkeys

By Stephen F. Ferrari[1]

The Amazon Basin is a primatological paradise, home to a truly amazing variety of species, ranging from the mouse-like pygmy marmoset to the comparatively gigantic woolly and spider monkeys, gangly denizens of the tree-tops. Between these two extremes, there are monkeys of all shapes, sizes, and colors, with extravagant hair styles, handlebar mustaches, bald heads, and comb-overs, as well as bug-eyed bug-eaters and frenetic gremlins. A motley crew, perhaps, but this treasure-trove of primatological diversity is mostly still waiting to be unraveled.

The Amazon is one of the world's last unexplored frontiers, a vast, sparsely populated region that guards countless mysteries and untold biological secrets. We have a good idea of the different types of primates that inhabit the region, but the exact number of Amazonian monkey species is less clear. During the first decade of the twenty-first century alone, no fewer than seven new species, and even a new genus (*Callibella*) were described. *Callibella* (now reclassified as *Mico humilis*) is a sort of missing link between the four-ounce pygmy and the "true" marmosets, veritable giants of just less than a pound in weight.

While the list of species is creeping towards the one hundred mark, the vast majority are still as mysterious to us in scientific terms as they were before they were discovered. Where do they live? How do they behave? What do they eat? Perhaps even more importantly, how will they cope with the reality of human "progress," the relentless march of the loggers, ranchers, and soybean farmers who are hacking their way ever deeper into the jungle, replacing the region's biological exuberance with monotonous pastures and plantations?

I was fresh from defending my Ph.D. dissertation when I first arrived at Belém, the sprawling Brazilian metropolis at the mouth of the Amazon, and I felt like an eager little boy who had just

[1]About the author: Stephen Ferrari graduated in Anthropology at Durham University in England, and earned his Ph.D. at University College, London, studying buffy-headed marmosets in southeastern Brazil. He subsequently moved to the Amazon region, where he spent 15 years researching the region's primate diversity. He now lives in northeastern Brazil, where his main research interest is the local titi monkeys (*Callicebus*).

Contact information: Departamento de Ecologia, Centro de Ciências Biológicas e da Saúde, Universidade Federal de Sergipe, Sao Cristovao, SE, Brasil, 49000-100, ferrari@pq.cnpq.br

Citation: Ferrari, S. F. 2014. "A Tale of Two Monkeys." In Strier, K. B. (ed.), *Primate Ethnographies*. Upper Saddle River, NJ: Pearson Education, Inc. (pp. 139–150).

been given the keys to the chocolate factory. But having the keys to the chocolate factory is one thing—finding your way around in it is quite another. I collected my Ph.D data in southeastern Brazil, where I could take the overnight bus to my study site. But I now faced a quite different reality, where distances were measured in days, and the simplest of trips through my primatological paradise could turn into a logistical nightmare, despite all the modern advances in transportation. Even half a century ago, the only way around most of the Amazon basin was by boat, meandering through endless river bends to get from one inhospitable, uncharted jungle to the next.

There is more than a little irony in the fact that, without the infrastructure that has accompanied the region's recent "progress"—the frontier towns, airports, and highways—many of our more interesting discoveries would have been difficult, if not impossible. The problem is that literally millions of square miles of the Amazon forest are located on what is known locally as the *terra firme*, the slightly higher, dry ground that separates the rivers. While floodplain habitats teem with life, their fauna and flora are quite distinct from those of the *terra firme*. So the early naturalists—including Alfred Wallace—had done little more than scratch the surface, or rather, around the edges of the region's biological riches, the vast majority of which remain untouched to this day.

In the late 1960s, however, the Brazilian government—at that time a military dictatorship—decided that it needed to occupy the country's vast northern frontier, and inaugurated an ambitious scheme to colonize the Amazon, a pristine wilderness about the size of western Europe. Initially, there was little controversy, and even less opposition. In those environmentally naïve days, the government was able to garner enormous loans from the World Bank to finance its lunacy, in particular, the so-called "megaprojects," the most controversial of which are the hydroelectric dams. As the world's largest hydrographic basin, the Amazon would seem to have an almost unlimited potential for the generation of hydroelectric energy, but in practice, the region's flat, low-lying topography constituted a major drawback.

The turning point came when the government decided to build a dam to supply Manaus, the metropolis at the remote center of the Amazon basin, which had become a free trade zone and a major industrial center. The city's factories needed electricity, but the region around Manaus is as flat as the rest of the Amazon pancake. In fact, while it is about a thousand miles upriver from the Atlantic Ocean, Manaus is only 300 feet above sea level. To compensate for the lack of gravity, the engineers from Eletronorte, the federal corporation responsible for the region's power grid, simply decided to create as large a reservoir as possible. Worse still, they chose a site called Balbina, which was located within the reservation of the Waimiri-Atroari, a fiercely defiant people who had been almost totally wiped out by disease and armed conflict and were only just settling into an uneasy rapport with Brazilian society.

In many ways, Balbina was just another megaproject, but as the 1980s kicked in, the environment had suddenly become big news, and the Amazon was on the crest of the planet's attentions. Brazil was also emerging from two decades of military rule and beginning to find its democratic feet. Eletronorte immediately became an environmental pariah, the archetypal faceless conglomerate displacing people and animals to flood vast areas of pristine forest. Whatever its environmental implications, to call Balbina a white elephant would be an understatement of biblical proportions. While its turbines still spin—generating barely a fifth of the electrical power produced by other reservoirs of similar size—Manaus now depends on Venezuela to satisfy its energy needs. Balbina was not only Eletronorte's greatest environmental fiasco, but also its ultimate engineering debacle.

Ironically, it was Eletronorte's subsequent project, at Cachoeira Samuel ("Samuel Falls") in the western state of Rondônia, which gave me my first real opportunity to come to grips with the region's biodiversity. Eager to placate both the World Bank and Brazilian public opinion,

FIGURE 13.1   The finished Samuel dam. **Photo credit:** Acervo Eletrobras Eletronorte.

Eletronorte had gone to great lengths to ensure that its environmental policies at Samuel were beyond reproach. Among other things, they had established a reserve—the Samuel State Ecological Station—adjacent to the reservoir, which was supposed to allay its impact on the local biota, and had earmarked a substantial budget to support long-term environmental studies within its 175,000 acres, which included sponsoring fieldwork like my own.

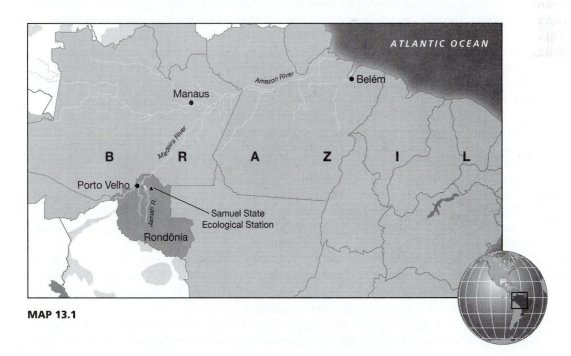

MAP 13.1

Rondônia is an intriguing region, not only for its untold biological and anthropological riches, but also for its fascinating history and prominent role in the colonization of the western Amazon basin. Among other curiosities, Rondônia is home to the Devil's Railroad (*Ferrovia do Diabo*), a forerunner of the many megalomaniacal white elephants of the second half of the twentieth century.

At the height of the rubber boom, towards the end of the nineteenth century, landlocked Bolivia was desperate to export the latex being produced in its Amazonian territories. The only viable route was the Guaporé River, which forms the country's border with Brazil, the problem being the twenty waterfalls that impede the passage of riverboats. This stretch of the river could be bypassed by a railroad, although it would need to pass through Brazilian territory. The Bolivian government negotiated a solution with Brazil, which was not unlike that which brought Alaska into the Union. The railroad was part of the payment for the 59,000-square-mile chunk of Amazon forest now known as the Brazilian state of Acre. While it was officially Bolivian territory at the time, Acre had been occupied by Brazilian rubber tappers.

Laying the 230 miles of track took more than five years and the lives of 6,000 workers who fell victim primarily to tropical diseases such as malaria and yellow fever. Legend has it that there is a body buried under each railroad tie. But this isn't the worst part of the story by any means. By the time the devil's work was done in 1912, the Amazonian rubber boom had all but fizzled out as cheap latex from Malaysian plantations began to flood the international market. In other words, the railroad was redundant the moment it was inaugurated, in the best tradition of the grand old pachyderms of the Amazon basin.

By comparison with this demoniacal railroad and other, more recent extravaganzas, the Samuel reservoir was a runty pale-pink baby elephant, sitting discreetly in a quiet corner of the Amazon forest. It nevertheless had its own role in local history. At the peak of the rubber boom, the area surrounding the reservoir had also been occupied by rubber tappers, who had expelled the original native residents. As the boom went bust, the rubber tappers moved out, and nobody moved in. The area was pristine, virtually untouched by human hands in almost eighty years.

Untouched, that is, until Eletronorte had come blundering in over the horizon to bulldoze a pair of enormous dykes out of the red Amazon earth. It was Balbina all over again, albeit on a much reduced scale— "only" about two hundred square miles of forest were to be flooded. But this was enough to displace thousands of unsuspecting animals from their once-tranquil forest, many of which—in particular, the monkeys—had to be rescued from the rising waters.

I arrived at Samuel towards the end of the flooding and was immediately both shocked and fascinated by the scenes that greeted me at the fauna rescue station. The monkeys were perhaps the saddest of the refugees, with their brooding, expressive faces and doleful eyes peering out from dark, hidden corners. I was shaken from my melancholic state of mind as I reached the penultimate cage door where a couple of small, dark shapes darted furtively towards my face. I stepped back instinctively but warmed immediately to the inquisitive little teddy-bear faces, heads cocked slightly to focus on me with their piercingly curious eyes. They were saddle-back tamarins (*Saguinus fuscicollis*), one of the most widespread and adaptable primates of the western Amazon basin.

They were surprisingly tame and barely blinked as I moved to within a couple of inches of the wire mesh that separated us. I later learned that they were so tame that they would sometimes be seen scampering curiously over parked Eletronorte bulldozers. Such behavior would be virtually unimaginable in any other wild rainforest monkey.

Much as I enjoyed meeting the tamarins, I was far more interested in making the acquaintance of their marmoset cousins, my scientific specialty. (I had studied the buffy-headed marmoset,

FIGURE 13.2   Much of the original forest has remained standing for many years after the reservoir was flooded. **Photo credit:** Provided courtesy of Stephen F. Ferrari. Photo taken by the late Liza Veiga.

Callithrix flaviceps, for my Ph.D. dissertation.) The tamarins' behavior seemed like a good omen, but I soon discovered that the local marmosets were as shy and reclusive as the tamarins were extroverted and had been captured only very rarely during the rescue operation. While I was a little disappointed not to see any marmosets, I couldn't help feeling a certain satisfaction at the idea that most of my little friends had been spared the trauma of the rescue.

Like stereotypical dog owners, primatologists tend to champion the merits of "their" species at scientific meetings as though they were noble family ancestors. I am no exception. I am a marmoset man, and let no one dare speak ill of the poor defenseless wee creatures. As the world's smallest monkeys, marmosets (*Callithrix*, *Cebuella*, and *Mico*) might look like little more than skinny little squirrels, but they have a fascinating lifestyle that I like to compare with our own in many ways. They are among the few animals able to produce their own food, for example, which provides them with many of the benefits of human agriculture.

They do this very much like the rubber tappers of the western Amazon. They gouge into the bark of certain species of trees and lianas to provoke the flow of plant gums, the edible equivalent of latex. They are able to gouge through the hardest of barks with their specialized front teeth—their jaws are like sharp little chisels—and digest the sticky substance efficiently in an enlarged and convoluted cecum, something like a grotesquely inflated appendix.

By producing their own food, marmosets are able to provide themselves with the basis for a stable family life in which husbands, uncles, aunts, cousins, and siblings all chip in to help with the raising of the young. In most cases, the mother will only take the infants to suckle them. A very civilized arrangement, if you ask me, at least from the mother's point of view.

While marmosets are found throughout most of Brazil south of the Amazon River, two species are virtually never found together, and they almost never coexist with their slightly larger tamarin cousins. Samuel turned out to be one of the few locations where they inhabit the same forest. Eletronorte's offer to sponsor a field trip felt like getting my very own golf cart to roam the chocolate factory.

After surviving an overnight flight, which stopped at half the one-horse towns in the Amazon basin, followed by an official visit to the corporation's sprawling installations (which involved shaking the hands of everyone from chief dam engineer to assistant monkey-catcher), I found myself crammed into a dusty old pickup barreling down the long, straight red line of the eastern dyke. The scenery was stark: a thick, red line bulldozed out of the green wall of the forest to our left, with a thin gray slab of water to our right.

After an eternity of rumbling gravel and billowing dust, we suddenly hit the cool, welcoming shade of the forest where the dyke abruptly turned into a muddy, winding country lane. I shrugged off my sweaty stupor instantly and began to strain my eyes for a glimpse of something interesting. This was hardly likely—the rusty iron monster would have put the fear of all the forest gods into even the most courageous of its inhabitants—but, as luck would have it, we eventually caught a fleeting glimpse of some small dark shapes darting across the road ahead.

The truck slid to a gravelly halt, and I tumbled down into the dust, eager for my first contact with the local fauna. My enthusiasm subsided as I recognized the excited chatter of some tufted capuchins (*Cebus apella*) as they disappeared into the forest. Not that these monkeys are uninteresting—on the contrary. Their behavioral complexity is second only to that of the chimpanzee, but they are among the most common and widespread primates of the Amazon basin, so they weren't very high up on my wish list.

A few miles later, the road came to an abrupt halt, literally in the middle of nowhere. Trails wandered off in three directions, and I chose the one that seemed most promising, for no better reason than the fact that it went straight ahead. It turned out to be a wise choice because I was almost immediately rewarded with the faintest of high-pitched whistles wafting through the treetops like a fleeting, almost imperceptible breath of wind. It would probably have seemed like insignificant bird twitter to most people, but I knew exactly what it was. A good ear for a vocalization is a prime requisite for a field primatologist, especially one who studies the smaller monkeys. Even the larger ones like the capuchins are almost invariably heard before seen and, more importantly, heard before they see the observer, which can make all the difference for successful tracking.

I waited, breathless and silent, for a second whistle. It was weaker than the first but emanated from a new position, and I was able to get a bearing. Luckily they were moving parallel to the trail in the direction of the road, so I was able to track them efficiently from a safe distance. They wandered closer to the trail, and I caught a glimpse of a branch swaying under the weight of a pint-sized monkey and then some fleeting shadows. I heard the chitter-chatter of excited voices. My cover had been blown, but the monkeys didn't seem to be that upset by my presence, and in fact, they continued on a beeline to the edge of the trail where I could finally focus my binoculars on something more than a shadow.

I aimed at a dark shape and when I focused, I found a familiar, teddy-bear face staring back at me. I would obviously have preferred a marmoset, but I wasn't complaining. The tamarin watched me serenely for a few moments before moving on at a tranquil pace. A second monkey popped up onto the same branch and followed the first one just as calmly. A youngster, half the size of the others, stopped to stare at me nervously for an instant but then scampered off after the others without glancing back. They really were amazingly docile animals.

FIGURE 13.3   A secretive denizen (*Mico rondoni*) of the Samuel forest.
Photo credit: Kurazo Okada.

As a fourth tamarin hopped up onto the branch, a ghostly shape suddenly appeared right next to it. I did a double-take, wondering if the jet lag and endless diplomatic meetings hadn't taken their toll on my mental faculties. But no, the image was real enough. It was a monkey, the same size as the tamarin, but a photographic negative, a pallid reflection of its dark, cuddly companion.

It was obviously a marmoset, but like none I had seen before. I was used to the fluffy types with elaborate hair styles that inhabit the mountainous forests of southeastern Brazil. This one was a skinny little devil, sparsely covered with silvery-white hair, but its strangest feature was its face, a bizarrely pink, bare face, with all the charisma of a church gargoyle. If the tamarins were as cute as teddy bears, the marmosets had all the charm of a forest goblin.

But beauty is in the eye of the beholder, and I was enthralled by this first encounter. I couldn't say the same for the marmoset. After studying me nervously for a couple of seconds, it came to the conclusion that I was some weird, hairy predator that was best avoided and hopped nimbly over the inert body of the tamarin to disappear off into the treetops. Then I noticed a different sound, an odd, whimpering sigh which I eventually discovered was the contact call of the marmosets. Recognizing these ghost-like whispers helped me to know where the marmosets were, even if I couldn't actually see them—which was almost invariably the case, unfortunately.

I knew they were there, often within a few feet of an unflustered tamarin or a few yards of me, but I was rarely able to grab more than a fleeting glimpse of a shadowy shape before it flitted away into the hidden depths of the vegetation. While I became instant friends with the tamarins, the marmosets never treated me as anything more amicable than a potential threat at a tolerable distance.

My salvation was a quirk in the tamarins' behavior. Whereas most primate species tend to keep to themselves, going about their daily business in discrete groups, saddle-back tamarins are association specialists and can be found living in tightly knit communities with other tamarin species throughout most of the western Amazon basin. These polyspecific associations, as they are called, are extremely systematic and appear to evolve under specific circumstances, where they result in certain benefits for at least one of the species involved. Marmosets are not known for this type of behavior, not least because, as we know, they are almost never found in the same forest as other marmoset or tamarin species, and associating with larger, faster monkeys would most likely be counterproductive.

Studies of tamarin associations have pointed to two main benefits for the species involved. One is the better detection of potential predators due to the doubling of the number of eyes and ears on the lookout for danger. The other benefit relates to the monkeys' foraging behavior, where these same extra eyes and ears can help locate and defend resources, such as fruiting trees, more efficiently.

Fruit may be important, but hunting prey is probably the principal factor here. Marmosets and tamarins are expert insectivores and are especially adept at catching large, mobile arthropods, in particular, grasshoppers. Grasshoppers rely on camouflage to avoid detection, but once they have been disturbed, their last resort is to hop as fast and far away as possible. While they do have wings, grasshoppers are gliders rather than fliers, and within the confines of the rainforest, they tend to ricochet noisily through the vegetation, making themselves painfully obvious to an attentive insectivore.

The more primates that are foraging together, then, the more prey are flushed and the more juicy insects are captured. As gliding grasshoppers (and similar prey, such as stick insects and tree-frogs) normally fall downwards through the canopy as they attempt to escape, the monkeys foraging lower down in the forest—normally the saddle-backs—get the better part of the deal. This is not a coincidence. Wherever and whenever saddle-backs associate with other tamarins, they always occupy the lower forest strata—it is an intrinsic, nonnegotiable part of the deal.

This is the main behavioral component of a complex of traits that contributes to the separation of the two species' niches, a necessary prerequisite for their peaceful coexistence. This includes the difference in body size—saddle-backs are barely two-thirds the size of other tamarins—and foraging behavior. While other tamarins typically sift through the vegetation for signs of prey, saddle-backs spend a good deal of their time scampering over tree trunks and investigating crevices in search of hidden insects.

One final, decisive detail is the fact that the principal predators of tamarins are birds of prey, which capture unsuspecting monkeys by swooping down on them from the sky above. This means that the animals in the higher part of the canopy also tend to be more exposed to potential predators. So the lowly saddle-backs clearly enjoy the best of both worlds, while the higher tamarin species definitely gets the raw end of the deal.

The marmosets represented a somewhat different deal. Not only are they the same size as saddle-backs, but they also prefer the lower strata of dense jungle habitats. On paper, then, they looked more like ecological competitors than foraging partners, but it was clear from our first encounter that the two species had some kind of working relationship. I was able to confirm this over the subsequent weeks, although I spent most of my time watching tamarins and listening for the marmosets. The saddle-backs played things by the book, moving deftly through the dense underbelly of the forest like a well-trained platoon of insectivorous guerillas, while the marmosets appeared to fill the ecological role of the larger tamarin species.

The saddle-backs were simply marvelous, a primatologist's dream. Whereas it would normally take two to four months of diligent tracking to prepare a group for behavioral monitoring, the saddle-backs were ready and waiting on our first morning together. By the same token, the marmosets were a living nightmare, and I doubted it would have been possible to habituate them in an even remotely adequate fashion after four years of tracking, let alone four months.

My plan was to monitor the tamarins and hope that their tranquil attitude towards human observers would eventually wear off on the marmosets. It seemed like a forlorn hope, but I have found that surprising things can happen in the field with a little patience and a lot of persistence. In the meantime, I focused all my attention on the tamarins, and I was far from disappointed by their antics. Their behavior was textbook saddle-back, and I was fascinated by their foraging technique. They would spend much of their time scurrying up and down the enormous trunks of trees such as the Brazil nut (*Bertholletia excelsa*), which has a thick, furrowed bark much like that of an oak. Curious in the extreme, they would investigate each nook and cranny of the bark with interminable patience, peering into fissures, inspecting knot holes, and poking their hands vigorously into dark crevices.

Now and again, a commotion would erupt as a spindly arm emerged from a hole with a large, boisterous insect on the end of it. A four-inch grasshopper can be a tricky handful for a nine-inch monkey, but they are expert insectivores and immobilize their prey instantaneously with a bite to the head. The successful hunter immediately becomes the center of attention, the focus of sharp, eager eyes. The youngsters squeal in anticipation and close in, hoping for some leftovers. They often get lucky—sharing food with the juveniles is one other special characteristic of the behavior of these small monkeys.

The marmosets were invariably there, somewhere. Like the opposite of good children, I could always hear them but almost never see them. On one notable occasion, however, the joint task force arrived at an enormous acacia (*Parkia pendula*) tree, which had a vast, spreading crown full of fruit. The fruits are like enormous bean pods, which hang under the crown on long stalks—hence the species name *pendula*. The pods themselves are dry and unappetizing, but they exude drooling blobs of edible gum that can provide a healthy snack for a hungry little monkey. As quick as a flash, they had spread out into the vast crown, and I suddenly realized just how large it was. They were tiny dark specks hopping along great black girders of boughs silhouetted against the clear blue sky.

As they scattered through the treetop, I finally got a full picture of the association. I counted nine tamarins and eight marmosets, not including carried infants. This was a fairly average arrangement. The inventory was important because, while I would often see four or five tamarins at a time, I don't think I had ever spotted more than a single marmoset at any given moment.

They reached the gummy pods, which were about the same size as an adult monkey, by edging cautiously along the thin stalks, upside down, anchored firmly by their feet. They licked the gum up avidly with their long, thin tongues, apparently oblivious to the fact that they were literally face-to-face with a sheer drop of more than a hundred feet to the forest floor.

After half an hour or so of gorging themselves on this sticky feast, the whole crowd of them slipped back into the denser vegetation for a well-earned siesta. Later on in the afternoon, I followed the tamarins as they foraged in the undergrowth of a shady forest dell. A couple of them were scampering up and down a small trunk right next to me, literally within arm's reach. Suddenly one of them stopped. He perched on the side of the trunk suspended on his clawlike nails and stared straight at me. We were eye-to-eye, six or seven feet apart, and as I gazed into the depths of those little honey-almond eyes, I suddenly understood why the saddle-backs were so tame. It was part of their deal, an integral component of their specialization for a communal way of life. Natural selection had molded their behavior to the point where they are instinctively tolerant of any mammal that was obviously not a predator, be it a marmoset, another tamarin, or a rather sweaty and disheveled *Homo sapiens*.

My little friend cocked his head as if to agree with my conclusions, and then he hopped further on up the trunk to the crown of the tree. It was a small tree, perfectly formed, with a dense, spherical crown some twenty feet from the forest floor. I spotted some round, green fruits, which looked like custard apples (Annonaceae), each about the size of a small peach.

The tamarin trotted nimbly along a horizontal branch until he reached a fruit and stopped to pick at it with his tiny, elongated fingers. I wasn't sure why he didn't just bite a chunk right out of it, but before he could make up his mind, a gangly black shadow came crashing down from above. I almost fell over backwards in surprise, and when I recovered my wits, I found that the tamarin's place in the treetop had been usurped by a large black-faced spider monkey (*Ateles chamek*), who grabbed the fruit with a long, spindly arm and rammed it unceremoniously into its mouth, sending chunks of green peel spinning every which way.

In what seemed like the same instant, the twenty-pound monkey bounced upwards, grabbed a branch with its amazingly long prehensile tail, and then rushed back up from where it had come in a whoosh of shaking branches. The poor little tamarin was nowhere to be seen, and I could only hope he had made it to safety in time. Despite the rudeness of the spider monkey's behavior, it was more typical of the relationship between species than the tamarins' instinctive tolerance. It's the basic law of the wild—the bigger species almost always have the upper hand over the smaller ones.

The tamarins wreaked a vengeance of sorts the following day, however. It had been a routine day: the marmosets upstairs, the tamarins downstairs, a breakfast of juicy grasshoppers, and a brunch of small red fruit followed by a tranquil midday siesta. We were foraging for insects in the flaccid mid-afternoon heat when something strange happened. The shift in behavior was almost imperceptible at first, but I suddenly realized that most of the tamarins had disappeared, leaving me in the almost exclusive company of the surreptitious marmosets.

Breaking from the usually tight-knit association, the foremost tamarins had hurried on ahead, forming a vanguard that was now signaling back to the stragglers with the characteristic whistles used for long-distance communication. When we finally caught up, it didn't take me long to understand what had happened. They had made a beeline for a marmoset gum-feeding tree, which was heavily pockmarked with gouge holes.

The tamarins were scurrying all over the tree, darting purposefully from hole to hole, but as soon as the marmosets turned up, they made themselves scarce. The marmosets spread out in an orderly fashion, moving nimbly up and down the thickly scarred trunk. This was the first and last time I had what I would consider an adequate view of them, such was their concentration on the task in hand. They were going from hole to hole, inspecting them for gum deposits, but finding absolutely nothing. The tamarins had sucked them dry.

Their whimpering sighs became a poignant lament, a lilting whisper of frustrated indignation. I had unexpectedly stumbled upon the final secret of the saddle-back-marmoset association— the tamarins appeared to be parasitizing the marmosets' gum-producing abilities. This was a cruel twist to the story for the marmosets. Gum is a "fallback" food for these small monkeys, a standby resource that helps them get through periods when fruit is in short supply. Producing gum demands time, energy, and know-how, so having their supply usurped by their supposed associates was a double blow and potentially a source of considerable hardship for the poor, unassuming marmosets.

As if to confirm this, they suddenly stopped vocalizing altogether, as if mourning their loss, and the forest was filled with an eerie silence.

This seemed to stack the benefits of association even higher in favor of the saddle-backs, and the relationship between the two species increasingly appeared to be more exploitative than mutual. I was able to confirm my suspicions a few years later, when the state government invited me to survey the region's biodiversity. My team and I surveyed 21 sites in northern Rondônia, and we found tamarins at most of them; the marmosets, however, were very thin on the ground, or even in the treetops, for that matter, and we were able to confirm their presence at only four locations.

My hypothesis is that the saddle-backs are actually out-competing the marmosets in an undeclared ecological war and may even be taking over their territory. Their exploitation of the marmosets' gum-holes may be the critical point here because it not only confers a considerable ecological advantage on the tamarins, but perhaps more importantly, it represents a major deficit for the marmosets. As for any subsistence farmer, crop failure can result in considerable hardship, and persistent failure may even force migration. The marmosets may simply find it impossible to coexist with the tamarins at many sites.

While I never did get very intimate with the marmosets in the field, I always felt there was something special about them, and after some meticulous detective work, which included detailed morphological and genetic analyses and the careful mapping of geographic distributions, my colleagues and I came to the conclusion that they represented a distinct species. It wasn't so much a firework-popping discovery as a correction of the original classification, which had identified the species as *Mico emiliae*, which we now know occurs only some 300 miles east of Rondônia. But it did mean that my own association with the marmosets from Samuel would go down in posterity, because they are now known formally by their full name of *Mico rondoni* Ferrari, Sena, Schneider, & Silva Junior, 2010.

FIGURE 13.4   The author, Steve Ferrari, in the field. **Photo credit:** Sirley Baião.

The final twist to this tale is that this brand new species is already listed as vulnerable to extinction by the International Union for Conservation of Nature (IUCN). This is because the species is not only restricted to a relatively small area of northern Rondônia but is also quite rare. In fact, if my hypothesis about the tamarins is correct, *Mico rondoni* may be the only monkey species being driven towards extinction by a nonhuman primate (*Saguinus fuscicollis*), rather than the ubiquitous and destructive *Homo sapiens*.

Suggested Readings

Ferrari, S. F., and E. S. Martins. 1992. "Gummivory and Gut Morphology in Two Sympatric Callitrichids (*Callithrix emiliae* and *Saguinus fuscicollis weddelli*) from Western Brazilian Amazonia." *American Journal of Physical Anthropology* 88: 97–103.

Ferrari, S. F., L. Sena, M. P. C. Schneider, and J. S. Silva Junior. 2010. "Rondon's Marmoset, *Mico rondoni* sp.n., from Southwestern Brazilian Amazonia." *International Journal of Primatology* 31: 693–714.

Lopes, M. A., and S. F. Ferrari. 1994. "Foraging Behaviour of a Tamarin Group (*Saguinus fuscicollis weddelli*), and Interactions with Marmosets (*Callithrix emiliae*)." *International Journal of Primatology* 15: 373–387.

Oliveira, M. M., A. B. Rylands, S. F. Ferrari, and J. S. Silva Jr. 2008. *Mico rondoni*. In IUCN 2013. IUCN Red List of Threatened Species. Version 2013.1 <www.iucnredlist.org>

Terbogh, J. 1983. *Five New World Monkeys: A Study in Comparative Ecology*. Princeton, NJ: Princeton University Press.

Acknowledgments

The fieldwork described in this essay was made possible through the support of Eletronorte, the Goeldi Museum, DHV Consultants, the Rondônia state government, and the Brazilian National Research Council (CNPq). Many people contributed to the study, but I would especially like to thank Rubens Ghilardi, Jr., Horacio Schneider, Iracilda Sampaio, and Ernesto Cruz.

14

There's a Monkey in My Kitchen (and I Like It)
Fieldwork with Macaques in Bali and Beyond

By Agustín Fuentes[1]

In July 1999 I was sitting under the immense banyan tree in the central plaza of the Padantegal Monkey Forest in Bali, Indonesia, when the most dominant of the three macaque groups at the site began moving up into the trees and the terraced hillside above the main temple. Cautiously, the temple group we had labeled "group 3" meandered, tentatively, in to take their place. Ten of my twelve students followed the group, slowly walking behind the individual monkeys they were observing, madly jotting down notes and trying to avoid eye contact with the multitude of young monkeys scurrying about their feet and occasionally grabbing at their water bottles and dangling binoculars. Pulling out my notebook, I noticed the adult female we had named "Teardrop" trailing by about 30 feet from any other monkey. She had a white birthmark in the shape of a tear just below her left eye, and she always seemed to be set apart from the rest of the group. My attention switched to Arnold, the dominant male, and Short-tail, the alpha female, as they teamed up to take a cluster of papaya leaves and a prized half coconut from two low-ranking males. Then I noticed Teardrop again: She had sat down about 10 feet from me. A few staccato alarm barks took my attention as a dog tried to run through the plaza but was chased by the "boys," a fluid group of between five and twelve young male macaques that seemed to always be causing a ruckus somewhere in group 3. When I glanced back to my right I noticed that Teardrop was sitting about 3 feet from me, seemingly staring at a leaf on the ground and absent-mindedly scratching her side. I scanned the plaza to get an idea of the groups' spread and starting writing down the locations and noting the clusters of females and young. Then, I felt a slight warmth on my right thigh. Looking down I noticed that Teardrop was sitting right next to me, her left hand on

[1]About the author: Agustín Fuentes, trained in Zoology and Anthropology, is a Professor of Anthropology at the University of Notre Dame. His research delves into the how and why of being human. Current projects focus on cooperation and community in human evolution, ethnoprimatology and multispecies anthropology, evolutionary theory, and interdisciplinary approaches to human nature(s). Recent books include "Evolution of Human Behavior" (Oxford) and "Race, Monogamy, and other lies they told you: busting myths about human nature" (U of California).

Contact information: Department of Anthropology, University of Notre Dame, Notre Dame, IN 46556, USA, afuentes@nd.edu

Citation: Fuentes, A. 2014. "There's a Monkey in My Kitchen (and I Like It): Fieldwork with Macaques in Bali and Beyond." In Strier, K. B. (ed.), *Primate Ethnographies*. Upper Saddle River, NJ: Pearson Education, Inc. (pp. 151–162).

FIGURE 14.1   The author (Agustín Fuentes) with macaques in Bali. **Photo credit:** Devi Snively.

my thigh. She was looking away—I held still. Slowly, over the next few minutes she calmly leaned into me. We did not look at each other, nor did we move, for about ten minutes. Then she got up, looked around, cast a sideways glance at me, and walked away.

During the next few years we would discover that this was a typical behavior for Teardrop. Unable to have offspring, she was never quite able to work herself into any of the clusters of females and young that made up the social core of the group. But she did, on occasion, sidle up next to humans and lean into them, sometimes even groom their hair. Obviously, as an observer one is not supposed to interact in such a manner with the monkeys, but she had a way of sneaking up and settling next to you, such that getting up would have drawn attention from the other group members and caused more of a problem than sitting there. As a monkey, she needed physical and social contact to live. As a macaque, she was sly enough to realize that if she could not get it from her group mates, there were plenty of large-bodied, relatively hairless, somewhat less savvy primates to get in a bit of contact time with when she wanted it.

This was an early and important insight into the world of cross-species relationships between humans and other primates. Teardrop and all of the other macaques at the temple forest of Padang-tegal taught me many lessons, the most important being that monkeys don't read textbooks, and therefore they don't always behave according to our preconceptions about them. They are dynamic and complex social beings. The only sure way to learn about, and understand, the amazingly rich and intricate life of other primates is to be with them, to observe them, in the place they live.

My introduction to primates occurred when I was juggling too many majors, protest sit-ins, concerts, parties, and all the other bits of being an undergraduate student at the University of

California, Berkeley, in the mid-1980s. One late summer day I was sitting in the first lecture of a primate social behavior class taught by the anthropologist Phyllis Dolhinow. She stood up in front of the class and launched into a description of the lives of a female langur and then a female chimpanzee, revealing the social intrigue, the raising of young, the dealing with adult males and other females, the search for food every day, and the complicated and amazingly exciting life of being a primate. That was it. My search was over and I was hooked. I whittled down my majors to two (anthropology and zoology), and with Professor Dolhinow's help and guidance, I finished my undergraduate career and began my graduate studies at UC Berkeley in Biological Anthropology.

Within three years of that influential lecture, I flew across the Pacific to Indonesia to spend two months travelling the archipelago in search of a field site to study primates in the wild for my Ph.D. One of my first stops was Birute Galdikas' site at Tanjung Putting, Kalimantan, on the island of Borneo. I spent a few weeks looking at macaques, chasing fleeting glimpses of leaf monkeys, and living with a camp full of researchers, local assistants, and a lot of real, live, and large orangutans. The reality, wild and yet fascinating, of the interface between all of these worlds, primates, people, research, conservation, political and economic realities, languages, and beliefs stuck with me.

Humans and other primates share a very long and complicated relationship. More than just us hunting them, more than just our species and their species competing for food and space, we have actually shared and helped shape each other's ecologies, health, and evolutionary histories. My experiences in the field have been the main forces that led to my involvement in/commitment to the emerging field of ethnoprimatology. My primate ethnography is about experiences in the intriguing landscape at what we call the "interface" between macaque monkeys and humans. This refers to the behavioral, ecological, social, and historical realities of the places where people and other primates overlap in space and time, sharing ecologies and histories. My core research in this area occurs in three different locations: Bali, Gibraltar, and Singapore.

BALI: MY BASIC TRAINING IN THE HUMAN-MACAQUE INTERFACE

In 1989 and 1990 I visited research sites across Indonesia, settling on the ultra-remote Mentawai islands for my dissertation work. Between 1990 and 1996 my primary focus was on the primates of the Mentawais, but every time I travelled to Indonesia I spent a little time on the island of Bali, specifically with the long-tailed macaques (*Macaca fascicularis*) and the people of the Padangtegal Monkey Forest. Most people know this site by the neighboring village of Ubud, which is a famous arts tourism destination. The monkey forest is often associated with Ubud, but in actuality it belongs to the village of Padangtegal. My first publication was on the unusual object manipulations of the macaques at the monkey forest, and there was something about the place that kept me coming back—I just wasn't sure what it was yet.

In 1996 I took my first tenure track job as an assistant professor at Central Washington University-CWU, and realized that it was time to move into a new research program that could form the infrastructure for a long-term research investment, provide a training ground for undergraduate students, and integrate my interests from anthropology, biology, and primatology. It took maybe about three days of consideration before I decided to try and start up a project at Padangtegal.

During the early to mid-1990s, I had collaborated with Professor Bruce Wheatley of the University of Alabama, Birmingham, on the project he had been running at this site. Bruce's interests focused not solely on the monkeys, but also on their relations to the local Balinese and

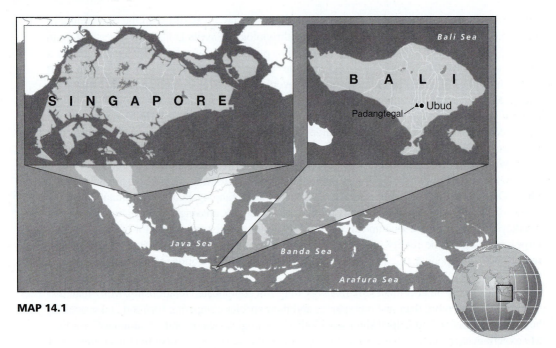

MAP 14.1

their roles in Balinese Hindu beliefs, temples, and as important parts of the tourist economy. His work formed the perfect jumping off point for my new project. After discussions with him I contacted his main colleague at the local Universitas Udayana and set up a pilot study and a field school for the summer of 1998. This became a core formative experience in my research, my education, and my life.

Collaborating with the newly founded Primate Research Institute, or Pusat Kajian Primata, at Universitas Udayana (UNUD-PKP), and the priests and temple management committee at the Monkey Forest in a busy and developed central Balinese town was a very different experience from the much more isolated conditions of Mentawais. Instead of being on the edge of the known world, days from any village of size and such basic things as hospitals, stores, or phone lines, I was now smack dab in the middle of a modern, bustling Indonesian and Balinese town. The tourist infrastructure was substantial, the monkey forest pulled in some income of its own, the human density was over 600 people per square kilometer, and in the midst of all of this lived more than 100 macaques, divided into three social groups, at a temple site with a small forest surrounded by villages, rice crops, and roads. Also, my collaborators at the UNUD-PKP were degreed veterinarians, virologists, and researchers, scientific colleagues tied into a global world, different from the Mentawai villagers who had never seen a computer, a paved road, or even a multistory building.

The crux of the matter at Padantegal was that the people and the monkeys shared space but also competed for it. For nearly five centuries, people and monkeys had overlapped in this same space. The local Balinese used the temple grounds on a daily basis—sometimes for small prayers, other times for enormous ceremonies. The macaques lived in and around the temple forest, moving out of the Balinese's way when necessary and reaping the benefits of the edible offerings left after ceremonies. The monkeys occasionally raided the surrounding rice fields and small shops and restaurants. However, starting in the early 1990s, thousands of tourists from around the world began coming to the Monkey Forest, taking pictures, wandering around the plazas and temples, and, occasionally, stepping on macaques' tails. The macaques took advantage of the tourists, who often had bags of food, water bottles, and an assortment of shiny glasses, hats, and knick-knacks within easy reach. As tourists increased, so did the number of shops and food stalls near the forest and the opportunities for monkey-human conflict. It was in the midst of this changing social and ecological reality that our project began.

That first field season was an eye opener. In June 1998 I flew out with my team of eight undergraduate students from the United States and my partner, who was the project videographer. A French graduate student met us at the site. We spent nearly two months observing the monkeys and interacting with our colleagues and the local villagers and temple staff. I learned an amazing amount about teaching, training undergraduate students, research methodologies, and international collaborations. We had every up and down imaginable—great successes and a few real problems—but ended up with an amazing data set. We were also on hand as the Indonesian economy tanked, and the dictator of nearly thirty years was overthrown! In addition, we produced a successful documentary video that chronicled the whole experience and can be found in many university libraries (*Primates like Us*, Dir. Devi Snively, Berkley Media LLC).

The biggest take-home for me was the realization about a new kind of primatological research project that blends cultural anthropology and primatology and many more "-ologies": the field of ethnoprimatology. I finally understood what kept me coming back to Bali: Monkeys and humans shared more than space—they live together, have lived together, and, unlike in many other places, they might do so successfully into the future.

The focused work at Padantegal ran from 1998 to 2003, and the larger Balinese Macaque Project, which expanded the fieldwork from the site of Padantegal to encompass the entire island, ran through 2007. During that time period I moved from Central Washington University to the University of Notre Dame, continued with a range of research and field school projects, collaborated with a wider array of colleagues, and made many, many friends. During this ten-year period many other researchers joined the project ranging from cultural anthropologists, primatologists, and geographers, to economists and virologists, to medical doctors and population geneticists. From it all I learned that watching and thinking about monkeys, and collaborating with and training humans, is difficult, but extremely rewarding. I also gained an awareness of the incredibly deep and complicated connections between the peoples, the monkeys, and their shared ecologies. I learned many things in Bali, but four stick in my mind: (a) management matters, (b) primates are amazingly complex, (c) the human-macaque interface can tell us a lot about ecosystems, and (d) science, especially fieldwork, is never conducted outside of a cultural context. Let me briefly illustrate these lessons with examples.

Let's start with the amazingly complex and fascinating social behavior of these macaques. During the five years of focused behavioral and ecological data collection at Padantegal, I was constantly modifying our methods and reappraising what I "knew" about primates. For example, in college I learned that macaque male dominance hierarchies are relatively rigid, involve a lot of fighting, and that they relate to mating success with females. I had also learned that male macaques show little interest in infants and that macaque monkeys do not use tools like chimpanzees. Every one of these assumptions, seen as primatological "facts" in the 1980s and early 1990s, was changed in some way during my observations. Males did fight and the dominance hierarchies were easily observable, but they were also really dynamic and subject to all sorts of twists and turns. Our detailed observations of three males who became alpha animals showed us that each one did so in a totally distinct manner. One held sway through sheer aggression and intimidation, vigorously attacking everyone (human and macaque) around him. Another gained

FIGURE 14.2 Crab-eating macaques of the Padangtegal Monkey Forest, near Ubud, Bali. **Photo credit:** Agustín Fuentes.

status by avoiding males and spending all of his time with females, mating and grooming with them until all the females in the group backed his bid to supplant the alpha male. This also showed us how the social backbone of groups, clusters of related females, could use their social capital to cause changes in the group structure. The third male did fight, but rarely by himself— rather almost always with three other males at his side. The surprising thing was that once alpha, he never mated. He rejected females' advances nearly 100 percent of the time, preferring to hang out and play with young juveniles or to groom females (and other males!) instead. Many of the males, not just high-ranking ones, showed great interest in youngsters, holding them and even carrying them. We even observed one case of a young mother passing away and an adult male adopting her young infant and raising it successfully.

From my earliest work at the site in 1990, I realized that these macaques were using rocks and sticks in ways that my coursework-based training told me they wouldn't. One female used twigs and leaves to groom others. Many youngsters stacked rocks, washed food and other items by rubbing them on rocks, and dug up bits of roots with rocks. While not as complex or exciting as chimpanzee tool use, recent work has definitely demonstrated that this species of macaque can and does use tools in a wide variety of ways.

Not surprisingly, management of the population was a core concern for the local Balinese. In 1998 there were 122 monkeys in three groups at Padantegal. In 2002 there were 204. By 2010 there were more than 500 in five groups. This population growth reflects the "success" of the research project and the reality that human-macaque relationships are complicated. Over the years, my students, the UNUD-PKP staff, and I worked closely with the temple manager, Pak Wayan Selamet and his staff to improve conditions for both the monkeys and the tourists. Based on the data on human and monkey behavior accumulating from our research, we curtailed the feeding of high-fat and high-carbohydrate foods by tourists and initiated monkey feeding plan in which the temple staff provisioned the monkeys at multiple locations with diverse and nutritious foods. While not stopping conflicts between monkeys or between monkeys and people, our efforts made them much more manageable and improved the experience for humans and macaques alike.

We also realized that, as Bruce Wheatley and colleagues had noted before, the local version of Balinese Hinduism played a role in shaping how the macaque-human interface played out. The core role for Hanuman, the monkey king, and his macaque minions in Hindu myths and many Balinese dances and plays created a sort of cultural backdrop predisposing the Balinese to a relatively generous view of macaques, especially those that live in and around temples. This enabled the Monkey Forest management team to rapidly and effectively influence the local attitudes and behavior towards the macaques and helped smooth over conflicts that arose as the population grew. The UNUD-PKP delivered veterinary assistance, and together we monitored the macaque population for changes in behavior, health, and ranging. Each year we went over the data with the temple management staff and made ourselves available to them as a sounding board and a working group so that the data were immediately and directly applied to the real-time needs of the local populations; the situation improved all around, and the tourist income from the forest grew dramatically; however, so did the monkey population. At the same time, the surrounding towns grew and tourist-related business increased, leading to more hotels and restaurants increasing the lure for monkeys waiting to get into their kitchens and trash dumps. This growth continues through today and a new research project, led by the Belgian primatologist Fany Brotcorne, is currently working with the Monkey Forest management to understand and deal with the spoils of management success: a super-healthy growing macaque population and a finite amount of space.

During my work at Padangtegal I saw the intrinsic importance in the human-macaque relationship, with monkeys, tourists, and locals dancing through intricate relationships that had behavioral, health, economic, religious, and possibly even evolutionary implications. This pushed me to expand the analysis of human and macaques on Bali across the island. In collaboration with biologists Hope Hollocher and Kelly Lane, our team created an overview of the whole island, mapping macaque populations and the human landscape. This made it look like the ways in which the Balinese used and perceived the land had huge effects on the shape and structure of macaques' lives. We had to look further to see the big picture. In collaboration with primate pathogen experts, population geneticists, biologists, and computer scientists, we sampled DNA and macaque and human pathogens, developed a very intensive computer analysis, and eventually realized that centuries (or millennia) of interaction between humans and macaques in a shared island ecosystem has shaped the bodies and behavior of both (probably more so for the macaques than the humans, however). The human-macaque interface is an important ecosystem in Bali, one that has to be studied at multiple levels to get any real idea of what is actually going on behaviorally, ecologically, or evolutionarily.

Unfortunately, not all of the outcomes from the project were as positive or as encouraging as the data. Working with colleagues from the UNUD-PKP and dealing with Indonesian regional and federal governmental agencies forced me to realize how privileged I was to have the kind of financial and resource-rich infrastructure that I had back in the United States. Even as a graduate student I had better access to books, articles, and grants than the majority of Indonesians practicing primatology. As a professor my pay was much higher, my ability to generate research funding much better, and my support from the university much deeper than that available to my Indonesian colleagues. These kinds of inequalities are extremely common in the world of professional primatology and until recently were not usually brought to light in published articles and in the training of students. The legacy of colonialism and the disparities between nations are part of the human ecosystem and cannot be ignored, no matter how one tries. In primatology this intrinsic inequality can create disequilibrium and cause problems for collaborations via misguided expectations and perceptions of gain on the part of the collaborators and ignorance of social, political, and economic realities (and histories) by the North American or European primatologists. Expectations, cultural barriers, economics, politics, and miscommunication/perception can seriously impede research progress and hinder collaborations from reaching their maximum output, effectiveness, and truly equitable outcomes. The Bali project was no different. After many years of fruitful, and sometimes frustrating, collaboration, it was these kinds of discordances in perception, goals, and the role of economic versus intellectual partnerships that ultimately led to the end of my work in Bali, Indonesia in 2007.

GIBRALTAR AND SINGAPORE: EXPANDING THE MACAQUE-HUMAN INTERFACE STUDIES

Macaques and humans overlap in fascinating and complicated ways in many other areas on the planet. I chose two of these, Gibraltar and Singapore, as my next field sites. Gibraltar drew me in, as it was on the Iberian Peninsula (with Spain and Portugal), had a multicentury interface between macaques and humans, and is the only place in Europe with free-ranging primates. Singapore is an island in Southeast Asia with a lot of humans and a robust population of *Macaca fascicularis*, like Bali. Unlike Bali, however, Singapore is one of the highest-density urban environments on the planet and one of the most developed places in the world. I thought it would make a particularly interesting comparative context for the Bali data.

Gibraltar is the small British colony at the very southern tip of the Iberian Peninsula. Claimed by Spain but controlled by the British for the last 300-plus years, the city of Gibraltar sits along the western slopes of the Rock of Gibraltar, upon which approximately 240 Barbary macaques (*Macaca sylvanus*) live in the Upper Rock Nature Reserve. These macaques (called "apes" by the locals, probably due to their lack of tails) have occupied the rock for at least 400 years and probably much longer. They are one of the main tourist attractions of Gibraltar, and hundreds of thousands of visitors interact with them every year. However, a few of the macaque groups also range into the city of Gibraltar and the small town of Caleta Bay on the eastern slope of the rock, where they raid garbage cans, sneak into peoples' kitchens, and generally annoy the residents closest to the reserve.

In the summer of 1989, before I had visited Indonesia, I was spending time with my family in Madrid, Spain, and decided to pop down to Gibraltar to visit the monkeys and chat with a Gibraltarian primatologist who had been studying them. The positive sensations of that visit, although it was brief, stayed with me for the next 15 years. By 2003, as I was winding down the Padangtegal-focused fieldwork, and had just moved to the University of Notre Dame, I wanted to develop a new field site to continue my focus on human–monkey interactions and take groups of undergraduate students for field schools and as part of research teams. Gibraltar's location next to Spain, my ancestral home, and a species of macaques that has interacted with people there for centuries made Gibraltar a very attractive choice. I decided to visit again, and contacted the NGO managing the monkeys—the Gibraltar Ornithological and Natural History Society (GONHS)—to see what we could come up with. Apart from a few articles published on the human–macaque interface in Gibraltar in the early 1990s, no studies were ongoing, and GONHS was very interested in facilitating more work. That settled it. Since 2004 I have conducted two field schools, two smaller-scale research trips, and directed a number of independent student research projects

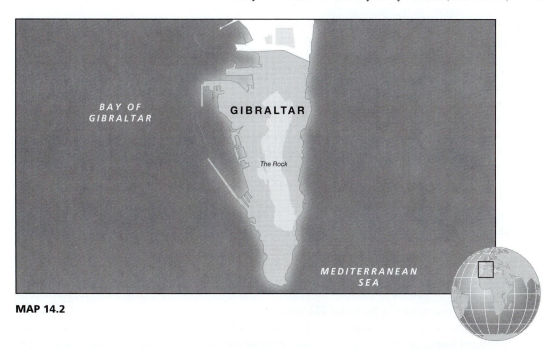

MAP 14.2

FIGURE 14.3   Barbary macaques have lived in proximity with humans on the Rock of Gibraltar for centuries. **Photo credit:** Agustín Fuentes.

there. My collaborators include some of my previous colleagues from the Bali project, GONHS, and both local and international veterinarians.

I decided to extend the interaction study from Bali by building a comparative data set with the Gibraltar macaques. This kind of approach allows us to see what behavior patterns might be specific to local ecologies, and different macaque species, and what might be shared across sites, ecologies, and species. Interestingly, the larger and more powerful macaques of Gibraltar were much calmer and less aggressive, with few conflicts and almost no biting, in their interactions with humans compared to those on Bali. The explanation for this mixes aspects of behavioral differences in these species of macaques (*M. sylvanus* versus *M. fascicularis*) with local management styles, tourist behavior, and the structure of the landscape.

These findings reinforced the lessons of Bali: There are no simple explanations, and the human-monkey interface is influenced by many different variables. However, there were a few fascinating similarities, for in both studies (1) adult male macaques and adult male humans were the most interactive and the most aggressive; (2) adult male macaques also got most of the tourist-provided food and young monkeys got the least; and (3) adult female humans were most likely to receive aggression from monkeys. While we are still examining the causal factors in these similarities, most of our results point to a heavy influence of human cultural patterns and the macaques' abilities to interpret them and exploit them, combined with common patterns of dominance hierarchies in the genus *Macaca*.

It appears that tourist nationality, feeding pattern and control by the monkey managers, and the role of tourist guides (in Bali) and their Gibraltar counterparts (taxi drivers) also influence the behavioral patterns that we observed. For example, in Bali we found that tourists from countries with no monkeys were slightly more likely to be bitten, and this was even more extreme for females from Northern Europe. In Gibraltar, where nearly all the tourists were from Europe, there were only slight differences between nationalities, but larger ones based on whether the tourists came on foot, via taxi, or a bus from visiting cruise ships. In both locations, the number-one predictor of having a conflict with the monkeys was carrying food and trying to keep the monkeys away from it. In Gibraltar taxi drivers initiated a majority of the interactions with macaques, and in Bali, tour guides had substantial influence on the quality and outcome of human–macaque interactions for their tour groups.

While macaques raided shops, hotels, and homes at both sites, the overall response and the range of responses by humans were much greater in Gibraltar than in Bali. At both sites the macaques are valuable economic resources and play some role in local myths. For the Balinese the inclusion in religious mythology is very deep and intertwined with art and social life, whereas in Gibraltar they are part of a political history related to the British control of the territory and are as often maligned as pests as they are seen as an integral component of Gibraltar's physical and historical landscape.

Jumping from Bali to Singapore seemed like a natural experiment in the making. Initial fieldwork in 2006, 2007, and 2009 set the stage for this project, which is ongoing today. As noted earlier, the macaques are the same species as in Bali (*M. fascicularis*), but the context is remarkably different. Singapore is a tiny island country of millions of people at the Southern tip of the Malayan peninsula, just above the equator, that simultaneously has one of the most modern cities in the world and about 1,800 macaques. While most of Singapore is high-rise buildings, shopping districts, expressways, and industry, the center of the island has some substantial areas of rainforest, and small forest patches are found throughout.

Singapore is a terrific comparative project for the Bali data—with the same macaque species but in a markedly different ecological context. Also, because Singapore is wealthy and quite well developed with regard to infrastructure (better than most places in the United States), and my collaborators are with the National Parks Board, the Singapore Zoo, and the local, well-funded universities, there are none of the problems associated with inequities and disequilibria found in Indonesia. This makes working there both fairly easy and quite productive.

The data from our few field seasons in Singapore demonstrate how absolutely important social and ecological contexts are. Given the infrastructure of Singapore, the social control exerted by the government, and the regular and efficient management of natural areas, Singapore has the highest density of people per macaque but the lowest rate of interactions and conflict of any of the three sites. The groups of macaques are smaller than in Bali, and rather than living in temples, the monkeys in Singapore live in forest patches in parks and near housing complexes, and even roam free on the grounds of the Singapore Zoo. The really interesting aspect of the human-macaque interface here is as follows: How do the monkeys and humans co-exist in such a dense urban environment? Humans living near parks complain about monkeys raiding their garbage cans and stealing into their kitchens, but our observations showed very little of that actually happening (at least when we were watching). The trick to solving this puzzle, it seems, is to get really high-quality data on where the monkeys actually go and what they actually do. So starting in 2011, along with Amy Klegarth, Lisa Jones-Engel and colleagues, I experimented with placing satellite GPS collars on a few monkeys, which worked extremely well. We are also collecting fecal samples to replicate the genetics and pathogen studies from the Bali project, which should give us some real insight into the history of the Singapore macaques and of *Macaca fascicularis* across Southeast Asia. The next few years should result in some spectacular data about monkeys living, successfully, in and around one of the highest-human-density places on the planet.

Take-Home Points

Since 1989 I have spent many years in different field conditions, watching monkeys, chasing monkeys, watching people, and interacting with them all. My experiences showed me how naïve I had been about primate behavior and about the politics/economics of conducting field research. Before going into the field, I had completed coursework and behavioral research on primates in captivity, and I had spoken with fieldworkers and read copious amounts of the primatological and anthropological literature—all of which I realized was important background once I found myself in the field and had to really learn what to do. I encourage all of you who are thinking of entering the field of primatology to prepare as best you can. Learn as much as possible about the people and places where you'll be working—the language, history, and ecology—and be prepared for the moment near the start of your first field season when you realize what Socrates meant when he said, "As for me, all I know is that I know nothing."

Watching primates can teach us much about the world and about ourselves. I am convinced that we can benefit substantially from studying other primates who live alongside humans. There are extremely few places on the planet where human impact is not felt, and almost all primate populations exist in anthropogenic ecologies. As we look forward into the twenty-first century, extinctions of some primate species are inevitable, but conservation efforts will continue for many others. However, if we can glean relevant information from primates, like macaques, who have co-existed alongside people for centuries or more, we might be able to switch our focus from conservation of primates in general to management of the human–other primate interface. As humans we have a cognitive capacity to alter the planet like no other species and to reflect on what that means. We are primates, and we owe it to ourselves and our primate cousins to work hard for a sustainable future.

Suggested Readings

Fuentes, A. 2002. "Monkeys, Humans, and Politics in the Mentawai Islands: No Simple Solutions in a Complex World." In Fuentes, A., and L. D. Wolfe (eds.), *Primates Face to Face: The Conservation Implications of Human and Nonhuman Primate Interconnections*. Cambridge University Press (pp. 187–207).

Fuentes, A. 2010. "Naturecultural Encounters in Bali: Monkeys, Temples, Tourists, and Ethnoprimatology." *Cultural Anthropology* 25 (4): 600–624.

Fuentes, A. 2012. "Ethnoprimatology and the Anthropology of the Human-primate Interface." *Ann. Rev. Anthropol.* 41:101–17, doi: 10.1146/annurev-anthro-092611-145808.

Fuentes, A., E. Shaw, and J. Cortes. 2007. "A Qualitative Assessment of Macaque Tourist Sites in Padangtegal, Bali, Indonesia, and the Upper Rock Nature Reserve, Gibraltar." *International Journal of Primatology* 28: 1143–1158.

Fuentes, A., A. L. T. Rompis, I. G. A. Arta Putra, N. L. Watiniasih, I. N. Suartha, I. G. Soma, I. N. Wandia, I. D. K. Harya Putra, R. Stephenson, and W. Selamet. 2011. "Macaque Behavior at the Human–Monkey Interface: The Activity and Demography of Semi-Free Ranging *Macaca fascicularis* at Padangtegal, Bali, Indonesia." In Gumert, M. D., A. Fuentes, and L. Jones-Engel (eds.), *Monkeys on the Edge: Ecology and Management of Long-tailed Macaques and their Interface with Humans*. Cambridge University Press, pp. 159–179.

Lane, K. K., M. Lute, A. Rompis, I. N. Wandia, I. G. A. Arta Putra, H. Hollocher, and A. Fuentes. 2010. "Pests, Pestilence, and People: The Long-Tailed Macaque and Its Role in the Cultural Complexities of Bali." In S. Gursky-Doyen and J. Supriatna (eds.), *Indonesian Primates, Developments in Primatology: Progress and Prospects*. Springer Science (pp. 235–248).

Acknowledgments

A list of all those who have helped and supported me across these last 20-plus years of fieldwork would be longer than the essay itself. So here is the abbreviated version: Let me thank my many colleagues at the University Udayana, particularly I. D. K. Harya Putra, Aida Rompis. I. Arta Putra, and Komang Gde Suaryana, the Institut Pertanian Bogor, Lembaga Ilmu Pengetahuan Indonesia, and Pak Wayan Selamet, the Padantegal monkey forest management committee, and the villages of Padantegal and Ubud for facilitating my work in Bali. I also want to acknowledge my many collaborators on the Bali project, especially Lisa Jones-Engel, Gregory Engel, Hope Hollocher, Kelly Lane, and many other folks from Central Washington University, University of Colorado, University of Guam, University of Notre Dame, and the University of Toronto. John Cortes, Eric Shaw, and Mark Pizarro, and all the GONHS staff who made the projects in Gibraltar so successful, and Benjamin Lee and colleagues at the Singapore National Parks Board, the Singapore Zoo, and Michael Gumert of Nanyang Technological Institute, who make working in Singapore a pleasure. I want to give special thanks to Amy Klegarth for her excellent, and pioneering, work on the Singapore and Gibraltar projects.

Partial funding for much of this field work came from Central Washington University, the University of Notre Dame Institute for Scholarship in the Liberal Arts, the National Science Foundation, the Waitt and National Geographic Foundations, and Conservation Inc.

15

Gorillas Across
Time and Space

By Martha M. Robbins[1]

In November 2009 I was making a field visit with Sosthène Habumuremyi, a Rwandan Ph.D. student who I was supervising. As we proceeded into the forest, I realized I was completely out of breath for two reasons. First, I was hiking uphill on a muddy trail at 10,000 feet altitude in the Virunga Volcanoes of Rwanda. Second, I was excited because I was going to see a gorilla that I hadn't seen in 17 years—Bwenge, the dominant silverback of a gorilla group monitored by the Karisoke Research Center of the Dian Fossey Gorilla Fund International. The very first time I saw Bwenge was the day after he was born in March 1990, only two months after I started my initial field work on gorillas. It was quite a thrill to discover a new baby gorilla, safely tucked away in his mother's arms, and he quickly became one of my favorite infants. His name means "intelligent" in the Kinyarwandan language. Unfortunately I hadn't been able to see Bwenge since I finished my Ph.D. field work in 1992. Despite wanting to continue research at Karisoke, it wasn't possible due to the war, genocide, and political instability that wreaked havoc on the region through the 1990s. I resumed collaborative research with Karisoke in 1998, but on projects involving analysis of their long-term database, which didn't justify getting past the tight restrictions on visiting the gorillas.

As we hiked along, I knew the gorillas were nearby because the dung piles we passed were getting fresher and fresher. I didn't care that I was getting stung by nettles, drawing up large, painful red welts on my hands and arms. The nettles brought back many memories, as did everything about the forest including the cool air and the pungent smell of the tangled mass of vegetation. Finally we saw branches shaking ahead of us, the one sign of gorillas from a distance in such a habitat, so I knew we had arrived at the group during their morning foraging session.

---

[1]About the author: Martha Robbins has been a research associate at the Max Planck Institute for Evolutionary Anthropology since 1998. Her research interests focus on the impact of ecological conditions on social behavior, reproductive strategies, and population dynamics. In addition to her research on the critically endangered mountain gorillas spanning more than 20 years, she has been involved with several projects studying western gorillas across Central Africa.

Contact information: Department of Primatology, Max Planck Institute for Evolutionary Anthropology, Deutscher Platz 6, 04103 Leipzig, Germany, robbins@eva.mpg.de

Citation: Robbins, M. M. 2014. "Gorillas Across Time and Space." In Strier, K. B. (ed.), *Primate Ethnographies*. Upper Saddle River, NJ: Pearson Education, Inc. (pp. 163–174).

I had to be patient for a bit longer, as we didn't see Bwenge for the first hour we were with the gorillas. Sosthène was studying some of the females in the group, so we were following them. Gorilla groups can spread out to cover an area larger than a football field when they are feeding, and visibility is rarely more than about 20 meters in vegetation that is taller than they or we are. Finally though, as we followed a female to the middle of the group, we could see the large head of a silverback sticking out of the vegetation. Slowly, Bwenge walked towards us, stopping about 10 meters away to have a look around his group. Bwenge had grown to be a majestic silverback, looking very much like his father, Titus, around his eyes, and a bit like his mother, Ginseng, in the shape of his nose. Given how he moved through the group and his interactions with the other gorillas, it quickly became obvious that he had acquired the same calm leadership style as Titus had, and I felt confident that his dominance tenure would last well beyond the two years already past. Following a short period as a solitary male, he had attracted seven adult females to join his group and already had sired three infants. I couldn't help but think how pleased I was that he had become a successful silverback, even though I certainly played no role in it. I reflected on all that had passed in his life and mine in the intervening years since I last saw him. Data collected from observations of Bwenge from birth to adulthood in his natural habitat contribute to our knowledge on gorillas in both a temporal and a spatial sense.

The primary reason field research is done on primates is not to sit around and watch cute, furry animals, or in the case of gorillas, to prove that we can dominate big, scary animals. As with any scientific discipline, researchers are interested in specific topics and questions. One topic that interests many primatologists and has been the driving force behind my research for the past two decades is to understand the diversity of patterns in sociality that we see among animals.

To understand the patterns of sociality, and because experiments are logistically and ethically difficult with most wild primates, we need long-term studies in different locations for a variety of species. One of the major premises of behavioral ecology is that variation in ecological

FIGURE 15.1   Bwenge as a dominant silverback in 2009 at the Karisoke Research Center, Volcano National Park, Rwanda. **Photo credit:** Martha M. Robbins.

conditions leads to variation in social behavior. Gorillas are interesting because they occupy such a wide range of habitats across ten countries in Africa. Currently gorillas are considered to be two species and four subspecies: Western gorillas (*Gorilla gorilla gorilla* and *Gorilla g. diehli*) and Eastern gorillas (*Gorilla beringei beringei* and *Gorilla b. graueri*). Gorillas pose many challenges for research: Habituating and continually monitoring them is time-consuming and difficult; gorillas are long-lived and take more than a decade simply to reach maturity; and sample sizes are inevitably small. In addition to the academic side of studying gorillas, we can't forget that they are critically endangered. Research on gorillas provides information to better understand their habitat requirements and patterns of population growth and decline, all of which are helpful for developing conservation strategies. In addition, understanding their social behavior provides information that interests the general public and tourists, which ultimately generates awareness and revenue for conserving them on both a local and international level.

Gorillas are one of the most studied primate species, but the vast majority of our knowledge about gorillas comes from the population that I refer to as the "extreme" gorillas—those of the Virunga Volcanoes, where Dian Fossey started the Karisoke Research Center in 1967. These are extreme gorillas because they live at one of the highest altitudinal ranges for any primate species, with a result being that their habitat is cool and contains almost no fruiting trees—very rare circumstances for primates—so the gorillas rely almost entirely on terrestrial herbaceous vegetation. Mountain gorillas are also extremely endangered; the Virunga Volcano population dipped as low as 250 individuals in the 1980s and, remarkably, has rebounded to nearly 500 gorillas in 2010, largely due to extremely intense conservation efforts even in the face of war and political instability.

By the time I began my graduate studies in 1990, these gorillas were extremely well studied, and dozens of scientific papers had been published about them by researchers including Dian Fossey, Sandy Harcourt, Kelly Stewart, and David Watts. I initially wondered what else could be learned about gorillas. Then I realized that even after twenty-some years of research on a long-lived, socially living species, we still hadn't seen the full diversity of possible social patterns, we had yet to fully understand what influenced this diversity, and that long-term research sometimes yielded surprises that made us question enduring assumptions. For example, when I started at Karisoke, it became immediately obvious to me that the gorillas had not read many of the publications written about them—gorillas were described as living in one-male social units, yet all three of the research groups contained more than one silverback adult male. Thus arose my Ph.D. project and my long-standing interest in the strategies used by males, particularly whether to disperse upon maturity and attempt to form a new social unit, or to stay in a group and "queue" (fight) for the alpha male position. While we still don't have all the answers, we can conclude from behavioral, demographic, and genetic studies that diversity in the social structure of male mountain gorillas arises from several interrelated causes including demographic stochasticity, life history traits, and the reproductive strategies of both males and females.

In 1998, I started a research position at the newly established Max Planck Institute for Evolutionary Anthropology in Leipzig, Germany. Concurrently, I looked beyond my fascination with the large, sexy silverbacks, and I began to focus more on females to gain a more complete picture of factors influencing variability among individuals and in the social system of gorillas. Because the food that mountain gorillas eat is so abundant and evenly distributed in the Virungas, and because dominance hierarchies among female gorillas are relatively weak compared to many other species such as baboons and macaques, we didn't expect to observe any relationship between dominance rank and female reproductive success. In contrast we did expect that as group size increased, female reproductive success would decline, especially given that some of the research groups had become extremely large, containing as many as 30–60 gorillas.

This work was possible through analysis of the demographic database, a compilation of all the births, deaths, and dispersal events among the Karisoke research groups spanning four decades. The database included the life details of more than 300 gorillas, which is quite a lot for a wild great ape, and required the efforts of many researchers. Much to our surprise, we found that group size had absolutely no effect on female reproductive success, so somehow the mountain gorillas are able to adjust their foraging patterns to accommodate large group sizes. Even more surprising, and contrary to theoretical predictions based on their abundant food sources, we found that dominance rank has a small, but nonetheless statistically significant impact on reproductive success; higher ranking females were more successful reproductively than lower ranking females. This unexpected finding then led us to question if maybe rank is a proxy for some other variable, such as body size, or if higher ranking females have some advantage while foraging despite their apparent lack of competition over food.

While the value of the long-term research at Karisoke is undisputed, I find it peculiar that until recently, the observations of the Virunga gorillas became "the norm" for all gorillas across Africa. It is equivalent to saying that what is "normal" for humans should be based only on observations of how a few hundred people live in the highest mountain regions of the Andes or Himalayas. In both cases, what we see in these high-altitude regions is only part of what is possible. The only way to know if the Virunga gorillas are "the norm" was to conduct similar research on gorillas living in different environmental conditions. One doesn't need to travel very far from the Virunga Volcanoes to find different ecological conditions that provide an opportunity to test for ecological variability leading to variation in social and demographic patterns.

The only other population of mountain gorillas in the world lives just 30 kilometers away from the Virungas, in Bwindi Impenetrable National Park, Uganda. In 1998, I began a research project in Bwindi in collaboration with the Institute of Tropical Forest Conservation. They had been monitoring one group of semi-habituated gorillas for almost ten years, but no one had taken

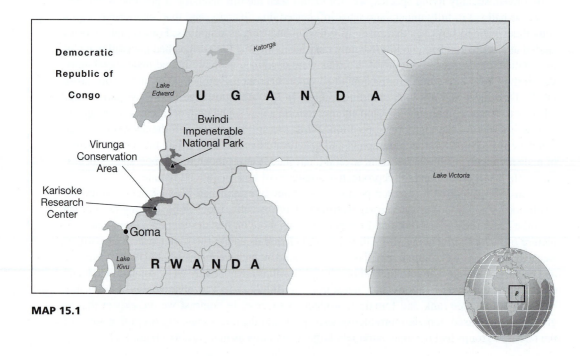

MAP 15.1

a particularly strong interest in them, and relatively little was known about them. Perhaps this was partially because of the conditions in Bwindi. The "Impenetrable" in the name of the park stems from the fact that the forest is an endless series of steep hills, all covered in a thick layer of herbaceous plants 1–2 meters high—a gorilla's dietary paradise, perhaps, but a field researcher's nightmare. In one corner of the Karisoke study area where the gorillas rarely went, the habitat was dominated by a plant, *Mimulopsis solmsii*, which grows in a dense tangle of woody stems, making it difficult to walk or even see the gorillas. I would dread when the gorillas ventured there. *Mimulopsis* is one of the most common understory plants in Bwindi; the forest is covered in it. Early on, I realized it was going to be either me or the *Mimulopsis*, and I think of this every time I throw myself against a wall of the stuff to try to follow a rapidly disappearing gorilla. Sometimes I think the gorillas eat it out of necessity—if they don't, even they won't be able to get through the forest.

Additionally, whereas Karisoke is located in the middle of the gorillas groups' home range, the research station where I work in Bwindi is located on the edge of the park, several kilometers from where the study group ranges. Here, to reduce the amount of time and effort to hike to the gorillas, we frequently use one of three base-camps. Our "camps" are very basic, with only a few tents and a fire to cook a huge pot of beans and potatoes, the daily staple. I had camped plenty by the time I got to Bwindi, but I quickly realized that in contrast to the workers at Karisoke who were accustomed to living in the same camp and working with expatriate women from having worked with Dian Fossey and others, the field assistants in Bwindi weren't accustomed to having a *mazungu* (Caucasian) woman sharing their camp. As a result, the lack of privacy and endless interest in my activities were sometimes difficult for me. Fortunately, I enjoyed the three-times-a-day ration of beans (and still do). The field assistants also didn't think that I could manage to work there; when I told them that I would initially be there for a year, their immediate response was to laugh and say that I wouldn't last more than a month.

Prior to my arrival, the field assistants' main task each day was to find the group of gorillas used for research. Through no fault of their own, many of the assistants were very nervous, if not outright afraid, of the gorillas. All across Africa, gorillas are known for charging and attacking people; their size can be intimidating. When I started, the "Kyagurilo" Group was about 80% habituated, but the assistants saw absolutely no reason to get any closer than 15–20 meters to the gorillas, which rarely provided me with anything more than an excellent view of bushes shaking as hidden gorillas moved underneath in the thick vegetation. Consequently, I spent much of my first year there accomplishing the last 20 percent of the habituation that enabled me to follow individual gorillas and make detailed observations on their social interactions, which I did partially by persuading the field assistants that I (and they) would not be killed if we got closer to the gorillas. Over time, they became convinced and grew to appreciate the value of such efforts. Fourteen years later, many of these assistants continue to work with me, and we can now laugh about the early days.

Despite these frustrations and the initially tough transition compared to Karisoke, working in Bwindi remains exciting. It is a very special place for me. One major ecological difference is that Bwindi gorillas consume fruit, which we discovered has implications for many aspects of their behavior in comparison with their Virunga colleagues: They travel more per day, they have larger home ranges, and they exhibit higher levels of competition over this clumped resource than over the herbaceous vegetation that makes up most of the Karisoke gorillas' diets. It also means we get to see the gorillas climb 20 meters or higher into the trees—and watching a 200-kilogram silverback climb to that height is a truly impressive sight. Research on the Kyagurilo group is the second longest running study on habituated gorillas, but even after 15 years of

FIGURE 15.2 The author, Martha Robbins, in Bwindi Impenetrable National Park, Uganda. **Photo credit:** Christophe Boesch.

data collection, we don't have the duration or the number of females to test for differences in group size and dominance rank on female reproductive success as we've done for the Karisoke gorillas. However, by combining the data from Kyagurilo Group with that from groups habituated for tourism in Bwindi, we have concluded that the interbirth interval (time between surviving births by females) is longer in Bwindi (5 years compared to 4 years at Karisoke). This means that the Bwindi population is unlikely to grow in size as quickly as the Virunga population, which is important for conservation management. We don't yet know the reason for this difference, but it is likely that ecological factors are at play. We wouldn't have realized that the Virunga gorillas have relatively short interbirth intervals in the absence of data from another population.

Gorillas have long life spans; females start reproducing at age 10, and males don't become mature until they are about 14 years of age. It takes a lot of time and patience to see changes in a gorilla group, and many that occurred in the Kyagurilo Group stand out in my mind. It was heartbreaking to see Zeus, the silverback who was dominant when I started in 1998, slowly be dethroned by the younger, stronger Rukina in 2004, which ultimately led to his death. At the same time, it was fascinating to see how Rukina maneuvered into the alpha position and gained acceptance of the adult females who previously had been loyal to Zeus. An adult female, Matu, who I thought was very old in 1998, surprised me by living until 2010; I still sometimes expect to see her doddering along in the back of the group. Shortly after Matu's death, Rukina moved the group into an area they had only rarely used in the previous 10 years, and two unhabituated females immigrated into the group. Four males who were boisterous juveniles in 1998 went from being playmates to adversaries, and they all eventually emigrated out of the group in 2009–2010 to become solitary males. I feel like I'm seeing old friends when we occasionally bump into any of them. Anthropomorphically speaking, I don't think Rukina feels quite the same way. Some things stay the same; two females have been high ranking since I began my research, and I still

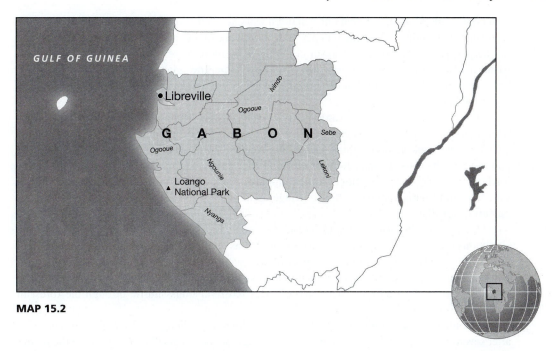

MAP 15.2

chuckle when I see them exchange aggressive vocalizations or light blows to reaffirm their displeasure with one another, even though they have spent more than 15 years primarily within 100 meters of each other. And the *Mimulopsis* has died off twice, following its 7–10-year growth cycles, opening up the understory of the forest and providing us with an opportunity to walk semi-unencumbered for a few months.

Despite all that we've learned in Bwindi, it provides information on only one more of the many populations of gorillas living in different environments across Africa. In 2005, in collaboration with Christophe Boesch, the director of the Primatology Department of the Max Planck Institute for Evolutionary Anthropology, we established a new study site in Loango National Park, Gabon, with the aim of habituating both western gorillas and chimpanzees in the same place. One rationale behind this project was to discover the social and ecological lives of western gorillas, therefore obtaining another piece of the puzzle needed to understand social diversity in primates. The forests that western gorillas inhabit are vastly different from the mountain gorilla's habitat. Western gorillas are one of the least known ape species, but our limited knowledge about them is certainly not due to the lack of effort by many researchers. Western gorillas are much more difficult to habituate than mountain gorillas because they are much more difficult to follow. There is very little understory vegetation in the forest, so they leave very few traces on the forest floor, making it difficult to "track" them. In addition, they move a lot further and can walk up to 3–5 kilometers a day. I knew of several failed attempts and had heard stories of habituating western gorillas taking five to ten years, so it was with some trepidation that I embarked on this project. In addition, I was juggling different projects and concerned about the additional travelling, but I saw the value of taking this new study on as a challenge.

While I could describe working in the Virungas versus Bwindi by comparing the Rocky Mountains and the Alps, starting to work in lowland forests of Loango with western gorillas was a bit like moving to a different planet. The lack of hills and mountains as well as very little understory vegetation means that one can often walk at a "city speed" of say, 4–5 kilometers per hour (instead of only 1–2 kilometers per hour, if you are lucky, in mountain gorilla terrain) and not be perpetually out of breath from climbing. And there were no *Mimulopsis* anywhere! I found the lowland forests very liberating, yet also sometimes claustrophobic and disorienting because they are flat and do not offer a larger view of the landscape as do the hills and mountains in Rwanda and Uganda.

Furthermore, one needs a wardrobe for every occasion. Mountainous terrain full of nettles, thick vegetation, and cool temperatures dipping into the 50s (Fahrenheit) or lower when it rains, calls for clunky hiking boots, thick socks, long-sleeved shirts, woolly sweaters and fleeces, rain jackets, and the most unsexy item of clothing that exists—rainpants. In contrast, the sultry lowland rainforests permit more tropical apparel, including t-shirts, shorts, and all-terrain sandals—all of which are called for to trudge up to one's waist through muddy swamps in hot pursuit of gorillas.

Loango is a beautiful lowland forest. It is located on the Atlantic Ocean, and one of the attractions it held as a study site was stories of gorillas along the beach and surfing hippos. Sections of the forest bring to my mind the idea of a "natural cathedral" with huge towering trees 30–40 meters high and buttresses stretching across the ground. We see forest elephants nearly every day, monkeys are everywhere, and colorful red river hogs shuffle through the forest in groups of 100 or more.

Habituating the gorillas has proven to be as huge a challenge as I anticipated, and even after seven years we still have a way to go. The dream of "beach gorillas" has become the reality of "swamp gorillas." (We have seen the unforgettable sight of gorillas on the beach, but rarely.) In the meantime, we have learned a great deal using indirect methods instead of direct observations on the gorillas. One should never underestimate the value of feces, which can tell you a lot

FIGURE 15.3 Rukina as dominant silverback sitting in the rain with Siatu (adult female) and Marembo (blackback) in Bwindi Impenetrable National Park, Uganda. **Photo credit:** Martha M. Robbins.

about the diet of an animal and can be used to extract DNA to create genotypes of the individual that left it behind. We've learned that Loango gorillas have a diet that is distinctly different from that of other western gorillas in other locations, adding to our knowledge on their ecological variability. Using genetic analysis, we've been able to estimate that there are about 100 gorillas in seven social groups in the study area. We've also been using remotely triggered "camera traps" to understand patterns of habitat utilization of the gorillas, chimpanzees, and elephants. To some degree, I feel like we are spying on the apes, but the possibilities of these surveillance techniques are amazing. These camera traps enable us to monitor many more groups and individuals in the long term than what is possible through habituation, therefore providing us with a systematic way to determine if the population of apes is increasing or decreasing.

Such a basic piece of information, change in population size, is not as easy to obtain as one may think, but crucial for understanding the impact of the major threats to gorillas as well as the effectiveness of different conservation strategies. Across Africa, the major threats to gorillas include habitat destruction, poaching, and disease, but they vary in intensity depending on the location. There are only about 900 mountain gorillas remaining in two small island populations of approximately 800 square kilometers. Their habitat is surrounded by one of the highest human population densities for a rural, agricultural area (~200–500 people per km^2). Fortunately, eating apes as "bushmeat" is considered taboo in these areas, so hunting directly for apes happens less often than in areas where western gorillas are found. However, poaching with snares is done to capture small antelope, and mountain gorillas can get their hands or feet caught in these snares, leading to severe injuries or death. Tourism, involving visiting a habituated group of gorillas and approaching them to within 10 meters, has proved to be hugely successful as a conservation strategy with more than 50,000 tourists visiting them per year and about two-thirds of all mountain gorillas being habituated. This, in combination with the high population density surrounding their habitat, makes them extremely vulnerable to the risk of disease transmission (particularly respiratory disease) from humans to gorillas. Thus, an added benefit to habituation is that the gorillas can be monitored closely on a daily basis and, in worst case scenarios, veterinarians can intervene in the field to remove snares or treat respiratory illnesses. Only through such intensive conservation strategies have mountain gorillas increased in numbers over the past four decades and have we been able to accumulate the data to monitor such changes.

In contrast to mountain gorillas, western gorillas occupy a vast area in central Africa, most of which has a relatively low human population density, but the forests they inhabit are in high demand for timber and other natural resources so their numbers are declining rapidly. There is little agriculture in these areas and people eat "bushmeat," including gorillas and chimpanzees. Tourism has developed on a small scale in only a few places because of the difficulty in habituating western gorillas, the risk of poaching, and the remote nature of the areas where they are found. Our current best guess is that there are somewhere between 50,000 and 150,000 western gorillas. Because of the size of the areas they inhabit (many forests more than 1,000 square kilometers, spanning several countries) and the difficulties of surveying these areas, we cannot be more precise with our estimate or know where they are declining most rapidly and why, or how to best prevent such losses. We're in a similar situation as if a shoe company didn't know how many shoes they produced or sold in a year and whether their success or failure depended on the quality of the product, their advertising, that their competitors went out of business, or something else entirely.

The importance of collecting long-term data and the value of making comparisons among locations makes collaboration an imperative part of any research or conservation effort. A common image of Dian Fossey is of a lone woman on a mountain, single-handedly studying and protecting the gorillas. Undoubtedly she was a pioneer in the field, and we owe her much for her dedicated work. However, times have changed, and collaborative work is recognized throughout all scientific disciplines as a more productive means of research. Only a small fraction of what we've learned about gorillas over the past two decades could have been gained by having just a handful of researchers spending all their time in a few remote study sites. I certainly don't have a time machine that enables me to be simultaneously in Bwindi, Loango, and Leipzig, Germany. Much of the data collection and field work has been done by hard-working local field assistants, volunteer research assistants, and graduate students. There are times I yearn for the early years when all I did was make observations on the gorillas, but I remind myself that much more can be done as a team. Additionally, some projects on gorillas are run by conservation groups that are more interested in direct conservation activities and focus less on research.

Fortunately, many of these conservation organizations see the value of research and are willing to collaborate with scientists, to the benefit of both parties. Yet, balancing the interests of research and conservation can sometimes lead to a schizophrenic feeling: One is trying to meet the pressures of being employed by a high-power research institute primarily interested in theoretical research topics and concurrently trying to meet the more practical demands of African park staff wanting to know how gorilla research contributes to management strategies and conservation. For example, understanding gestural communication may mean little to a park warden, whereas studying crop raiding is unlikely to lead to a new framework of primate socioecology.

One of the greatest benefits of working in many locations is that even after 20 years, I can go back to the Virungas or Bwindi with fresh eyes to see what the gorillas are doing that is new or unique to their population. We know several differences between populations of gorillas, but undoubtedly more remains to be discovered. For example, with western gorillas, groups rarely contain more than 20 individuals or more than one silverback, both of which occur in more than 20 percent of mountain gorilla groups. Grooming in mountain gorillas is not as common as in many other primate species, but, oddly, adult western gorillas have not been observed to groom one another. Several other differences among populations in behaviors used for communication, foraging, and social interactions are being revealed through long-term comparative studies. Such differences may be due to variation in ecology, but we also can't rule out the possibility that some of these behaviors are learned socially and may be indicative of "'traditions" in gorillas. Overall, having knowledge of more than one location provides broader perspective on each location. The whole becomes greater than the sum of the parts.

While we could gain much from indirect methods in Loango, one of the scientific goals of the study is to compare gorillas' social behavior with that of Karisoke and Bwindi gorillas, meaning that we need to succeed with habituation. In April 2011, I was spending the day with one of our Gabonese research assistants, Loïc Makaga, who has worked with us untiringly for the previous six years. We already had spent several hours patiently tracking the gorillas, with Loïc intensely concentrating on every broken branch and blade of grass, crossing swamps and large stretches of dried leaves. I'm still a novice at tracking western gorillas, so I'm pretty happy if I can spot a pile of dung or notice a footprint in the mud. Finally, we detected the pungent odor of a silverback and heard several loud "woof" barks, which was the silverback signalling his alarm at our presence. My heart started to race as I hoped that he wouldn't charge us. We advanced slowly, trying to ascertain whether the black shadows 30 meters away were gorillas or simply dark shadows of the forest. We stopped for a while, and then advanced by crawling until we saw the silverback resting 15 meters away. He was lying on his back and occasionally made soft "woof" barks. The low volume of these barks and his relaxed pose were signs that he was becoming increasingly tolerant of our presence. A few dark shadows, which were other gorillas,

FIGURE 15.4   Walking through a swamp in search of chimpanzees and gorillas in Loango National Park, Gabon. **Photo credit:** Christophe Boesch.

shifted behind him and I sensed that there were eyes watching us that we couldn't see. After a few minutes, a juvenile gorilla came into view near the silverback. Much to our surprise, the juvenile peered at us and walked towards us! He stopped after advancing a few meters but then continued to observe us with curiosity. The silverback didn't seem to mind this and, in fact, he rolled over into a more comfortable position. Loïc and I exchanged wide grins, delighted to think

FIGURE 15.5   Moutchi, juvenile gorilla in Atananga Group, Loango National Park, April 2011. **Photo credit:** Martha M. Robbins.

that we'd made one small step in habituating this group. The juvenile was soon christened by Loïc and the other field assistants as "Moutchi," meaning "intelligent" (coincidental, as they hadn't heard of Bwenge). At the time, I knew we still had a long way to go with the habituation, but my thoughts raced on to what we would discover from this group. I also couldn't help but hope that we would be observing Moutchi in 15 years as the dominant silverback of his own social group.

Suggested Readings

Harcourt, A. H., and K. J. Stewart. 2007. *Gorilla Society: Conflict, Compromise, and Cooperation between the Sexes.* Chicago: University of Chicago Press.

Head, J., C. Boesch, L. Makaga, and M. M. Robbins. 2011. "Sympatric Chimpanzees (*Pan troglodytestroglodytes*) and Gorillas (*Gorilla gorilla gorilla*) in Loango National Park, Gabon: Dietary Composition, Seasonality, and Intersite Comparisons." *International Journal of Primatology,* 32: 755–775.

Robbins, M. M. 2010. "Gorillas: Diversity in Ecology and Behavior." In *Primates in Perspective,* 2nd edition. Campbell, C. J., Fuentes, A., MacKinnon, K. C., Bearder, S., and Stumpf, R. M. (eds.), Oxford University Press, Oxford, pp. 326–339.

Robbins, M. M., M. Gray, E. Kagoda, and A. M. Robbins. 2009. "Population Dynamics of the Bwindi Mountain Gorillas." *Biological Conservation,* 142: 2886–2895.

Robbins, M. M., M. Gray, K. A. Fawcett, F. B. Nutter, P. Uwingeli, I. Mburanumwe, E. Kagoda, A. Basabose, T. S. Stoinski, M. R. Cranfield, J. Byamukama, L. H. Spelman, and A. M. Robbins. 2011. "Extreme Conservation Leads to Recovery of the Virunga Mountain Gorillas." *PLoS ONE,* 6: e19788.

Acknowledgments

I would like to thank the governments and national park services of Rwanda, Uganda, and Gabon for their permission and longstanding interest in the research described in this essay. None of the research could have been conducted without the assistance and persistence of many, many field assistants, volunteers, and graduate students for the projects; unfortunately, there are too many to name personally here. I also thank the various funding agencies and NGOs who have made much of this research possible, particularly the Max Planck Society. Lastly, there are several people to whom I am greatly indebted for inspiring me, guiding me, pushing me, and collaborating with me over the years for the projects I describe in this essay, namely, Chuck Snowdon, Karen Strier, Diane Doran, Christophe Boesch, Alastair McNeilage, Josephine Head, and Andrew Robbins.

16

Chimpanzee Reunion

By Craig Stanford[1]

Frodo and I had not seen each other in more than a decade. I had no expectation that he might remember me. I was just one of dozens of researchers who had spent time with the chimpanzees of Gombe National Park, Tanzania since the early 1990s. My research had been about the hunting behavior of the chimpanzees, and since Frodo was the most avid, fearless, and successful hunter of the Kasakela chimpanzee community, I had spent more hours in his company than with any other chimpanzee. Frodo also had a well-known habit of getting physical with the researchers. This is highly unusual; when we accustom wild primates to our presence, our goal is to be accepted as a neutral part of the landscape so we can quietly watch the goings-on in their lives. As Frodo grew up surrounded by human observers, he became quite fearless of them, and as he reached adulthood, he began to bully researchers and tourists. I had endured countless slaps, charges, and one memorable and scary encounter in which he had knocked me down, then briefly groomed my hair as I laid curled up defensively on the ground. Given our history, Frodo was not a chimpanzee easily forgotten.

After many years away, I had the opportunity to visit Gombe during a trip to East Africa in 2010. I approached the visit with some trepidation. After fifteen years away, I might not recognize the animals I had spent so much time watching. A new crop of young researchers was in place, and even the physical landscape was said to be altered. I had heard many stories about too many new buildings and too many tourists and other people in the camp. I wanted to see for myself what had changed and what remained the same. I also had my family in tow, including my oldest daughter who had spent time in Gombe as a toddler, and was now returning as an undergraduate. In the early years of my work I had been away from my family for many months at time. This was a chance to show my three children what had fascinated me so much about this place and its apes.

[1]About the author: Craig Stanford is Professor of Biological Sciences and Anthropology at the University of Southern California and Director of the USC Jane Goodall Research Center. He is best known for his research and publications on chimpanzee hunting and meat-eating in Gombe National Park, Tanzania, done in collaboration with Jane Goodall.

Contact information: Departments of Anthropology and Biological Sciences, University of Southern California, Los Angeles, CA 90089-0032, USA, stanford@usc.edu

Citation: Stanford, C. 2014. "Chimpanzee Reunion." In Strier, K. B. (ed.), *Primate Ethnographies*. Upper Saddle River, NJ: Pearson Education, Inc. (pp. 175–184).

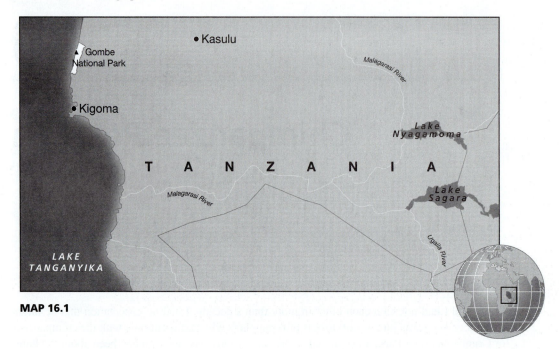

MAP 16.1

Gombe National Park, a ten-mile long sanctuary of hills and forest on the eastern shore of Lake Tanganyika, is synonymous with chimpanzee research, and with the most famed of all primate researchers, Jane Goodall. Her pioneering work is still the benchmark by which all other studies of wild apes are judged. When Goodall arrived on the shores of Gombe in 1960, she had no idea that she was beginning a life's work that would rank as the longest and most important study of animal behavior yet conducted. She documented the importance of kinship in chimpanzee society and showed that individual personalities matter enormously. Some male chimpanzees are shrewd manipulators who obtain social alliances, high dominance rank, or sex through their political skills. Other males are less political, being content to remain low-ranking their entire lives. Still others try, usually unsuccessfully, to use brute force to get what they want. Whatever the outcome, their individual personas dictate the courses of their long lives. This observation was touted by Goodall in the 1960s much to the dismay of many in the mainstream scientific community, who viewed animals as automatons. Primates are not hard-wired in the way that rodents and many other simpler mammals are, and Goodall was the pioneer in opening our eyes to this.

The term *ethnography* describes well the study of wild chimpanzees, because these apes and their relatives live long, complicated lives and display the sort of cultural diversity that defines humanity, albeit on a simpler scale. Their individual lives matter greatly in the larger life of the community. Frodo is a particularly influential chimpanzee. When he decides to hunt, others hunt with him. When he was an alpha male, he ruled the roost and others avoided encounters with him. He was a catalyst to the events around him in much the same way that a human political leader, chief, or headman influences events in his social sphere.

A key part of the ethnographic nature of chimpanzee field studies is immersion by the researcher into the minute-by-minute lives of the study subjects. In chimpanzee research, we follow the animals on their daily rounds, watch the most intimate moments of their lives, and carry

FIGURE 16.1 Habituation allows researchers to make detailed observations of the lives of wild apes. Here Frodo dines on a colobus monkey he has captured. **Photo credit:** Craig Stanford.

on the studies for many years and multiple generations. After fifty years of research at Gombe, we are only now seeing a fourth generation of chimpanzees grow up. This is because chimpanzees may live nearly fifty years in the wild, and into their sixties in captivity. You could accurately refer to the life of a chimpanzee as a career, in that it involves striving to reach a particular station in life, then struggling to maintain or improve it, all the while mating and traveling and feeding before the inevitable decline years. A field study of a year or two doesn't begin to uncover the many layers of an ape's world, built as they are upon decades of interactions with other members of their families and communities, and with the forest around them. They are, in this sense, very much like ourselves.

As the years stretched into decades, it became clear that chimpanzees were very much like us in other important ways. Once several long-term field studies in various parts of Africa had been conducted, comparisons could be made among chimpanzee societies. Researchers found that each population of chimpanzees exhibits a suite of behaviors that are unique. In some forests, chimpanzees make tools from twigs and blades of grass to "fish" for termites through tunnels in enormous earthen termite mounds. Hundreds of kilometers away, another chimpanzee population has never been seen to termite-fish. Instead, they gather stones from the forest floor and use them as hammers to crack open hard-shelled fruits. Tools are not the only learned traditions. Behaviors like the style and technique of grooming oneself and one another vary among chimpanzee populations. We do not believe there is a genetic component to this variation, nor do the learned traditions appear to be related solely to environmental differences between two forests. The technological and other traditions, if we saw them in human societies, would be called culture. While some anthropologists dispute the concept of culture applied outside the human

FIGURE 16.2   An infant chimpanzee in Gombe National Park can expect to be observed by human researchers nearly every day of its life. Such a long-term database is crucial to understanding the nature of primates that live such long and complicated lives. **Photo credit:** Craig Stanford.

species, primatologists embrace the concept as it applies to any suite of behavioral variations that seem clearly to be learned. Cultural primatology came of age once we had enough long-term studies to make meaningful comparisons, and it continues to shape and redefine our ideas about the ape-human continuum.

CHIMPANZEE HUNTING BEHAVIOR

It was once acceptable to discuss chimpanzee hunting behavior, along with a host of other behaviors, as though it did not vary from forest to forest. Today we know that along with the obvious nutritional reasons for obtaining calories, fat, and protein from prey, chimpanzee hunting is influenced by social factors that may vary from one population to another, making a unitary explanation unworkable. For example, cooperation appears to play a greater role in hunting success in western African rain forests than it does in eastern Africa. Perhaps the tall, continuous canopy of a rain forest places a higher premium on cooperative hunting. It may alternatively be that a learned tradition has emerged in some sites more so than in others. In general, we must consider a cultural role for any behavior that we see chimpanzees engaging in, given how important learned traditions are in chimpanzee society.

During my years at Gombe in the 1990s, my research had focused on hunting. Before Jane Goodall's work, we assumed that chimpanzees were entirely herbivorous, and her earliest reports of chimpanzees eagerly killing and eating monkeys, antelope fawns, and piglets were greeted with great skepticism. With more long-term studies, we now know that meat-eating is a routine part of the lives of nearly all populations, and that chimpanzees are avid and efficient predators when the opportunity arises.

Hunting is an excellent example of a behavior that must be learned over the course of years, by observing others around you doing it. While the desire for meat and for prey is a biological urge, the skills involved in acquiring meat are strongly cultural. In fact, chimpanzee hunting styles vary from one forest to the next, most likely due both to differences in the local environment and also to learned traditions of how to hunt. In some forests hunting is highly cooperative; in others, such as Gombe, it is distinctly less so. In some forests chimpanzees prefer adult colobus monkeys as prey; in Gombe they appear to selectively target babies, even plucking them from their mother's chests and allowing the mother to escape. I had begun my study with an interest in how chimpanzees' predatory behavior impacts their major prey, red colobus monkeys. Red colobus are 15- to 20-pound monkeys that are widespread across Africa and are favored prey for chimpanzees everywhere the two species occur together. I wanted to understand how this predator-prey system worked, and Gombe National Park was the perfect place to study it. The predators—the chimpanzees—were accustomed to being followed and watched at close range by researchers, so I knew I could see the action before and during a hunt. And red colobus are abundant at Gombe and often encountered by chimpanzees.

Studying hunting behavior is fascinating, exciting, and often heartbreaking. I habituated two groups of colobus monkeys to my presence; they were approachable enough that I was eventually able to sit under a tree and watch their spirited defense against a chimpanzee attack. This enabled to me know both the hunters and the hunted as individuals. It also meant I occasionally watched one of my chimpanzees killing and eating one of my colobus. On one memorable day during my study, the chimpanzees attacked and killed seven colobus from my main study group. Nearly one-quarter of the animals in that group were taken that day.

As chimpanzees forage, they knuckle-walk in a loose formation across the forest floor. When they happen upon a tree holding a group of colobus monkeys, the monkeys begin to give high-pitched alarm calls, while the hunters sit underneath seemingly evaluating the situation, the best strategy, and perhaps their odds of success. What happens next may depend on whether the chimpanzees are highly motivated to hunt and whether there are enough male chimpanzees present to mount an effective offense against a defense spearheaded by several angry male colobus. At Gombe, the usual goal of the hunt is the capture of one or more infant monkeys (at other sites adult colobus are preferred prey). But capturing an infant means getting past a group of male colobus, and they attempt to repel the attackers by leaping onto and biting them. Some male chimpanzees don't get involved in hunts often or are easily chased off by the monkeys. Others, like Frodo, are fearless and ruthless. Female chimpanzees also hunt, although not often and rarely successfully. They instead rely on males sharing with them after a kill is made. The hunter may chase down a mother monkey, leaving her to fight another day while plucking her infant from her arms. This is fascinating stuff, but also difficult to watch dispassionately. There were days when I would watch my chimpanzee study subjects catch, kill, and eat monkeys that were also my study subjects.

I found that while the Gombe chimpanzee diet comprises meat only as a tiny fraction compared to ripe fruits and other plant foods, chimpanzee predation has a major impact on red colobus population biology. During periods of frequent hunting, the chimpanzees could eradicate one-tenth of the entire colobus population. This would likely be unsustainable if it continued long term. Instead, hunting frequency was seasonal, and also cyclical and correlated with fluctuations in the average sizes of chimpanzee foraging parties. This turned out to be related to the greater propensity of male chimpanzees, who do about 90 percent of the hunting, to pursue prey when they are in larger parties. They also tend to be more successful when in larger hunting parties. The likelihood of hunting, and therefore the impact on the colobus population, was also tied to female chimpanzee behavior. When a female chimpanzee has a sexual swelling, males aggregate around her, party sizes swell, and hunts and kills become more frequent. One could argue therefore that female chimpanzee reproductive cycles have an impact on the local population of red colobus. This was a very unexpected outcome of the study, and one that engendered much debate and discussion among my colleagues and students. I was confronted by colleagues who argued with one of my assertions, that male chimpanzees sometimes use meat as a bartering chip to obtain more sex from females who want scraps of the meat they possess. Our evidence for this hypothesis was strong enough to be published in prestigious scientific journals, but it led to other studies that attempted to refute the notion. Most recently, a study in Tai National Park, Cote d'Ivoire, by Christina Gomes and Christophe Boesch showed that their male chimpanzees traded meat for sex with particular females over a long time period. That is, males who shared meat most liberally with females also received more matings from those females than did other males. So in at least some times and places, meat is a bargaining chip in chimpanzee sexual politics.

Chimpanzee hunting is not exactly comparable to predatory behavior by other social carnivores like lions and wolves. Unlike carnivores, chimpanzees mainly eat plant foods supplemented by animal protein. As omnivores, they must decide not only when to hunt, but how to balance their energy spent hunting, which is often energy wasted when prey escape, against energy spent searching for fruits and other foods.

GORILLAS

What I learned during my years at Gombe served me well when I moved to a new project in Bwindi Impenetrable National Park in neighboring Uganda. Bwindi is home to one of the two remaining populations of wild mountain gorillas. It is also home to a population of chimpanzees, which at the time I began my study we knew very little about. I traveled to Bwindi as a tourist following the end of my Gombe chimpanzee study in 1995, wanting simply to see mountain gorillas in the wild. But my visit to Bwindi inspired me to begin an entirely new study, which I began in earnest two years after the end of my work with Jane Goodall. I would continue my research on chimpanzee behavior and ecology, but this time instead of studying chimpanzees as predators, I would examine their relationship with the gorillas with which they co-existed at Bwindi. I worked with a Ugandan doctoral student, John Bosco Nkurunungi, and together with a team of assistants we slowly pieced together a portrait of co-existence between the two ape species.

Having the opportunity to observe chimpanzees and gorillas on the same day in Bwindi, sometimes even together in the same tree, provided starkly contrasting first impressions of the two apes. Male gorillas are about four times as large and heavy as male chimpanzees; even female gorillas are twice the size of the largest Bwindi chimpanzee. If chimpanzees live a high-energy life filled with sex and violence, gorillas are much the opposite. A researcher sees as much sex among gorillas in a typical month as a chimpanzee researcher may see in a single morning. The same applies to aggression. Bwindi gorillas travel in cohesive groups of eight to thirty animals, and individuals rarely stray more than a few dozen meters from the group. Chimpanzees, meanwhile, don't even live in groups. Their communities occupy defined territories, but on a given day it's impossible to predict how many might be traveling together in their temporary foraging parties.

But beyond the differences between the two species, we gradually discovered as many parallels as differences. Dian Fossey's pioneering work with mountain gorillas in the nearby Virunga Volcanoes had established a conventional wisdom about gorillas. This conventional wisdom did not, however, hold true for the majority of Africa's gorillas. Fossey found her gorillas to

FIGURE 16.3 In some forests in Africa, gorillas share their habitat with chimpanzees. This is an adult male silverback mountain gorilla. **Photo credit:** Craig Stanford.

be highly sedentary, eating an entirely foliage-based diet while browsing in dense meadows and thickets. At Bwindi, and in most other sites where gorillas are found, they eat nearly as much fruit as chimpanzees do. They climb tall trees in search of this fruit, contrary to the terrestrial ways of Virungas gorillas (perhaps because the latter live in a nearly fruit-free environment), and they travel much further each day than Fossey's gorillas did. Much of our research on chimpanzees and gorillas at Bwindi was therefore spent trying to identify the key behavioral and dietary differences between the two species that allowed them to co-exist in the same forest. After nine years of field research, we concluded that the forest at Bwindi, with its rich fruit supply and towering trees, strongly shaped Bwindi gorilla behavior and that differences between the gorillas of Bwindi and the Virungas are due to local environmental conditions, not genetic differences. There is limited evidence for cultural differences among gorilla populations too. For instance, gorillas in the Virungas and Bwindi both carefully handle the leaves of certain plant species that possess tough bristles that must be painful to chew. But the techniques of rolling up the leaves to avoid the bristles before ingesting them vary slightly between the sites. This is presumably because young gorillas grow up watching their mothers handle tough-to-eat foods, and they adopt the local technique.

FRODO

Back at Gombe, I spent several days following chimpanzees around and catching up on who had grown up, who had died, and who was now the alpha male. I finally encountered Frodo on my fourth day back. It was a bit of a shock. When I had last seen him in 1995, Frodo had been a strapping, handsome nineteen-year-old, entering his prime and as physically powerful and intimidating as a male chimpanzee can be. During my years away, I had kept track of Frodo through Jane Goodall and her many students and research assistants. He had risen to alpha rank at the age of twenty-one, supplanting his older brother Freud. He reigned for five years before losing his high rank and then wandered alone for a time—as ex-alphas often do—before slowly reintegrating himself into the community as a lower-ranking, but still influential male.

Now, fifteen years since I had last seen him and nearly a decade since he had been overthrown, Frodo was a shadow of his former self. His body, once enormously muscular and impressive, had lost much of its tone. His coat of hair had lost its sheen and his face looked grizzled and old. He was only 34—past-prime but not elderly in chimpanzee years by any means. He looked far older to me than his older brother Freud, who at thirty-nine looked essentially the same as when I had last seen him. Why had Frodo not aged more gracefully? I attribute it to a hard life in the fast lane, struggling to rise to alpha and then keep his status, combined with an undiagnosed health problem that had left him looking quite sick for a period after falling from alpha rank. As I watched Frodo and mused about his storied life, the expression "how far the mighty have fallen" seemed to fit him perfectly. Genetic studies of paternity among the Gombe chimpanzees have shown that Frodo had a high level of reproductive success not only during his reign as alpha male in the community, but also when he was a mere adolescent. He is a member of the vaunted "F" matriline that began in Goodall's early days with Flo, a venerable female whose daughter Fifi gave birth to Freud, Frodo, and five other sons and daughters.

Despite his grizzled appearance, Frodo is still a mighty hunter. Minutes after I first encountered him, he made a mad dash into a tree shading the staff camp to nab a young and inattentive colobus monkey. For the following two hours, as research assistants and tourists came by to watch, Frodo and his brother Freud sat munching happily on the chicken-sized lunch he had caught. Frodo did what any self-respecting chimpanzee hunter who is victorious in catching prey does; he shared nepotistically with his brother, and not with the several other male chimpanzees who were in the vicinity during the hunt's aftermath.

Frodo was not the only chimpanzee who had changed a great deal since my last visit. Many chimpanzees whom I remembered as babies have grown up. The current alpha is Ferdinand, whom I recalled as a cuddly little juvenile. Titan is a swaggering young adult male considered to be a likely future alpha. Like any high school reunion; it's a challenge to recognize anyone, including the chimpanzees I had spent so much time with. Many of the chimpanzees who were prominent members of the community in the 1990s have died and a few females have migrated to neighboring communities. Many of the conversations I had with the current field assistants centered around their stories about the new generation of chimpanzees, comparing them with my accounts of what the parents or older siblings of those animals were like.

There are important changes at Gombe that go beyond the chimpanzees themselves. As in any world-renowned conservation site for an endangered animal, the long-term health of the local environment in which the animals live is a key concern. I had heard rumors that new buildings, more tourism, poaching, and other problems had seriously impacted the Gombe chimpanzees' habitat. Although these are all legitimate worries, I was pleasantly surprised to find on my return visit that any negatives were outweighed by positives. Until the mid-1990s, local fishermen who ply Lake Tanganyika for *dagaa* (a small sardine-like fish) had lived in temporary beach camps in Gombe National Park. Their numbers grew year by year until their presence—along with their trash, their campfires, and their thatched shacks—created a serious public health menace. The chimpanzees and baboons, having lost their fear of humans, wandered into the fishermen's camps, ate from their trash heaps, and risked infecting themselves with everything from tuberculosis to scabies. After years of negotiation, the government had finally shifted the fishing camps to other beaches outside the park's boundaries. On my return visit, the tranquility and cleanliness of the beaches was a stark contrast to the 1990s. As tourism becomes a larger revenue earner for the Tanzanian government, the temptation to develop Gombe unwisely, with too many buildings and staff, must be tempered by the environmental impact concerns. All things considered, the park and the habitat are doing quite well fifty years after Jane Goodall first stepped out of a boat onto its lakeshore.

It's not possible to be concerned about conservation inside a national park without becoming involved in the areas surrounding the park boundaries. As Gombe National Park was being whittled into its current small dimensions by deforestation on three sides (the fourth side is the lakeshore), human issues began to press in. Today the village of Mwamgongo sits just north of the park boundary. *Schistosomiasis,* a parasite that lives in standing water and enters the body while people are bathing or swimming, is prevalent in the local lake water, as well as in many of the local inhabitants. Women have historically walked hours to collect fuel wood, a growing problem when much if not all of the available wood is now on protected park lands. The Jane Goodall Institute has become involved in villages near Gombe, including Mwamgongo, educating school children about environmental issues. The Institute plants trees to replace those cut by villagers and encourages the use of energy-efficient, low-technology stoves for cooking to reduce pressures on fuel wood and reduce the hours per day that local people must spend searching for it.

When I began my study of wild chimpanzees many years ago, it never occurred to me that I would be doing an ape ethnography when I studied chimpanzees or gorillas. Field biologists like to think of their work as empirical, data-oriented, and quite different in approach from what a cultural anthropologist studying human societies does. But looking back, my perspective has changed. Immersing oneself in the daily lives of my study subjects, paying close attention to the minute details of their lives, and trying to understand how the life of one chimpanzee or gorilla is connected to the lives of all the others in the group is ethnography. In fact, I have since had the opportunity to spend time among people living in traditional societies with my cultural anthropologist/ethnographer spouse, and I have seen first-hand the parallels between long-term studies of people and those of our closest kin, the great apes. This should come as no surprise, given the long, complicated, and richly detailed lives that all primates, human or nonhuman, live.

Like all good ethnographers, chimpanzee researchers care deeply about the future of their study site and its inhabitants. One cannot spend a career benefiting from work on an endangered species and not give something back to that species. This payback can be training host country students to carry on the research and conservation work, or applying field data about the animals to new and better conservation strategies, or publicizing the plight of the animals to raise awareness and fund-raising, for their protection. These days, most field primatologists become involved in all these efforts. Chimpanzees are not only endangered nonhuman primates. They are our next of kin, a window onto our evolution, and a mirror into which we all look seeking answers.

Suggested Readings

Goodall, J. 1986. *Chimpanzees of Gombe: Patterns of Behavior*. Cambridge, MA: Harvard University Press.

McGrew, W. C. 2004. *The Cultured Chimpanzee: Reflections on Cultural Primatology*. New York: Cambridge University Press.

Stanford, C. 2008. *Apes of the Impenetrable Forest*. (Primate Field Studies Series.) Upper Saddle River, NJ: Pearson Education.

Stanford, C. 2012. *Planet without Apes: Can We Save Our Closest Kin?* Cambridge, MA: Harvard University Press.

Acknowledgments

I thank Karen Strier for the invitation to contribute to this volume, and the staff of Gombe National Park for all their assistance during my years working there. My work in Gombe was supported by the National Geographic Society, the Leakey Foundation, and the Jane Goodall Research Center of the University of Southern California.

PART V

Changes with Time

17

Questions My Mother Asked Me

An Inside View of a Thirty-Year Primate Project in a Costa Rican National Park

By Linda Marie Fedigan[1]

It is a red letter day for our capuchin project in Costa Rica. After locating one of our study groups in its usual home range, a student and I notice that a young female named Kathy Lee (KL) has what appears to be a small grey lump on the back of her neck. Looking through binoculars, we can make out the body of a tiny infant slung across KL's upper back with its eyes closed and head hanging down in the crook of her neck, while KL forages with the rest of her group and leaps nonchalantly from tree to tree. We are excited because this is one of the first times that we have tracked a female from the day of her own birth through the birth of her first offspring. KL has many relatives in the group. She is the alpha female of the group and the eldest daughter of the prior alpha female that died a year earlier. As the day progresses, several group members approach KL to sniff and touch the new arrival. KL's sister seems particularly interested and stays close to the new mother-infant pair, grooming them when they rest. We feel some concern for this new infant because there has been instability among the adult males of the group and we know that male fighting can lead to the death of small infants. When the group decides to rest in the park's campground, we radio to other members of our team who are elsewhere in the forest and back at our research house to come see the new infant.

We are discussing the difficulty of sexing infant capuchins when a tour bus arrives in the campground and disgorges a group of people dressed in tank tops, shorts, and flip flops. Seeing us peering into the trees with binoculars, several of the park visitors rush over to us. A sighting of monkeys inevitably causes great excitement in tourists, who sometimes react counterproductively.

---

[1]About the author: Linda Fedigan's primary research areas are life histories of female primates, social relations between the sexes and population dynamics of Neotropical monkeys. She is the author and co-editor of several books (including: *The Complete Capuchin*, co-written with Dorothy Fragaszy and Elisabetta Visalberghi) and approximately 100 journal articles and book chapters. She has supervised 30 graduate degrees to completion and a number of her former graduate advisees pursue active careers in primatology at their own field sites.

Contact information: Department of Anthropology, University of Calgary, Calgary, Alberta, Canada T2N 1N4, Fedigan@ucalgary.ca

Citation: Fedigan, L. M. 2014. "Questions My Mother Asked Me: An Inside View of a Thirty-Year Primate Project in a Costa Rican National Park." In Strier, K. B. (ed.), *Primate Ethnographies*. Upper Saddle River, NJ: Pearson Education, Inc. (pp. 186–195).

Some of them shout "monkeys!" and start to run at them, and one visitor tries to throw bananas from his lunch at the monkeys "in order to see them better." Another stares at our sweaty field clothes and admires our "leg warmers" (snake leggings). The idea that we would wear anything to deliberately warm us up further on this sweltering 99°F day provides some comic relief. We explain that these tree-dwelling monkeys are habituated to the presence of people below them on the ground, but they need to speak and move quietly and also that capuchins eat the natural fruit of the forest rather than domesticated human foods. We loan them our binoculars and point out the new infant, and then they start to ask good questions: How many monkeys are there in the park? How long do they live? How old is the female with the new baby? How long have you been studying them? And why do you watch monkeys in this forest and country so far from home?

The last question in particular is a deceptively simple but profound one that I've been asked by everyone from my mother to my colleagues and students as well as journalists and the public when they learn that I am a primatologist. I have been leading a long-term study of white-faced capuchins in Sector Santa Rosa of the Área de Conservación Guanacaste (formerly Santa Rosa National Park), Costa Rica for very close to thirty years, taking note and keeping records as my favorite monkeys age and die, as the primate populations grow and stabilize, as the forest regenerates, as the park itself is transformed, and as local people and research team members come and go. I first visited Santa Rosa in 1982, looking for a protected forest in a politically stable country where I could bring students to study monkeys that would be relatively easy to see and habituate to observation. I feel enormously fortunate to have found a site that met these research objectives. But why have I continued with this project for so long? What motivates a person to conduct a 30-year study of monkeys in a tropical forest in Central America? I can provide several answers.

For one, I had been privileged early in my career to learn that a long-term dataset is a scientist's treasure trove. When I began to study primates in 1972, I focused on the Japanese macaques of Arashiyama, and my Japanese predecessor and mentor handed me 18 years of genealogical data on the monkeys in the group. A traditional tenet of Japanese primatology is that researchers work collaboratively and pass along their knowledge to new members of the research team. Thus, from the beginning, the Arashiyama macaques were not an anonymous horde of

FIGURE 17.1   The author, Linda Marie Fedigan. **Photo credit:** Christian Bruyère.

animals in my eyes. Instead, my mentor patiently trained me to recognize individual monkeys with names, birthdates, histories, siblings, and lineages as well as distinctive faces, voices, scars, and personality quirks. My understanding of these animals was so much enriched by the cumulative information from the researchers who preceded me that when I started my own field study of white-faced capuchins in Santa Rosa, I knew that one of my goals would be to produce a similar long-term life history dataset.

A second factor that has motivated my long-term capuchin monkey project is that I have always been drawn to questions about how and why some females, some groups, and some populations reproduce better than others over time. In long-lived primates, these questions can be properly answered only after decades of study. Compared to other vertebrates, most monkey species are long-lived animals. Japanese macaque females can live to be 32 years old, and female capuchins at Santa Rosa can live at least into their late twenties. (My colleague, Susan Perry, estimates that the oldest female capuchin at her neighboring capuchin study site lived to be 36 years old.) An individual monkey, matriline, group, or population can reproduce well for a few years and then fall on hard times and experience reduced reproductive success. Furthermore, I knew from studies of other primates that some of the most important phenomena, such as predation, infanticide, and the effects of natural catastrophes (e.g., hurricanes) are rare or recorded only after years of study. The fact that it takes great patience and much time to be rewarded with true insight into the lives and social systems of these animals is part of what drives me and my colleagues to keep watching, to never rest or be complacent that we fully understand our study subjects, and to look forward to the next astonishing thing we see them do or learn about them. It is also why, even after 30 years, they continue to surprise us.

Thirdly, at the time that I began my study of white-faced capuchins in 1983, little was known about their behavior and lives in the wild. I knew that I would have to start with the basics

FIGURE 17.2   Kathy Lee at 23 years of age. Like many older adult female "white-faced" capuchins, she has a fluffy white fringe of hair around her face. After first giving birth to Alien/Artemis at age seven, Kathy Lee has since produced ten offspring, four of which are known to be alive and two of which (male offspring) are suspected to be alive in groups outside our study area.
Photo credit: Fernando Campos.

(which included simply habituating study groups to the presence of continuous observers on the ground below them) and that it would be many years before I could address the questions about reproductive success and population dynamics that really interested me. Luckily, I came armed with persistence as one of my personality traits as well as two other advantages.

The first advantage is that my long-term study has been continuously supported by ongoing federal grants from NSERC (the Natural Sciences and Engineering Research Council of Canada). Although it is certainly competitive to obtain NSERC funding, the successful applicants receive five years of funding in each round, and NSERC places emphasis on funding the scientist (on the basis of their accomplishments and their career trajectory) as well as on funding the particular project that is described in the proposal. This makes it possible to plan and conduct a long-term study, indeed to plan a career of research. I have talked with many colleagues whose long-term field projects are constantly in jeopardy or have been terminated because of unpredictable interruptions in funding.

A second advantage that facilitated the success of my long-term study is that I established my research project in a national park where a world-renowned experiment in tropical forest regeneration was being simultaneously conducted. Three species of monkeys (capuchins, howlers, and spider monkeys) occur sympatrically in Santa Rosa National Park (SRNP), which is located on the Pacific coast of Costa Rica. SRNP was established in 1971 from reclaimed ranchlands and was one of the two first parks created in Costa Rica. In the early 1970s, efforts began to remove cattle, poachers, and squatters from the area. However, it was not until 1989 that the ecologist Dr. Daniel Janzen (who has made it his life's work to save the tropical dry forests of Guanacaste) successfully spearheaded a project to create a conservation area (a "megapark") by merging Santa Rosa with several small nearby parks and reserves. In the late 1980s, the Área de Conservación Guanacaste (ACG, www.acguanacaste.ac.cr) was created, and funds were raised to better protect the forest and its inhabitants from poachers and from the fires that ranchers had traditionally set every dry season to create more grassland for their cattle. Janzen also founded

MAP 17.1

the nonprofit Guanacaste Dry Forest Conservation Fund (http://gdfcf.org/) and raised funds to purchase almost all the ranches that surrounded the original SRNP and later to purchase large tracts of land on the neighboring volcanic slopes and most recently to purchase cloud forest and Atlantic rainforest on the eastern slopes of the mountains. The original Santa Rosa National Park, approximately 100 square kilometers in size, is now just one sector in a vast conservation area that is more than 170,000 hectares in size.

Santa Rosa was not the first place where I tried to establish a long-term study of primates. Before 1982, I had explored several possible locations and even started two projects that I had to abandon (one because the political environment was too unsafe at the time and another where the government was stable, but the animals were not protected). There were many reasons to choose to work in a national park in Costa Rica. The country is famous as a stable democracy with a strong environmental conservation ethic. The animals and their environment are protected by law, and the park service provides researchers with facilities (housing, labs) and services such as assistance with export permits and other legal requirements. And it provides a research community, a place where we can take the plants and insects that our monkeys are eating on a given day to the park's botanists and entomologists for help with identification. Additionally, Costa Rica has a proud history of supporting and maintaining its national parks and so we can work in Sector Santa Rosa of the ACG with some confidence that the park will continue to exist and be maintained as a protected area for the foreseeable future. Indeed, in 1999, it was declared a UNESCO World Heritage Site.

There are, however, also some constraints involved in working in a national park. The most obvious one is that in some seasons, there are many visitors to ACG, specifically to Sector Santa Rosa, which is located near a chain of beautiful beaches outside the park that have been developed recently for tourism. Introducing visitors to nature is, of course, one important reason for a park's existence. But visitors can bring their urban attitudes and behavior with them—playing loud music, driving vehicles too quickly on the park's single paved road, smoking in the forest, and generally not knowing how to behave in the presence of wild animals. Two of our five study groups have home ranges that encompass areas of the park (nature trails and a campground) where tourists get out of their vehicles and often interrupt the normal flow of a monkey group's day. When this happens, we stop collecting data and wait for the monkeys to move back into the forest away from park visitors.

There have been many changes to the national park where I have worked over the past 30 years and to the monkey populations residing in it. When I began my research there, Santa Rosa was a remote, seasonally burnt set of forest fragments affected by the traditions of neighboring ranchers, local poachers, and political instability in nearby Nicaragua. The federal offices of the National Park Service in San José, which initially ran its parks rather like a military operation, exerted an enormous amount of control. All the guards were middle-age men who were stationed on a rotating basis at parks across the country, usually far from their homes, and they wore green, military-type uniforms and rode horses to patrol the park against poachers and roaming cattle. Although they worked hard to protect the park, and some of them expressed interest in the local flora and fauna and in our study of its primates, they were not hired or educated as naturalists and conservationists. With the metamorphosis of Santa Rosa National Park into a sector of the Área de Conservación Guanacaste in 1989 came the hiring of local residents as caretakers of the different park sectors and of youthful, university-educated Costa Rican men and women who came to work in ACG because they wanted to be part of an exciting new conservation project to save the remaining tropical dry forest and to regenerate the native habitat from pasture land. One such recruit was Roger Blanco Segura, who came to ACG in 1985 as the assistant research coordinator, before being promoted to the Research Coordinator position that he has now held for 25 years. Roger Blanco has been an enormous help to our project and those of other researchers in the park, always finding ways to facilitate our work and guide us through the legal formalities. Quite simply put, our project and all that we have learned about the monkeys of Santa Rosa would not exist without him.

Along with the changes to the human context in which my project has taken place in Costa Rica over the past three decades, there have been many changes to the tropical dry forests of Santa Rosa. According to Dan Janzen, when the conquistadors arrived in the New World, more than half of the Mesoamerican forests were dry rather than rain forests. But today, virtually none of the original dry forest remains. Before the establishment of the park in 1971, people had greatly disturbed the habitat while attempting to make a living through logging, slash-and-burn horticulture, coffee and cotton agriculture, and cattle ranching. These activities had left a patch-work quilt of forest fragments surrounded by open fields that were either partly or completely cleared and then planted with crops or the African "jaragua" grass that sustains cattle. During the annual dry seasons, the ranchers had burned these fields to renew the grasses (a practice still widely followed elsewhere in the province of Guanacaste), and the fires had often burned into the forests. During the first decade that I studied monkeys in Santa Rosa, we were often called upon in the dry season to help fight the grass fires that raged into the park from neighboring ranches, using little more than brooms and shovels. Finally, in the early 1990s, as part of the creation of the ACG as a "megapark," a professional fire-fighting team became residents and employees of the park and since then, fires in ACG have come under much better control.

It takes seven to ten years without a fire for a field of grass to choke itself out and for the small woody seedlings to become established as trees. Dan Janzen has identified two dispersal patterns by which tree seeds are dispersed into regenerating pastures, leading to two types of new forest growth that offer different resource potential to herbivores: wind-dispersed patches of new forest, and vertebrate-dispersed patches of new forest. Wind-dispersed seeds are highly protected (often toxic) and unattractive to herbivores, and wind-dispersed trees do not provide much shade or fruit. If the pasture was created by clear-cutting of the trees, then seed-dispersing animals will cross the field only if they have to. But if the pasture was selectively cleared and a few fruit trees were left in place, then fruit-eating animals will travel into the pasture to eat from these trees and disperse the seeds across the pasture in their dung—thereby creating a vertebrate-dispersed patch of new forest. The home ranges of most of our study groups originally included several pastures of both types that the monkeys either skirted or ran across rapidly in order to travel from forest fragment to forest fragment.

Over the years, we have observed how the monkeys use these newly regenerating areas. It was very soon clear to us that the capuchins were much more attracted to former pasture land where big fruit trees had been left in place when the field was cleared. Both types of pastures have been slowly turning back into forest for the past 40 years since the park was established, and even the wind-dispersed patches of new forest growth are now used by the capuchins, mainly to forage for insects. One of the many rewarding aspects of my decades of research in Santa Rosa has been to actually observe a tropical dry forest begin to grow back from pastureland—to see tall (if skinny) trees and forest-dwelling animals residing where before there were only intro-duced grasses and scorched, desiccated fields. According to Dan Janzen, who has spearheaded so much of the regeneration work, it takes about 150–200 years to regrow a tropical dry forest (and 1,000 years to regrow a tropical rain forest). I will not live to see the full fruition of this regen-eration project, but it has been inspirational to learn that it is possible to begin to restore an eco-system like tropical dry forest, that had been brought to the edge of extinction.

Additionally, there have been many changes to the monkey populations over the past 30 years. When I first approached the Costa Rican National Park Service in San Jose back in 1983 for a permit to conduct research on the primates in Santa Rosa, they asked if I would count and monitor the number of monkeys in the park. The primates had not been censused for over a decade since a very early study by Curtis Freese, a Peace Corps volunteer who had been present when the park was created in 1971. I agreed, and in addition to collecting behavioral and ecological data on selected study groups, I began to conduct an annual parkwide census of the capuchins and howlers in the park every May through June for the first six years of my study, and then I switched over to biennial censuses and eventually to overseeing monkey censuses in the original Santa Rosa 100-square-kilometer area every four years. It is a major undertaking to count all the monkeys in a park. Many students and assistants have helped, and Dr. Kathy Jack, who is now co-director of the Santa Rosa capuchin project, has been my major collaborator on this part of the project.

During our first census in 1983, we located and counted 226 capuchins in 20 groups and estimated the total park population size at 318 capuchins. The estimated population size is larger than the number actually counted because we know we always miss some males that are moving between groups as well as a few groups that evade our search strategies in any given year. Most recently, in 2011, Fernando Campos, who led the census team, counted 532 capuchins in 35 groups, and we estimate the total population size at 613 capuchins. Thus, over this 28-year period, the capuchin population size has doubled. It has also grown at a fairly steady pace. In the same time period, the population of howler monkeys initially grew at a much faster rate than did the capuchin population (probably because howlers produce infants at an earlier age and more often), but then the howler population leveled off over the past decade and the 2011 census indicated that it had even decreased. Howlers are twice the size of capuchins (male howlers weigh 6.5 kilograms on average as compared to the capuchin male average weight of 3.3 kilograms) and unlike capuchins, we never find howlers resting or foraging in trees younger than 60 years or smaller than 63 centimeters in diameter at breast height. Perhaps because howlers require large, mature trees to accommodate their large body size, they have for now run out of suitable habitat in which to expand as the forests of Santa Rosa only slowly regenerate. It is also possible that other factors (e.g., cyclic yellow fever epidemics) are causing fluctuations in the howler population.

The even larger spider monkeys (adult males average 8.4 kilograms) are more difficult to census than the capuchins or howler monkeys because the spider monkeys live in ever-changing (fission-fusion) groups. Therefore we have had to estimate the density of spider monkeys in different areas of the park by using transect counts (a method whereby an observer repeatedly walks a line through the forest and counts the number of individuals they can see on either side of the path). These transect counts have shown us that spider monkeys definitely prefer old growth forest and larger patches of forest where it is easier for them to locate sufficient trees in fruit at any given time. Their frugivorous diet and need for a large home range is likely a major explanation as to why spider monkeys are the first of the three species to disappear when forests are disturbed by human activities and the last to return to regenerating forest fragments. Capuchins eat an omnivorous diet (insects, fruit, small vertebrates), and they have the smallest body size of the three species and are the first to use newly regrowing forest patches. We have found that capuchins will start to forage for insects in patches of forest that are only 25 years old, whereas we find spider monkeys at the highest densities in the Santa Rosa forest fragments that are at least 100 to 150 years old.

Along with documenting the fascinating process of how monkey populations return to regenerating forests, in recent years I have been able to begin answering the questions that fundamentally motivate me to study monkeys over the long haul and that first drew me to Santa Rosa: How and why do some females experience greater reproductive success than others?

I already knew from my earlier work on Japanese macaques that dominance rank and the inheritance of good genes and a certain amount of serendipity all play a role in the variable number of surviving offspring that different female primates produce. From capuchins, I further learned that several factors affect a female's reproductive success: the changing levels of resources available to her and her offspring over time; the number of supportive matrilineal kin that reside in her group; and the behavior of males, which can strongly influence the unfolding of a female's reproductive success over her lifetime. As part of their own drive to reproduce optimally, males may pursue strategies that negatively affect the ability of females to successfully rear their young. As my collaborator, Kathy Jack, and I have documented, male capuchins change groups every few years and form coalitions to drive rival resident males out of their groups. During these takeovers, females and their young are often wounded, and even very dominant ("alpha") females may lose their infants due to infanticide by nonresident males. In fact, because high-ranking females are more central to the group that is being invaded, they may be more vulnerable to male aggression during invasions than are the more peripheral, low-ranking females. In this way, "sexual conflict" (opposing strategies pursued by the two sexes to improve their respective reproductive success), can confound the effects of female dominance relations on their reproductive success. Female capuchins usually remain in their natal groups throughout their lives, residing with their young and their female kin. However, alpha females often form alliances with the resident alpha male and may disperse with him when he is inevitably defeated and driven out by new males. We have found that these dispersing females do not reproduce well in new groups away from their kin. We have also found that female capuchins produce more surviving infants when they reside in groups with higher proportions of adult males, presumably because the latter can resist takeovers by invading coalitions, whereas a single resident adult male cannot.

I also learned from our many years of study that capuchin females experience relatively slow life histories compared to many other monkey species. Capuchins have their first infants when they are between six and seven years old, pregnancy lasts for 5.5 months, and they give birth only every two to three years if the prior infant has survived. However, one-third of the infants born will die in their first year of life from various documented and inferred causes (predation, infanticide, parasites, contagious diseases). If a female's infant dies, she is likely to produce another one in about a year. Reproduction is energetically costly for female mammals, and lactation appears to be even more "expensive" for mothers than gestation, perhaps because the nursing infant is larger than the gestating fetus. Grainne McCabe and I found that lactating female capuchins at Santa Rosa eat more food items per hour (and, in particular, they consume more protein and fat) than do pregnant or cycling females. We also found that this pattern of lactating females taking in more energy than do other females climbs steadily over the first 8 weeks of the infant life, when the baby is growing rapidly, and then maternal energy intake starts to decline at the age when the infant begins to move around off its mother's body and is carried by others in the group. Alloparenting (when an infant is cared for by an individual other than the mother) and even allonursing (suckling an infant other than one's own) are quite common in white-faced capuchins.

Thus, Sarah Carnegie, Amanda Melin, and I had a pretty good clue that the costs of lactation might drive the seasonal timing of reproduction in our study females. As noted above, Santa Rosa and much of the surrounding sectors of ACG consist of tropical dry forest, which means that the habitat is highly seasonal with virtually no rainfall between mid-December and mid-May, during which time many of the trees lose their leaves. During the dry season, the capuchins continue to find some fruit to eat (for example, fig trees can produce fruit at any time of year), and the monkeys also turn to eating insects and small vertebrates (birds and their eggs, bats, lizards, squirrels, coati pups). There is some debate in the literature about whether females should time their mating/conception seasons or their birth seasons (and therefore lactation periods) to coincide with food abundance. If the *mating* season corresponds to periods of higher food abundance, that will provide better resources for pregnant females and for infants that are being weaned because their mothers have conceived again. On the other hand, if the *birth* season corresponds to periods of greater resources, that will provide energy to lactating mothers. Capuchins are not strictly seasonal breeders, but they do experience conception and birth peaks, and 60 percent of all infants are born in the four-month period of April through July. The peak in abundance of the kinds of fruits that capuchins eat occurs from April through September, virtually the same period as the birth and lactation season. Thus, we have concluded that many capuchin females time the births of their infants such that the most energy-expensive period of reproduction—lactation—occurs during the peak in the availability of food to nourish the mothers.

And what about the newborn infant of the alpha female, Kathy Lee, that we first observed soon after it was born? Over the subsequent weeks, months, and years, we determined that he was a male and observed him continuously until he disappeared at the age of seven years during a male takeover of his group. As a youngster, his odd and prominent habit of tilting his head and holding his tongue out on windy days (perhaps as a cooling mechanism?) led to him being named "Alien." Because he was a subadult when he disappeared at the time of the takeover that occurred during his seventh year, we thought he would likely have fought back against the invading males and might have been wounded and driven out of the group. Four years later, we added a new study group to our research project, a group that ranges to the north of our previous study area, and we thought that the alpha male of the new group (a male in his prime whom we named

FIGURE 17.3 Artemis at 15 years of age. Like many adult male capuchins, he has broad shoulders, a wrinkled forehead, and dark spots on his face that help us to identify him. Also like many older adult males, he has changed groups multiple times. **Photo credit:** Fernando Campos.

"Artemis") looked quite a bit like a grown-up Alien. We had collected fecal samples from Alien many years before for genetic analyses, and after we collected samples from Artemis, we were able to confirm that the two males were one and the same. We had located Alien again, 11 years after his birth. He remained as alpha male of the new study group for 5 years, before disappearing again during a recent invasion of outsider males. This time we asked ourselves whether he was killed during the takeover, as sometimes happens to alpha males, or was twice fortunate, and we will find him again one day, living in yet another group as an older male. His mother Kathy Lee, meanwhile, is still resident in her natal group, and in 2010, at the age of 22 years, she gave birth to her most recent daughter, whom we named Sage. Only time will tell the eventual fates of Kathy Lee and her offspring and of the growing monkey populations of Santa Rosa. Along with my graduate students and successors, I have every intention of continuing the project long enough to find out.

Suggested Readings

Carnegie, S. D., L. M. Fedigan, and A. D. Melin. 2011. "Reproductive Seasonality in Female Capuchins (*Cebus capucinus*) in Santa Rosa (Área de Conservación Guanacaste)." *International Journal of Primatology* 32: 1076–1090.

Fedigan, L. M., and K. M. Jack 2012. "Tracking Monkeys in Santa Rosa: Lessons from a Regenerating Tropical Dry Forest." In Kappeler, P., and D. Watts (eds.), *Long-term Field Studies of Primates*, Springer Press, Heidelberg (pp. 165–184).

Fedigan, L. M., and K. M. Jack. 2013. "Sexual Conflict in White-Faced Capuchins: It's Not Whether You Win or Lose." In Fisher, M. L., J. R. Garcia, and R. S. Chang (eds.), *Evolution's Empress: Darwinian Perspectives on Women*, Oxford University Press, New York (pp. 281–303).

Janzen, D. H. 2002. "Tropical Dry Forest: Área de Conservación Guanacaste, Northwestern Costa Rica." In Perrow, M. R., and A. J. Davy (eds.) *Handbook of Ecological Restoration, volume 2, Restoration in Practice*, Cambridge University Press, Cambridge, MA (pp. 559–583).

McCabe, G. M., and L. M. Fedigan. 2007. "Effects of Reproductive Status on Energy Intake, Ingestion Rates and Dietary Composition of White-Faced Capuchins (*Cebus capucinus*) at Santa Rosa, Costa Rica." *International Journal of Primatology* 28: 837–851.

Perry, S. 2008. *Manipulative Monkeys. The Capuchins of Lomas Barbudal*. Cambridge, MA: Harvard University Press.

Acknowledgments

I thank the Costa Rican National Park for permission to work in SRNP from 1983–1989 and the administrators of the Área de Conservación Guanacaste (especially Roger Blanco Segura) for allowing us to continue research in the park through the present day. Over the thirty years of this project, many people have contributed to the census and life history database on the Santa Rosa monkeys and I am very grateful to all of these students, colleagues, and local assistants. Research described in this chapter complied with all institutional and government regulations regarding ethical treatment of our study subjects. My research has been supported by ongoing Discovery Grants from NSERC (Natural Sciences and Engineering Research Council of Canada) and by the University of Calgary and the Canada Research Chairs Program.

18

Male Bands in the Amazonian Rainforest

By Anthony Di Fiore[1]

We set off into the forest on a surprisingly cold, damp morning for the Amazon. It had rained hard the night before, and now a thin, misty layer of fog draped over the treetops. With sunlight just beginning to peek above the fog, we scrambled up a muddy, sharp ridge to the west of a clearing that had been made a few months before by a U.S. oil company. Well, I scrambled—pulling myself up the steep slope with the help of saplings, rotting tree roots, and one spiky palm that I didn't notice in the dim light until it was too late—while my companions, four Waorani hunters not much older than I, plus one of their young sons, had none of my difficulty. They talked softly in Wao and occasionally with me in broken Spanish, while climbing easily up the ridge top where they paused for me to catch my breath.

This was one of a series of days that I spent with the hunters in the summer of 1994 to delimit the northern and southern boundaries of the patch of forest where I was to do my dissertation research on the natural history of woolly monkeys. Surrounding us was the huge expanse of Ecuador's Yasuní National Park, currently the largest and most pristine patch of ostensibly protected natural rainforest in western Amazonia. Yasuní is a gem of a place, located at the base of the Andes, right on the Equator. The region hosts an insanely high diversity of neotropical organisms—birds, mammals, plants, reptiles, and invertebrates. You name it, the diversity you find in Yasuní exceeds global records, and many of these organisms are endemic, occurring nowhere else in the world.

After resting for a few moments, my companions and I walked roughly southwest on the ridge along an old game trail that the Wao had used for generations. From the clearing

[1]About the author: Anthony Di Fiore is a biological anthropologist with wide-ranging interests in the social behavior, ecology, population genetics, and phylogenetic history of New World monkeys. His research combines long-term field-work at study sites in the Yasuní Biosphere Reserve in western Amazonia (one of the most diverse tropical forests on Earth and home to 10 species of nonhuman primates) with molecular genetic analysis, which allows him to address topics that are difficult to explore in observational studies alone, including questions about dispersal behavior, gene flow, mating patterns, and the fitness consequences of individual behavior.

Contact information: Department of Anthropology, University of Texas at Austin, Austin, TX 78712, USA, anthony.difiore@austin.utexas.edu

Citation: Di Fiore, A. 2014. "Male Bands in the Amazonian Rainforest." In Strier, K. B. (ed.), *Primate Ethnographies*. Upper Saddle River, NJ: Pearson Education, Inc. (pp. 196–206).

MAP 18.1

where we started, we heard the growl of a big generator firing up and then the repetitive "boom, boom, boom" of a perforation drill punching an oil well into the ground below the jungle. The noise grew fainter as we headed deeper into primary forest, gradually giving way to more friendly forest sounds—the periodic band-saw buzz of cicadas, the low rumble of a passing giant orchid bee, the Chihuahua-yelping of two toucans calling back and forth across

FIGURE 18.1 Adult male woolly monkey at the Tiputini Biodiversity Station, Yasuní National Park, Ecuador. **Photo credit:** Dylan Schwindt, courtesy of Anthony Di Fiore.

our trail. At one point, we walked through a lek, or breeding display ground, of screaming pihas, nondescript, almost impossible-to-see birds with an ear-piercing three-note whistle that resembles a catcall.

This day was not exactly how I had envisioned spending time during my third month of dissertation fieldwork. I'd already cut and mapped trails, set up botanical transects to collect information on forest phenology, and I was now smack in the middle of habituating the groups of monkeys I would eventually study. But a few days before, while following a group of woollies with my field assistant (another Wao named "Capitán" Juan Nenquimo), I had run into one of the men I was now with. Capitán and I were within a few hundred meters of the new oil company road standing under a pair of adult female woolly monkeys and their kids. The monkeys were plowing through a tree crown full of "mango de monte," a delicious wild drupe with a sharp, sweet taste almost like passion fruit when we heard a couple of unmistakable blasts coming from about 100 meters away. Capitán looked towards the shots, yelled something in Wao, and took off running through the forest in that direction. I followed, and after a few of minutes of frantic crashing, caught up to him arguing back and forth in Wao with Mingui Ahua, a local hunter, and a young boy who was accompanying him. The Wao language is not the most mellifluous one to begin with, and their conversation was loud and intense, bordering on aggressive. "Tell him to stop shooting!" I panted in Spanish to Capitán and tried to catch my breath. "Tell him we're studying the monkeys. Don't shoot at them!" Capitán kept arguing with Mingui for a few minutes, then turned to me and said in Spanish, "He says he doesn't care. He's hunting for a feast."

Mingui stepped away from us and began moving in the direction of some of the woolly monkeys that we could still hear in the area. We followed him about 10 meters back. "Listen, stop, please!" Capitán and I yelled. Another shot, and then a few moments later, a crash as a monkey fell to the ground. Mingui walked over to the animal, picked it up, and then purposefully traced his way back through the forest, not looking at us, to the bodies of three more adult woolly monkeys he had managed to down in as many shots in the minutes before we had caught up with him. Capitán and I kept following behind Mingui, haranguing him, until he and the boy threw the four monkeys over their shoulders and headed out to the road.

Over the next few days, after conversations with my advisor and seriously considering giving up on my dissertation work, I met with Mingui and some of the other local Wao to try to work out how I might continue to work in the area—which fell within the hunting grounds of the local families—without worrying about them killing the animals I was there to study. Contract anthropologists from the local oil company's division of "Community Relations" suggested a possible way forward, one that I later realized was typical for the company to use when they wanted something from the locals: Pay them off. I was anxious to get on with my work, so I agreed to give each of the local hunting families a stipend of food every month as a "site use fee" in exchange for their not hunting in the area and for helping me encourage other local hunters also to refrain. Like any negotiation about territory and space among the Wao, this involved a formal excursion to walk and mark the borders. So here we were, a few days later, setting up the study area boundaries that Mingui, along with Wampi and Nambai (his half-brothers and the only other adult men from his settlement), would theoretically respect and help me to police.

For the Wao men I was with, our walk in the forest seemed an entertaining distraction from what they might otherwise be doing—manual labor for the oil company. And for me it was a fun distraction, too. Although I was none too fond of Mingui (given that our first contact was when he shot four monkeys in about ten minutes), out on the trail with Wampi and Nambai and a boy I think was Nambai's son he was a pleasant, even entertaining companion. My initial efforts on the trail to try to explain to them why I wanted to follow woolly monkeys and study them were awkward, almost foolish sounding. Me: "They're related to people!" Wampi: "Of course! They look like us." Me: "And no one knows much about them." Mingui: "Ha! Not true! We know all about them!" Me: "And they make great subjects for testing socioecological models about primate grouping patterns." All of my companions: "Huh?" In fact, a year before, while looking into a different place to work, another Wao elder had denied me the chance even to talk with him about studying monkeys in his group's hunting zone. The reason? I was told that he was incredulous that someone who wasn't a hunter would want to follow monkeys, so he thought I must have something else up my sleeve.

Things got more comfortable on the trail when the men began telling me forest stories of their own. Wampi, whose Spanish was the best of the bunch, described how when he was a boy, he went hunting in this same area with his father, and they ran across and somehow pissed off a jaguar, who came toward them. Wampi's father managed to position himself and his son on the side of a sapling opposite from the jaguar and thus dodge the cat's swipes at them, all the while beating it over the head with a stick until it gave up and walked away. I decided to never make a jaguar angry, and have so far succeeded, although I have pissed off plenty of fer-de-lances and peccaries.

After we had walked for a couple of hours, the men became more reserved. We were now traveling through an area they knew less well, and all the men quieted down and looked around carefully as we walked. Here, they told me, was the chance of running into other people in the forest—not Wao who were "civilized" (as the men I was with described themselves) but the more "savage" and "belligerent" Tagaeri, a small splinter group of Wao descended from a warrior

FIGURE 18.2 Wampi, one of the local Wao hunters who worked as a field assistant.
Photo credit: Dylan Schwindt, courtesy of Anthony Di Fiore.

named Taga, who decided, soon after missionaries first contacted the Wao back in the 1970s, that he wanted nothing to do with Westerners. In subdued voices, the men took turns telling me about their families' contacts with the Tagaeri since the split—of male relatives being killed, of women being abducted and forced to marry into Taga's clan, of retaliation parties their relatives had organized to go after the Tagaeri. I was told—made to promise, in fact—that if I ever came across any indication of other people in the area I would leave the forest immediately and go talk with them. Such signs might include barefoot footprints far from the road, old campsites with thatched palm dwellings, or isolated fields of yucca. More ominously, they described warnings that might be placed on my trails—like a pair of crossed spears lashed together with vines— which they said was an unmistakable message to turn around and get out.

Throughout our hikes—but especially when we were talking about the Tagaeri—I was struck by how closely Mingui, Wampi, and Nambai coordinated their activities in a way that seemed natural, intimate, and almost unconscious. They finished each other's sentences, and consulted quietly with few words and with subtle hand gestures about which way to go, when and where to stop and rest, and so on. And when the sky went dark and big, heavy raindrops began to fall, the men fanned out wordlessly and, each with a machete, quickly collected a set of large fronds from understory palms. They came back together near a pair of parallel saplings, and in about three minutes wove a 2-meter tall lean-to that they then used as a shelter from the storm for the next hour. They stayed far drier and cooler than I did, curled up under a thick, plastic, and yet strangely-not-waterproof poncho. Later that day after the rain, when we stopped for a rest, Nambai and the boy who had tagged along with us ducked down to a nearby stream. There Nambai offered advice and help as the kid fished for a freshwater stingray they had spotted sliding along the bed of the stream. After the boy had pinned the ray to the stream-bottom with a spear he had made from a nearby sapling with a couple of deft machete cuts, Nambai helped him finish it off, collect it from the stream floor, and remove the venomous tail spine before packing it in leaves to carry back with us—all without exchanging more than a few touches and a couple of *sotto voce* words in Wao.

Over the next two years, as I conducted my dissertation work in the area with the agreed-upon boundaries, I would meet with Mingui, Wampi, Nambai, and their families semi-regularly to give them the food that was my part of our deal, and I'd occasionally give them rides along the road. For the most part, the Wao seemed to respect our accord, but there were slips. Once, I had a tense run-in with Nambai, who had gone into the study area with a gun and startled another graduate student who was following woolly monkeys. Another time we came upon a group of Wao, some from the local community among them, who had shot a puma crossing the road and then followed it into the study area to finish it off. But overall the deal seemed to work out. When other hunters, from further south along the road, came up one time and went into the site, the hunters I knew took them aside and cautioned them about respecting that area.

Beyond these contacts, from time to time my team hired Wampi to help us follow monkeys or reopen trails, as he showed the most interest of the local folks in what we were doing and got a huge kick out of the fact that we could recognize and had named the animals individually: "That female's called 'Effie'? Why don't you call her 'Lunch'? Jejeje!" And Capitán, who was not from the region, worked with me for the better part of a year before he had to leave Yasuní. The reason why is a long story, but the short version is that he was kicked out of the park by the oil company, long after he stopped working for us, for taking part in a Wao strike against the company. Periodically, the local Wao would cut down trees and block traffic on the oil company road in order to protest something the company had done or simply to make things inconvenient. On one occasion, the strike was more serious and resulted in vandalism at some of the facilities, and rumor has it that Capitán helped the locals commandeer a company vehicle and drove some of the vandals up and down the road, thus prompting his expulsion. Reflecting on it now, I think Capitán must have learned to drive a manual transmission by practicing shifting for me from the passenger seat as we drove our decrepit Land Cruiser over 14 kilometers of gravel road from the research camp out to the field site each morning.

Capitán and Wampi usually seemed quite content to be in the forest, getting paid to help me track the monkeys as I learned my way around the site and how to follow the animals on my own. Most of our conversations on those days centered around our respective histories—them growing up in the forest in the 1970s and 1980s in lowland Ecuador, me in suburban Virginia—and on the quiet treasures of the forest around us. I remember being regaled with stories of ocelot hunting, of relatives who'd been bitten by venomous snakes, and of plants and poultices used to treat various tropical infirmities. Capitán once showed me how to make a whistling projectile launcher from the rubbery leaf and stem of a particular kind of understory plant. "My dad taught me this when I went hunting with him as a kid," he said, and I spent the next month practicing making them myself. Wampi would call in toucans with a small trumpet made from a rolled leaf while we sat listening for monkeys, and once, when I was thirsty, he sliced through a fat vine, which disgorged a steady flow of clear liquid. "Bejuco de agua" (water-vine). "Drink it." They showed me which palm nuts to break to find refreshing coconut water inside. It was impossible not to be fascinated. Their questions of me invariably centered around my wealth and status as an "extranjero gringo," and no amount of protest could convince them of my true identity as a penurious graduate student. "How much did your binoculars (then my most prized and extravagant possession) cost?" "If I wanted to visit you in the U.S., how much would it take to get there?" "How many days' travel away is this 'California'?" "Have you met the president?" "Can I have your watch?"

Only a couple of times did they ask why the heck I was there, in remote Ecuador, wanting to study monkeys. "What's so special about them?" This was a hard question to answer, I found, without sounding to my ears like an eco-nut. "Well," I would say, "monkeys reproduce very slowly . . . female woolly monkeys, for example, only have a baby every three years or so . . . only a little faster than people do. And they don't start reproducing until they are seven or eight years old! So, monkey populations are really easily overhunted. Once population size gets low, it's hard to recover."

I talked with Wampi once about empty forests—forests without monkeys or other large animals, many of which are likely to be important seed dispersers for tropical plants. We were resting on a small saddle between two ridges, listening for monkeys, and Wampi chopped idly at a rotting tree stump with his machete. "Woolly monkeys eat, like, 250 different kinds of fruits [even in Spanish, I tended to stick "like" into the middle of my sentences] and to swallow and then poop out the seeds of many of them. That's how plants get their seeds moved away from parent trees . . . no monkeys, no plant reproduction." I talked about fragmentation, too, as seen throughout eastern Ecuador where petroleum exploration, logging, commercial agriculture, and human colonization associated with all of these has and continues to lead to fragmentation across the lowlands. "Woolly monkeys and especially spider monkeys need a lot of area to roam in. When new roads and farms go in, the monkeys can lose a lot of land then not have enough area to survive. Some monkeys may do okay, but not woolly monkeys or spider monkeys."

"Okay." Then I would get asked, "But what's important about woolly monkeys and spider monkeys?" Here it got more difficult, but I tried to explain how these monkeys, in particular, were interesting to me because of the kinds of groups they live in:

"With most monkeys," I said, "like the 'barisos' (squirrel monkeys) or 'machines' (capuchins), the females make up the social core of a group. But not in the 'chorongos' (woolly monkeys) or 'maquisapas' (spider monkeys). There, the males make up a group's core. Females leave when

FIGURE 18.3   Adult female spider monkey from the Proyecto Primates Research Area, Yasuní National Park, Ecuador. **Photo credit:** Dylan Schwindt, courtesy of Anthony Di Fiore.

they become sexually mature, but males are philopatric—they stick around in their natal groups and hang out, as adults, with their male relatives.

"This is a very rare, special pattern . . . seen only in a few kinds of primates: in people, in chimpanzees (which are closely related to people), and in a few, special primates like woolly monkeys and spider monkeys in South America. That's why I am here, really, to study how and why these primates are different and to maybe understand something about male kinship and cooperation that we can apply to thinking about human social behavior."

"And don't you have forests in your country? Why come here?"

"Yes, we have forests, but not tropical rainforest like this," I said. "And we have no wild primates."

Wampi was silent for a minute, maybe thinking about this, then flashed me a grin, grabbed his machete and said, "Vamos."

At the time, I could not have imagined that I would still be motivated by these questions 11 years later. Yet, there I was, back in Yasuní one unusually hot midsummer afternoon in 2005, with Andres Link, then one of my graduate students, chasing a subgroup of white-bellied spider monkeys as they bee-lined from feeding tree to feeding tree. For the past few months, we had been working on habituating the spider monkeys at a new research site in the area: the Tiputini Biodiversity Station, which is downriver from where I had done my dissertation work on woolly monkeys and is more protected from hunters. Spider monkeys move through the trees more quickly than woollies, and on that day we had followed two adult males, Juan and Geronimo, from the core of our main study group's range, far to the west of where we currently were. It had been a dogged, nonstop chase of close to a kilometer, and another three males had joined the

FIGURE 18.4   Andres Link (left) and the author (right) standing on the banks of the Río Tiputini in the summer of 2005 after spending a morning running after unhabituated spider monkeys. **Photo credit:** Anthony Di Fiore.

party en route. Finally, they all seemed to be settling down and were casually feeding and resting on thick branches about 20 meters up in the midcanopy. Our respite was short-lived. One by one, the males stopped feeding or stood up, moved to the edge of the tree crown, and filed out of the tree in a single column heading straight east. They moved deliberately, fast, and almost silently, traveling low in the canopy, keeping about 10 meters between one another, and showing none of the raucousness and exuberance that often characterizes spider monkeys' locomotion.

Andres and I followed the males for about an hour as they moved straight towards the edge of their territory and then beyond, finally turning south in a long, arcing path that took them through an area of forest we had never seen them visit before. They finally stopped along the edge of the river that borders our study site, well outside their usual stomping grounds. There, they spread out over approximately 100 meters of riverfront, climbed up high in different trees, and then spent the next fifteen minutes or so loud calling back and forth before going quiet and resting again. We thought we heard loud calls of another group of spider monkeys, coming from deep in the forest on the other side of the river.

This was our first close-up observation of a male "patrol," and over the past seven years we have recorded several dozen more. Patrols typically involve the same basic pattern of behavior: Multiple males (usually most of the adult and subadult males in the group), and sometimes a few females as well, coalesce into a single, coordinated subgroup and then travel along the edge of the group's territory or through the rarely visited boundary zone that seems to exist between group territories. Alternatively, the subgroup may make a temporary incursion or "raid" into the territory of an adjacent group, sometimes visiting a resource patch (like a mineral lick) deep inside another group's range. During patrols and raids, if males from another group are encountered, the reaction is almost invariably hostile, with members of the different groups exchanging vocalizations and sometimes charging or aggressing against one another physically.

Since 2010, our spider monkey research has been focused primarily on the behavior of males—on their cooperation and competition within and between groups, and particularly on the patrols, raids, and aggressive intergroup encounters that are among the more obvious interactions that males have. The functions of these behaviors are not nailed down, but it's easy to list some possibilities. Males may use patrolling to mark the boundaries of a shared territory (although, unlike for some pack-living canids, there's not much compelling evidence that this idea holds any weight for spider monkeys). Alternatively, males may patrol to regularly monitor their territory boundary and better detect and repel possible intruders. They might also use patrols and/or raids to seek out and possibly kill rival males from other groups, or to try to lure females away from other groups to join their own. In any case, males' collective boundary patrolling and participation in intergroup encounters is a clear example of how male spider monkeys from the same group can be remarkably tolerant of one another—and even work together—while at the same time being antagonistic to males from other groups.

As I had told the Wao hunters, male spider monkeys tend to be philopatric. This means that they typically do not disperse from their natal groups, and males from the same group can be closely related to one another. In fact, our recent genetic work has demonstrated that the males in the group Andres and I were following are indeed relatives. It is perhaps not surprising, then, that intragroup relationships among males tend toward the tolerant. That's not to say that males from the same group don't compete with one another. Given the limited reproductive opportunities available to males, it is impossible to imagine that some subtle form of competition doesn't take place—but if it's there, it's not often overt or easy to see. That's also not to say that kinship is essential for male cooperation within groups. Our genetic data suggest, in fact, that some adult male spider monkeys are not closely related to the other males from their group, but they still participate in collective intergroup aggression anyway.

Between groups, all bets are off. Intergroup encounters are almost always tense and hostile. Especially when very different-size subgroups of males meet, escalated violence tends to ensue, as males from the larger subgroup cooperatively chase and harass the males from the smaller one. The same kind of intergroup hostility—and the same increased risk of escalation as the power differential between groups increases—has also been reported in studies of east African chimpanzees, and, importantly, humans. Thus, all three of these taxa (spider monkeys, common chimpanzees, and humans), interestingly, converge in various fundamental aspects of their behavioral biology: in their patrilineal and patrilocal pattern of social organization, in the prevalence of female dispersal/exogamy, in the importance of social bonding and cooperation among males from the same group, and in males' xenophobia and intolerance of same-sex rivals in other groups.

Since Andres and I have been working on male social interactions in spider monkeys, we have been struck time and again by these strong convergences. My own "boundary patrol" with local hunters when I first began working in the field mimics in many ways the patrols we've been studying among spider monkeys, from the cooperative participation of male kin (though kinship clearly isn't essential for cooperation, as I was assimilated into the male Wao "in-group"), to our fear of the real or imagined "other" that might or might not have been encountered.

Not surprisingly, in the years since I started working in the Yasuní region, my relationships with and attitudes towards the Wao—and particularly with the few male hunters that I first met 18 years ago—have changed dramatically, from ones marked by suspicion and hostility on both sides, to tolerance and, at least on my part, occasional moments of affection. I realize, too, that I have known these men for as long as I have been an adult. The boy who accompanied us on our boundary treks in the mid-1990s has to be in his late twenties or early thirties now, and the men, only slightly older than me, in their late forties. Over these years, Nambai, Mingui, and Wampi have all had kids and raised those kids to adulthood or near-adulthood, while their community and the other ones in the area have grown in size through immigration and improved health care. For a while, another, older, male relative named Tihue moved into the area, and I confess I always found him the most delightful of the local men to talk with, even though I knew he was an avid hunter who may or may not have heeded our no-hunting agreement. Tihue would tell me, in Wao-punctuated Spanish, about many of his extended hunting trips and of the spectacular things he had seen—mega-groups of 100-plus white-lipped peccaries, woolly monkeys staring down and mobbing a jaguar, and so on. I often wasn't sure I believed or even whether I fully understood what he was telling me, but he did so with such enthusiasm that it was hard not to feel it myself. And I found it hard to reconcile Tihue's engaging personality and gentle disposition towards nature with the stories I had heard of his participation in bloody revenge raids against the Tagaeri in his youth. Nambai, too, who terrified me (and lots of other people) 20 years ago strikes me now as a doting father and grandfather. Last time I saw him, perhaps two years ago, he proudly told me about the new outboard motor his son had just bought and about his newest grandchild. I find it poignant that we're all still walking around and working in the same forests as we were 20 years ago.

It may be my imagination, but I felt a sea change in how I was perceived by the Wao in the early 2000s, after my first daughter was born. During my summer 2002 field season, I took pictures of my family with me and wound up standing alongside the river one afternoon talking with Wampi and a couple of other Wao, and I asked if they wanted to see my pictures. Wampi knew my wife from years before, and I showed him pictures of her holding our daughter: "Oh,

FIGURE 18.5 The author (Anthony Di Fiore) showing photos of his family to the children of his field assistants. **Photo credit:** Margaret Metz, courtesy of Anthony Di Fiore.

she's blonde, like your wife." "What's her name?" "How old is she now?" "When will you have a boy?" I was peppered with questions, not just from Wampi but from the other folks standing around as well. Later, some of the Wao women came up to me and asked to see the pictures, too, which was the first time anyone other than the men or young children had ever spoken to me or smiled at me. Now, as the community has grown and as I work farther away from my old field site, when I make a trip to Yasuní, I see fewer and fewer of the Wao whom I know. When I do see them, it's not monkeys we talk about anymore, but our families and relatives. It seems we all share an interest in kinship dynamics after all.

Suggested Readings

Bass, M. S., M. Finer, C. N. Jenkins, H. Kreft, D. F. Cisneros-Heredia, S. F. McCracken, N. C. A. Pitman, P. H. English, K. Swing, G. Villa, A. Di Fiore, C. C. Voigt, and T. H. Kunz. 2010. "Global Conservation Significance of Ecuador's Yasuní National Park." *PloS One* 5:e8767.

Campbell, C. A. 2008. *Spider Monkeys: The Biology and Behavior of the Genus Ateles.* New York: Cambridge University Press.

Di Fiore, A., and R. C. Fleischer. 2005. "Social Behavior, Reproductive Strategies, and Population Genetic Structure of *Lagothrix lagotricha poeppigii.*" *International Journal of Primatology* 26: 1137–1173.

Di Fiore, A., A. L. Link, C. A. Schmitt, and S. N. Spehar. 2009. "Dispersal Patterns in Sympatric Woolly and Spider Monkeys: Integrating Molecular and Observational Data." *Behaviour* 146: 437–470.

Kane, J. 1995. *Savages.* New York: Knopf.

Peres, C. A. 2000. "Effects of Subsistence Hunting on Vertebrate Community Structure in Amazonian Forests." *Conservation Biology* 14: 240–253.

Robarchek, C. A., and C. Robarchek. 1998. *Waorani: The Contexts of Violence and War.* Fort Worth, TX: Harcourt Brace College Publishers.

Acknowledgments

I would like to thank the Ecuadorian Ministerio de Ambiente for its long-term support of primate research in the Yasuní region as well as the directors and staff of the Yasuní Scientific Research Station and the Tiputini Biodiversity Station for generous logistical assistance in the field. Heartfelt thanks are also due to Kristin Phillips, Andres Link, Eduardo Fernandez-Duque, and many students and research assistants for their humor and camaraderie in the field. I am also very grateful to the members of the Waorani communities of Guiyero and Tiimpuca for allowing us to study primates on their lands. This research has been supported, in part, by grants from the Harry Frank Guggenheim Foundation, the National Geographic Society, the Wenner-Gren Foundation, the L.S.B. Leakey Foundation, and the National Science Foundation (grant BCS 1062540).

19

Blue Monkeys and Bridges
Transformations in Habituation, Habitat, and People

By Marina Cords[1]

When I first set foot in the Kakamega Forest in western Kenya, 34 years ago, I had never seen a wild monkey before. Armed with new binoculars and gumboots, I followed Thelma Rowell down a muddy trail. Thelma, my doctoral supervisor, was here to introduce me to the forest she had chosen as a promising study site. It became clear immediately that sensitive ears were essential for studying monkeys here: The first sign of my subjects was their alarm chirps, which I initially mistook for bird calls. Eventually we located the source, and I was able to pick out the two species of guenons that are common in the forest—blue monkeys and redtail monkeys. Only a few individuals were visible, and they were widely scattered: They stared at us from the top of the canopy, bobbing their heads and chirping. By midday, I wondered if I would be able to collect enough data to answer my research question, which focused on the adaptive value of mixed-species associations of these two guenons. Would I see enough monkeys? Would I see them do something other than make alarm calls? Only later in the afternoon did we see more than a few of them at a time: In fact, it seemed that suddenly there were blue monkeys in all directions, challenging my expectation that they lived in small groups of 10 to 20, as had been reported before. Thelma suggested, "Maybe they don't live in groups at all." She was prone to provocative statements, but in this case, it seemed a surprisingly reasonable proposal: We observers could not detect a group center or edge, much less a direction of movement. As I planned to follow particular groups, studying their movements and feeding patterns and relations with groups of redtails, my inability to distinguish a group was a problem.

Fast forward 29 years. The same binoculars are still around my neck, although now the blue monkeys are sometimes so close that I cannot focus them properly. I've gone through many

[1]About the author: Marina Cords is a professor in Ecology, Evolution and Environmental Biology at Columbia University, New York City, and part of the New York Consortium in Evolutionary Primatology (NYCEP). She has focused her research on the social behavior and ecology of monkeys in the Kakamega Forest, using observations supplemented by laboratory investigations.

Contact information: Department of Ecology, Evolution & Environmental Biology, Columbia University, New York, NY 10027, USA, mc51@columbia.edu

Citation: Cords, M. 2014. "Blue Monkeys and Bridges: Transformations in Habituation, Habitat and People." In Strier, K. B. (ed.), *Primate Ethnographies*. Upper Saddle River, NJ: Pearson Education, Inc. (pp. 207–217).

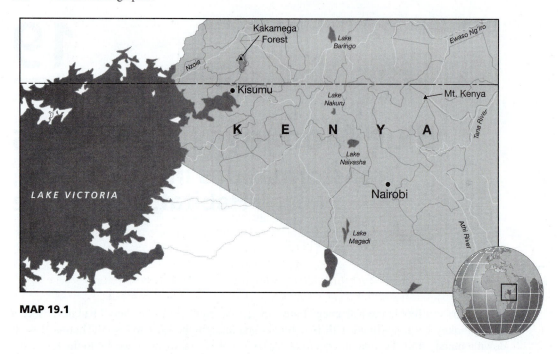

MAP 19.1

pairs of gumboots. It is morning and I've just caught sight of the resident adult male in one of our four blue monkey study groups: It's my turn to follow this particular group, whose identity is clear once you recognize individuals and realize that a group's amoeboid movements are in fact concentrated within a particular area. Even without the binoculars, I can see that the resident male is holding something red in his hand. I gulp as I get a better view: It turns out to be the bottom half of an infant blue monkey, and he is holding it like a goblet, occasionally licking the bloody rim in the middle of what would have been a torso. Infanticide has been reported in blue monkeys, but we've never seen any direct sign of it here in Kakamega, although there have been a few suspicious occasions when a male harassed a new mother, whose infant then disappeared. Don't jump to conclusions, I warn myself: Maybe the infant belongs to a neighboring group, a victim in the sometimes violent intergroup encounters that punctuate blue monkey life. I know exactly how to tell if this is within-group infanticide: I have to find the mother of the only young infant in the study group. Her infant is so young that she carries it almost constantly. But where to find her? Being moderately low-ranking, she tends to frequent the outskirts of the group. I walk around to get a sense of where the group members are located, and then I quickly find her, with no infant clinging. By the end of the day, I've verified that this case of apparent infanticide has all the hallmarks of sexually selected male behavior.

So much was different at these two points in time: our understanding of the most basic elements of natural history, the number of animals monitored, and our ability to distinguish and locate them. Even the focus of research, constrained by what was actually feasible, had shifted: I started out investigating sociality between species, but moved on in later years to study variation among individuals within their groups. (Why were only some males infanticidal? How did dominance rank affect the social life of females?) At the root of most of these differences was the gradual habituation of the animals to human observers. Habituated animals have a reduced tendency to flee when people are near. Habituation allowed me to identify and make detailed observations of individuals. Recognition of individuals made group identification possible and also highlighted differences among group members. My research on guenons at Kakamega is deeply connected to the process and outcome of habituation. Habituation, in turn, is related to the animals' perception of danger.

Early in my study, all the monkeys were very wary of humans and didn't differentiate the humans they encountered. Such a reaction was not surprising given the way local people treated monkeys at the time. A monkey close by was invariably the target of a rock or stick; not surprisingly, the monkeys kept their distance. During the first months of the study, I learned to follow monkeys without "pushing" them by coming too close; I also wore the same army-green clothes every day, and consciously avoided raising my arms in ways that might suggest I was about to throw an object. Over the first year of study, the monkeys gradually lost some of their fear, and I occasionally had opportunities to study—with binoculars—the details of their faces and the hairs at the ends of their tails, which helped me to begin to distinguish individuals.

Habituation was a noticeable process over fifteen to twenty years. Just a few months after I had selected a study group of each species, Thelma returned for a visit. The monkeys initially chirped and climbed to the treetops after spotting us together, but over the course of a few days, they began to treat us interchangeably. Similar clothing, haircuts, and behavior around them probably helped. Indeed, the first time I put on a blue sweater and popped a red umbrella in the rainy season, there was a chorus of chirps and rapid flight through the canopy; but eventually, they seemed to learn that I was okay, even in unusual clothing. The next noticeable step in their habituation occurred when students from the University of Nairobi joined our field team in 1981. The monkeys had no experience with African observers: The Africans they knew threw stones and sticks, and the monkeys behaved as if this was what they expected of the visiting students. We muttered in disbelief about our "racist" monkeys, who seemed more perturbed by the Kenyan

FIGURE 19.1 Grooming is the main form of affiliative behavior in blue monkeys, a female-bonded species in which female kin stay together for life. Grooming is not limited to kin, however: This couple is unrelated. Once the monkeys were better habituated, distinguishing physical characteristics were easier to observe, facilitating individual identification. **Photo credit:** Marina Cords.

students than by white-skinned American visitors. But after about a month, they accepted the Kenyan students as equivalent to Thelma and me. Importantly, they continued to distinguish the monkey-watching Kenyans from other Kenyans who passed by on the forest trails.

By the mid-1990s, the monkeys learned to make another distinction among the passers-by. We had by then focused our study on blue monkeys, and picked up a second blue monkey study group, and both groups began to cross a dirt road that ran through the forest. The groups were growing, and the forest across the road provided a supplementary foraging area. For both the monkeys and me, crossing the road was a nerve-wracking experience in those early months. Serving as a route to the offices and health center in the nearby forest station, the road had pedestrian traffic throughout the day. Monkeys crossing the road had to come down low in the vegetation on either side, but when passing boys and young men detected them there, they seemed invariably to throw stones, presumably finding that monkeys made good targets. I was often behind the front line of the group, in the thick vegetation and invisible to people on the road, but I was forced to dodge these missiles along with the monkeys. Women and girls did not throw stones, and the monkeys soon picked up on this sex difference. When the pedestrians were female, the monkeys usually continued their activities—mostly feeding—in the low vegetation along the road, and even scampered across occasionally. However, when even an individual boy or man walked down the road, the monkeys climbed up to the treetops as he approached and returned to lower branches only after he had passed on. Clearly the monkeys were learning to be more specific in their judgment of which humans were dangerous.

As the monkeys began to cross the road regularly, sometimes daily, they encountered local people much more often than before, and these occasions brought me into greater contact with the local population as well. In earlier years, my days were spent deeper in the forest, and I met

FIGURE 19.2 Monkeys learned to avoid danger when crossing the road, and people learned to stop throwing stones. Nowadays, monkeys will cross the road even when people are present, but they still keep their distance, and will linger on the road only when it is empty, as here. In the forest, however, well-habituated animals come to the ground more often in certain locations, and do not mind the proximity of the monkey-watching team. **Photo credit:** Marina Cords.

FIGURE 19.3   The Kakamega Forest has supplied surrounding families with various products for generations. A common sight along the roads is women carrying firewood. It is permitted in some areas to collect fallen branches from the ground. **Photo credit:** Marina Cords.

people infrequently. They passed through the forest for many reasons—gathering firewood, mushrooms, or honey, moving cows through to a local grassland, or just taking a short-cut—but they generally went about their business with no attention to the monkeys, which were high in the trees. The monkeys also reacted very mildly to these passers-by. My usual contact with people in the forest consisted of an exchange of verbal greetings, sometimes after they had recovered from the shock of finding a foreigner hidden in the greenery. On the road, however, where the monkeys had to come low to cross, the people noticed them more often. On many occasions, as the rocks started flying in our direction, I would bash through the vegetation to reach the road and accost the stone-throwers. My visible presence invariably stopped the stones, and if the person didn't just flee in horror at seeing an angry *mzungu* ("European") emerge from the bush, I was able to engage in conversation about stone throwing. The men were usually a little sheepish about why they threw stones, admitting they had no particular reason to do so. I would explain that the monkeys were under study, and dodging stones made research difficult. It surprised me that local people had any understanding, and apparently great respect, for research. Perhaps the realization that someone did care, someone who had come from far away and returned year after year, helped make an impression.

It is still amazing to me that, within a few years, the stone throwing stopped entirely. Nowadays, there is ever more traffic on this road, but when passers-by detect monkeys, they either ignore them or take the time to observe them for a few minutes. This happens even when the research team is not visible: Often it is mothers with small children—heading to or from the dispensary for vaccinations—who take the time to introduce their children to the local wildlife.

This change in attitude and behavior likely reflects several developments. First, beginning in 1997, I began to work with Wilberforce Okeka, a forest guard but also a forest *fundi* (expert) whose expertise was often appreciated by tourists. One German visitor supported Wilberforce's vision to begin educating local children about the forest, in hopes that knowledge would foster appreciation and a desire to conserve. Wilberforce started the Kakamega Environmental Education Program, or KEEP, with Saturday meetings on the grass outside his government-issue bungalow. Though not formally trained beyond the eighth grade, Wilberforce read voraciously and was a natural teacher. Over the next decade, with support from organizations both outside and within Kenya, KEEP developed enormously, attracting more and more children to the Saturday classes, increasing its educational outreach activities to surrounding schools, and developing new conservation-related programs focused on bee-keeping, tree nurseries, and tourism. Wilberforce tapped into a wellspring of enthusiasm on the part of experienced forest guides, as well as young and eager forest neighbors who were welcomed and taught by the more knowledgeable members (a number of these young members joined my research project). News of KEEP's existence and its message traveled to the larger region around the forest, and new branches popped up. KEEP's development was both cause and effect of a more explicit local awareness of conservation as an issue, and of the forest as a system that involved not only trees, whose value as sources of timber had long been obvious, but also the other forest organisms.

Second, I suspect that our long-term research was also a factor in changing the attitudes of local people towards monkeys. Our working habits were decidedly peculiar in the context of local norms: We worked ridiculously long days, didn't break on weekends and holidays, and often appeared to be standing around doing almost nothing, our eyes focused on monkeys who also appeared to be doing nothing of interest, and even while it drizzled. I know that our work was a source of puzzlement (and sometimes laughter), but I suspect that it was also a signal that something about these monkeys was important enough to warrant all that attention. In Kenya, university professors are still held in high regard, and over the years, the continual reappearance

FIGURE 19.4 Conservation resource center for use by the Ikuywa KEEP branch, completed in 2008. This is the third conservation center built for this community-based conservation organization. The author (Marina Cords) is standing, far right. **Photo credit:** Courtesy of Marina Cords.

of a professor from the United States sent a message that something in this forest was of value. On a day-to-day basis, many individual interactions of our field team with local people likely made a difference. Some involved the local Kenyan assistants, explaining their jobs and what they knew about the monkeys to their friends, families, and visitors; some moonlighted as tourist guides on off days. Less directly, many visitors or passers-by would run into members of our team, obviously engrossed in the tasks of close observation, sample collection, and recording what we saw. Many wanted to peek through our binoculars, or peered over our shoulders to see the "book" that we were writing (i.e., our field notebooks).

One of my most memorable interactions of this sort occurred in 2005, when I was caring for a two-month-old orphan blue monkey that a KEEP member had found one morning on a road, several miles from our study area. For about two months, this young monkey was part of our research team, and contributed unwittingly, but hugely, as a goodwill ambassador. He simply came along into the forest, either sitting or sleeping in a net bag outfitted with a small foam pad, or hopping around on our boots and the surrounding vegetation when we remained in one place for a bit. It surprised me how often people passing by did not notice his presence. One day, however, a grandmother, daughter, and granddaughter approached me on the Station Road, where I was watching one of the study groups. The granddaughter spied the infant monkey and informed her older relatives. All three stopped and looked in both wonderment and disbelief, at which point they caught my attention; I approached and held the little monkey so that they could see it better. The grandmother, in her fifties, was amazed at the hands, so much like those of humans. But when the young monkey yawned, exposing its pink tongue and mouth and the rows of little white teeth, she was overcome with astonishment. She had never realized the similarity of a monkey to a human. To me, in turn, it was shocking to think of *not* knowing about this close phylogenetic relationship.

For many who study nonhuman primate behavior, an important motivation derives from the close relationship of their subjects to humans. While always aware of that connection, my interest in these animals came from a different perspective. Trained in biology rather than anthropology, I studied primates because they exemplified social living, and the balance between cooperation and competition that such living entails.

My initial research focus, on mixed-species groups, reflected an aspect of guenon sociality that was often mentioned, but little researched at the time. Most African forests include multiple guenon species, and they often associate together, but more was known about mixed flocks of birds and schools of fish, for whom cooperation served to improve personal safety or foraging success. To investigate the costs and benefits of polyspecific association in blue and redtail guenons, I aimed to follow a study group of each species, and kept records of the location and behavior of group members as their group moved separately from and together with a heterospecific group. It took several months to identify study groups, and initially, my success was completely dependent on finding a particular unmistakable individual: Only then did I know it was "my" group. Finding particular individuals was serendipitous in the early years: Observation conditions were poor, always involving distances of tens of meters, and positive recognition of an individual often required a particular view (say, head on) that might not occur. As I learned to identify the members of my main study groups, I also worked with a local expert, Jackson Gutwa, to learn to recognize about a hundred species of plants that the monkeys ate; this enabled me to record their dietary habits. This process was a lesson on two fronts, in fact, for not only did I learn to identify plants (and to appreciate their many roles in traditional medicine), but I also learned that local people could see the world quite differently from me.

To avoid intruding too much on Jackson's time, I set up a field test for plant identification by marking dozens of trees along a particular route through the forest. I tied inexpensive nylon twine around the trunk, and fitted a plastic tag on the twine, recording the tree number with permanent ink. I intended this to be a temporary test array, and deliberately chose bright colors of twine and tags so that I could easily locate each test tree, and recover all materials for removal once I had learned the tree identifications. My testing array proved to be considerably more temporary than I had anticipated, however, and it was not because I was particularly adept at learning tree IDs. Indeed, on only the second time out on the test route, I realized that some of my tags were no longer in place. However, it was not until several weeks later, when I found a guinea fowl caught in a snare, that I realized how unimaginative I had been in considering why those tags were missing, and how differently people could view "worthless" twine and the forest's wildlife: The bird's leg was caught in a noose of bright yellow nylon! Evidently, my research area was another person's hunting ground, and my tree tags had morphed into his hunting equipment. The guinea fowl that I was always thrilled to see—they came in impressive coveys of up to 70 individuals, and made exhilarating rattling calls like tambourines—were a tasty meal for him, and my actions might be increasing his catch. Fortunately, I was able to release the guinea fowl, and immediately removed all remaining tree labels. Scouring the area revealed no other snares, but I wondered if others might be farther afield.

Perhaps the greatest mismatch of interests between a primatologist and local people concerns hunting of the study subjects, rightfully called poaching when it is illegal. In my years in Kakamega, evidence of poaching has been scattered, and I suspect only a few people have been involved. Nevertheless, sightings of guinea fowl and duikers (small antelope) have become far less common over the last three decades, likely the consequence of unsustainable hunting activity. While many local people were affected by the conservation message of KEEP, it did not reach all members of the community.

Throughout the first 25 years of my study, there was only scattered evidence of blue monkey poaching: brief sightings of retreating men carrying bows and arrows, unconfirmed reports by local people, and disappearances of animals last seen near hostile crowds, angry about actual or suspected crop-raiding. This low background level of hunting, along with the more casual stone-throwing mentioned earlier, was likely why monkeys were wary of local people in the first place.

In 2008, some of our study animals began to frequent areas of the forest that were new to them and to us. This change in ranging area apparently resulted from anthropogenic changes to the environment, specifically the installation of power lines along a second road that crossed the study area. Before, monkeys had crossed this road easily through overhanging branches. But after 15 meters of forest along one side of the road was razed to install poles and cables, there were no treetop passageways, and monkeys seemed unwilling to cross 30 meters of open ground in an area with considerable foot and bicycle traffic throughout the day. This road bisected one group's home range, so when it became an essentially impermeable barrier, the size of the accessible range was much reduced. I believe that this is why this monkey group began to use new areas of the forest: It needed a larger food-supplying area. A part of the new area, comprising two adjacent plantations of exotic trees, turned out to be particularly dangerous from the perspective of poaching.

The physical structure of these plantations certainly contributed to the danger here. The treetops were relatively low, and because it was essentially a monoculture, there was also much less three-dimensionality to the canopy. On the ground, a human could look directly at the tallest branches, without any foliage from smaller trees in the way. Monkeys therefore had very limited escape routes in this type of forest. Adding to their difficulties, if they tried to retreat to more natural forest with a taller, thicker canopy, they had to cross a wide track, and the crossing itself put them even more in harm's way because there were few branches that functioned as crossing "bridges," and these were just a few meters above the ground, where monkeys were more vulnerable.

These plantations were also dangerous because their well-trodden foot- and cow-paths increased contact with humans, and some of the humans passing by—more than in other parts of our study area—were poachers. Perhaps this partially reflects the fact that the plantations were far from the forest station, where forest guards were based. We witnessed parts of several poaching events here, allowing us to understand the poachers' tactics. Sometimes a gang of men and boys surrounded a monkey in a tree and hurled sticks at it. It seemed unlikely that such a stick would kill a monkey, but the frantic rush of the animals to get away from the threat clearly exposed them to danger. A combination of speed, fear-induced mistakes (not quite making a leap), and many animals fleeing at once (sometimes causing branches to snap off, or congesting limited escape routes and thus hindering escape) led individuals to flee inefficiently, and seemed to heighten the risk that they might land on or near the ground where escape is more difficult. Another more common hunting tactic was to use dogs, whose barking and frenzied chase similarly panicked the monkeys and set them to error-prone flight. The hunting dogs were much faster on the ground than were monkeys in the tree, and any monkey falling to the ground with dogs in the vicinity was at extremely high risk. The attacks we witnessed stopped when hunters noticed us, and we never actually saw a monkey being caught; however, animals sometimes disappeared after loud encounters with barking dogs and alarm calls from monkeys that we heard from a distance and could not reach in time. Once, hours after such an attack that we heard but did not see, we found a fresh carcass on the ground with no wounds or other obvious clues suggesting a particular cause of death. We knew that this senior female had not fled from the attack with the rest of her group, which crossed the track to leave the plantation. Presumably dogs would have eaten her if they had the chance, so her lack of external wounds suggested that she had fallen to the ground after the dogs had left. We wondered if she succumbed to heart failure *after* the stress of the attack, even though she had safely weathered it.

While encounters with poachers were upsetting for monkeys and monkey watchers alike, we learned more about how the monkeys adjust assessments of danger and respond accordingly, a lesson that began with the population's habituation. The monkeys learned quickly to use additional cues of danger to modify their behavior. For example, although they were attracted to the plantation forest for feeding, they appeared to time their visits to avoid the daily march of cattle, herdboys, and dogs en route to and from a distant grassland. The cows were heralded by the sound of their bells, audible over a long distance and well before the cows actually came into view. Monkeys did not cross into the plantation forest in the morning until after the bells had passed, and then often did so immediately, suggesting that they waited until the coast was clear. While in the plantation, the monkeys also were extraordinarily quiet. Even when they fled at a distance from the sound of approaching people or dogs (unlike the cattle-herders, who passed through twice a day every day, other people appeared more regularly), they moved *silently* across the track from the plantation to the taller, more natural forest. This silent flight was uncharacteristic: Anywhere else, alarm calls would have preceded or accompanied the retreat. The suppression of calls suggests voluntary control, and supports other observations of non-human animals that suggest their calls are not automatic, involuntary responses to internal states such as fear, as was once believed. The fact that this study group adjusted its behavior to local conditions in a matter of weeks also speaks to the monkeys' acute sensitivity to danger and their ability to modify their responses rapidly and adaptively.

Unfortunately, our team has made little progress in decreasing the danger level to monkeys in the plantation forest. We continue to find snares in the vicinity, and every now and again, we hear hunting dogs. Perfectly healthy-seeming animals continue to go missing on occasion, and their abrupt disappearance suggests predation: Whether this is predation by human poachers or natural birds of prey is much harder to say. Hunters in this part of Kenya know that their acts are illegal and are of course reluctant to be identified by, much less to speak to, our research team. Sometimes we recognize the hunting dogs, but it has been difficult to identify their owners. To the extent that our presence protects the monkeys, we have to worry whether hunting activity has just moved to other groups without human observers.

Additional research questions have arisen as a result of the monkeys moving into the new forest area after the power lines were installed. Shortly after the study group began to use the dangerous plantation forests, it fissioned, and a year later, one of the daughter groups fissioned again. Two of the resultant groups have continued to use the plantation forests to this day, although their home ranges include safer areas as well. The fissions have produced relatively small groups, whose members would seem to be at a disadvantage in terms of shared vigilance for danger: Other studies of primates have reported larger groups where predation risk is higher. At the moment, we are uncertain whether our assumptions about danger are wrong—perhaps a smaller group is advantageous if the strategy for confronting enhanced risk is to be cryptic—or other factors, such as reduced competition for food, are favoring the smaller groups. We are also curious to know how well females frequenting these less-natural forests are reproducing. Increasingly, primate habitats around the world are less pristine, more fragmented, and likely to include more non-"natural" habitat. Our study animals seem to want to use these plantations, despite their evident dangers, to feed on trees native to Australia and Southeast Asia. What does this mean for their nutritional balance, and ultimately for their reproduction and survival? Can areas of plantation forest contribute useful habitat to the species, and if so, how do those benefits balance out with risks? These are a few of the questions that our research continues to address.

Suggested Readings

Cords, M. 1987. "Mixed-Species Association of *Cercopithecus* Monkeys in the Kakamega Forest, Kenya." *University of California Publications in Zoology* 117: 1–109.

Cords, M. 2008. "Face-offs of the Female Kind." *Natural History* 117: 22–27.

Cords, M. 2012. "The Thirty Year Blues: What We Know and Don't Know about Life History, Group Size and Group Fission of Blue Monkeys in the Kakamega Forest, Kenya." In Kappeler, P., and D. Watts, *Long-Term Studies of Primates*. Berlin: Springer.

Cords, M., and J. L Fuller. 2010. "Infanticide in Blue Monkeys (*Cercopithecus mitis stuhlmanni*) in the Kakamega Forest, Kenya: Variation in the Occurrence of an Adaptive Behavior." *International Journal of Primatology* 31: 409–431. doi: 10.1007/s10764-010-9400-z

Fashing, P., N. Nguyen, P. Luteshi, W. Opondo, J. Cash, and M. Cords. 2012. "Evaluating the Suitability of Planted Forests for African Forest Monkeys: A Case Study from Kakamega Forest, Kenya." *American Journal of Primatology* 74: 77–90.

Foerster, S., M. Cords, and S. Monfort. 2011. "Social Behavior, Foraging Strategies and Fecal Glucocorticoids in Female Blue Monkeys (*Cercopithecus mitis*): Potential Fitness Benefits of High Rank in a Forest Guenon." *American Journal of Primatology* 73: 870–882.

Acknowledgments

I am grateful to the Government of Kenya (Office of the President, Ministry of Education, Science and Technology and National Council for Science and Technology) for permission to study the Kakamega monkeys, and to the University of Nairobi Zoology Department, Moi University Department of Wildlife Management, Masinde Muliro University of Science and Technology Department of Biological Sciences and Centre for Kakamega Tropical Forest Studies, and the Institute for Primate Research (National Museums of Kenya) for local sponsorship. I thank the foresters and local staff of the Kakamega Forest Station for their friendly cooperation over three decades.

Funding was provided by the National Science (NSF-GF, SBR 95-23623, BCS 98-08273, BCS 05-54747, BCS 10-28471) Ford, Leakey, Wenner-Gren and H. F. Guggenheim Foundations, AAAS-WISC, the University of California Research Expeditions Program, and Columbia University.

For introducing me to the field site and getting me started on what turned out to be a very long-term study, I am indebted to Professor Thelma Rowell. For assistance in learning the ways of the forest, I thank Jackson Gutwa, Wilberforce Okeka, and Benjamin Okalo. Many field assistants, students, and colleagues helped to keep the field project running over the years, including long-termers P. Akelo, M. Atamba, S. Brace, B. Brogan, C. Brogan, N. Cohen, S. Förster, A. Fulghum, M. Gathua, K. Gaynor, J. Glick, C. B. Goodale, F. Hardy, M. Hirschauer, J. Kirika, K. MacLean, S. Maisonneuve, C. Makalasia, C. Mitchell, N. Mitchell, S. Mugatha, J. Munayi, C. Oduor, C. Okoyo, J. Omondi, B. Pav, K. Pazol, A. Piel, L. Pollack, S. Roberts, E. Shikanga, D. Shilabiga, and E. Widava. Many, many others have provided much valued assistance for shorter periods, both in Kenya and New York. Thanks to all.

20

The Evolution of a Conservation Biologist

By Colin A. Chapman[1]

There is little doubt that the earth's biodiversity and ecological systems are gravely threatened. For example, in 2010 the Food and Agriculture Organization of the United Nations estimated that 16.1 million hectares of forest was lost per year globally in the 1990s, and the majority of this was lost in the tropics (15.2 million ha/year). Such large numbers are hard for me to comprehend, but this is about the size of the state of Florida. The conservation situation with respect to primates is similarly very grim, if not worse. Approximately half of the nearly 600 species and subspecies of primates living today are in danger of going extinct. In fact, one subspecies in West Africa, Miss Waldron's red colobus, may already be extinct. For the last two decades, I have studied what I would argue is the only viable population remaining of another endangered species of red colobus monkey (*Procolobus rufomitratus*) at Kibale National Park, Uganda, where my wife and I work.

Although I have dedicated much of my life to the conservation of primates and the ecosystems in which they live, my commitment has evolved over time as I witnessed the plight of primates and tropical rainforests around the world. My father tells a story about when I was very young and was losing at a game of Scrabble. He spelled out "primate," and I asked what it meant. He told me what primates were and why they were interesting. According to my dad, I then

[1]About the author: Colin A. Chapman received his joint Ph.D. in the Departments of Anthropology and Zoology at the University of Alberta. He spent 2 years at McGill and 3 years at Harvard University doing postdoctoral research. Colin served as a faculty member in Zoology at the University of Florida for 11 years, and returned to McGill in 2004 to take up a Canada Research Chair Tier 1 position in Primate Ecology and Conservation, is a Fellow of the Royal Society, and a Killam Research Chair. Given the plight that primates have suffered as a result of deforestation and hunting, he has focused his research and conservation efforts on primates. He is a Research Associate of the Wildlife Conservation Society, an honorary Lecturer at Makerere University in Uganda, and has been instrumental in funding and maintaining the Makerere University Biological Field Station.

Contact information: Department of Anthropology and McGill School of Environment, McGill University, 855 Sherbrooke Street, West Montreal, Quebec, CANADA H3A 2T7; and Wildlife Conservation Society, 2300 Southern Boulevard, Bronx, NY 10460 USA, colin.chapman@mcgill.ca

Citation: Chapman, C. A. 2014. "The Evolution of a Conservation Biologist." In Strier, K. B. (ed.), *Primate Ethnographies*. Upper Saddle River, NJ: Pearson Education, Inc. (pp. 218–227).

FIGURE 20.1   Red colobus from Kibale
National Park, Uganda.
Photo credit: Jessica Rothman.

stated that I wanted to watch monkeys, and I have never seriously deviated from that path. In fact, the only time I ever questioned whether I would conduct research on primates until a nice old age was when I met a male elephant in the forest in Kibale. The bull decided that he did not like all the noise I was making cutting a trail, and I had absent-mindedly gotten about 15 meters from the elephant when he charged. Elephants can run fast, and I think that the only thing that saved me was that I ran into the swamp, where the heavy elephant would have sunk quickly into the mud had he followed me. There might have been a few other close escapes involving poisonous snakes and large cats, but I lived through those, too.

After doing an undergraduate project that paid me to travel from Edmonton, Alberta, to Guatemala by bus (a bus ride with many stops that took months and covered over 6,100 kilometers) and then flying to St. Kitts in the Caribbean in search of primates, I settled on St. Kitts as a study site for my master's research. I focused on how ecological conditions influenced behavior and ranging of the St. Kitts vervet, a species of monkey that was introduced onto the island in the seventeenth century, coming over on slave ships associated with the sugarcane industry. This was a wonderful introduction to the world of primatology. Linda Fedigan, my supervisor from the University of Alberta, had conducted research on a particular group of primates before me, so when I started to work on them, they quickly habituated to my presence, and the juveniles would often come within a couple of meters and "peep" at me as if to ask, "What are you doing here again?". However, if a stranger got within 100 meters, the group faded into the vegetation, becoming invisible to all.

Late one night, I was woken up by a friend who worked as guide taking people on treks up the volcano. He had come to tell me that he had heard that a juvenile vervet from my group had been captured. At this time in St. Kitts' history, a biomedical group was conducting research on vervets in captivity. While I was ethically opposed to this sort of research, as a master's student I was not in a position to do much about it. But we had come to an agreement that no animals would be taken from the area that our study group inhabited, so at first light, I raced on my motorbike to the facility to ask about the fate of this juvenile. The researchers were very kind and apologetic; they called in the trapper and we learned that he had trapped the juvenile in the home range of our study group. The senior researchers asked me what I wanted to do. I was not entirely sure, but I figured that as the juvenile was still in quarantine and thus had not likely been exposed to any diseases, I wanted to reintroduce him to the group. I literally put the little male into my backpack (yes, he bit me), rushed to my field site, and searched for the group. I found them in one of their favorite resting areas and as I got close, the juvenile started giving calls. A number of animals approached me but were still more than 10 meters away. When I opened my backpack just a little, the juvenile began calling much more intensely, and a female came within 5 meters, calling continuously. Then I opened the bag all the way. The juvenile ran out and was immediately picked up by a female, and they both disappeared into the bush. I had the sense to cut hairs on the side of the captured juvenile so that I would be able to recognize him again, and to my relief, he was still with the group when I left the island a number of months later.

With more experience under my belt, looking back I am not certain I did the right thing, particularly with a present-day understanding of disease transmission. I think luck was with me then, though, and it seemed to have worked out. And it was this experience that likely pushed me towards a life of conservation. Sadly, the home range of my vervet monkey group is now the site of a luxury hotel. Maybe some of you reading this essay have stayed at this resort without knowing the history of the area, or if not the exact one on St. Kitts, then perhaps another one that also led to losses of primate life.

After my experience in St. Kitts, I thought seriously about my academic career. I never doubted my goal was to study primates in the wild, but I wondered how I would do it. Dr. Fedigan had recently started research in a protected area, Santa Rosa National Park, Costa Rica, and it made sense to go there, along with my wife, for our PhD research projects. Santa Rosa is a wonderful place with three species of primates: cebus monkeys that show complex social relationships; howler monkeys with fascinating diet choice; and spider monkeys with an amazing prehensile tail and grouping patterns that change in complex manners over the day.

After the first year of studying the basic ecology of all three of these species, I became fascinated in a side project dealing with what determined the size of primate groups. My ideas were relatively simple. Various researchers had suggested that grouping confers such predictable benefits that differences in group size can be explained by the disadvantages. The most accepted potential cost of grouping is that by being a member of a group, animals experience reduced foraging efficiency. This is either because animals fight over food, or one animal in a group simply beats another to the food; thus, when the second animal comes for the food, there is simply none left. In both of these situations it is thought that competition over food leads to animals having to travel farther.

Animals must forage over an area that can meet their energetic and nutritional requirements. It follows that an increase in group size will increase the area that must be traveled to find adequate food supplies. Thus individuals must travel farther and expend more energy if they are in larger groups, rather than in smaller groups. With an increase in the time spent traveling, a point is approached where the energy spent in travel exceeds that obtained by feeding, and smaller groups become advantageous. The first time I presented these ideas, my lab mates thought it was a silly idea and that I should abandon this line of research. This might have been due to the fact that I explained it poorly or that it was a relatively new and unusual idea. However, my work over the years and that of others has provided general support for these ideas.

It was while I was trying to wrap my head around what determined the size of primate groups that I again came face to face with conservation issues. Costa Rica is known in tour guides as the "Garden Spot of Central America" because it has such an extensive system of parks and reserves, but outside of those parks the land has often been terribly degraded. When I was in Santa Rosa, a well-known field biologist named Dr. Daniel Janzen was trying to buy land to extend the park. My wife and I surveyed these areas because we thought that if we could demonstrate their potential for supporting primates, he would have a good fund-raising tool. Much of the landscape consisted of badly damaged grasslands that had once been forest 30 meters tall, but there were still some small forest fragments and riverine forests and it was in these areas that we often found all three of the monkey species that were present in Santa Rosa. It was clear that if one could restore the forest, like Dr. Janzen was trying to do, one could help the monkey populations in significant ways.

To the best of my knowledge, the term conservation biology was introduced as the title of a conference organized by biologists Bruce Wilcox and Michael E. Soulé at the University of California, San Diego in La Jolla, California in 1978. This was before I had ever been to the field or seen my first wild primate. Arguably, the field of conservation biology did not become well recognized until after 1987, when the journal *Conservation Biology* was first published. At this time I was completing my doctoral degree and surveying the degraded habitats neighboring Santa Rosa.

I continued to work in Costa Rica for my first postdoctoral study, but in 1989, the opportunity to conduct a second postdoc in Kibale came through. Everyone thinks that my wife and I made the decision to start working in Uganda as the next step of a well-planned research program; however, this could not be farther from the truth. In reality, we had applied for postdoc positions in Panama, South America, South East Asia, and Africa; we were just very lucky that each of our respective proposals to work in Uganda came through. My wife's research and conservation efforts focused on fish and freshwater systems, while mine focused on primates and tropical forests. After working for almost three years with Richard Wrangham on chimpanzees and trying to understand how changing ecological conditions affected group dynamics in chimpanzees, I began to pick up where a long-term researcher, Tom Struhsaker, had left off with his study of the endangered red colobus monkeys. My wife and I have conducted research on these monkeys ever since.

We thought that assessing determinants of red colobus abundance would be valuable in managing this population. To do this we conducted intensive population density surveys to determine primate numbers at six locations in Kibale that were on average 12 kilometers apart. These sites were all connected by continuous forest, so primates could easily disperse between them.

Red colobus were present at all of these locations; however, their lowest density was at an undisturbed and very diverse location in the middle of the park, and they were abundant in disturbed and logged locations where tree density was low. This pattern was not easily interpreted in light of forest structure because we expected that primate biomass would be related to food availability and therefore greater in the least disturbed area. We decided to examine the relationship between monkey density and food supply. This included watching redtail monkeys, a fruit-eating species, as well as the red colobus, a leaf-eating monkey, in these six locations for about 4,000 hours (the equivalent to working at an 8-hour-a-day job for almost two years) to determine their important foods.

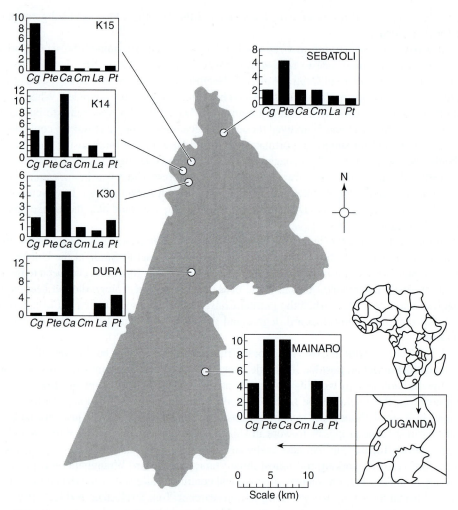

FIGURE 20.2   Map and density of the common primates found in different areas of Kibale National Park, Uganda. (Figure courtesy of Colin A. Chapman.)

We found a fairly strong positive relationship between the abundance of the fruit-eating redtail monkeys and their food, but the relationship for the red colobus held only if one undisturbed and very diverse site in the middle of the park, known as the Dura River site, was excluded. We knew that Tom Struhsaker had seen an epidemic that killed a number of red colobus back in the 1970s and we saw a male die of apparently the same disease in 2013, so it was possible that this population was still recovering from the effects of a past disease. However, it bothered us to not understand an outlier like this. Were we missing something?

We started to consider the possibility that primate abundance might be affected by more than the availability of food, with food quality being a likely candidate. Unlike most primates, colobus monkeys have a specialized alkaline forestomach capable of digesting leaf material. Previously, Katie Milton had proposed that leaf selection in howler monkeys, another leaf-eating monkey, was related to how digestible a leaf was relative to its protein levels. Others extended

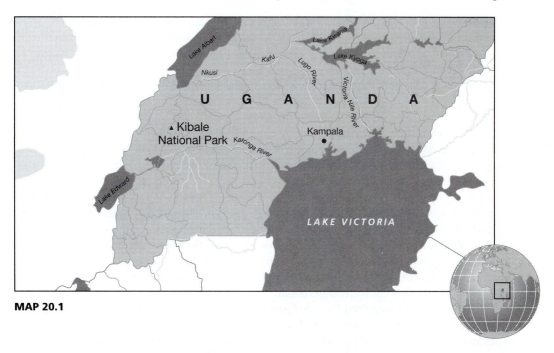

MAP 20.1

this idea and suggested that if easily digestible mature leaves (i.e., low in fiber) were plentiful in an area where other, more-preferred foods were lacking, the site could support a relatively large population of colobines. When we quantified the average protein-to-fiber ratio of mature leaves at our sites in Kibale, we found was that it predicted the differences in red colobus abundances. The low abundance of colobines at the Dura River site finally made sense, for although this site had an abundance of food, it was of low quality.

No conservation biologist in his or her right mind should make conservation decisions based on four data points, so over the next 6 years, we examined the generality and predictive power of the relationship between protein-to-fiber ratios and colobine abundance by adding our biomass and leaf chemistry values to five previously published values and to a set of values we collected in five forest fragments. We found that a whopping 87 percent of the variance in colobine biomass could be attributed to the quality of the foods at a site.

It was extremely satisfying to discover that colobus abundance was predicted by the quality of the foods available to them (or a strong correlate of this) because we could use this information to engineer solutions to conservation issues. It does not take a Ph.D. to conclude that primate populations can be protected more efficiently if we decrease logging or bushmeat hunting, but finding subtle, unexpected, or cascading effects of anthropogenic disturbance and using this information to construct informed management plans is a major challenge. That is why it was so rewarding to be able to start applying our findings about the importance of protein-to-fiber ratios in primate conservation. For example, this knowledge of their dietary preferences would allow one to restore an area to make it very suitable for endangered colobus by planting the highest-quality species of trees. Such habitat restoration may soon become a big element of tropical conservation as a result of changing international agreements about how countries can offset carbon emissions that increase global warming by restoring "natural" forest and storing carbon in trees. As many countries have trouble meeting the carbon emission reductions that they have pledged to make, they can live up to their previous agreement, while not cutting emissions by buying carbon. Basically, a country can pay for the reforestation of areas, and the carbon in those trees is taken off what the country emits so that it achieves its promised reduction levels.

We know almost nothing about how climate change will influence primates—which species will prosper or which will go extinct. We do know that some estimates suggest that the climate could warm by 5.8°C this century. Primates will be affected by either climate-induced loss of particular plant species or changes in flowering and fruiting cycles. It has been estimated that 81 to 97 percent of the 5,197 African plant species studied will have distributions that will decrease in size and/or shift in location, many to higher altitudes, and 25 to 41 percent of plant species will lose all their area by 2085.

A second area in which to apply this understanding about colobus food quality is in logging operations. We would like to influence logging companies by instructing them not to cut down trees that have particularly high protein-to-fiber ratios to reduce the impact of logging on the colobus. Realistically, logging companies will take the trees with the best market value. However, one could hopefully convince them to directionally fell trees that they do cut away from trees with high protein-to-fiber ratios. Often over 50 percent of the trees killed in a logging operation are not cut for timber, but are incidental damage. Directional felling is a large component of what is required for a logging concession to receive certification from groups such as the Forest Stewardship Council, which facilitates the reduction of damage in logging operation, and the certification facilitates logging companies being paid more for the timber they sell.

Logging operations as well as bushmeat hunting and expanding human populations have increased the risks of infectious disease transfers between humans and other primates. The sudden appearance of diseases like SARS and swine flu, the devastating impacts that diseases like Ebola have on both human and wildlife communities, and the immense social and economic costs created by viruses like HIV underscore our need to understand the ecology of infectious diseases. Given that monkeys and apes often share parasites with humans, understanding the ecology of infectious diseases in nonhuman primates is of paramount importance. In the last couple of years, my colleagues (particularly Tony Goldberg), students, and I discovered that red colobus monkeys have three unknown simian retroviruses, including a new form of the SIV virus (the progenitor of HIV). We also found serologic evidence for a novel like poxvirus in red colobus and have shown that anthropogenic disturbance promotes bacterial transmission among humans, livestock, and primates. With primate habitat loss averaging approximately 200 square kilometers a day, humans, domestic animals, and primates are forced into closer contact, which contributes to the emergence of novel infectious diseases. A particularly poignant example comes from Minkebe Forest in the Democratic Republic of Congo, where Ebola caused not only human deaths but also a decrease of at least 90 percent in the gorilla populations. In collaboration with my student, Ria Ghai, and Tony Goldberg, we are now using novel genetic techniques to examine if and potentially how readily *Trichuris* (a very common intestinal parasite) and malaria are transferred among primate species, including humans. To our knowledge this has not been done for a community of primates that includes humans. If transmission is frequent, this will dramatically change concerns over spatially separating nonhuman primates and people and lead to significant modification in both conservation and public health strategies.

Doing good conservation work is not just the application of information on the plant and animal communities; rather success depends on acceptance by the local human community of the ideas coming out of academic efforts. It is not surprising that we have gotten to know the local community well during the 24-plus years we have worked in Kibale. They welcomed us warmly during the entirety of our research. Several members of the community worked with us from the very beginning of the project; one was born in the backseat of the truck as we were racing the mother to the hospital. One day when we were working far from our base camp, a truck just like ours drove off the road and over a cliff. The driver, a 2-meter-tall, red-haired white man with a beard, was killed along with a passenger. Based on this description, the locals thought that my wife and I had been killed. Once the community found out we were not dead, they threw a party for us to, as they said, "welcome us back from the dead." It was the nicest funeral for ourselves we had ever attended.

We wanted to give something back to these kind people, so we asked our closest friends in the community what they regarded as their most pressing needs; almost universally the request was for jobs. We could not hire the whole community or even a significant part of it (more than 6,000 people are within easy biking distance of the field station), so we went to the second need on their list, health care. After payday or the sale of their crops, the people in this community make essential purchases and then pay for making improvements to their houses or for their children's school fees. Thus, within a week they are often out of readily available cash. If a child gets sick, it costs over a day's labor to go to a clinic. They often do not have the cash on hand, so they wait. It is only when the child is very sick that they ask friends and neighbors for a loan and then go to the clinic. We verified the importance of the local community`s need for health care and the reason it was ranked number two in their list of what they needed the most by studying the health situation in depth. It quickly became clear that medical services were desperately needed in the area. For example, life expectancy in Uganda is only 45 years; 26 percent of children under the age of 5 are malnourished; 30 percent of all deaths among children between the ages of 2 and 4 are caused by malaria that could be easily treated or prevented; and many of the diseases are waterborne, as people typically collect water for drinking, water their cattle, and wash their laundry at the same water source—usually the only water source available. Thus, our objective became to build a medical health center just within the borders of Kibale National Park to provide the communities surrounding the park with reliable health care that is close at hand and affordable and to maintain strong positive park–people relationships.

With the efforts of many undergraduate and graduate students, we raised the funds to work toward our objective. Within two years, the Kibale Health and Conservation Centre was functioning. It is staffed by a full-time nurse and a second nurse who concentrates on outreach to the schools, and it is visited regularly by a medical doctor and AIDS counselors. To make the service affordable, there is no charge to see the nurses or doctor, who are paid with funds raised in North America. Patients pay only for treatment (e.g., malaria drugs), and if they cannot pay at the time, they are asked to come back on payday. We thought that the local people would see the health centre and the benefits coming from it as a benefit of the park and have the cascading effect of decreasing the illegal bushmeat hunting and the collection of firewood that still occurs in the park. In keeping with our academic spirit, we are now testing the impact of the Centre on people's health knowledge, which should improve from the outreach, as well as looking at changes in attitudes toward, and actions related to the park. It is estimated that the Centre provides vital health care and education to more than 6,000 people, so the potential for positive impact is very real.

After a couple of decades of working with tropical primates in the field, I am optimistic about conservation. It is very obvious that human actions endanger many primates and that

FIGURE 20.3   Kibale Health and Conservation Centre. The Centre was established by Drs. Colin and Lauren Chapman as a means of expressing their thanks to the local community that had been so welcoming to them during the time they have spent in Uganda and we are eagerly looking forward to working with this community over the next couple of decades.
Photo credit: Colin A. Chapman.

great effort needs to be made to conserve the forests they inhabit. However, the rate of forest loss is declining, a great deal is now known about primate diseases, and programs to decrease the size of the bushmeat industry are succeeding. These advances should not make us reduce our efforts—rather our knowledge offers great opportunities to make significant contributions to primate conservation. We now have clear guidelines as to the actions that need to be taken. Certainly many questions need to be addressed to make primate conservation a reality: What will direct human depopulated areas towards a process of ecological recovery? What are effective measures to reduce the transmission of diseases between people and nonhuman primates? How is it possible to reduce the national and international trade in bushmeat? How will climate change impact specific regions and their primate species? These questions provide the foundation for research programs that will make a real difference and will generate the information needed to construct informed conservation/management plans. It is a very exciting and challenging time for people interested in primate conservation; there is sufficient background information to ask really thrilling and meaningful questions, and the tide has turned so that there is a real willingness to fund and bring about significant change. I sincerely hope that some of you who have read my story of how I became involved in primate conservation see how things have changed in the last couple of decades, become excited about the current possibilities, and invest your time and energy to conserving primates and their habitats. Good luck.

Suggested Readings

Chapman, C. A., and C. Peres. 2001. "Primate Conservation in the New Millennium: The Role of Scientists." *Evolutionary Anthropology* 10: 16–33.

Chapman, C. A., T. R. Gillespie, and T. L. Goldberg. 2005. "Primates and the Ecology of Their Infectious Diseases: How Will Anthropogenic Change Affect Host-Pathogen Interactions?" *Evolutionary Anthropology* 14: 134–144.

Cohen, M. L. 2000. "Changing Patterns of Infectious Disease." *Nature* 406: 762–767.

Acknowledgments

This research has been funded by a great many funding agencies. I would like to single out National Geographic for taking risks on fun ideas, Wildlife Conservation Society for being with us in the initial years, and the National Science and Engineering Research Council of Canada for its flexibility in funding. I would like to especially thank Lauren Chapman for being with me throughout the years, the graduate students for making things fun, and the Uganda field assistance for all the help and knowledge, particularly our program directors Dr. Patrick Omeja and Dr. Dennis Twinomugisha.

21

Studying Apes in a Human Landscape

By Jill D. Pruetz[1]

I will never forget my first day back with the chimps in May 2011. I had left my study group in December 2010 after an eight-month field season, the longest time I had been able to spend with them since I first began my study of Fongoli chimps in 2001 in southeastern Senegal, West Africa. As I arrived at the chimp party, which was gathered around a feeding tree at Maragoundi ravine, I got the usual second glances (barely noticeable) that told me they had indeed noticed I hadn't been here in a while, yet I was no stranger. For the first time, though, I was greeted by a pant-hoot from two-year-old Aimee. She and her mother sat on the edge of a feeding tree crown, seemingly hesitant to enter because of the dominant males there, and I assumed Aimee's pant-hooting was because she was excited about the prospects of eating. But as she finished her loud call, she turned and looked down at me and held her hand out, as if for reassurance or greeting— or both. Her mother seemed to try and stifle her loud and frankly inappropriate pant-hoot, if it was indeed directed at me, but whether she was worried about Aimee associating too closely with me or inciting the ire of the dominant males feeding nearby, I wasn't sure. I smiled but could do little else, for both scientific and practical purposes. A little more than a year earlier, I had actually carried Aimee back to her group after my project manager had rescued her from poachers in the nearby town. Whether she remembered me from that incident in particular or was just behaving as one normally would when someone (some chimp, usually) who hadn't been seen in a while reappeared, or even whether she just wanted someone to share her excitement that day is something I'll never know. I do know it was one of the best moments of my life and the best homecoming I've had at Fongoli.

[1]About the author: Jill Pruetz is the Director of the Fongoli Savanna Chimpanzee Project, which has been ongoing since 2001. She is the Walvoord Professor of Liberal Arts & Sciences at Iowa State University. She established the nonprofit organization Neighbor Ape in 2008 in order to aid the conservation of chimpanzees in Senegal as well as contribute to the well-being of humans living alongside them.

Contact information: Department of Anthropology, Iowa State University, Ames, IA 50011, USA, jillpruetz@yahoo.fr

Citation: Pruetz, J. D. 2014. "Studying Apes in a Human Landscape." In Strier, K. B. (ed.), *Primate Ethnographies*. Upper Saddle River, NJ: Pearson Education, Inc. (pp. 228–237).

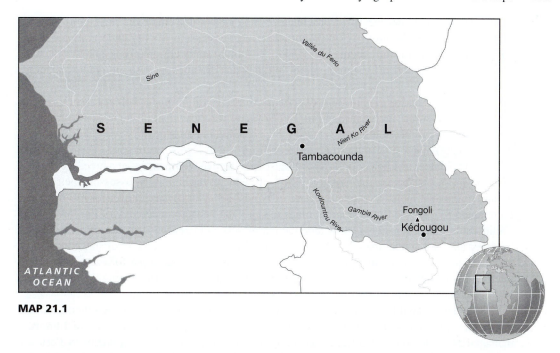

MAP 21.1

This recollection of my reencounter with Aimee illustrates the complicated relationship I have had with the Fongoli chimpanzees over the years. If I were to throw my scientific protocol to the wind, for example, which maintains that we are to ignore the chimpanzees unless we feel significantly threatened, I would have reached out to Aimee literally, as a sign of reassurance when she appeared to direct her pant-hoot to me. However, this might result in even more directed behaviors from Aimee or other chimpanzees, and the goal of habituation is to be ignored by the subject, influencing their behavior as little as possible. I first became interested

FIGURE 21.1   Adult female Fongoli chimpanzee Natasha with her infant Pistache. **Photo credit:** Adrien Meguerditchian.

in studying wild chimpanzees after I volunteered and then became employed at a facility housing captive chimpanzees in south Texas. Before that, when I was a university undergraduate, I had no particular desire to study them. A lot of people want to study chimpanzees, and they look so endearingly silly in those TV commercials, but they just did not appeal to me. That was before I had met one.

I had been looking to gain some experience working with primates before I went to graduate school and, surprisingly, an opportunity came my way less than an hour's drive from my university (at that time, Southwest Texas State University, in San Marcos, Texas; later shortened to Texas State) and a little more than an hour from where I grew up in south Texas. It was a chance to volunteer as a behavioral psychologist with captive chimpanzees at a breeding facility. My job was to contribute to the psychological well-being of the chimps by assessing their behavior and trying to stimulate positive and species-typical behavior. It was all over for me after that. I attempted to stay true to my original plans to study the behavioral ecology of the New World Callitrichids, small monkeys that include the marmosets and tamarins, because of their unusual behavior and biology compared to most other monkeys. However, I could not shake how I felt about chimpanzees. Nothing I had read about chimpanzees prepared me for experiencing the intelligence and emotions of a primate so similar to humans. It was so intriguing, it drew me like nothing ever has, before or after that moment when I connected with them.

I thought I should still try and pursue my study of Callitrichids in graduate school, so I left the chimps after a year and landed a position with Paul Garber at the University of Illinois. I managed his field study of moustached tamarins (*Saguinus mystax*) in Amazonian Peru for almost six months before I even set foot on Illinois soil. This time in Peru reinforced my love for fieldwork, but it also reconfirmed my desire to work with chimpanzees. This was easier said than done. While chimpanzees are among the most intensively studied wild mammals, gaining entry to a project as a student is fairly difficult. Competition for a student position with the principal investigator of a site is intense; getting into a site as someone else's student is even harder.

Ultimately, I took advantage of another option that allowed me to finish my degree while spending two years in the field in Africa, albeit not with chimpanzees. I applied for and was chosen to manage a research project on patas monkeys (*Erythrocebus patas*) and vervets (*Chlorocebus aethiops*) led by Lynne Isbell, then of Rutgers University and later of the University of California at Davis. I lived for a little more than two years in Kenya and really hated to leave. I loved the open savanna woodland environment I worked in there, and I decided that this was the type of environment in which I wanted to study chimpanzees.

After studying patas monkeys and vervets on the savannas of Kenya for two years for my doctoral dissertation research, I realized that combining my love of chimpanzees with my love of a savanna habitat would be the perfect setting. The solution, I decided, would be to start my own site. My undergraduate advisor encouraged me to approach Dr. William (Bill) McGrew, then of Miami University, the former director of the longest study of chimpanzees in a savanna habitat, at Mt. Assirik, Senegal in the 1970s. Bill helpfully finagled a postdoc for me and, along with his primatologist wife Linda Marchant, we surveyed chimps in Senegal in the year 2000. During one of my forays to survey outside of the Parc National du Niokolo Koba (PNNK) where Bill had previously worked, I encountered a site about 50 kilometers east and to the south of Mt. Assirik that seemed especially promising based on the density of chimpanzee sleeping nests. It was there that I began my long-term study of the Fongoli chimpanzee community the next year.

I'm sure each field primatologist has his or her hardship stories. In fact, right now, in April 2012, I'm writing as I sit by the side of the dirt road near Kedougou, Senegal, waiting for my project manager to fetch someone to help me put a new tube in my motorcycle tire so I can get back to my base camp. I would have had all of the necessary tools if I hadn't run out of money too early in the month, which is not an infrequent occurrence. I can trace this story of woe back to the frustrating accounting system that I have to deal with—or perhaps it's combining the U.S. system with that of Senegal. A flat tire is a relatively minor inconvenience typical of the myriad little things one needs to deal with in the field, but it prevented my project manager from taking a night off from the educational workshops he conducts. As it was, we were able to have a brief business meeting after discovering that I had a tube only for the rear tire, so he had to send the mechanic back to town again for a front tire tube. While he was gone, I got back to my writing.

Each field site is different, and no matter how you plan, based on your previous experience, something new and different always crops up. I did my first stint in the field in Belize, Central America, on an archaeological research project and field school. I absolutely loved the fieldwork but not cleaning myriad pieces of pottery along with the other necessary tasks. The thought of analyzing them further steered me away from archaeology and towards primatology, which had really clicked with me as an undergraduate. My next experience in the field was studying moustached tamarin monkeys in Peru as a first-year graduate student, and although both the Belize and Peru field sites were hot and humid, each brought its own challenges. The hike out through a mangrove swamp to our archaeological site was more difficult than following tamarins through the forest in Peru, but my days began much earlier—by 4:30 a.m.—so that I could get to the monkeys before they moved away from their sleeping trees. Food was varied and delicious in Belize, prepared for us in by a local Mayan woman, while in Peru we subsisted off a very bland diet and sometimes ran out of food. Both Belize and Peru had a diverse and pesky insect fauna, but each also had amazing experiences to offer that offset the hardships. Seeing pink dolphins in the Amazon River was a spectacular experience, and walking through an ancient Mayan burial ground while a storm gathered was equally amazing.

The same can be said for each subsequent site I have worked at: Kenya's central highland district was characterized by animals that made me feel as if humans had not yet made their mark there, and a number of those animals could quickly take your life. Costa Rica's wet forests, where I have taught summer field schools for mainly undergraduates contemplating a career in primatology, were among the most beautiful I have been in, but the swampy terrain is one of my least favorite substrates from which to observe primates. Nicaragua's dry forests, another place where I have taught field schools, provided a beautiful setting for studying howling monkeys as they ranged in the foothills of one of two volcanoes that made up the island of Ometepe, but the itching brought about by a species of plant whose pollen was blown through the walls of our cabins was almost unbearable. Panama's swampy archipelago is an amazing group of islands, but the Raffia swamps proved almost impossible to navigate, especially with a group of students intent on following howling monkeys. Comparatively speaking, the semi-arid savanna-woodland of southeastern Senegal is one of the most difficult climates I have worked in because of the intense heat and frequent illnesses one must face, but the chimpanzees I am studying there are worth all of the discomfort.

I bring up the subject of physical challenges first because they are something that most fieldworkers think about but that are impossible to anticipate or avoid. For example, becoming severely ill in a faraway place that lacks health care on a par with what Western scientists are used to can be one of the greatest challenges to a person's resolve. I've had malaria more than a dozen times, and although I was fortunate to have recovered each time, it is not an illness to be trivialized, given how many people die of this disease yearly and the long-term effects it can have on one's health.

The mental and emotional toll that fieldwork can take on a primatologist may be equally challenging. Many people like me study animals in part because the process provides some sense of fulfillment. I suspect that many primatologists who would gladly spend their day with 32 chimpanzees would feel much less comfortable in the company of the same number of humans, each of whom you may have to actually interact with, rather than observe quietly from the outside. Nonetheless most fieldworkers recognize that our work is impossible without the aid of local people. Therefore, I believe that a general anthropological background is invaluable in going about the usually delicate process of invading some stranger's place so you can study a prosimian, monkey, or ape that lives nearby. Although legally the local people had no land rights, I still asked their permission before I started work at Fongoli. Without their consent and assistance, my project could not be successful.

Many of those local folks have names for the flora and fauna that can be helpful if you want to identify the plants and animals by their scientific names. The local people also usually have some knowledge of the habits of the subjects you will be studying. This was one of the main reasons why I employed the village hunter when I began my work at Fongoli, and he did not disappoint me. One of the first places he took me was to a small cave where he claimed chimpanzees stayed. Now, that sounded fantastic and would be a first for chimpanzees if it were true! If only I could just report what he told me, but I knew I would need some sort of scientific proof, so I set up wildlife cameras. The chimpanzees were too clever to be caught on camera, but I finally used trace evidence of hairs, feeding remains, and knuckle prints in caves we swept out to demonstrate that, indeed, chimpanzees at Fongoli really did use caves to cool off in the dry season, even before they were habituated enough to my presence to allow me to watch them come and go from the caves. If it weren't for my guide, I wouldn't have learned about this cave use until several years later, when we could finally observe the chimpanzees' movements at close range.

Working closely with people in southeastern Senegal and living in a village provides a real support system, which can be crucially important in a number of ways. In our village of Fongoli, it is typical to visit ill people extensively. While this can actually be somewhat taxing to the ill person, it means that someone is looking out for you. My senior field assistant is also the acting chief of our village and serves as an important intermediary between our project and the chief of the largest village in the vicinity of the chimpanzees' home range. Culturally, his role facilitates the working relationship between my project and the people living alongside the Fongoli chimpanzees. For example, the people of the village of Djendji, which is within the chimpanzees' home range, began being more careful about disturbing the chimps at an important waterhole near their village when we began communicating with them about our research and the significance of this water source to the chimpanzees. Crops were no longer planted as close to the water source, and villagers now generally avoid an area upon detecting chimpanzees, if possible. Before I began my study at Fongoli, chimpanzees were not necessarily persecuted, despite the fact that they raided people's beehives, but if other people came from Mali to shoot a chimpanzee for medicinal or other reasons, there was little resistance by the village authorities. That changed once we began a relationship between our project and the people living alongside chimpanzees here.

Despite the many reasons to work with people that live alongside or near the primates we study, establishing these relationships was initially a challenge. I would say I'm socially awkward on my best days, even when communicating in American English, my native tongue. For a significant period during my childhood I was horribly shy, barely speaking at all in front of strangers. I've since overcome that shyness, but language skills are not my *forte*, which made it hard for me to pick up the local French, which is one of the national languages of Senegal. It is amusing, humbling—and frustrating—to be so inarticulate in a society that prides itself in speaking multiple languages. Indeed, my project manager speaks nine languages and his English, which he learned since beginning work with me, is now better than my French.

Communicating with the local people was only one of my concerns on my first trip to Senegal in 2000. My initial plan had been to resurvey the chimpanzees that my postdoc advisor had previously studied while he and his wife went to the Democratic Republic of Congo to study bonobos (*Pan paniscus*). Due to political constraints, they had to shift their work to chimpanzees at Mt. Assirik, Senegal, and Bill's past experience at the site during this critical time in my research plans was invaluable. Having directed the Stirling African Primate Project (SAPP) for four years in the late 1970s, Bill was familiar with the relatively neglected PNNK, in the same area where the Mt. Assirik chimpanzee population was located. It would have taken me much more time and effort to find the old SAPP campsites and surveyed valleys if Bill had not been there to guide me.

Our surveys of the Mt. Assirik area turned up a healthy count of chimpanzees based on extrapolations from the density of sleeping nests. All great apes construct sleeping platforms at night, and most of the time they build new nests each night. Nest density, then, gives us an idea of ape density, and it seemed like this was high both inside and outside of the PNNK. Nonetheless, the chimpanzees we encountered inside the park's boundaries exhibited extreme fear and flight behavior. Their behavior contrasted with the more relaxed behavior we witnessed in chimpanzees outside of the park during the few brief encounters we had with there. Similar to those inside the park, chimpanzees on the outside left the area when they saw us but the urgency of their flight was very much reduced compared to park chimpanzees. I attributed this difference to the fact that when chimpanzees in Senegal survive outside of protected areas, it is usually because the local people living alongside them do not hunt them. The chimpanzees' behavior indicated that they considered humans a part of their ecosystem, and although it was still preferable to avoid humans, humans were not as threatening to them as they were to the park chimpanzees. This made me consider the advantages of establishing a permanent research site somewhere other than inside the park.

Niokolo Koba National Park is much less frequently visited compared to South or East African parks, such as Serengeti National Park in Tanzania, where I once saw more than thirty tourist safari vans gathered around a single leopard. By comparison, during our eight-week stay in the Mt. Assirik area of the PNNK, which is somewhat removed from the single tourist lodge in the park, we saw about one tourist vehicle per month. Chimpanzees in the Mt. Assirik area are more likely to encounter poachers with guns than wildlife tourists, as poaching has always been of concern to PNNK officials and has only gotten worse as the population of this region of Senegal has increased, in part because of immigration from neighboring countries. This, together with the difficulty of convincing granting agencies that chimpanzees could be habituated in a savanna habitat (in the words of one anonymous reviewer, "What makes you think you can do this when no one else has been able to?"), led me to conclude that focusing on the Fongoli chimps would be my best option. Being less fearful of humans, I predicted they would be easier to habituate than chimpanzees living in the park.

We know now that one of the biggest hazards of habituating primates in general and great apes in particular to the presence of humans is the risk of transmitting diseases to them. In fact, the situation has become so dire that in certain areas the research paradigm has shifted from a hands-off to a hands-on approach to allow for interventions such as vaccinating the apes against human transmitted diseases. For this reason, I have adopted a very conservative observation protocol at Fongoli. This includes coming no closer than 10 meters to an individual and trying to

FIGURE 21.2 Author following a party of Fongoli chimpanzees across a fallow field, illustrating the anthropogenic nature of some of Fongoli chimpanzees' home range as well as a typical follow distance. **Photo credit:** Courtesy of Jill Pruetz.

maintain even greater distances, if at all possible. I also require anyone who goes out to watch the chimps to wear surgical masks if they are less than 11 meters from an ape in order to reduce the risks of airborne illnesses such as the common cold, which can easily turn into pneumonia for a young chimpanzee. Disease contraction is less of an issue with primates that are less closely related to humans, but the goal of reducing an observer's effect on the study subject also requires an acceptable approach distance. For the patas monkeys and vervets I studied in Kenya, we also kept 10 meters distance from our focal subjects. With more arboreal primates, such as New World monkeys, maintaining such minimum distances is often less of a problem.

Of course, our study subjects do not read our observation protocols and, in the case of the Fongoli chimpanzees, we often have to get up and move when an individual comes too close to us. If an ape appears to be merely passing by, we don a surgical mask and wait. If that ape appears to want to sit 2 meters from you, like David the current beta male (and aspiring alpha) often does, we gather our things and leave. With someone like David, this can be a tricky procedure, however. An untimely move (too soon after or just as he arrives) may be interpreted as a signal that he is supplanting you. This is great for his self-esteem and his quest for alpha male position, but it could also stimulate him to engage in more direct—and dangerous—threats. Depending on the species studied, threats from the primates themselves vary. Vervets are small-bodied primates (about 4–5 kg) yet they can be quite aggressive, and I would not want to be bitten by one of them. Some primates also make distinctions between the sexes when they threaten human observers. Male vervets selectively redirected aggression towards the female research assistants in Kenya, despite the fact that at least I was taller than my male Kenyan field assistant. Threats from arboreal monkeys may be loud (as in the case of howler monkeys), but are usually less of a safety problem.

Besides the risk of transmitting diseases, allowing a chimpanzee to become so habituated to us that they lose all fear or any inhibition of touching us can be mutually hazardous. As much as we think we might like to play with infant chimpanzees, they would quickly assess just what weaklings we humans are. This has happened at study sites where ape–human contact was allowed, before we knew about the real dangers of disease transmission. Although David's comfort in approaching us is fairly benign at this point, the status quo could easily change if anyone makes a mistake or if one of the well-habituated youngsters that has grown up with us becomes even less inhibited than David. We discourage all contact, for both our own and the chimpanzees' safety. If they were ever to display aggression to the local people that live alongside them, the chimpanzees would surely lose out.

I was most intrigued by the fact that chimpanzees were one of the last large mammals left in the Fongoli area and that humans and chimpanzees apparently coexisted relatively peacefully. In large part, this is due to the cultural beliefs of local people, who consider hunting and eating chimpanzees taboo. A master's student, Kerri Clavette, studied folk tales involving primates among the various groups of people living alongside chimpanzees in southeastern Senegal. Most groups, including the Beudick, Bassari, Fulani, and Malinke, portrayed chimpanzees as arising from humans who had somehow lost their way, for example, by fishing on Friday when it was forbidden, or escaping a circumcision ceremony. Nonetheless, other groups of people don't have these same taboos. People from Mali appear to hunt chimpanzees, and reports maintain that

FIGURE 21.3 Adult male David (in background, against boulder) has used me to shake off an aggressive pursuit by an older male who would not come as close to me. In that case, David brushed my leg—the only contact, as far as I know, other than the rescue and return of baby Aimee and the retrieval of orphaned infant Toto that we have had with any of the Fongoli chimps so far. By press time, David had achieved alpha status. **Photo credit:** Joshua Marshack.

people from Guinea do as well. As more and more people move in from neighboring countries to take advantage of the booming mining industry, they will add to the pressures that a human population has on wildlife, and this is one of the most significant threats looming to chimpanzees in Senegal today.

There have been many changes over the years at Fongoli, but, in terms of conservation issues, there have been distinct shifts in what threatens chimpanzees most. When I began my research in 2001, the chimpanzees had been living alongside humans here for hundreds, if not thousands of years, and it quickly became apparent that farming per se was not an issue as long as the human population density remained low, even though the changes that humans brought to the landscape were very visible. An issue that quickly became apparent was the nonsustainable gathering of wild plant foods by local people, which was communicated to me by Peter Stirling, who grew up in Senegal as the son of missionaries, was interested in wildife and conservation, and ultimately earned a degree in anthropology. I met Peter when I began my study, and he later worked for me briefly on my project. He provided me a lot of insight to the cultures in southeastern Senegal, and he informed me of problems he was familiar with, such as intensive gathering of the wild plant fruit *Saba senegalensis* by local people and people from the nearby town of Kedougou. While we focused on these problems early in the project, these gathering practices took a back seat to other conservation issues when, in 2006, sheep herds began infiltrating the area from northern Senegal and Mauritania, and the herdsmen's cutting of trees became our most worrying problem. More recently, as small-scale or artisanal gold mining increased, more people stopped farming their fields as well as gathering wild foods, so that previous conservation concerns diminished even more, and local communities have come together to restrict herdsmen's use of their lands, making mining our utmost concern today.

According to my current Ph.D. student, Kelly Boyer, who is conducting her dissertation research in the nearby Faleme region of Senegal, illegal hunting seems to be on the rise, perhaps to supply miners with food, making the issue even more complicated. Charcoal production in the chimpanzees' home range appears to be increasing and could also impact the woody biomass of the area, especially given the increasing human population in the area. In just 11 years of the Fongoli Savanna Chimpanzee Project, then, the major conservation concern has shifted at least three different times, with various related problems coming into play, indicating that any attempt to solve such problems necessitates being as flexible as the chimpanzees are themselves.

I began my research at Fongoli with the goal of habituating the chimpanzees for scientific study but spent equal effort attempting to understand the complexities of human and chimpanzee interaction. After habituation, my focus was concentrated on scientific study for several years, but it quickly became apparent that conservation concerns had to remain a priority, given the changes occurring in the human population in Senegal. This is feasible on a large scale only with the assistance and collaboration of students and colleagues, and with an expansion of our conservation efforts. While I have monitored the chimpanzee community north of Fongoli via nest and feeding traces study and other indirect methods, I have no plans to habituate this group. This is mainly an ethical decision on my part. The responsibilities and implications of habituating a second community of chimpanzees in this area where they are sympatric with humans prevent me from taking this step. However, in collaboration with Senegalese primatologists, I hope to habituate a community of chimpanzees for long-term study inside the Niokolo Koba National Park, near the Mt. Assirik site, one of the last protected areas of Senegal where these apes are likely to survive. I believe a strong research presence there in collaboration with the Parks Department will significantly reduce poaching in the area, and these poachers focus currently on large ungulates, including endangered species. Scientifically, the Mt. Assirik chimpanzees are interesting because they are less affected by anthropogenic changes to their environment, such as the extermination of most of their predators, as is the case at Fongoli. In reality, the chimpanzees at Fongoli are not likely to survive much longer than I will, given the human pressures they face and their intrinsically low birth rates. Initiating another project on chimpanzees that range within a legally protected area where relatively little human pressure affects them seems our best bet at ensuring the survivorship of this species in Senegal. As more people become concerned over the welfare of savanna chimpanzees, however, perhaps we can turn around the decline in this species in Senegal. The fact that cultural practices have so far protected Senegal's chimpanzees is encouraging and highlights the need to work closely with local stakeholders in the conservation of their natural resources.

Suggested Readings

Goodall, J. 1986. *The Chimpanzees of Gombe: Patterns of Behavior*. Cambridge, MA: Belknap Press.

Pruetz, J. D., and D. Kante. 2010. "Successful Return of an Infant Chimpanzee to Its Natal Group after a Poaching Incident." *African Primates* 7: 35–41.

Pruetz, J. D., and P. Bertolani. 2007. "Savanna Chimpanzees Hunt with Tools." *Current Biology* 17: 1–6.

Pruetz, J. D., and P. Bertolani. 2009. "Chimpanzee (*Pan troglodytes verus*) Behavioral Responses to Stresses Associated with Living in a Savanna-Mosaic Environment: Implications for Hominin Adaptations to Open Habitats." *Paleoanthropology* 2009: 252–262.

Stanford, C. 1998. *Chimpanzee and Red Colobus: The Ecology of Predator and Prey*. Cambridge, MA: Harvard University Press.

Acknowledgments

I would like to thank the Republic of Senegal and especially the Eaux et Forets of that country for kind permission and assistance in conducting research in Senegal. Funding has been granted to the Fongoli Savanna Chimpanzee Project by Iowa State University, National Geographic Society, Wenner-Gren Foundation, Leakey Foundation, National Science Foundation, USAID-Senegal, Primate Conservation Inc., American Society of Primatologists, Ted Townsend, and the Ellen Walvoord Professorship in Liberal Arts & Sciences at Iowa State University. In Senegal, Dondo Kante, Mboule Camara, Michel Sadiakho, and Waly Camara contributed greatly to the research project. Numerous students have also contributed greatly to the Fongoli project, including S. Lindshield, K. Boyer, S. Bogart, A. Piel, A. Clanin, P. Bertolani, M. Gaspersic, F. Stewart, M. Cook, C. Clement, S. Johnson-Fulton, and M. Waller, as project managers. Other students that added to the success of the Fongoli project include J. Marshack, E. Wessling, C. Tourkakis, M. Robinson, M. Howells, P. Knutsen, K. Clavette, and A. Socha. Janis Carter, Souleye Ndiaye, and Peter Stirling have each been invaluable to the project. Our conservation program through Neighbor Ape has benefited greatly from numerous donors, including the late Dorothy Pruetz, without whom I could have done none of my work.

APPENDIX

Tables of Cross-Referenced Regions, Species, and Key Topics and Concepts

The essays in this volume offer complementary perspectives that can be aligned in a variety of ways. The three tables in this Appendix highlight some of these alternative alignments, transcending the themes into which the book is partitioned. The 21 essays are cross-referenced according to Geographical Regions and Study Sites (Table I), Primates Studied (Table II), and Key Topics and Concepts (Table III). I used the keywords provided by each of the authors to lay the foundation for the tables; then the listings were expanded to include other essays for which a particular keyword also seemed to apply. Although this process may have resulted in some unintended imbalances or omissions, I hope that the tables will nonetheless serve as useful organizational guides and stimulate readers to find other connections in these stories.

TABLE I   Geographical Regions and Study Sites (*Essay number. Author*)

Field Sites

AFRICA

2. *Moore, 3. Nash, 9. Beehner & Bergman, 10. Henzi & Barrett, 15. Robbins, 16. Stanford, 19. Cords, 20. Chapman, 21. Pruetz*

Congo Basin: *15. Robbins*

Virunga Volcanoes: *15. Robbins*

EAST AFRICA: *2. Moore, 3. Nash, 9. Beehner & Bergman, 15. Robbins, 16. Stanford, 19. Cords, 20. Chapman*

Ethiopia

Awash National Park, Ethiopia: *9. Beehner & Bergman*
Simien Mountains National Park, Ethiopia: *9. Beehner & Bergman*

Kenya

Gede Ruins National Monument, Kenya: *3. Nash*
Kakamega Forest, Kenya: *19. Cords*

Rwanda

Karisoke Research Center, Rwanda: *15. Robbins*

Tanzania

Gombe National Park, Tanzania: *2. Moore, 3. Nash, 16. Stanford*
Ugalla, Tanzania: *2. Moore*

Uganda

Bwindi Impenetrable National Park, Uganda: *15. Robbins, 16. Stanford*
Kibali National Park, Uganda: *20. Chapman*

SOUTH AFRICA: *9. Beehner & Bergman, 10. Henzi & Barrett*

Botswana

Moremi Game Reserve, Botswana: *9. Beehner & Bergman*
Okavango Delta, Botswana: *9. Beehner & Bergman*

South Africa

Western Cape Province, South Africa: *10. Henzi & Barrett*

TABLE I (*Continued*)

WEST AFRICA

15. Robbins, 21. Pruetz

Gabon

Loango National Park, Gabon: *15. Robbins*

Senegal

Fongoli, Senegal: *21. Pruetz*
Mt. Assirik, Senegal: *21. Pruetz*

MADAGASCAR

Antserananomby, Madagascar: *4. Sussman*
Berenty, Madagascar: *4. Sussman*
Beza Mahafaly Special Reserve, Madagascar: *3. Nash*
Kirindy Forest, Madagascar: *12. Kappeler*

ASIA

2. Moore, 6. Huffman, 11. Reichard, 14. Fuentes, 17. Fedigan

India

Mt. Abu, India: *2. Moore*
Ranthambhore National Park, India: *2. Moore*

Indonesia

Bali, Indonesia: *14. Fuentes*

Japan

Arashiyama, Japan: *6. Huffman, 17. Fedigan*
Iwatayama, Japan: *6. Huffman*
Kyoto, Japan: *6. Huffman*

Singapore

14. Fuentes

Thailand

Khao Yai National Park, Thailand: *11. Reichard*

CENTRAL AMERICA

5. Glander, 17. Fedigan, 20. Chapman

Costa Rica: *5. Glander, 17. Fedigan, 20. Chapman*
Guanacaste Province, Costa Rica: *5. Glander, 17. Fedigan*

SOUTH AMERICA

1. Strier, 7. Snowdon, 8. Fernandez-Duque, 13. Ferrari, 18. Di Fiore

AMAZON

7. Snowdon, 13. Ferrari, 18. Di Fiore

ATLANTIC FOREST

1. Strier

Argentina

Formosa Province, Argentina: *8. Fernandez-Duque*

Brazil

Samuel State Ecological Station, Rondonia: *13. Ferrari*
RPPN Feliciano Miguel Abdala, Caratinga, Minas Gerais: *1. Strier*

Colombia: *7. Snowdon*

TABLE I	Geographical Regions and Study Sites (*Essay number. Author*) (*Continued*)

    Ecuador: *7. Snowdon, 18. Di Fiore*
Yasuní National Park, Ecuador: *18. Di Fiore*
Peru: *7. Snowdon*
Captive Sites
EUROPE
    12. Kappeler, 14. Fuentes
German Primate Center: *12. Kappeler*
Gibraltar: *14. Fuentes*
NORTH AMERICA
Duke Lemur Center, Durham, North Carolina: *4. Sussman, 12. Kappeler*
University of Wisconsin-Madison, Wisconsin: *7. Snowdon*

TABLE II	Primates Studied (*Essay number. Author*)

APE
    2. Moore, 3. Nash, 11. Reichard, 15. Robbins, 16. Stanford, 21. Pruetz
AFRICAN APE
    2. Moore, 3. Nash, 15. Robbins, 16. Stanford, 21. Pruetz
    Chimpanzee (genus: *Pan*): *2. Moore, 3. Nash, 16. Stanford, 21. Pruetz*
      Savanna chimpanzee: *2. Moore, 21. Pruetz*
    Gorilla (genus: *Gorilla*): *15. Robbins, 16. Stanford*
ASIAN APE
    Gibbon (genus: *Hylobates*): *11. Reichard*
    White-handed gibbon: *11. Reichard*
    Pileated gibbon: *11. Reichard*
OLD WORLD MONKEY
    6. Huffman, 9. Beehner & Bergman, 10. Henzi & Barrett, 20. Chapman
Baboon (genus: *Papio*): *2. Moore, 3. Nash, 9. Beehner & Bergman, 10. Henzi & Barrett*
    Chacma baboon: *9. Beehner & Bergman, 10. Henzi & Barrett*
Blue monkey (genus: *Cercopithecus*): *19. Cords*
Gelada baboon (genus: *Theropithecus*): *9. Beehner & Bergman*
Langur (genus: *Semnopithecus*): *2. Moore*
Macaque (genus: *Maccaca*): *6. Huffman, 14. Fuentes, 17. Fedigan*
    Barbary macaque: *14. Fuentes*
    Crab-eating macaque: *14. Fuentes*
    Japanese macaque: *6. Huffman, 17. Fedigan*
    Snow monkey: *6. Huffman*
Red colobus (genus: *Procolobus*): *16. Stanford, 20. Chapman*
NEW WORLD MONKEY
    1. Strier, 7. Snowdon, 8. Fernandez-Duque, 13. Ferrari, 17. Fedigan, 18. Di Fiore
CALLITRICHID
    7. Snowdon, 13. Ferrari, 21. Pruetz
    Marmoset (genus: *Mico*): *13. Ferrari*
    Pygmy marmoset (genus: *Cebuella*): *7. Snowdon*

TABLE II *(Continued)*

    Tamarin (genus: *Saguinus*): *7. Snowdon, 13. Ferrari*
    Cotton-top tamarin: *7. Snowdon*
    Saddle-back tamarin: *13. Ferrari*
Capuchin monkey (genus: *Cebus*): *17. Fedigan*
Howler monkey (genus: *Alouatta*): *5. Glander, 17. Fedigan*
Muriqui (genus: *Brachyteles*): *1. Strier*
Owl monkey (genus: *Aotus*): *8. Fernandez-Duque*
Spider monkey (genus: *Ateles*): *17. Fedigan, 18. Di Fiore*
Woolly monkey (genus: *Lagothrix*): *18. Di Fiore*
STREPSIRRHINE
    3. Nash, 4. Sussman, 12. Kappeler
Bushbaby (Genus: *Galago*): *3. Nash*
Lemur: *4. Sussman, 12. Kappeler*
    Ring-tailed lemur: *4. Sussman*
    Common brown lemur: *4. Sussman*
Sportive lemur (Genus: *Lepilemur*): *3. Nash*

TABLE III Key Topics and Concepts (*Essay number. Author*)

Academic disciplines
    1. Strier, 2. Moore, 3. Nash, 4. Sussman, 6. Huffman, 7. Snowdon, 14. Fuentes,
    17. Fedigan, 19. Cords, 20. Chapman
Activity rhythms
    8. Fernandez-Duque
Age at first birth
    1. Strier, 11. Reichard
Alternative tactics
    2. Moore
Anthropogenic activity
    4. Sussman, 19. Cords, 20. Chapman, 21. Pruetz
Anthropogenic ecology
    14. Fuentes
Babbling, parallels to human infants
    7. Snowdon
Behavioral change
    1. Strier, 6. Huffman, 17. Fedigan, 19. Cords
Behavioral development
    3. Nash, 6. Huffman, 7. Snowdon
Behavioral ecology (see Socioecology)
    1. Strier, 2. Moore, 4. Sussman, 5. Glander, 8. Fernandez-Duque,
    10. Henzi & Barrett, 15. Robbins, 17. Fedigan, 18. Di Fiore, 20. Chapman,
    21. Pruetz

TABLE III Key Topics and Concepts *(Essay number. Author) (Continued)*

Behavioral flexibility

 1. Strier, 10. Henzi & Barrett, 14. Fuentes, 16. Stanford

Behavioral innovation

 6. Huffman

Behavioral tradition

 6. Huffman, 16. Stanford

Biodiversity

 3. Nash, 20. Chapman

Biodiversity hotspot

 11. Reichard

Biological markets model

 10. Henzi & Barrett

Bushmeat

 15. Robbins, 20. Chapman

Captive breeding

 7. Snowdon

Captive and wild studies of primates

 3. Nash, 7. Snowdon, 12. Kappeler

Career trajectories (or paths)

 2. Moore, 3. Nash, 4. Sussman, 5. Glander, 6. Huffman, 8. Fernandez-Duque,
 11. Reichard, 14. Fuentes, 20. Chapman, 21. Pruetz

Cathemerality

 8. Fernandez-Duque

Census

 1. Strier, 17. Fedigan

Coalitions

 2. Moore, 17. Fedigan

Coastal fynbos

 10. Henzi & Barrett

Cognition

 12. Kappeler

Communication (language, understanding)

 1. Strier, 4. Sussman, 6. Huffman, 7. Snowdon, 11. Reichard, 14. Fuentes,
 18. Di Fiore, 21. Pruetz

Community-based conservation

 7. Snowdon, 8. Fernandez-Duque, 19. Cords

Conservation

 1. Strier, 2. Moore, 3. Nash, 4. Sussman, 5. Glander, 7. Snowdon,
 8. Fernandez-Duque, 10. Henzi & Barrett, 11. Reichard, 12. Kappeler, 13. Ferrari, 14. Fuentes,
 15. Robbins, 16. Stanford, 17. Fedigan, 18, Di Fiore, 19. Cords,
 20. Chapman, 21. Pruetz

TABLE III   (*Continued*)

Conservation biology

    5. Glander, 20. Chapman

Conservation education

    1. Strier, 7. Snowdon, 8. Fernandez-Duque, 19. Cords

Cooperation

    18. Di Fiore

Cooperative breeding

    7. Snowdon

Cooperative problem solving

    7. Snowdon

Copulation call

    11. Reichard

Corridor, forest

    1. Strier

Cultural behavior

    6. Huffman, 16. Stanford

Cultural context

    1. Strier, 4. Sussman, 6. Huffman, 8. Fernandez-Duque, 14. Fuentes, 21. Pruetz

Deforestation

    12. Kappeler, 13. Ferrari, 16. Stanford

Demography

    1. Strier, 8. Fernandez-Duque, 15. Robbins

Determinants of primate abundance

    20. Chapman

Development (human activities)

    4. Sussman, 13. Ferrari

Disease

    15. Robbins, 20. Chapman, 21. Pruetz

Dispersal

    1. Strier, 2. Moore, 8. Fernandez-Duque, 11. Reichard, 17. Fedigan, 18. Di Fiore

Eco-tourism

    5. Glander, 15. Robbins, 16. Stanford, 17. Fedigan

Ecology

    4. Sussman, 10. Henzi & Barrett, 15. Robbins, 16. Stanford

Endangered species

    1. Strier, 7. Snowdon, 12. Kappeler, 15. Robbins, 16. Stanford, 20. Chapman

Ethics

    1. Strier

Ethnoprimatology

    14. Fuentes

TABLE III (*Continued*)

Health
   14. Fuentes, 16. Stanford, 21. Pruetz
Health clinics
   20. Chapman
Hormonal controls of fatherhood
   7. Snowdon
Hormones and stress
   9. Beehner & Bergman
Human dimensions
   1. Strier
Hunting, by primates
   16. Stanford
Hunting, of primates (see Poaching)
   15. Robbins, 18. Di Fiore, 19. Cords, 20. Chapman, 21. Pruetz
Hydroelectric projects
   13. Ferrari
Individual recognition
   1. Strier, 6. Huffman, 9. Beehner & Bergman, 11. Reichard, 19. Cords
Infant care
   7. Snowdon, 8. Fernandez-Duque
Infanticide
   2. Moore, 5. Glander, 10. Henzi & Barrett, 19. Cords
Insectivory
   13. Ferrari
Intergroup encounter
   11. Reichard, 18. Di Fiore, 19. Cords
Intergroup violence
   2. Moore, 18. Di Fiore
International collaboration
   1. Strier, 6. Huffman, 14. Fuentes
Interspecific association
   13. Ferrari
Interspecific avoidance
   4. Sussman
Japanese primatology
   6. Huffman, 17. Fedigan
Kinship
   6. Huffman, 12. Kappeler, 17. Fedigan, 18. Di Fiore
Learning, parenting skills
   7. Snowdon

TABLE III   Key Topics and Concepts (*Essay number. Author*) (*Continued*)

Learning, social

6. Huffman, 7. Snowdon, 12. Kappeler

Life histories (see female life history)

1. Strier, 5. Glander, 8. Fernandez-Duque, 11. Reichard, 12. Kappeler, 17. Fedigan

Local expert

4. Sussman, 18. Di Fiore, 19. Cords, 21. Pruetz

Local people

1. Strier, 2. Moore, 4. Sussman, 5. Glander, 6. Huffman, 8. Fernandez-Duque, 9. Beehner & Bergman, 11. Reichard, 14. Fuentes, 17. Fedigan, 18. Di Fiore, 19. Cords, 20. Chapman, 21. Pruetz

Long-term demography

1. Strier, 5. Glander, 11. Reichard, 17. Fedigan

Long-term field research

1. Strier, 2. Moore, 5. Glander, 6. Huffman, 8. Fernandez-Duque, 11. Reichard, 12. Kappeler, 15. Robbins, 17. Fedigan, 18. Di Fiore, 19. Cords, 20. Chapman, 21. Pruetz

Male bonding

1. Strier, 18. Di Fiore

Male encounter vocalization

11. Reichard

Male groups

2. Moore, 18. Di Fiore

Mate guarding

9. Beehner & Bergman, 11. Reichard

Mating systems

6. Huffman, 7. Snowdon, 8. Fernandez-Duque, 12. Kappeler, 17. Fedigan

Microchips

5. Glander

Moist evergreen forest

11. Reichard

Monogamy

8. Fernandez-Duque, 11. Reichard

Multimale group

11. Reichard

Natal dispersal

11. Reichard

National park

16. Stanford, 17. Fedigan, 18. Di Fiore, 20. Chapman

Night tree

11. Reichard

Nocturnal primate

3. Nash, 8. Fernandez-Duque, 12. Kappeler

TABLE III   (*Continued*)

Noninvasive methods
   1. Strier, 2. Moore, 7. Snowdon

Nongregarious primates
   3. Nash

Nutrition
   20. Chapman

Nutritional stress
   9. Beehner & Bergman

Oxytocin and affiliation in pair bonds
   7. Snowdon

Pair bond
   8. Fernandez-Duque, 11. Reichard

Pair living
   11. Reichard

Patchwork family
   11. Reichard

Paternal care, male infant care
   7. Snowdon, 8. Fernandez-Duque, 14. Fuentes, 15. Robbins

Paternity
   12. Kappeler, 15. Robbins

Patrols
   18. Di Fiore

Plantation forest
   19. Cords

Pneu-Dart, Inc.
   5. Glander

Poaching (see Hunting, of primates)
   2. Moore, 11. Reichard, 15. Robbins, 18. Di Fiore, 19. Cords, 20. Chapman,
   21. Pruetz

Politics, political instability
   12. Kappeler, 14. Fuentes, 15. Robbins, 17. Fedigan, 21. Pruetz

Population density
   2. Moore, 17. Fedigan, 20. Chapman, 21. Pruetz

Population differences
   3. Nash, 6. Huffman, 7. Snowdon, 8. Fernandez-Duque, 9. Beehner & Bergman,
   10. Henzi & Barrett, 12. Kappeler, 14. Fuentes, 15. Robbins, 16. Stanford,
   20. Chapman

Population dynamics
   1. Strier, 5. Glander, 12. Kappeler, 15. Robbins, 17. Fedigan

Population growth
   1. Strier, 5. Glander, 14. Fuentes, 15. Robbins, 17. Fedigan

TABLE III Key Topics and Concepts *(Essay number. Author)* *(Continued)*

Population persistence

1. Strier

Protected reserve

1. Strier

Radio collars, satellite collars

3. Nash, 8. Fernandez-Duque, 12. Kappeler, 14. Fuentes

Reproductive concession

10. Henzi & Barrett

Reproductive success

6. Huffman, 15. Robbins, 17. Fedigan

Reproductive suppression

7. Snowdon

Safe capture

5. Glander

Savanna

2. Moore, 21. Pruetz

Seasonality

6. Huffman, 17. Fedigan

Sexual activity

6. Huffman, 10. Henzi & Barrett, 11. Reichard

Sexual conflict

10. Henzi & Barrett

Sexual selection

8. Fernandez-Duque, 9. Beehner & Bergman, 12. Kappeler, 19. Cords

Social behavior

1. Strier, 6. Huffman, 11. Reichard, 12. Kappeler, 15. Robbins, 19. Cords

Social grooming

7. Snowdon, 9. Beehner & Bergman, 10. Henzi & Barrett, 11. Reichard

Social learning

6. Huffman, 7. Snowdon

Social organization

2. Moore, 4. Sussman, 7. Snowdon, 10. Henzi & Barrett, 20. Chapman

Social stress

7. Snowdon, 9. Beehner & Bergman

Socioecology (see Behavioral ecology)

1. Strier, 2. Moore, 3. Nash, 4. Sussman, 5. Glander, 9. Beehner & Bergman, 10. Henzi & Barrett, 15. Robbins, 20. Chapman

Solitary foragers

3. Nash

Species identification

3. Nash, 13. Ferrari

TABLE III   *(Continued)*

INDEX